THE EVOLUTION
OF AMERICAN
URBAN SOCIETY

THE EVOLUTION OF AMERICAN URBAN SOCIETY

THIRD EDITION

HOWARD P. CHUDACOFF
Brown University

JUDITH E. SMITH
Boston College

PRENTICE HALL, Englewood Cliffs, New Jersey 07632

Library of Congress Cataloging-in-Publication Data

Chudacoff, Howard P.
The evolution of American urban society.

Includes bibliographies and index.
1. Cities and towns—United States—History.
2. Urbanization—United States.   3. United States—
Social conditions.   I. Smith, Judith E. (date)
II. Title.
HT123.C49   1988   307.7'6'0973   87-18720
ISBN 0-13-293689-5

Manufacturing buyer: Raymond Keating
Cover photographs: Library of Congress; Reconstructed View of
  Cahokia by Valerie Waldorf, courtesy Cahokia Mounds
  Historic Site, Collinsville, Illinois; Judith E. Smith
Cover design by Suzanne Bennett and Associates

©1988, 1981, 1975 by Prentice Hall
A Division of Simon and Schuster
Englewood Cliffs, N.J. 07632

Printed in the United States of America

10 9 8 7 6 5 4 3 2 1

ISBN 0-13-293689-5   01

Prentice-Hall International (UK) Limited, *London*
Prentice-Hall of Australia Pty. Limited, *Sydney*
Prentice-Hall Canada Inc., *Toronto*
Prentice-Hall Hispanoamericana, S.A., *Mexico*
Prentice-Hall of India Private Limited, *New Delhi*
Prentice-Hall of Japan, Inc., *Tokyo*
Simon & Schuster Asia Pte. Ltd., *Singapore*
Editora Prentice-Hall do Brasil, Ltda., *Rio de Janeiro*

To my parents,
Mildred and *Irving Chudacoff*
and to the memory of my grandparents,
Jennie and *William Saferstein*

To my parents,
Edward A. and *Beth K. Smith*
and to the memory of my grandparents,
James and *Sarah Smith* and *J. Harry* and *Sadie Kulakofsky*

C

Contents

8 Contested Cities: The Politics of Growth in an Age of Suburbanization, 1945–1974, 260

9 Prospects for Urban America: 1974–1986, 294

Index, 309

Preface

This third edition of *The Evolution of American Urban Society* presents some substantial changes from previous editions. Most importantly, Judith Smith has been included as a coauthor and has brought to the book some needed and significant perspectives. An accomplished urban and social historian, Professor Smith has enhanced this volume with new material on immigrant and working class life, racial minorities, and women's experience. We have thus added new sections throughout the book while retaining the original framework of the first two editions, which most students and instructors seemed to appreciate. We also have tried to bring the material up to date, both by adding material from recent scholarship to every chapter and by revising the final three chapters so as to account better for political, social, and economic developments of the past decade. As in earlier editions, this volume includes chapter-by-chapter bibliographies that are intended to aid readers who might seek further information on specific topics and that include new scholarly works.

Since the first edition of *The Evolution of American Urban Society* appeared in 1976, American cities have experienced turbulent times: the decline of central cities, the revival of central cities; the hope of educational and economic opportunity, the reality of drugs and homelessness; the rise of Sun Belt cities and decline of Frost Belt cities, then the slippage of Sun Belt cities and renaissance of Frost Belt cities; and much more. Behind all these patterns remain the challenges, the joys, the disappointments, and the innovations that have made American cities and their people such exciting objects of historical analysis. This book is their story.

We wish to express our appreciation to John V. Moeser for his assistance in reviewing the text.

Judith Smith would like to acknowledge the careful and thorough research assistance of Robert Macieski, whose scholarly rummaging through the past broadened the range of materials on which this third edition has been able to draw. Donna Penn and Nancy Palmer also provided critical research experience. She would also like to thank her husband, Larry Blum, and her children, Ben and Sarah Blum-Smith, whose support was invaluable to this undertaking.

Howard P. Chudacoff
Judith E. Smith

THE EVOLUTION
OF AMERICAN
URBAN SOCIETY

1

Urban America in the Colonial Age, 1600–1776

URBAN BEGINNINGS

The history of city building on the North American continent preceded the arrival of the Europeans. Tribes in the Mississippi Valley had built a city known as Cahokia, which is estimated to have had a population of thirty-five thousand. Artifacts recovered at Cahokia indicate the existence of far-flung trading networks, specialization of crafts, and clustered housing and markets, although by the time of European colonization the urban civilization of these tribes had largely disappeared. Similarly, archaeological evidence of a Huron town in the Great Lakes region has uncovered more than one hundred large structures that probably housed a total population of between four and six thousand people. The Huron town was larger than the average European village of the sixteenth century and larger than all but a handful of European colonial towns in America even after one hundred fifty years of colonization.

The Europeans who colonized North America were from the beginning urban-minded people, linked to commercial markets. Even the earliest explorers in New England had viewed the new land in terms of the commodities it yielded or promised to yield. Although "commodity" had earlier been defined as articles that were useful to people, now its meaning was as an object of commerce, owned for the sole purpose of being traded away at a profit. A whole continent of forests, plains, and deserts opened before the colonizers, but before they could plunge into that wilderness they needed central places for trade, for defense, for government, and for worship. Thus they created cities—places that functioned to organize and protect populations and to accumulate and disseminate goods and communications.

The Native American City of Cahokia   This photograph is based on a reconstruction of Cahokia painted by Valerie Waldorf. At the center of community life was the large earthenware temple which rose to a height of one hundred feet. Cahokia artisans mass produced knives, salt, and stone hoe blades for local consumption and export. Note the outlying farms surrounding the more densely settled areas. Cahokia may have been a crossroads of trade and water travel in the heartland of North America. *(Cahokia Mounds Historic Site, Collinsville, Illinois.)*

Each of the major colonizing nations contributed to America's urban heritage. As the Spanish, who arrived first, overthrew the powerful Indian empires of Central and South America, the explorers rebuilt settlements on the ruins of what once had been lavish capitals. Cartagena, Mexico City, Lima, and Bogota grew on these sites, some holding as many as fifty thousand inhabitants by 1700, a size that dwarfed all colonial cities to the north.

The Spanish also developed a formal system of town planning that they applied to their colonies in both North and South America. This was the Laws of the Indies, an enactment of 1583 that synthesized earlier practices of settlement, some from Roman times. The Laws specified uniform requirements for town location, street layout, and land use, and they shaped urban beginnings in Florida and the American Southwest. Early maps of Saint Augustine, San Antonio, and San Diego show how the Laws influenced a common design of rectangular blocks, straight streets, and right-angle intersections grouped around a large, central plaza. La Villa Real de Santa Fe, founded in 1610, was the earliest of these planned communities, and for many years Santa Fe served as an administrative center for New Spain's farthest northern frontier. Spanish colonization intended to distinguish among types of settlements; "pueblos" were to be centers of commerce and colonization; "missions" were established for the goal of religious conversion, and "presidios" were military outposts. But such distinctions often faded once actual settlement occurred. For example, San Antonio was originally established at the headwaters of a river on the site of a native American village. Called Yanaguana by the native people, it was rechristened in 1691 with a wooden cross as San Antonio. A band of seventy-two soldiers, settlers, and monks came to settle in San Antonio in 1718, and a quarrel between the chief military leader and the missionary priest led to separate settlements of a presidio and the mission later famous as the Alamo. Presidios were established at San Diego in 1769, San Francisco in 1776, Los Angeles in 1781, and Santa Barbara in 1782, but soon house and farm buildings sprang up beyond the walls of the presidio proper, and the military communities looked indistinguishable from the civil settlements of the pueblos.

In contrast to the Spanish, the early French explorers came not as colonizers but as individuals seeking personal gain. As traders, however, they needed centers for the exchange of goods, so they founded commercial ports along the waterways of colonial North America's perimeters. In the North and West, they built Quebec, Montreal, Detroit, and St. Louis, towns of varied design that usually conformed to the topography of the area. These places acted as staging points for fur traders and missionaries who combed the Great Lakes and Mississippi River regions in the early 1700s. In 1722, Sieur Jean Baptiste de Bienville founded New Orleans near the mouth of the Mississippi. Designed as a large, walled settlement with square blocks and an open field on the waterfront, New Orleans became a great commercial center later in the century when settlers spilled across the Appalachian Mountains and toward the western river valleys.

The oldest of great American cities was founded by Dutch settlers who, like the Spanish, brought elaborate urban plans with them. In 1625 a group of colonists from the Dutch West India Company arrived on Manhattan Island with intentions to build a trading center called New Amsterdam, complete with a twenty-five-foot-wide main street and a central marketplace. Although the Dutch used New Amsterdam mainly as a fur trading center and made little effort to develop its harbor, the town soon would become one of the continent's great seaports.

These projects remained as important precedents for future American cities, but the English colonies along the North Atlantic coast, more than any other colonies, created and shaped American urban life. It was especially in the several settlements along or near the Massachusetts shore that the urban frontier began. These towns combined Puritan notions of social and religious harmony with the inward, village orientation of agrarian peasant society to create a kind of corporate communalism, a collective attitude and local identification that laid the foundations for the development of an urban spirit. The town of Boston, however, recast the mold. According to the precepts of John Winthrop, the colony of Massachusetts

Bay was to be "as a Citty upon a Hill," a place that bound people together in the sanctification of God. But when in 1630 the settlers relocated from Charlestown across the Charles River to Boston in order to take advantage of the better water quality there, they began a process that was to swell and diversify population and expand economic activity, thereby obliterating Winthrop's vision. For Boston was to become more than an agrarian-based town: its harbor and natural location as a commercial and administrative hub turned it into a prosperous, worldly city whose interests spilled over the bounds of "a Modell of Christian Charity."

In subsequent decades several other cities developed similarly along the Atlantic coast harbors to the south, all sustained by trade. In 1639 a group of religious dissenters founded Newport on the Island of Rhode Island, ostensibly as a haven for the persecuted. The site they chose had the best harbor in southern New England, and it was this geographical advantage rather than religious tolerance that assured the town's existence. When the British took New Amsterdam from the Dutch in 1664, they inherited the finest natural port in North America and quite naturally preserved the commercial functions of the city as well as making it the capital of the New York colony. In 1680 proprietors of the Carolina colony moved their chief settlement from a marshy location to a peninsula jutting out between the Ashley and Cooper rivers in order to utilize its harbor and more healthful environs. The settlement, named Charles Town (later Charleston), soon became the largest and wealthiest town in the southern colonies. And in 1682 William Penn chose the site for Philadelphia 100 miles up the Delaware River where it was joined by the Schuylkill. This was to be not only the capital of the Pennsylvania colony and the most extensive experiment in city building that the colonies had yet witnessed, but also a place intended as "the most considerable for merchandize, trade, and fishery in these parts."

There were and would be others—Providence, Albany, New Haven, Baltimore, Williamsburg, Norfolk, Savannah—but throughout the colonial period the five cities of Boston, Newport, New York, Philadelphia, and Charleston were the largest and most influential. Although their origins spanned a half century, these five cities resembled each other in several important ways. Most fundamentally, all were ports. As depots for arriving immigrants and as transfer points for resources and products going to and coming from other parts of the world, they all linked their fortunes to the sea. In addition, all had planned beginnings, and all were products of the same civilization. Except for Newport, all originated in intent and leadership in London and Amsterdam, both centers of societies that judged cities to be necessary and desirable. Thus it is not surprising that the Dutch and particularly the British established settlements that assumed characteristics of genuinely urban places: the concentration of people, resources, and ideas. The colonial cities represented for the colonizers the transfer of "civilization"—an urban environment and the activities associated with it—from the Old to the New World.

Because the major colonial cities were commercial and administrative centers, thus attracting inhabitants as much by natural economic forces as by official policy, they all grew rapidly, as the following population figures reveal.

	1690	1742	1775
Boston	7,000	16,382	16,000
Philadelphia	4,000	13,000	24,000
New York	3,900	11,000	25,000
Newport	2,600	6,200	11,000
Charleston	1,100	6,800	12,000

None of the American port towns could compare with even the secondary commercial centers of western Europe such as Lyons, which had reached forty-five thousand in the 1530s, or Norwich, which had grown to nineteen thousand by the 1570s. The port towns were small because they served regional populations that were still themselves limited and because the risks of trade, the lack of development in the agricultural hinterlands, and the low level of credit available to the seaport entrepreneurs limited the opportunities for growth of a market economy on a scale comparable to European commercial capitals. Still, this surge of urban population satisfied British mercantile objectives of centralization for the sake of control. Indeed, the Crown had encouraged the growth of towns because such concentrations of population facilitated the defense and government of the colonists.

But the size and economic opportunities of these cities also prompted activities that stretched the intended limits of colonial administration and eventually threatened the colonial system. As links in the mercantilist system, the colonial ports collected and dispatched raw materials such as grain, rice, fish, furs, and lumber, needed by England, and received the manufactured wares of British merchants for American consumption. Thus most lines of communication extended from individual cities to the mother country rather than among the colonies themselves.

It was not long, however, before the colonial towns bred their own merchants and tradesmen who began to look to the interior settlements in search of markets for locally produced as well as imported goods. Consequently, each city began to cultivate its own commercial hinterland, an activity that turned the colonial ports into small mercantilist powers themselves and enabled them to expand their economies beyond English goals of simple self-support. Just as the colonial mercantile relationship to England drained the colonies of raw materials and what little silver currency circulated, the cities began to draw products and coin from the countryside.

Colonial Amsterdam, 1660   This extraordinary map is a redrawing by John Wolcott Adams and I. N. Phelps Stokes of the Castello Plan of New Amsterdam, first drawn in 1660. The street leading out from the fort and into the undeveloped area is Broadway. The road along the fortification separating the settled area from the unsettled land is Wall Street. *(I. N. Phelps Stokes Collection. Prints Division, The New York Public Library, Astor, Lenox and Tilden Foundations.)*

As early as the 1640s, Boston traders tightened commercial ties westward and southward to Springfield and Hartford and along Long Island Sound, and by the eve of the Revolution inland trade had become an important concern to all of urban America. In Rhode Island, for example, a Providence merchant, Welcome Arnold, shipped processed lime—a necessity for the production of mortar and plaster—not only to Boston, New York, Philadelphia, and Baltimore, but also to smaller settlements in the New England interior. Arnold added retail consumer goods to his inland lime traffic, and he helped attach a broad hinterland to Providence that choked off any potential expansion by Newport, enabling Providence to surpass Newport's size and become New England's second city by 1800. This quest for domestic markets sparked intercity commercial rivalries that gave American urbanization a spirited quality.

The importance of commerce partly explains why most major colonial cities were in the North. With the exceptions of Charleston and, to a lesser degree, Savannah and Norfolk, the South lacked the deep, safe harbors that benefited northern ports. But unlike the North, the South had many rivers that were navigable far inland. Ports were therefore less important in the South, because trading ships did not have to stop at the coast to transfer cargoes to wagons and smaller boats that could travel into the interior. Also, the southern economy, tied to staple-crop agriculture, tended to be more self-sufficient and less dependent on trade than that of the more diversified North. Southern plantations produced much of their own food and clothing, and the region's wealth was invested more in labor than in commerce and industry. Finally, because a large proportion of southern residents were slaves and indentured servants rather than laborers who received wages, there were relatively fewer people in the South with expendable incomes for commercial exchange.

Size and commercial activity, combined with benign neglect on the part of England, also forced the colonial cities into the expansion of self-government. Most towns were created by charters of incorporation granted by the king or the provincial government. These charters defined the form and scope of local administration. Gradually, every colonial city except Charleston assumed self-management of local affairs, acquiring power either by piecemeal grant or by charter revision. Philadelphia and (after 1664) New York, capitals of proprietary colonies, resembled English cities in that they were municipal boroughs, incorporated by royal charter and administered by a mayor and some kind of council. The dominant English tradition of urban self-government was the closed municipal corporation, which reflected the particular commercial focus of cities. Political privileges were not connected to residence but rested in the hands of those who had skills or property, and the vast majority of local officials were chosen from the commercial classes, chiefly merchants and artisans. In Philadelphia, many officers served for life, and in New York City the same officials were generally reelected year after year. Local ordinances were concerned with regulating and promoting trade. In an economy of scarcity, municipal corporations meant to enforce community norms of commercial conduct. Most ordinances concerned such issues as limiting entry into certain skilled crafts, establishing standard weights and measures, fixing prices for locally produced goods, and controlling the quality of those goods. In New York City and Philadelphia the municipal corporation fixed a just price for bread and set the fees that carters could charge. Most city revenues were derived from license fees and rental of market stalls.

In contrast the affairs of Boston and Newport were attended to in town meetings, an institution that resembled the assemblies of rural England yet grew out of Puritan congregationalism. Several times a year all male residents (freemen) of the town would meet to conduct local business—to elect officials, pass laws, levy taxes, and settle disputes. The more open structure and broader fiscal and administrative powers of Boston and Newport made their governments more efficient than those of New York and Philadelphia. Town meetings were thus symbols of order as well as agencies of government. However, they took place only a few times a year. In between, "selectmen"—chosen as executive officials—assumed governmental duties. Their power over appointments, judiciary decisions, and administration often diminished the initiative of the town meeting. The same men, usually those of high standing in both the marketplace and the church, tended to monopolize the councils of selectmen. Deep-rooted traditions of deference in Boston as well as in other colonial cities meant that a community's wealthiest and most well-established men stood for election and were returned to political office year after year. Political factions or parties were considered dangerous, and municipal elections were not seen as forums for expressing differing political ideologies. Nor was political representation understood as expressing competing social, residential, or economic interests. Elections were a traditional means of confirming existing patterns of social order.

Throughout the colonial era the government of Charleston remained in the hands of the provincial assembly that appointed commissioners to manage the affairs of the city. The assemblymen and commissioners often did not live in Charleston, and they represented interests that were seldom sympathetic to the city's welfare. The particular form of urban rule in Charlestown burdened the city with the least responsive government of the five ports. But in all the colonial cities the patterns of urban government in the seventeenth century supported deferential attitudes toward authority.

PROBLEMS OF GROWTH

The urban settlements of the British colonies did not seem much like cities in the early 1700s. Cattle grazed behind crudely built houses, and hogs wallowed in muddy streets. Urban dwellers of different classes, religions, ethnic backgrounds, and occupations lived crowded together along the streets nearest the harbor and wharves. No one could remain anonymous in a place whose boundaries extended no more than a mile in any direction. Paper money was scarce, so people often bought things by bartering with something they had grown or made. The church provided the principal social community for men and women beyond their family and work lives; there were no newspapers, theaters, or other diversions. Oral discourse rather than written or printed words shaped communication among people, and a combination of superstition and belief in the Bible's prescriptions for behavior prevailed.

Yet, almost from their inception the local governments felt the pressures of urban growth. Many of the physical and social problems that nag modern urban society appeared in every colonial city. Although the practical experience and technological tools for their solution were lacking, each town improvised, adjusted, and borrowed methods of response from England and from each other. Initially, individual citizens took steps to remove inconveniences, but quite early they combined and made collective efforts, often surrendering private initiative to government directive. The cities were still small enough and most of their problems so simply defined that most people could comprehend the consequences of alternative solutions (including the alternative of neglect) without having to confront the dilemma of defining public interest. Most colonial city dwellers could appreciate the unity of collective action and accept the exercise of regulatory powers by government.

Urban organization requires efficient transportation and communications, so it is not surprising that town governments devoted much effort to determining where, how, and when new streets should be constructed. In every city—including Philadelphia, where gridiron street patterns had been established prior to settlement—individuals had laid out new roads and paths where they were needed. As a result, narrow streets wound incoherently through some districts. In the 1700s, government intervened, and the construction of new streets became accepted as a function of public policy, even though such roads were merely open stretches cleared of obstructions. In New York City, officers of the municipal corporation looked to private persons to assume the cost of laying out roads as well as filling in swamps, digging wells, erecting bridges, dredging harbors, and building wharves. The city's control of public property made it possible for the municipal corporation to impose these responsibilities on individuals.

The laying of streets, however, involved more than locating a route, removing tree stumps and rocks, and, occasionally, paving with gravel and cobblestone. Mud and stagnant water impeded traffic and threatened health, causing drainage to become a related concern. Boston was most successful in meeting this problem: after 1713 the city began grading streets so that they slanted from the middle to side gutters. By the 1760s other cities had initiated drainage projects. The cities dealt with related problems as well. The governments of Boston, New York, and Newport fined builders who attempted to erect structures in paths of traffic. Several towns constructed and maintained bridges over streams and marshes. These intrusions of public authority met with little resistance from private citizens.

Once the streets, sewers, and bridges were built, the difficulties were far from over, for as the colonial cities grew, so did their traffic. The streets were not only transportation routes but also play areas for children and foraging grounds for hogs, dogs, and cattle. By the middle of the seventeenth century, congestion and accidents were common nuisances on city streets. To protect pedestrians and playing children, several towns levied fines for riding at fast gaits on city streets and for failure to keep horses and other draft animals under tight rein.

Regulations could not lessen the amount of traffic, however, and in an attempt to ease the pressure, cities built more streets, undertook grading and paving projects, and paid more attention to street cleaning. The best streets were those of Boston and Newport, whose governments could levy taxes for highway improvements. Other cities had to depend upon private means or other sources of public funds, such as fines, license fees, or lotteries. Where projects were elaborate, as in Boston, full-time laborers were hired at public expense. Most cities, however, followed the English custom of requiring each householder to devote a certain number of days each year to labor on public works or hire a substitute. In Charleston slaves did most of the public work, and in Boston each free Negro was forced to work on the roads eight days a year instead of doing watch duty, from which blacks were prohibited.

Tossing refuse onto the streets had been one of the bad habits of European city dwellers, and colonial Americans were no more restrained. Their streets quickly became cluttered with human and animal waste, ashes, bones, shells, and other rubbish. The cities, beginning with Boston and New Amsterdam, responded by passing laws prohibiting the indiscriminate disposal of trash. A report from Boston in 1652 noted:

> At a meeting of all the Selckt men, it is ordered that no person inhabiting within said Town shall throw forth or lay any intralls of beasts or fowls or garbidg or Carion or dead dogs or Cattle or any other dead beast or stinkeing thing, in any hie way or dich or Common within this neck of Boston, but ar injoynened to bury all such things that soe they may prevent all anoyanc unto any. Further it is ordered that noe person shall throw forth dust or dung or shreds of Cloth or lether or any tobacco stalks or any such thing into the streets.

But such measures proved impossible to enforce and ineffective as deterrents. Only Boston made any public provision for regular street cleaning, hiring a number of scavengers to haul away street rubbish, but this service was abandoned after 1720 because of mounting costs. Nonetheless, American streets probably were cleaner, better constructed, and better lighted than most of their European counterparts. As early as the 1690s Philadelphians had begun to light lamps in front of their homes at night. Their example was followed by residents of other cities, and by the middle of the eighteenth century local governments had begun to raise and allocate money for public street lighting.

Streets and traffic caused only inconvenience; fire threatened existence. Indeed fire was one of the most feared hazards of urban life, and necessitated public regulations that were less imperative in the countryside. Most buildings in colonial American cities were sited close together and were made of wood, so once started, a blaze was hard to confine. Lacking advanced technology, local authorities could take only limited and precautionary measures, such as prohibiting smoking out of doors, regulating storage of gunpowder and other combustibles, and establishing standards for construction of roofs and chimneys. These last provisions formed the

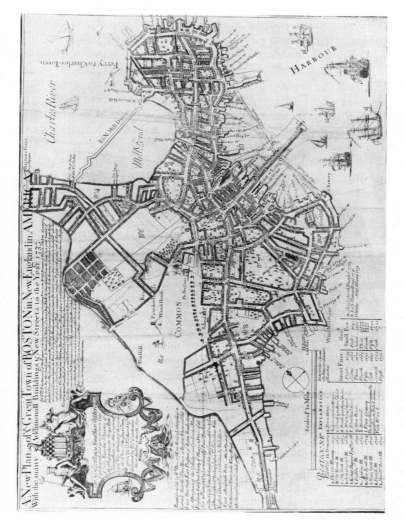

Boston, 1773 This plan, drawn by John Bonner in 1733, includes the Long Wharf, which stretched some 1,500 feet into the harbor and contained shops and warehouses. As time passed, spaces between the other wharfs and docks were filled in, and the wharfs were joined to make room for new buildings. Throughout its history the city of Boston has constantly reclaimed space from areas formerly covered by water. *(The John Carter Brown Library, Brown University.)*

first American building codes and included prohibitions on reed and straw roofing, and on wood and plaster chimneys. Authorities also attempted to eliminate potential fires by limiting places in which brush or rubbish could be burned and forbidding construction of wooden buildings in the center of town. In 1649 Boston adopted the English curfew, requiring all house fires to be covered or extinguished between 9 PM and 4:30 AM. Nearly all American towns adopted the European tradition of community responsibility for extinguishing fires. Each city contained at least one volunteer fire company comprising private citizens and organized as a protective and social agency.

Unfortunately the towns did not react to such urban dangers as fires until after a disaster had occurred. This was to be a recurring pattern in American urban history. Destructive or disruptive events usually provoked some civic reform, but then the concern would dwindle to apathy until another disaster struck and galvanized a new spirit of action. After the first of the "great" fires struck Boston in 1653, public alarm prompted the first urban fire code in colonial America. The measure required every householder to keep a ladder, at his own expense, to facilitate fire fighting. The town also bought ladders and hooks, and officials assumed the authority to order the leveling of any burning structure. Few other precautions were taken until 1676, when another conflagration threatened to destroy all of Boston. After it was extinguished, the town bought a fire engine from England and appointed a supervisor and twelve assistants to operate it. Even these measures were not enough, for in 1679 one of the worst fires in American history swept Boston, ravaging most of its commercial section. This disaster forced officials to tighten fire regulations and to organize the city into districts for more efficient fire control. Other towns acted similarly to meet the threat of fire, but Boston's many destructive fires resulted in regulations and equipment among the most advanced in the world.

Protection was another problem emerging in the young cities. The seamen, transient laborers, and others attracted to the ports by the promise of jobs engendered by the market economy threatened the orderly world of family and communal governance. Urban life necessitated some type of agency to preserve the peace and protect property. At first, private citizens organized volunteer patrols. Subsequently, most police forces copied the European system of daytime constables and night watches appointed daily and paid for by the public. Although the duties of the watch differed from town to town, they consisted mainly of apprehending criminals, maintaining order—controlling brawlers and drunks—and watching for fires.

Constable and watch duty, required of every male citizen, proved to be a thankless and dangerous job, and as time passed, increasing numbers of townsmen tried to evade service. The wealthy could hire a substitute or pay the fine for not serving. Thus, most early police were laborers, tradesmen, and artisans—those who could least afford to contribute time from their daily livelihoods. Colonists' experiences while quartering the British Army made them acutely aware of the abuses of power that could be taken by a standing army, and they were thus unwilling to create a permanent, professional police force. By the middle of the eighteenth century average city dwellers faced rising danger to person and property from street riots, drunken brawls, and petty thievery. But they did not yet perceive this situation as a significant threat, and they remained uncommitted to the idea of a formal agency of law enforcement. Although crime in the colonial towns seems to have been less severe than in English cities and on the Continent, the failure to establish an institution of urban order has haunted American cities to the present.

Notions of public health in the seventeenth and eighteenth centuries were probably more primitive than those of fire and police protection. The germ theory of disease had not yet been established; most people believed noxious vapors from stagnant water and decaying material caused sickness. Nevertheless, regulations that attempted to eliminate these vapors by controlling garbage disposal—a task at first left to hogs that roamed the streets—and prohibiting pollution of streams and ponds removed some of the breeding places of disease-carrying pests. Local laws were enacted prohibiting citizens from dumping refuse and filth in certain public places, and men were hired to carry away trash and human waste. Most cities eventually passed measures that regulated the location and depth of privies and graves and confined tanneries and slaughterhouses to one part of town. Measures controlling the disposal of waste were enacted with little, if any, objection to the use of governmental authority.

Town dwellers feared infectious diseases as much as fires, and once an epidemic began it was hard to stop. All the colonial cities except Charleston were located away from the climate and diseases of the tropics, but all were seaports and therefore vulnerable to epidemics brought in by infected seamen, vermin, and insects. Smallpox was the most frequent and dreaded danger, threatening every city. Boston and Charleston suffered most severely from this disease, experiencing epidemics that killed hundreds at a time. But as with fire, misfortune helped to create progressive policy, for by the 1760s Americans were beginning to accept inoculation as the best preventive measure. Fevers, dysentery, and other diseases were also prevalent, and the cities combated them by requiring inspections of entering ships and refusing landing to those on which sickness was found. Boston was the first city to establish quarantine regulations, and by the early 1700s most other cities had followed its lead. In spite of limited medical knowledge, by 1770 city officials had succeeded remarkably well in controlling most major scourges except yellow fever, which continued to plague eastern and southern cities until the twentieth century.

Another problem of urban growth was the large number of indigent residents, whose care became a major responsibility of each city. Poverty has never been a problem peculiar to cities, but it took on new meaning in the urban context. In the early years of settlement the incidence of poverty was quite low, especially relative to English towns. Generally, widows, orphans, and disabled people, impoverished by circumstances beyond their control, were the ones who required assistance. Colonists accepted the seventeenth-century English notion of public responsibility for the support of dependent classes. Poor relief accounted for much of local government expenditures. People in need remained with their families or in the homes of neighbors and were provided with clothes, firewood, and bread.

As the towns grew, their involvement with market forces beyond their control brought increasing economic uncertainty—good times and bad times, high and low wages, periodic unemployment. A temporary glut on the market could bring a drop in commercial revenues that could quickly expand the number of residents without food or firewood. The burden of manpower and resources expended in the European wars of 1689 to 1697, 1702 to 1713, and 1739 to 1747 and the inflation caused by emergency issuance of paper money hurt a growing part of the urban population. Periodic unemployment, rising prices that outstripped wages, and war taxes that fell with unusual severity on the lower classes created poverty that was no longer the situational condition of the aged, widowed, or crippled but now a problem that touched the seasonally unemployed, war veterans, new immigrants, and migrants from inland areas seeking employment in the cities. Poverty was particularly visible in the cities, their being much more densely populated than the countryside. In Boston, relief expenditures for the poor rose from 500 pounds in 1700 to 4,000 pounds in 1736, and in New York from 250 pounds in 1698 to 5,000 pounds in the 1770s. As the cost of poor relief increased, Boston, New York, and Philadelphia built almshouses in the 1730s in an attempt to reduce the cost of caring for the growing number of poor citizens by sheltering them under one roof and in some places by having the willing poor support themselves by picking okum, weaving cloth, and making shoes. These institutions also housed sick poor who could not work and the "Vagrant & Idle Persons" who would not work and were therefore classed as criminals. Some officials stigmatized those on relief by requiring them to wear or carry badges designating their status as paupers. Another form of relief consisted of assigning ("binding out") the needy to private businesses in a form of indentured servitude.

Many cities tried to minimize pauperism—as well as their tax money spent on the poor—by restricting immigration. Philadelphia, New York, and nearly all the New England towns had provisions requiring the registration, bonding, or inspection of all newcomers. Those who had no friends or relatives to vouch for them or who lacked visible means of support were ordered away. As the cities grew in size, however, so did the need for laborers and the opportunity for anonymity. By the early 1700s immigration restrictions were breaking down, and many places were openly encouraging immigration.

Public relief efforts were increasingly supplemented by aid from private agencies. In the eighteenth century, organizations such as the Scots Charitable Society in Boston and New York, the Carpenters' Company in Philadelphia, and the Fellowship Society in Charleston, as well as churches and wealthy individuals, made substantial contributions to the alleviation of poverty. Still, as time passed, the number of urban poor grew even larger. The proportion of a colonial city's population assisted by public or private money at any one time is difficult to discern. But it seems that for every relief recipient several more lived at the subsistence level and received no aid and that poverty plagued American cities from the very beginning.

Attempts by the colonial cities to solve their problems highlight a curious, but also typical, intertwining of private interest and public welfare. On the one hand, problems were common to all cities. They were predicaments of urban life, of many people living close together, and they required community regulation of formerly private activities. As one historian has written, "In the country a man might construct his home, build his fire, dig his well, erect his privy, and dispose of his rubbish without thought for the well-being of his neighbors, but in town these became objects of community concern and gradually of civic ordinance. In the country a man might be little affected by the poverty or wrong-doing of others, but the towns soon discovered their civic duty in the combatting and control of these social evils."[1] Many of the problems of health, fire, water, and communications were insoluble at the time, and colonial city dwellers simply tried collectively to minimize them and then to adjust as technological and scientific developments offered solutions. Social problems such as disorder and poverty remained baffling. Nevertheless, a kind of public unity plus the inheritance of a European tradition of public endeavor enabled colonial cities to meet their problems and to set precedents for future urban generations.

THE SOCIAL MOSAIC

Between 1690 and 1740 the small colonial seaports grew into commercial centers that rivaled British provincial ports such as Hull, Bristol, and Glasgow. Like their counterparts abroad, by the end of the seventeenth century the towns of colonial America were not only experiencing similar problems, but were also developing similar social mosaics that set them apart from the surrounding countryside. Racial, cultural, and religious diversity jumbled urban society while economic distinctions sliced through it. With the exception of the New England towns, restrictions on immigration seldom worked; the English composition of most cities was quickly diluted by other groups.

By the early 1700s blacks were almost as numerous as whites in Charleston, and there were substantial numbers of blacks in cities all the way up the coast to Boston. Scotch-Irish and Germans constituted important segments of the populations of Philadelphia and New York, where they met the growing need for laborers, but their presence challenged shared English assumptions. The cities contained a more diverse society than could be found in rural areas and also housed more institutions for the entertainment, edification, and refreshment of their residents. The increasing population provided the cities with human and economic resources for the creation of educational facilities and the dissemination of information from the outside world.

Most colonists migrated or descended from European society, where a distinct hierarchy of status prevailed, and they accepted the existence of social differences in America. In fact, a stratified society was justified as being sanctioned by God. Thus a Boston merchant asserted in 1700 that God "hath Ordained different degrees and orders of men, some to be High and Honourable, some to be Low and Despicable, some to be Monarchs, Kings, Princes, and Governours, Masters and Commanders, others to be subjects, and to be commanded." From the beginning an ordered social structure crystallized in colonial America, but it operated differently in the cities than in the country. In the cities the greater development of the market meant more opportunity to accumulate wealth. But it also created growing inequalities between those whose extensive resources allowed them to take risks and make profits and those whose modest resources made them more vulnerable to economic fluctuation.

Although the lines between the major status groups were often blurred, colonial urban society can be said to have consisted of four such groups, distinguished by male occupation and wealth. In the top rank were wealthy merchants and investors, plus an occasional clergyman or government official. These generally were men who had become wealthy from overseas and inland commerce or had accumulated enough capital to use in lucrative moneylending or land-rental businesses. Merchants often did more than buy and sell goods. In a time when banks, law offices, and construction companies were rare, merchants used their money and influence to assume the role of banker, legal arbitrator, and land developer. As historian Gary Nash has argued, those who controlled mercantile endeavors gained a disproportionate share of economic power in colonial cities through their impact on the flow of marketable goods, shipbuilding, credit facilities, and urban real estate.[2]

Men in the top status group controlled most of the local wealth (which consisted primarily of property) and filled the higher positions in local government. As time passed, they seemed to procure proportionately more of the wealth than those in the lower ranks. According to data compiled by Nash, in 1687 the wealthiest 10 percent of Boston's population controlled 46 percent of the taxable wealth. By 1771 the top 10 percent owned 63 percent. In Philadelphia, over a comparable period, the richest 10 percent of the population increased its holdings from 46 to 72 percent of that city's taxable wealth.[3] In Boston and Philadelphia, as well as in other cities, this upper order was neither a closed aristocracy nor a monolithic social class. Its membership was both large and diverse, including men who had advantages of birth and position as well as those who had risen from a lower rank. Throughout the colonial period, wealth, more than birth, was the principal criterion for admission to this upper group.

Wives of wealthy merchants had lives that were very different from women in the countryside. One of the benefits of residing in a town was the availability of a pool of female workers who could be hired as servants. Supervision of domestic labor was an involved and time-consuming activity. But because wives could send servants to buy and prepare food and could hire seamstresses to create clothing, they had more time to write letters and diaries and to engage in rounds of social visiting. Daughters in well-to-do eighteenth-century households were the only American women at the time who could accurately be described as leisured. They did not have to help with household work, so that they were free to sleep late, learn music and dancing, and read the latest novels. In cities, because goods were available for purchase, household production decreased as wealth and privilege rose. Once urban women were able to buy things like tea, milk, butter, candles, linens, cloth, coats, and gowns, the seventeenth-century mode of housewifery symbolized by the spinning wheel became increasingly a badge of lower status.

Although the wealthy capitalists wielded considerable power, the lower ranks better embodied typical colonial urban life. Beneath the merchants and their allies was a large, diverse, fluctuating population of craftsmen, retailers, minor jobbers, and innkeepers that constituted the middle class. Among the craftsmen and retailers were coopers, who provided barrels and kegs that were essential for shipping and storage; carpenters and woodworkers, who provided housing and furnishings; food dealers; metalsmiths; and printers. These individuals carried on local manufacturing and merchandising in the preindustrial city, running the one-man shops that predominated in every town. Often they were aided by an apprentice, indentured servant, or wife. Individual shopkeepers and craftsmen generally lived and worked in the same house.

Within most of the crafts a wide range of wealth and status existed, reflecting the hierarchy within each craft from apprentice to journeyman to master craftsman. The range of wealth was thus related to age but also to the possibilities within each craft. Artisans working with precious metals were more likely to earn a comfortable living than were cobblers, and house carpenters were more likely to become property owners than were tailors and stocking weavers. Artisans hoped to earn a "competency," enough money to live in relative comfort, and in every city the average artisan or shopkeeper usually owned enough property to vote, often also holding a minor office. Shopkeepers' and artisans' wives probably did not have to spin or weave, but occasionally they assisted their husbands in business, acting in place of their husbands in case of absence or death. They had responsibility for food preparation, which often included cultivating a garden and raising poultry. Daughters and wives also sewed extensively to keep their families clothed.

The expansion of the economy and the opportunity to rise in importance by acquiring wealth attuned colonial city dwellers to bourgeois standards. But such conditions also made the middle classes vulnerable to economic dislocation: their position on the social scale rose and fell over time, depending on economic developments. The early years of urban growth offered lucrative opportunities for small-scale investors and entrepreneurs. As the cities grew, however, so did the size and specialization of their economic operations. By the middle of the eighteenth century larger businesses were squeezing small investors out of high-return areas such as commercial shipping. Between 1687 and 1771 the proportion of taxable wealth owned by Boston's and Philadelphia's middle classes declined while the percentage owned by the upper segments rose. Evidence indicates that economic opportunities of the urban middle class in most cities became restricted until westward expansion and the dawn of industrialization in the early 1800s opened new avenues for advancement.

The third economic group consisted of a growing number of unskilled laborers, mariners, and some artisans. These people owned little or no property. Many were transients, earning a living on the docks and at sea or moving from town to town in search of work. They loaded, unloaded, and were the crew on ships that linked the seaports with the commercial world of Europe and the West Indies. Other laborers dug wells, paved streets, and hauled wood and other goods. Their wives and daughters took in washing, kept boarders, spun at home, and served as seamstresses and housekeepers for middle- and upper-class families. Many working-class families lived in crowded two- or three-room cottages at a bare level of subsistence, but in labor-scarce cities some could command high wages and acquire property. Geographical mobility and chances for improvement precluded the development of a permanent proletariat in the colonial cities. The entrance to most crafts remained open, and local restrictions on newcomers failed to prevent working-class families from migrating. Still, cities housed much higher proportions of poor and propertyless people than did rural areas. By the close of the colonial period the poor constituted between 20 and 30 percent of many a city's population—though the percentage was smaller in southern towns, where large numbers of slaves reduced the proportion of white laborers. The fortunes of the urban working classes were especially sensitive to economic fluctuations. If the local economy was expanding, they could subsist and even improve their lot. But whereas economic uncertainty and decline brought sacrifice and deprivation to the middle and upper classes, the working classes struggled for survival.

Indentured servants were positioned below free labor and above slaves in the social structure. Indentured servitude was closely linked to immigration, because most indentured servants traded four or seven years of labor for passage across the Atlantic and on arrival were sold at the docks to the highest bidder. They were an important part of the labor force in New York and Philadelphia. In the early years of urban settlement, many indentured servants were probably kin of emigrating Englishmen who paid their passage in return for their labor. Later, German and Scotch-Irish servants and redemptioners provided the vast number of bound white laborers. By the 1730s, German and Scotch-Irish indentured servants were most numerous in Philadelphia. There they worked not just in households but in ropewalks, shipyards, bakeries, and liveries and by the mid-1740s constituted more than one-fifth of the city's white male work force.

A rising standard of living and mobility up and down the social scale, however limited, was possible for about four-fifths of colonial city dwellers—a sizable majority. But the remainder, consisting of blacks and Indians, both slave and free, formed a permanent, inescapable lower class. In the Southwest the availability of Indian labor near the mission at San Gabriel was one of the main attractions prompting northern Mexican colonists to found the city of Los Angeles. Indian slaves could be found in several northern towns, although by 1715 the difficulties of dealing with native Americans in bondage led Massachusetts, Rhode Island, and Connecticut to pass laws forbidding importations from Charleston, the center of the Yamasee slave trade. African slaves were the most common form of bound labor everywhere. By the end of the seventeenth century, free laborers, apprentices, indentured servants, and slaves probably constituted as much as half of the urban labor force. In 1690 about one in nine Boston households included at least one slave, and in 1698 over one-third of New York households had slaves. Although the Quakers who dominated Philadelphia later repudiated slavery, earlier settlers freely bought and sold slaves. After 1714, sizable numbers of slaves were imported into all the northern port towns. By 1750 about one-fifth of all Boston families owned slaves. By 1746 an estimated one-half of New York households owned a slave.

In Charleston, Baltimore, New York, and Boston, slaves did much of the heavy manual work and provided most of the domestic service. Slave ownership was almost universal among the urban elite; costumed slave coachmen and livery grooms were a common way of visibly displaying wealth. Newspaper advertisements in New York City for skilled black slaves suggest that some members of the artisan class had prospered sufficiently to substitute slaves for apprentices. In all of the ports, urban slavery moved steadily from the households to the docks, warehouses, and shops, where slaves worked as mariners and in crafts connected to shipbuilding, in the ropewalks, shipyards, and sail manufactories. The importance of these slaves to the growth of cities increased during the eighteenth century.

Northern urban slavery was characterized by particular patterns that distinguished it from slavery in the Chesapeake Bay area and low-country south. For one thing, northern slavery was disproportionately urban. During the eighteenth century, between one-fifth and one-fourth of the slaves in New York colony lived in New York City; one-third of the slaves in New Hampshire and Massachusetts lived in Portsmouth and Boston, and nearly half of Rhode Island's black population lived in New-port. Crowded urban housing conditions forced slaves into back rooms, lofts, and occasionally makeshift alley shacks. Under these circumstances few masters held more than one or two slaves, and masters discouraged their slaves from establishing families. As a result there were more male slaves than females in the cities, especially in the early years, and black women had fewer children than did white women. The inability or unwill-ingness of urban masters to support large households of slaves put a severe strain on black family life, but it also encouraged masters to allow their slaves to live out, hire their own time, and thereby gain a measure of independence and freedom.

In the cities, slaves tended to live and work in close proximity to whites. With that proximity, slaves gained first-hand knowledge of their masters' world, and they also rubbed elbows with working-class whites in taverns, cockfights, and fairs where poor people of varying status mingled. This knowledge of white culture in combination with the job opportunities provided by the complex northern economy, the close ties between master and slave, and the social life of city streets helped urban slaves to make better lives for themselves. In the eighteenth century some urban slaves informally enjoyed the rights to hold property of their own, to visit friends, live with their families, or hire their own time.

The cosmopolitan nature of the cities also sped the transformation of African to Afro-American. In the early years of northern urban slavery, most slaves did not arrive directly from Africa but came through the West Indies or the mainland South. This seasoning in slavery had worked to destroy ties to African tribal culture but had also prepared urban slaves to turn urban opportunities to their own advantage. Between 1732 and 1754, slaves were imported into the cities directly from Africa. The large num-bers of newly arrived Africans reawakened urban Afro-American slaves to their African past by providing direct knowledge of West African society. Northern black slaves designated their churches "African" and called them-selves "Sons of Africa." They showed their new knowledge of African cul-ture most clearly in the celebration of Negro Election Day, a West African ritual festival of role reversal celebrated commonly in New England and middle-colony towns in the mid-eighteenth century. Celebrations took different forms in different communities, but everywhere a day of merrymaking that drew in blacks from the surrounding countryside culminated in the selection of black kings, governors, and judges. While the black governors held court, adjudicating minor disputes, slaves paraded and partied, dressed in their masters' clothes and mounted on their masters' horses. Negro Election Day celebrated a momentary release from bondage and also acknowledged leadership within the black community. Northern whites, confident of their own control over the institution of slavery, not only aided Election Day materially but sometimes joined in themselves. In these interstices of urban life, slaves developed strong and cohesive Afro-American traditions that would sustain future urban black communities.

In southern port cities like Charleston and Savannah, urban Afro-American slaves' extensive knowledge of white culture contrasted sharply with the survival of West African tribal traditions in the plantation areas identified by a black majority. The coastal cities needed workers to transport and process the plantation staples, to serve the hundreds of ships that docked at the wharves, to run the planters' urban households, and to satisfy the planters' taste for luxury goods. Slaves did most of this work. Throughout the eighteenth century, slaves constituted more than half of the population of Charleston and other low-country ports. Probably nothing arrived at or left these cities without some black handling it. Black artisans also played a large role in urban life, employed by master craftsmen in every variety of work. Black artisans labored along the waterfront as shipwrights, coopers, and ropemakers and also in the higher trades as silversmiths and cabinetmakers. In addition, black women controlled much of the marketing in the low-country ports, mediating between slave-grown produce from the countryside and urban consumption.

Mobile, often skilled, and occasionally literate, southern urban slaves understood the white world and, like their counterparts in northern cities, used their knowledge to enlarge their independence. They hired their own time, earning wages, kept market stalls, occasionally even opened shops, lived apart from their masters, and rented houses of their own, sometimes even keeping families intact. In these activities, urban slaves visibly assumed the white man's privileges. Some slaves gained special positions as a result of intimate sexual relations with white masters, and the small free-mulatto population of Charleston was the product of such relationships. In Charleston the considerable size of the slave population relative to the white population made slaveholders much less sanguine than their northern counterparts about the existence of an independent black community, but even though restrictions and regulations attempted to limit the autonomous space for black communal institutions, the small black communities that developed below the bluff in Savannah and along Charleston's Neck confirmed the growing independence of urban Afro-American culture.

Urban life, with its varied activities and social contacts, was less regimented for a slave than servitude in the country, but it remained restrictive. By the early 1700s most towns had passed a number of ordinances, such as curfews and prohibitions on certain purchases, limiting the private activities of all blacks, slave and free. Actual slave insurrections in New York City in 1712 and at the Stono River in South Carolina (20 miles from Charleston) in 1739 and rumors of slave conspiracy in New York City in 1741 inspired whites to react with terror and execution, exposing the violent coercion that lay just beneath the surface of white paternalism. After the 1712 revolt thirteen slaves died on the gallows; one was starved to death in chains; three were burned at the stake; one was broken on the wheel; and six committed suicide. Mounted whites who stopped the march of rebels from Stono on its way south to Florida killed several slaves and set their heads on mileposts along the road. In New York in 1741 eighteen slaves and fourteen whites were sentenced to be tortured and hanged; thirteen slaves were condemned to burn to death at the stake, and another seventy were transported to the West Indies. In addition, local lawmakers passed slave codes that strictly regulated slaves' freedom of movement and stripped away many of their rights.

Women, like slaves, were viewed as dependents whose existence depended on their place within the household. Commonly accepted norms of family hierarchy, female submission, and mutual obligation dictated the nature of relations between wife and husband, just as they ordered those between man and God, slave and master, child and parent. The nuclear family was the central focus of colonial society, even more than in England, because migration had severed individuals and families from their wider kin connections. As dependents, women generally were assumed to be incapable of expressing autonomous political or religious opinions. An adult woman's authority derived from her role as mistress of the household; under her husband's supervision she directed the household's daily affairs, and should fate or circumstance prevent her husband from fulfilling his role as head of the household, the wife could appropriately stand in his place without really changing the patriarchal order of society.

Colonial governments increasingly legalized the status of women as deputy husbands by passing statutes that allowed women some limited powers to run businesses in the absence of their husbands. The laws were not an endorsement of women's economic independence; rather they were a means of keeping women whose men were dead or absent from relying on public relief. Nevertheless these laws facilitated women's economic activity, and they implicitly supported the idea that it was possible for a married woman to have a separate estate. Although the proportion of self-supporting working widows (and increasingly, spinsters) in the eighteenth century never exceeded 10 percent of the adult female population, they congregated in the towns and cities. In Boston as early as the 1740s, 13 percent of the city's 16,000 residents were widows, "almost all of them poor," according to the town records.

In both the seventeenth and eighteenth centuries some working widows managed trades inherited from their husbands, at least until sons could replace them, and were therefore found in every type of occupation— including that of mortician, blacksmith, and reporter. But most working women were employed in trades connected to household production and in ventures they started themselves, usually catering to female clients. In Baltimore, 8 percent of the city's households were headed by women in 1796, and two-thirds of these were widows, less than half of whom worked to support themselves. The rest were spinsters, almost all of whom worked. Although their number included the occasional printer, mill owner, and speculator, positions they invariably inherited when they became widows, most of Baltimore's working women, like those elsewhere, entered the wide array of trades originating in domestic work. Women were not only seamstresses and laundresses but dyers, starchers, soap and candle makers, lacemakers, and mantua makers. As shop proprietresses, they dealt in china, groceries, pastries, dry goods, millinery, and hardware. As in other cities, they ran inns, boarding houses, and taverns. Indeed, by the end of the eighteenth century women held the majority of liquor licenses in most towns. Women ran dame schools and small boarding schools and worked as midwives, wet-nurses, and domestic servants, usually earning less in wages than unskilled white men or hired out male slaves, barely eking out a living for themselves and their children.

The continuing development of the market economy in the cities and the resultant specialization in economic life began a process that heightened the distinction between the world of men in the marketplace and the world of women in the home. In wealthy families in the North and South, use of servants for cooking and cleaning reoriented women's domestic activities to child rearing, and the importance of women's maternal functions began to be recognized. In nothern dissenting families the special concerns of Quakers and Puritans with children's spiritual upbringing had the same effect of emphasizing the role of women in their maternal capacity. Historian Mary Beth Norton has found that by the time of the Revolution, urban women's knowledge of family property was limited to the furnishings of the houses in which they lived, unless they were widows or had worked outside the home, while rural women's household tasks sometimes gave them access to information about family property in fields and livestock. Men's knowledge of household accounts and household purchases was similarly limited.[4] Norton's findings suggest that men and women did indeed inhabit different worlds and that the distinctive qualities of urban life sharpened the boundaries separating men's and women's daily lives.

The variety within the colonial urban population fostered new social institutions and modified old ones. An institution that was particularly affected by urbanization was the church. The initial period of growth of American towns was one in which religion pervaded every aspect of human life. Churches influenced political and economic affairs and absorbed social life as well. Whether in the Puritan North, the Anglican South, or the more divided middle colonies, the clergy were held in high esteem and exerted power over family life, education, and government. Religion defined and enforced social discipline.

As time passed two developments peculiar to urban growth threatened the supremacy of organized religion in the colonial cities. Population growth and diversity spurred the multiplication of rival sects, which broke down religious unity. Baptists, Presbyterians, and Anglicans contested Quaker preeminence in Philadelphia and Congregational hegemony in the New England cities. Particularly in New England, Puritan ministers could no longer command communal deference, since many families imitated the British aristocracy and joined the Church of England. The evangelical revivals known as the Great Awakening of the late 1730s and 1740s broke with great force in the cities, where crowds congregated by the thousands to hear the charismatic George Whitefield and others who followed him assault traditional sources of authority and permanently shatter the monopolistic hold of the educated clergy on religious discourse. Cosmopolitanism and economic opportunity provided other townspeople with several alternatives to church attendance. Secular activities and amusements increasingly lured some people away from the church, provoking Cotton Mather to lament with characteristic alarm that "the peculiar Spirit and Error of the Time [is] *Indifference* to *Religion*." Although church membership grew absolutely in nearly every city, it rose slowly and as a result the gap between a town's total population and its total church members continually widened.

As colonial towns grew, taverns began to intrude upon the church's share of people's time. Open to all men, these public houses were the most egalitarian of all colonial establishments. All classes came here to drink, eat, talk, and hear the news of the day. But the taverns served more than mere social functions; they were centers for the discussion of politics, transaction of business, distribution of broadsides and pamphlets, and delivery of mail from visiting ships. As the number of taverns multiplied and as members of various social groups began seeking out people of their own sort, many establishments acquired a reputation for catering to one class or another. But in most cities formal distinctions between taverns did not exist. Of course the services provided were only for men; it was highly improper for a respectable woman to be seen tipping a cup of grog. Malt could justify God's ways to men, but women had to look elsewhere.

By the end of the seventeenth century taverns and groggeries had become the most flourishing centers of urban life. However, their informality and profusion of rum and other alcoholic beverages also made them natural locations for disorder and vice. In response to rising complaints most towns adopted the English policy of licensing establishments. This did not diminish the number of public houses—by the 1720s there were over a hundred licensed taverns in Boston, and in the peak year of 1752 New

A Colonial Tavern This trade card advertises the reopening of a prominent tavern in Newburyport, Massachusetts. Such establishments performed vital, but often overlooked, functions for colonial city dwellers. (Courtesy of The American Antiquarian Society.)

York authorities issued 334 licenses—but it did give the town governments some measure of control. On the other hand, licensing resulted in the rise of many "speak-easies." Coffeehouses and inns also became important centers for social, political, and commercial activity. In New York, for example, the Tontine Coffeehouse served as the merchant's exchange, and the Exchange Coffeehouse was the clearinghouse for many real-estate transfers.

In addition to all of the activities of the public houses, cities offered the vast majority of educational and cultural opportunities in colonial America. Family and church had the primary responsibility for education, and most children still learned to read at home, but supplementary schooling, initiated by parents on an informal basis, was fairly widespread. Following the lead of Boston, many cities supported some type of public school by the

1720s, and they all could boast several private schools for the wealthy as well as religious and charity schools for the poor. Even Indians and blacks could obtain learning, however limited, from English missionary groups such as the Anglican-based Society for the Propagation of the Gospel in Foreign Parts. At the same time, scores of bookstores appeared in the larger cities, and the colonial bookseller became instrumental in the spread of literary culture. Private libraries could be found in the towns and country, but cities, notably Boston and Philadelphia, pioneered the establishment of public libraries. Not only did the cities house and distribute written works, but they also printed them. By 1700 Boston, Philadelphia, and New York had presses that were producing books and pamphlets of secular and religious prose and poetry. More important, these printers supplied almanacs, blank forms, and newspapers, all vital to urban life. In the eighteenth-century seaports the printing and distribution of political pamphlets, minutes of legislative proceedings and assembly votes, instructions to assembly representatives, and special election pamphlets had the effect of broadening the conception of politics, giving all literate colonists access to the examination and discussion of controversial issues previously only within the reach of the political elite. And because the cities housed almost all of the museums, scientific associations, concerts, theaters, and artists, they dominated science and the arts as well as the publishing and dissemination of literature. John Smibert, the noted eighteenth-century American portrait painter, worked in Newport and Boston; plays and dance exhibitions were increasingly popular in New York and Charleston; and writers from all five colonial cities contributed scientific papers to the *Philosophical Transactions* of the Royal Society.

CITIES IN THE AMERICAN REVOLUTION

While colonial cities were generating common internal problems and complex social structures, they remained appendages of the British Empire, founded and governed as nodes in a larger administrative and economic network. For over a century American city dwellers lived outwardly at peace with the mother country, but beneath the relatively calm surface three forces were gnawing away at the foundations of British mercantile control. First, in order to meet immediate problems of local organization and services, the colonial towns had developed their own institutions. These institutions exercised considerable authority over local ordinances, taxes, and finances because the Crown and Parliament were uninterested in devoting attention to every detail of colony management, or were unable to do so. This situation was particularly true of Boston, where the town meeting influenced so many local matters. By 1750 every one of the dozen or so other major colonial towns had also achieved some degree of governmental independence, and they jealously protected it. Second, colonial merchants had managed to coexist with the restrictive Navigation Acts by arranging with sympathetic customs collectors to pay only a fraction of the required duties or by evading the law altogether and engaging in illicit trade. Thus much of the trading community acquired and expected profits outside of the mercantilist system. Such profits were not always assured, though. When British creditors demanded payments before American merchants were able to comply, or when local or foreign customers were unable to pay on time for goods delivered, a credit crunch staggered commerce. Such instances, however, prompted Americans to search even more avidly for new markets, outside the British colonies as well as inside. Third and perhaps most important, many colonial townsmen came to view their self-government and commercial independence as the most natural and just system for them, and any interference with it as illegal and tyrannical.

The Peace of Paris, which ended the French and Indian (Seven Years') War in 1763, signaled a new era during which new British policies agitated these forces and converted them into the sparks of American independence. At the end of the war Great Britain faced the tasks of organizing her newly enlarged empire abroad and relieving economic pressure at home caused by the soaring costs of colonial defense and administration. Thus in 1764 Parliament, under the leadership of George Grenville, passed the Molasses Act, attempting for the first time to raise revenue in America. This measure clamped down on smuggling and provided for stricter enforcement of a new, though reduced, molasses duty. Since 1733, the duty had been sixpence per gallon; now it was to be threepence. The Stamp Act followed in 1765, the first direct internal tax ever laid on the colonies. It required revenue stamps, costing from a halfpenny to upwards of twenty shillings, to be attached to all newspapers, almanacs, broadsides, pamphlets, advertisements, licenses, bonds, leases, and numerous other legal documents and commercial papers. These acts hit cities the hardest, affecting merchants, lawyers, and printers directly and artisans, shopkeepers, tradesmen, and laborers indirectly. The repeal of the Stamp Act in 1766 did not lighten the burden, for in 1767 Parliament passed the Townshend Acts, adding import duties to glass, lead, paper, paint, and tea.

It is not surprising, then, that cities provided the arenas for much of the resistance to new British policies. The earliest and most organized activity came from the merchants. For them the Peace of Paris brought not only restrictive legislation but also the demise of wartime prosperity, which had been derived largely from trade with England's enemies. The merchants' first reaction was to try to recapture evaporating profits by encouraging more inter- and intracolonial trade. In April 1764 some Boston merchants organized the Society for Encouraging Trade and Commerce Within the

Province of Massachusetts Bay, and in the following months New York and Philadelphia merchants formed similar associations. The same year, several prominent New Yorkers revived the Society for the Promotion of Arts, Agriculture and Economy (which had existed briefly forty years earlier) to encourage more local manufacturing, which could ostensibly offset the Navigation Acts and the high prices of imported goods. Leaders of other cities followed this example. None of the efforts worked: they failed to change not only Parliament's policies but also the skewed balance of trade that drained the colonies of hard money, the only medium accepted by royal tax collectors and London creditors. Therefore in 1765 merchants, particularly in the northern cities, adopted new tactics—boycotts and the nonimportation of British goods—and they formed associations to petition Parliament and the Crown for relief, to enforce nonimportation agreements, and to communicate ideas and activities to other colonies. It was this community of interests, activated in the 1760s but dating back to the seventeenth century, that coordinated resistance against the British and tied the first knots of American union.

These early protest activities included few notions of American independence. Merchants wished mainly to revive the conditions that had existed before 1763 and that had brought prosperity to traders in every city except Boston. To be sure, the merchant community was not unified. Some merchants, such as Thomas Hutchinson and his brother-in-law Andrew Oliver, were deeply enmeshed in British mercantile trading networks and obligated by profitable royal connections as well as their own financial interests to support parliamentary policies. Men like Hutchinson and Oliver lived a life-style modeled on that of the British aristocracy and favored more, rather than less, British presence in America. Other merchants, however, had won wealth and position from smuggling as well as legitimate trade, certainly without any help from the mother country, and cared little about the English social hierarchy. In fact, as their protests to economic restrictions mounted, they became increasingly antimonarchical and resentful that royal appointments and restrictions stood in the way of their exercising political power commensurate with their economic resources. Still, until the 1770s most merchants were concerned far more with profits than with independence.

Just as debate among the merchants was beginning to break up the previously unquestioned consensus concerning the prerogatives of British government, debate among merchants and artisans continued over who would rule at home. English norms of deferential politics had been profoundly challenged in periodic upheavels and surges of divisive political partisanship. In Boston as early as 1689 a thousand townspeople used the opportunity of William and Mary's return to England to resist the usurpation of local prerogatives by Sir Edmund Andros, pouring into the streets, forming militia units, and surrounding the Town House. A committee of safety, consisting primarily of merchants and clergymen, assumed control and imprisoned Andros. This unusual mobilization of ordinary people led to demands for a broadened suffrage and left in its wake continued questioning of the proper relationship between rulers and ruled.

Similarly in the late seventeenth century, tensions between Dutch and English and elite and plebian segments of New York's population surfaced during the few years in which Jacob Leisler, a militia officer of German origin, established an interim government admidst the power vacuum created by the Protestant revolt going on in England. Shortly after their assumption of power, the Leislerians freed imprisoned debtors in New York. Then they called for the election of justices of the peace and militia officers and petitioned the crown for a charter "in the like manner and with the same or more privileges as Boston," clearly aiming for a more participatory system. Leislerian mobs went so far as to attack the property of some of New York's wealthiest merchants. But when a newly appointed royal governor arrived in March 1691, Leisler surrendered the government. He was tried and found guilty of treason by an all-English jury, but the ethnic and class tensions that surfaced during his reign persisted. In Philadelphia between 1684 and 1689 a religious schism split the Quaker community and expressed not only religiously inspired but also widely felt political and economic grievances. While citizens in Boston, New York, and Philadelphia may have denied the legitimacy of factional politics, their ready involvement in political divisions revised deeply held notions of deferential politics.

All during the eighteenth century, political and economic questions continued to divide the urban community. How much paper money should be issued and would it be redeemed to benefit wealthy creditors or poor debtors? How best might Boston intervene in the provision of food stuff: to ensure a profit for provisioners or to make food available to city dwellers at the lowest costs? Could the Morris faction successfully challenge the political hold of Governor Cosby in New York? Could Penn's proprietary party be dislodged from power in Philadelphia? These were the issues that aroused the urban electorate and transformed the spirit of urban politics from hierarchy and deference to contentiousness and participation.

The factional mobilization around these issues, the heightening of partisanship through the distribution of inflammatory political broadsides, pamphlets, and newspaper articles, the fluctuations between prosperity and hard times, war-inflated prices, and scarce money prompted artisans, shopkeepers, and small merchants to organize as political actors. These groups encountered the additional challenge of upper-class resistance to their ambitions to enter the local political arena. Nevertheless most craftsmen qualified for the franchise, and by using leverage at the polls, they wedged their way into both legal and extralegal agencies. The nonimportation agreements and boycotts of the 1760s and 1770s hurt those artisans particularly dependent on trade with England, such as shipwrights, but benefited many more who could manufacture for the gentry who had previously bought imported goods. In Philadelphia, artisans were filling half or more of the vacancies for local office by the 1770s, and in Charleston in 1769, artisans assumed one-third of the positions on a Committee of Enforcement of a boycott against the Townshend Acts. Relations between merchants and artisans were often acrimonious, but many could agree on boycotts and nonimportation. In the end, both sought to advance their own interests, and increasingly their objectives were the same—relief from British oppression.

The grievances of the poor and propertyless classes also intensified in the twenty-five years before the Revolution, but these groups could not vote on political issues of the day, and none held office in colonial cities. High prices and unemployment were particularly severe in the 1760s, and thousands who lived at or near the subsistence level faced calamity. Jobs were even more scarce in cities where British troops were stationed, such as New York and later Boston, for many soldiers bolstered their meager pay by underbidding local laborers and artisans for employment. Moreover the British navy continued to forcibly impress, or draft, American seamen and laborers for service on British ships, arbitrarily carrying off any able-bodied breadwinners and angering and frightening whole communities. Historian Jesse Lemisch has estimated that one night in 1757 a force of 3000 British soldiers operating in New York pressed some 800 men, about one-fourth of the city's adult male population.[5] Several hundred men were subsequently released, but the scope of the raid reveals the impact that mass impressment could have on a city.

Even without the vote the lower classes had a powerful way to express their political voice. When the rich would not act to relieve suffering in a period of economic decline, common people felt justified in taking collective action. In Boston the widespread feeling that older ideals of community well-being were being sacrificed to new standards of entrepreneurial freedom, and individual gain activated the crowd. In 1710, because of Queen Anne's War, grain prices were higher in the West Indies than they were in Massachusetts, even though there was a bread shortage in Boston. When grain merchant Andrew Belcher decided to avail himself of the opportunity to sell at these higher prices, ordinary Bostonians descended on Belcher's loaded ship, sawed through the rudder, and later tried to run it aground. Three years later the crowd again punished Belcher, who still insisted on his right to profit without regard to the cost to the community. This time, crowds attacked and emptied his warehouses, shooting the lieutenant governor when he tried to intervene. In 1727 a crowd of Bostonians destroyed a controversial public market that appeared to offer unfair competition to small retailers.

The lower classes used the same kinds of protest demonstrations against what were viewed as unjust British interventions in American affairs. A crowd battled against impressment by British naval officers for three days in Boston in 1747, threatening and attacking naval officers and their press gangs; another crowd manhandled and intimidated customs officials and destroyed custom house officials' property in Boston in 1768. Still another crowd battled British soldiers in New York's Liberty Hill riot in 1770. In many circumstances the crowds acted with the tacit approval of men of higher position. But the inclusiveness of the crowd, drawing women, children, servants, and black people into insurrectionary activity, and its empowering of otherwise dispossessed people always contained the threat of wider social revolt. In responding to the hated Stamp Act, crowds in many cities seemed dangerously close to unsettling public order. In 1765 Boston crowds went beyond their goal of intimidating stamp distributor Andrew Oliver by burning and beheading his effigy, attacking Oliver's house, and exacting a public promise from him not to fulfill the duties of his office. Nine days later the crowd attacked the homes of several customs officials and then settled some old scores with Thomas Hutchinson by demolishing his elaborately built house. Hutchinson had long been a supporter of local and British policies that fell with particular severity on the lower classes. In New York City, crowds pushed merchants to go beyond

New Hampshire—Stamp Master in Effigy This woodcut, produced fifty years later, shows a crowd parading the effigy of the New Hampshire stamp distributor through the streets of Portsmouth in 1765, carrying a coffin to symbolize the death of the Stamp Act. *(Metropolitan Museum of Art, Bequest of Charles Allen Munn 1924. [24.90.1566a])*

New Hampshire

the more passive resistance of a boycott and nonimportation strategy into openly defying Parliament by continuing commerce without any stamps. In Charleston in late October, 1765, an organized crowd shouting "liberty, liberty and stamp'd paper" forced the resignation of the South Carolina stamp distributor. By November 1 when the Stamp Law was to go into effect, not a single stamp distributor in the colonies was willing to carry out the duties of his office, due in large part to the crowd activities in colonial ports. In most cities the merchant-gentry regained the revolutionary initiative as the impending armed struggle with the British drew near, but crowd activism was an enduring legacy of eighteenth-century urban life.

One city—Boston—epitomized all the elements that were pulling the American colonies away from the mother country. Boston, alone among American cities, did not experience population growth after 1740, and its economy had been floundering since the early 1700s. Not only did Philadelphia and New York undercut Boston's commercial dominance, but also nearby rivals such as Providence, Portland, Salem, Gloucester, and Lynn raided her regional hinterland, already too small to support the amount of interior trade that blessed cities to the south. Boston's early acceptance of public responsibility for social welfare became a liability as expenses and taxes soared in response to the mounting numbers of poor and the city's heavy commitment to municipal improvements. While costs rose and opportunities diminished, the city lost its attractiveness—its population declined from 16,382 in 1743 to 15,631 in 1760. The economic maladies that only brought discomfort to other cities in the 1760s aggravated existing sores in Boston.

As described above, the crowd in Boston had been active throughout the eighteenth century. During the Stamp Act crisis, protest occurred in other cities, but after the repeal of the Townshend Acts in 1768, crowd activities receded except in Boston. There activities of the Sons of Liberty, particularly the harassment of customs officials, provoked the British into sending two regiments of troops. The presence of troops only deepened anxiety on both sides, and the tension burst on the night of March 5, 1770, when a line of soldiers fired into a jeering crowd in front of the Customs House, killing five and injuring six. Radicals such as Sam Adams were quick to capitalize on the "Boston Massacre," spreading word of all (and some extra) gory details throughout the colony and down the Atlantic Coast. Although not the first clash between troops and colonists, the Boston Massacre not only deepened anger and resentment in Boston but also raised fears in other cities that they would be the next recipient of British brutality.

Boston became the center of resistance three years later in a confrontation over the Tea Act, in which Parliament had granted a virtual monopoly of the American tea trade to the British East India Company. When the first three ships carrying tea arrived at Boston Harbor in December, 1773 Sam Adams and his associates summoned an extralegal mass meeting whose results are well known—the Boston Tea Party. This gathering, which technically was not legal, attracted some five thousand people, nearly one-third of the city's population and the largest mass assembly in the city's history. As the meeting adjourned on the night of December 16, a number of men wearing Indian costumes boarded the ships and dumped their tea into the bay. The reaction of the British to this threat to imperial authority was an important catalyst in changing colonial resistance into rebellion. Parliament closed the Boston port and asserted its colonial prerogatives in a series of four "coercive" acts, which limited town meetings and elections in all of Massachusetts, provided for the quartering of troops in the colony's towns, removed the prerogative of the towns to try British officials accused of crimes in America, and organized a provincial government in Quebec without a representative legislature.

Only the Port Act punished Boston directly; the other measures reinforced the power of Parliament and the Crown along a broader spectrum. But they all struck at the two most cherished aspects of urban life—self-government and commerce. By choking off the city's economic bloodstream and its organs of self-government, Parliament not only deepened desperation in Boston but also threatened the other cities. Bostonians now faced certain ruin of the remainder of their commerce. Moreover, their town meetings and local elections had been reduced to meaningless exercises. All their attempts at reform and redress had failed. As G. B. Warden has observed, Sam Adams now "had little trouble in persuading his neighbors and countrymen that England was 'making war' against every colonial right, and destroying every traditional means of security and self-preservation."[6] It was not difficult to spread the fear that if the British could tether the freedoms of Massachusetts colony and Boston, they could do the same to other colonies and cities. When Adams and the Committee of Correspondence sent an appeal to Philadelphia and New York asking all Americans to join a boycott of all trade with Great Britain, New York merchants responded by organizing the Continental Congress, which not only conceived American independence but also nurtured American union. Surely, to quote Richard C. Wade, "in this perspective, the American Revolution began on the cobblestones of Boston rather than on the rolling greens of Lexington."[7]

The predicaments of the cities did not alone cause the American Revolution; the final break with England resulted from a number of forces that had merged at various moments in history. Yet the cities were instrumental in the timing and the organization of the Revolution not only because they bore the weight of British policy, but also because they possessed the facilities and human resources to implement resistance and then rebellion. Their meeting houses provided forums for debate and protest, their printing shops helped spread news and propaganda, and their taverns and coffeehouses furnished workshops where logistics were planned.

Women in cities were critical to the success of the Revolution, despite

Crowd Tactics of Urban Revolutionaries   This drawing depicts Boston townspeople protesting the tea tax by tarring and feathering and roughing up the excise tax collector. The background left shows the famous tea party. At the right is the Liberty Tree with a crumpled paper labeled Stamp Act upside down on its trunk and a hanging noose on its limb. Attributed to Philip Dawe. *(Colonial Williamsburg Foundation.)*

their formal status as dependents without political voice. They were central to the boycotts of imported products and later to the production of household manufactures. Their operation of businesses in their husbands' absences allowed the cities to keep functioning during wartime. Women took part in revolutionary crowds and in New York countered war-time price inflation by forcing storekeepers to charge just prices. These activities did not expand the boundaries of women's sphere but rather took place in the shady areas where household and community interests overlapped and at a historical moment when household and community life were politicized. Neither interest in politics nor patriotic contribution enabled women to become full citizens, but the Revolutionary years were shaped by women's as well as men's activities.

The separation of the thirteen colonies from Great Britain mirrored a process that had been going on in the dozen or so American cities for nearly one hundred years. The residents of each town had cast off traditional notions of deference and had replaced them with politics both more contentious and more participatory, and these lay at the heart of new revolutionary understandings of representation. Urban citizens had developed a sense of community and an allegiance to a particular place where older visions of commonwealth mingled with newer visions of individual enrichment. Motivated by familiar ideals of public interest and newly developed conceptions of self-interest, merchants and mechanics could urge resistance to new British taxes and ultimately to the British empire itself. In the process of freeing themselves, urban dwellers found that they had moved beyond beliefs in preordained destiny and were heady with new thoughts of freedom, the perfectibility of humanity, and the desire to shape their own futures. By the 1770s, common interests and grievances, aided by increased intercolonial communication, had spread these concepts of community, individualism, and personal agency beyond particular cities to encompass all the colonies. Thus cities, with their experience of collectivism, opportunity, and diversity, not only kindled but fed the flames of American independence.

BIBLIOGRAPHY

Early contact between native Americans and European explorers and colonists is analyzed in Gary B. Nash, *Red, White, and Black: The Peoples of Early America,* 2d ed. (Englewood Cliffs, N.J.: Prentice-Hall, 1982) and William Cronon, *Changes in the Land: Indians, Colonists, and the Ecology of New England* (New York: Hill and Wang, 1983). Studies of colonial urban growth and government include Carl Bridenbaugh, *Cities in the Wilderness: Urban Life in America, 1625–1742* (New York: Ronald Press, 1938); Bridenbaugh, *Cities in Revolt: Urban Life in America, 1743–1776* (New York: Capricorn Press, 1956); Sylvia D. Fries, *The Urban Ideal in Colonial America* (Philadelphia: Temple University Press, 1977); Jon C. Teaford, *The Municipal Revolution in America: Origins of Modern Urban Government, 1650–1825* (Chicago: University of Chicago Press, 1975); John W. Reps, *Town Planning in Frontier America* (Princeton, N.J.: Princeton University Press, 1969); and Carville Earle and Ronald Hoffman, "The Urban South: The First Two Centuries," in *The City in Southern History: The Growth of Urban Civilization in the South,* eds. Blaine A. Brownell and David R. Goldfield (Port Washington, N.Y.: Kennikat Press, 1977).

The cities of Boston, New York, and Philadelphia have received particular attention from colonial historians. Gary B. Nash's richly detailed study of the development of popular political consciousness in the century preceding the American Revolution focuses on these cities: *The Urban Crucible: Social Change, Political Consciousness and the Origins of the American Revolution* (Cambridge, Mass.: Harvard University Press, 1979). Other studies include Darret Rutman, *Winthrop's Boston: A Portrait of a Puritan Town, 1630–1649* (Chapel Hill, N.C.: University of North Carolina Press, 1965); G.B. Warden, *Boston: 1689–1776* (Boston: Little, Brown, 1970); Thomas J. Archdeacon, *New York City 1664–1710: Conquest and Change* (Ithaca, N.Y.: Cornell University Press, 1976); Hendrik Hartog, *Public Property and Private Power: The Corporation of the City of New York in American Law, 1730–1870;* and Sam Bass Warner, Jr., *The Private City: Philadelphia in Three Periods of Its Growth* (Philadelphia: University of Pennsylvania Press, 1968). On education in colonial New York, see Carl Kaestle, *The Evolution of An Urban School System: New York City, 1750–1859* (Cambridge, Mass.: Harvard University Press, 1973). See also James Henretta, "Economic Development and Social Structure in Colonial Boston," *William and Mary Quarterly* 22(January 1965):75–92; and Alan Kulikoff, "The Progress of Inequality in Revolutionary Boston," *William and Mary Quarterly* 3d ser., 28 (July 1971): 375–93, 400–11.

On urban slavery in this period see Ira Berlin, "Time, Space, and the Evolution of Afro-American Society," *American Historical Review* 85(February 1980):44–78; Berlin, "The Revolution in Black Life," in *The American Revolution: Explorations in the History of American Radicalism*, ed. Alfred F. Young (De Kalb: Northern Illinois University Press, 1976), 349–82; Joseph P. Reidy, " 'Negro Election Day' and Black Community Life in New England, 1750–1860," *Marxist Perspectives* 1(Fall 1978):102–117; and Ira Berlin and Ronald Hoffman, eds., *Slavery and Freedom In the Age of the American Revolution* (Charlottesville: University Press of Virginia, 1983).

The situation of women in colonial urban America is discussed in Nancy Woloch, *Women and the American Experience* (New York: Alfred A. Knopf, 1984), chap. 2; Mary Beth Norton, *Liberty's Daughters: The Revolutionary Experience of American Women, 1750–1800* (Boston: Little, Brown, 1980); Norton, "The Evolution of White Women's Experience in Early America," *American Historical Review* 89(June 1984):593–619; Laurel Thatcher Ulrich, *Good Wives: Images and Reality in the Lives of Women in Northern New England, 1650–1750* (New York: Alfred A. Knopf, 1982).

A number of community studies of New England towns have provocative implications for the urban context. They include John Demos, *A Little Commonwealth: Family Life in Plymouth Colony* (New York: Oxford University Press, 1970); Philip T. Greven, Jr., *Four Generations: Population, Land and Family in Colonial Andover, Massachusetts* (Ithaca, N.Y.: Cornell University Press, 1970); Kenneth A. Lockridge, *A New England Town: The First Hundred Years* (New York: W.W. Norton & Co., 1970); Michael Zuckerman, *Peaceable Kingdoms: New England Towns in the Eighteenth Century* (New York: Alfred A. Knopf, 1970); Edward M. Cook, Jr., *The Fathers of the Town: Leadership and Community Structure in Eighteenth Century New England* (Baltimore: Johns Hopkins University Press, 1976); and Stephen Innes, *Labor in a New Land; Economy and Society in Seventeenth Century Springfield* (Princeton, N.J.: Princeton University Press, 1983).

Works elaborating the roles of city inhabitants and economies in the years preceding the Revolution include Gary B. Nash, *The Urban Crucible: Social Change, Political Consciousness and the Origins of the American Revolution* (Cambridge, Mass.: Harvard University Press, 1979); Jesse Lemisch, "Jack Tar in the Streets: Merchant Seamen in the Politics of Revolutionary America," *William and Mary Quarterly* 25(July 1968):371–407; Charles S. Olton, *Artisans for Independence: Philadelphia Merchants and the American Revolution* (Syracuse, N.Y.: Syracuse University Press, 1975);

Stephen E. Lucas, *Portents of Rebellion: Rhetoric and Revolution in Philadelphia, 1765–1776* (Philadelphia: Temple University Press, 1976); Edward C. Papenfuse, *In Pursuit of Profit: The Annapolis Merchants in the Era of the American Revolution* (Baltimore: Johns Hopkins University Press, 1975); Charles G. Steffen, *The Mechanics of Baltimore: Workers and Politics in the Age of Revolution, 1763–1812* (Urbana: University of Illinois Press, 1984). See also Gary B. Nash, "Social Change and the Growth of Prerevolutionary Urban Radicalism," in *The American Revolution: Explorations in the History of American Radicalism,* ed. Alfred T. Young (De Kalb: Northern Illinois University Press, 1976), 3–36; Paula S. Baker, "The Domestication of Politics: Women in American Political Society, 1780–1920," *American Historical Review* 89(June 1984):620–47.

ENDNOTES

[1] Carl Bridenbaugh, *Cities in the Wilderness: Urban Life in America 1625–1742* (New York: Ronald Press, 1938), 93.

[2] Gary B. Nash, *The Urban Crucible: Social Change, Political Consciousness and the Origins of the American Revolution* (Cambridge, Mass.: Harvard University Press, 1979), 18.

[3] *Ibid.,* 395.

[4] Mary Beth Norton, "Eighteenth Century Women in Peace and War: The Case of the Loyalists," *William and Mary Quarterly,* 3d ser., 33(July 1976):386–409.

[5] Jesse Lemisch, "Jack Tar in the Streets: Merchant Seamen in the Politics of Revolutionary America," *William and Mary Quarterly* 25(July 1968):371–407.

[6] G. B. Warden, *Boston, 1689–1776* (Boston: Little, Brown, 1970), 293–94.

[7] Richard C. Wade, "The City in History—Some American Perspectives," in *Urban Life and Form,* ed. Werner Z. Hirsch (New York: Holt, Rinehart, and Winston, 1963), 63.

2

Urban Life in the New Nation, 1776–1860

THE COMMERCIAL REVOLUTION

The process that generated urban growth continued long after the thirteen colonies merged into the American Union. Only now migration, economic change, and technological advance broadened the scale and quickened the pace. Whereas only five major and about fifteen secondary cities constituted urban America in the colonial period, scores of towns sprouted and blossomed between the Revolution and the Civil War. When the first federal census was taken in 1790, there were only 5 cities with 10,000 or more inhabitants. In 1830 the number had risen to 23, and it had reached 101 by 1860. The number of people living in urban places mushroomed from 201,655 in 1790 to 6,216,518 in 1860, approximately one-fifth of the national population. New cities filled in much of our modern urban network, stretching from Buffalo to Seattle, from Mobile to San Francisco. By pulling the line of settlement across the continent, by steering the national economy, and by attracting the talent and leadership that tamed the West, these cities, like their predecessors on the Atlantic Coast, influenced the course of national development.

Established eastern ports still dominated the urban scene as the young republic grappled with the problems of independence, although Baltimore surpassed Newport as one of the top five cities. But in the 1780s new difficulties compounded those that had nagged city dwellers since 1763. Merchants found themselves deprived of the economic advantages and protection they once had taken for granted as members of the British mercantile system. The middle and lower classes faced shortages of housing and consumer goods, accompanied by rises in prices, unemployment, and rents. During the winter of 1783–84 one-seventh of Philadelphia's population received public charity. A severe economic depression deepened the predicaments of all classes between 1785 and 1787. Since hard money and precious metals remained as scarce as before the Revolution, states began to issue paper money of varying value. Lack of uniform standards of this paper money and its uncertain worth tangled commercial exchange. In addition, contests over the content and quality of money in circulation sparked conflicts between capitalists who wanted a stable currency and debtors who wanted more paper money. These tensions often took a geographical shape, as mercantile and commercial interests dominated in the urban and more densely settled eastern regions and cash-poor farmers populated the western frontiers of the new republics. The most acute struggle occurred in 1786–87, when a band of nearly two thousand debtor farmers from western Massachusetts led by former Revolutionary War captain Daniel Shays threatened a federal arsenal and halted court proceedings in which the state was trying to seize property for nonpayment of taxes. The farmers dispersed only after merchants from the eastern part of the state hired a militia to hunt them down.

Philadelphia in the Federal Era This view of Second and Market Streets in 1799 pictures the city's main intersection with the Court House in the left foreground and the steeple of Christ Church in the background. At the time, Philadelphia was one of the largest and most elegant of American cities. Engraving by W. Birch & Sons. (*I. N. Phelps Stokes Collection. Prints Division, The New York Public Library. Astor, Lenox and Tilden Foundation.*)

The hands of those who were already interested in replacing the Articles of Confederation with a stronger central government were strengthened by incidents such as the Shays rebellion. Those involved in overseas trade and foreign affairs were the first to agitate for a new governing instrument that would facilitate commerce. Significantly, urban mercantile classes, intent upon promoting trade and economic stability, played a leading role in the formation and adoption of the Constitution. Although only 5 percent of all Americans lived in cities, twenty of the fifty-five delegates to the Constitutional Convention in Philadelphia in May, 1787, were city dwellers, and another twenty, mostly lawyers and merchants, had extensive urban contacts. The new Constitution the delegates hammered out protected mercantile interests by granting Congress the powers to tax, to borrow and coin money, and to regulate commerce and centralized economic decision making by prohibiting the states from levying their own tariffs, coining their own money, or issuing bills of credit. States were explicitly prohibited from re-

L'Enfant's Plan of Washington D.C. Most of this plan was incorporated in the construction of the capital. Note the imposition of wide, diagonal avenues on the gridiron layout. Although a few new towns adopted variations of this plan, most developers in the nineteenth century preferred a strict gridiron street system because it was easier to construct and made lot sizes more uniform. *(The John Carter Brown Library, Brown University.)*

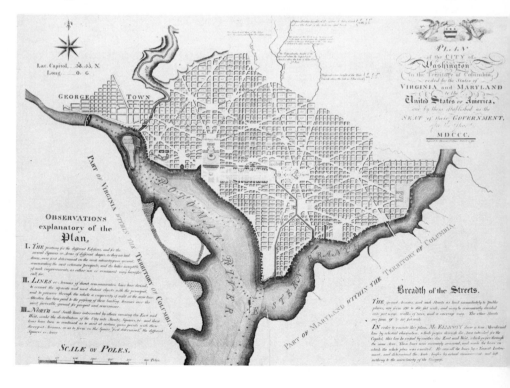

sponding to popular pressure like that generated by the Shays insurgents to relieve debtors of the obligations of their contracts.

When the Constitution was sent to the state ratifying conventions, city interests lined up on the side favoring adoption. Urban artisans hoped that a stronger national government would support domestic manufacture. Urban support of the press meant that of a hundred or more newspapers printed in the 1780s, only a dozen opposed the Constitution. Cities, towns, and their tributary regions in every state voted for delegates who supported the Constitution, while areas dominated by small subsistence farms chose delegates who opposed it. New Hampshire's coastal and Connecticut River towns, commercially linked to Boston, helped swing the state in favor of ratification, and New Hampshire became the ninth and deciding state to accept the Constitution. New York City and its surrounding counties threatened to secede from the state if it did not ratify. Virginia's eastern tidewater regions, including Norfolk, were joined in support of ratification by areas of what became West Virginia that were developing commercial outlets to the Ohio River.

Commercial recovery for the new nation was underway by the end of the 1780s. Population increases and territorial expansion were catalysts of economic growth. Everywhere there were expanded sources of supply, new commercial and manufacturing patterns, and increased numbers of participants in the market economy. A remarkable spread of interstate and interregional trade would soon generate demands for new roads and canals. At the same time, expanding trade and improvements in inland transportation turned farmers into businessmen; formerly self-sufficient farmers began to grow just one or two cash crops for market. Between 1790 and 1820 the nation's farm population grew at about the same rate as its city population. Farmers sought out commercial markets, and inland cities sprang up to process and ship farm products, sometimes even to turn them into finished goods for sale back to the farmers.

WESTWARD EXPANSION

The path of western settlement illustrated this dynamic interaction between cities and countryside. Cities accompanied and even preceded the frontier, acting as commercial outposts and depots from which settlement radiated. The growth of cities made western crops more marketable and boosted the value of western farmland. In turn, expansion of the farming frontier spurred the growth of cities as market and exchange points. Along the Ohio and Mississippi river valleys the towns of Pittsburgh, Cincinnati, Louisville, Lexington, and St. Louis formed what historian Richard Wade termed an urban frontier, planted in the late 1790s before the surrounding soil was broken for cultivation.[1] Like their colonial predecessors, these cities were founded as commercial centers by commercial-minded people.

The Urban Frontier   This lithograph of Pittsburgh in 1849 shows the city about a half century after its founding on the triangle of land between the Allegheny and Monongahela Rivers. Note how important a river location was for a young, commercial city. Lithograph by Tappan and Bradford after a drawing by B. F. Smith, Jr. *(I. N. Phelps Stokes Collection. Prints Division, The New York Public Library. Astor, Lenox and Tilden Foundations.)*

A generation later the city-building process repeated itself in the Great lakes region. By 1840, Buffalo, Cleveland, Detroit, Chicago, and Milwaukee had emerged as important western cities and had fostered settlement in the Old Northwest. Commercial growth supported manufacturing, and as demand for finished goods began to rise in interior America, these cities developed industrial bases to complement their commercial functions. Pittsburgh produced glass, Louisville textiles, Cleveland iron products, and Chicago agricultural implements. In the far west and the southwest the 1834 Secularization Proclamation altered the status of the vast tracts of mission lands and stimulated the commercialization of agriculture and the growth of cities. After the Civil War, railroad connections would enable southwestern cities like San Antonio, El Paso, San Diego, and Los Angeles to serve as commercial exchange centers in relation to their surrounding countrysides.

The South had its own process of urban development, structured by the needs of staple crop agriculture, particularly cotton and tobacco, and, after 1850, by limited processing industries. Baltimore, Charleston, Savannah, Mobile, New Orleans, Memphis, St. Louis, and Louisville were major cities ringing the South by 1840, each joined to its hinterlands by commercial connections stretching inward along the South's abundant navigable waterways. Southern urban economies revolved around the cultivation, marketing, and processing of a staple crop for its eventual delivery in a northern port. The dependence of southern merchants on New York City in particular for marketing, shipping, and credit inhibited the growth of parallel facilities in southern cities and drained capital from the region, thus limiting the extent of urbanization in the South.

This common pattern of commercial foundations and good transportation connections characterized city origins in the United States in the colonial era and the early nineteenth century. But expansion of the market prompted an additional source of urban growth in the later period—land speculation. Although historians have directed much attention to the speculation in western farmland, they have often neglected the urban dimensions of this activity. The nineteenth century witnessed a mania of city building in this country as energetic and sometimes shifty entrepreneurs bought and plotted land for new towns and then sold it for hefty profits to other eager speculators who hoped the property would appreciate even more. It was this kind of expectation that produced spectacular land booms, such as the one in Chicago during the 1830s. Here a choice 80-by-100-foot lot that sold for $100 in 1832 brought $3,000 by 1834, and this price soared to $15,000 the following year. As one observer remarked, "Every man who owned a garden patch stood on his land and imagined himself a millionaire." But this inflationary process could also have adverse effects. For every urban venture that succeeded, several did not. Some failed for lack of leadership, some for lack of money, some for excess of floodwaters. Many an optimistic urban speculator from the East came West holding a deed, only to find his property in the midst of a mosquito-infested swamp. Still, both the successes and the failures reveal that western speculation was as much urban as rural.

Growth in older and newer cities strained established forms of municipal government. The closed municipal corporation with its power to fix labor costs and the price of commodities like bread seemed in the early nineteenth century to impede commercial growth. What had once seemed necessary to protect the "commonwealth" now appeared to be a limitation on freedom of enterprise and the rights of economic liberty. Municipal price regulation gradually collapsed, and municipally controlled markets disappeared. Local businessmen campaigned for new city charters that would give the government powers to raise more revenue through taxes and to borrow money that could be spent on municipal improvements that supported expansion of the market economy. Although there was some popular opposition, most charters of incoporation were revised between 1820 and 1860 to allow communities to spend money on improved water supplies and firefighting equipment that could protect capital investment in warehouses and workshops, harbor improvements, canals, turnpikes, and eventually railroad connections. Newer cities of the Ohio Valley and the Great Lakes consciously emulated the institutional approach of older seaports. The government of Lexington sent a leading citizen to Philadelphia to inspect the street lighting system, and Pittsburgh sent a delegation to Philadelphia, Baltimore, and New York on the same mission. The city council of Cincinnati ordered its board of health to consult officials in Boston, New York, Philadelphia, and Baltimore for recommendations on construction of a sewer system. Charters of western towns intentionally included the same regulatory and taxing powers as those in the East.

The duplication of these forms and functions coupled with commercial and cultural ties bound eastern and western cities into a national urban network where sectional differences were blurred. Chicago, Baltimore, and Philadelphia resembled each other more closely than they resembled their surrounding countryside. But common interests and experience did not necessarily breed cooperation. Trade had accounted for the growth of almost all early American cities. Each successful urban center established an economic domain in its immediate vicinity in the first half of the nineteenth century, but commercial expansion was an ever hungry process that pushed cities to continually search for more markets. Inevitably such forays resulted in collisions between cities that laid claims to overlapping hinterlands. The resulting rivalry aptly dubbed "urban imperialism" by Wade has been an important dimension of urban interaction from the early 1800s to the present.

The urge for urban growth was linked to a goal of predominance, and these two forces made early nineteenth-century urbanization an aggressive, dynamic phenomenon. People believed that their city had to keep growing to prevent economic stagnation and to stay ahead of rival cities. Increased immigration, markets, and transportation connections fed upon one another to produce a "multiplier effect," an endless spiral that spun off greater and greater profits. In the 1820s, for example the young towns of Cleveland and Sandusky vied for the northern terminus of a canal between the Ohio River and Lake Erie. Although Sandusky had more natural advantages, the Ohio legislature chose Cleveland, primarily because that city's businessmen were able to exercise more political leverage, through bribery as well as through normal persuasion. This victory set in motion a chain reaction that accelerated Cleveland's growth. The canal enabled Cleveland to attract more businesses, consequently providing employment opportunities and spurring population growth. Because of these factors, the city provided a natural transfer point when railroads began to crisscross the Midwest. New transportation links fostered *more* business, *more* population growth, *more* markets, and so on. Contests similar to the one between Cleveland and Sandusky took place hundreds of times in the West and South as upstart towns fought for such prizes as the location of a county seat, the site of a railroad or canal terminus, a college, or a land office.

Eventually rivalries crossed geographical boundaries as larger cities clashed over hinterland markets. Here is where urban imperialism had national impact, for competing cities contributed to the construction of a national transportation network that rearranged axes of trade and politics.

Construction of the Erie Canal (1817–25), which linked the Hudson River to the Great Lakes, not only tied a large portion of growing western markets to New York, but also provoked Philadelphia, Baltimore, and Boston into constructing their own transportation lines into the West. The results included a maze of turnpikes, canals, and, ultimately, the Baltimore and Ohio and the Pennsylvania railroads. Competition between Charleston and Savannah and between New Orleans and Mobile prompted rapid railroad construction in the South. When Chicago businessmen obtained railroad connections to the region beyond the Mississippi River while their rivals in St. Louis remained committed to river transportation, a shift in the direction of western trade resulted. Instead of following water routes to St. Louis and then to the port of New Orleans, by the 1850s products from the West increasingly moved over rail to Chicago and from there often as far east as New York. Although competition between larger cities did not leave any one contestant completely vanquished, feelings of urgency and fears for survival enveloped every rivalry. As one Philadelphia businessman remarked when the state chose to construct a water and land transportation route between Philadelphia and Pittsburgh, the premium was on speed "before the commerce has acquired the correspondence and habitude that are so difficult to break."

Urban promoters attempted to create a loyalty to place that could personify cities to their residents and transcend conflicts of interest between businessmen and workers. A railroad or canal claimed to serve not only the interests of residents of Baltimore, Philadelphia, or Chicago but also "Baltimore," "Philadelphia," and "Chicago" as entities themselves. Private capital was scarce, so many projects were financed with state and local funds, making entrepreneurial interests the same as public interest. This urban chauvinism combined with the speculative nature of urban growth to produce "boosterism," the optimistic—indeed pompous—promotion of a city in heroic language. Boosters used rhetorical metaphor to project continuity from the present into the future and spoke of dreams as reality. It was this spirit that led a booster of St. Louis to predict that "we have but commenced to tell the wonders of a city destined in the future to equal London in its population, Athens in its philosophy, art, and culture, Rome in its hotels, cathedrals, and grandeur, and to be the central commercial metropolis of a continent."

In San Diego, boosterism entailed a drive to separate the Anglo community residentially and commercially from the old Mexican pueblo. Beginning in the 1850s, Richard Henry Dana, author of the popular *Two Years Before the Mast,* led San Diego's Anglo merchants in a campaign to promote the "New San Diego" by attracting Anglo settlers and investors and building new hotels and a wharf. Within a few years of the establishment of the new town in the 1860s the old pueblo settlement had been emptied of Anglo merchants and residents.

Often boosters themselves were enthusiastic and enterprising entrepreneurs, who hitched their private fortunes to the quick development of their city—the more the city grew, the better for individual profit making. William B. Ogden's investments in land and railroads in Chicago made him a multimillionaire and helped simultaneously build Chicago from a village of a few thousand people when he arrived in 1835 to a metropolis of nearly half a million when he died in 1877. Dr. Daniel B. Drake, whose writing and work brought fame to Cincinnati, planned and invested in canals and railroads there. Boosters' premium on growth contributed to the unplanned expansion of American cities. Emphasis on speed resulted in the hasty construction of railroads with little concern for future operability or safety. Booster rhetoric could be used by con artists interested more in a fast buck than city building. But boosters also helped to create institutions that were public resources as well as personal monuments; Ogden and Drake participated in every public enterprise undertaken by their respective cities—bridges, sewers, parks, hospitals, libraries, and medical colleges.

PROTOINDUSTRIALIZATION AND CHANGES IN URBAN SOCIAL STRUCTURE

The commercialization of the countryside and growth of manufacturing in the cities preceeded in tandem. Farmers were busy raising cash crops needed to buy everyday necessities from urban craftsmen who manufactured guns, shoes, woolen cloth, furniture, wagons, and farm tools. Increased demands for such goods paved the way for changes in the organization of production. In the eighteenth century, master craftsmen and journeymen had produced goods directly for individual customers; thus a shoemaker made and sold shoes in the same room. In the nineteenth century, shoemakers were producing for a broader more impersonal market. The business of selling shoes was separated from the process of making shoes, and the process of making shoes was subdivided into many steps, each requiring less skill than the integrated process had formerly. Even before the development of mechanization and factories, control over production fell from shoemakers to merchant capitalists who had the cash and credit resources to arrange the purchase of raw materials, organize large-scale production, market the finished product, and await delayed payment. Similar developments among coopers, building tradesmen, metal workers, tailors, hatters, clothiers, and boat builders diluted traditional skills, expanded the size of the work group, and passed control of profits and the work process to merchant capitalists.

Before the 1840s most manufacturing in American cities was confined to two types of products: (1) consumer items, such as refined sugar, leather goods, and distilled products, that merchants could exchange for meat, grain, and cotton in the West and South; (2) commerce-serving items, such as ships, sails, paper, and barrels. However, along some New England rivers and streams mechanized textile mills were beginning to establish genuine factory organization, and communities were emerging around them. Many of the mill towns in Connecticut, Massachusetts, and Rhode Island never grew beyond a few hundred people, most of them landless agrarians or families who split their time and personnel between millwork and farming. A few places grew larger, among them Chicopee and Holyoke, both founded by an organization of investors called the Boston Associates. The most famous project financed by the Boston Associates was Francis Cabot Lowell's industrial experiment at Lowell, Massachusetts, where he recruited New England farm girls to work and live in a tightly regulated and paternalistic mill community.

The factory system brought tremendous changes in work wherever it took hold. Use of mechanized devices instead of hand tools made ownership of the means of production almost impossible for wage earners, because only the wealthy could afford to invest in costly machines, especially those that were run by water or steam power. The use of machines to break down production into simple repetitive tasks meant that most workers no longer needed as full a range of craft skills or had responsibility for the quality of the item produced. The pace of the machines regimented the workday in a way artisans had never experienced. Called to work by the bell, prohibited from talking to other workers, producing at the speed of the machines, and disciplined by foremen, factory workers could not slip off to go fishing, share a round of ale, or compete in foot races, as artisans' control over their workday had accustomed them to do.

Still, in many cities the factory system coexisted with traditional small-scale manufacture, because swelling urban populations continued to create demand for the products and services of many crafts. As a result, in these cities the number of workers in traditionally small-scale occupations increased along with the number of factory workers. Historian Bruce Laurie has identified five different types of production coexisting in antebellum Philadelphia: factories powered by steam or water, not-yet-mechanized central shops employing twenty-five or more workers, small sweatshops employing from six to twenty-five workers, small neighborhood artisan shops where fewer than six toiled, and individual outworkers who did piecework in their homes.[2] In Providence, Rhode Island, where textile, base metal, and precious metal industries were developing at a rapid pace in the 1840s, the number of consumer-serving tradesmen such as smiths, bakers, cabinetmakers, carpenters, carriage makers, engravers, and masons increased by almost 50 percent during the same period. Table 2-1 illustrates the growth of these artisan occupations in Providence between 1845 and 1850. It also reveals the extent of population movement the city experienced. Of the 387 tradesmen listed in 1850, 215, or 56 percent, had not

TABLE 2-1 Growth of Artisan and Retail Services in Providence, Rhode Island, 1845–50

OCCUPATION	NUMBER LISTED IN 1845	NUMBER LISTED IN 1850	NEW IN 1850
Artisans and Services			
Bakers	11	16	11
Blacksmiths	33	55	20
Cabinetmakers	9	13	4
Carpenters	65	91	54
Carriage Makers	16	23	14
Engravers	9	17	11
House Painters	29	38	22
Masons	17	28	14
Printers	6	9	5
Shoemakers	52	72	45
Tinsmiths	17	25	15
Total	264	387	215
Retailers and Services			
Brokers	16	23	13
Coal Dealers	14	21	10
Commission Merchants	27	37	27
Confectioners	19	15	10
Druggists	8	13	7
Fancy-Good Dealers	8	14	9
Furniture Dealers	7	15	10
Jewelry and Leather Dealers	18	25	9
Lumber Dealers	20	21	13
Marketmen and Merchants	66	105	83
Milliners	29	40	26
Paint and Paper Dealers	12	13	4
Shoe Dealers	31	32	22
Stove Dealers	6	19	16
Total	281	393	259

Source: *The Providence City Directory* (Providence, R.I.: H.H. Brown, 1845 and 1850).

been listed five years earlier. Some of these men may have been apprentices or children too young to have been listed in 1845, but undoubtedly most were newcomers to the city, for Providence's population increased by 30 percent between 1845 and 1850. During this period the same patterns occurred with regard to the city's retailers, such as confectioners, grocers, druggists, and dry-goods merchants, who increased in number by over 40 percent. By 1850 nearly two-thirds of retailers had arrived or entered their business since 1845. To be sure, in some places, particularly in northeastern mill towns, an industrial working class constituted a large proportion of the population. But in larger and more diverse cities the occupational distribution retained a more varied character.

The expansion of the urban economy meant that the rich were growing richer and the poor were growing poorer. Analyses of urban social structure in the middle third of the nineteenth century have revealed that small numbers of people were accumulating large proportions of the available wealth. In Boston, where 5 percent of the population had owned 44 percent of all taxable property in 1771, the richest 4 percent owned 59 percent of the wealth in 1833 and 64 percent by 1848. In New York the upper 4 percent owned 49 percent of the wealth in 1828 and 66 percent in 1845. Similar concentrations of wealth could be found in Philadelphia, Brooklyn, Baltimore, St. Louis, and New Orleans. Every city contained families with lofty fortunes who had maintained or increased the wealth accumulated by their forebears. Housed in mansions, transported in private carriages, clothed in the finest fabrics, fed the choicest delicacies, waited on by servants, entertained in exclusive clubs, the wealthiest urban residents could remove themselves from contact with the new urban masses. The middle and lower classes could advance by acquiring property or by moving into shopowner or skilled-craft occupations. But such attainments were precarious. National economic panics and depressions, which occurred almost regularly—1819, 1837, 1857—and the growing scale of many businesses snuffed out the chances of many a small investor. Thus even though upward economic and occupational mobility seems to have remained fairly stable in places such as Boston and Philadelphia between 1830 and 1860, downward mobility increased.

Near the lower end of the social spectrum, pressures of city life weighed heavily. Wages rose slightly between 1820 and 1860 but remained pitifully low in relation to prices. Daily pay for unskilled workers rose from 80 or 90 cents a day in the 1840s to slightly over a dollar a day in 1860. Factory workers received even less. Spinners in textile mills, for example, received an average of only $2.73 a week in 1842; by 1860 they were drawing only $2.85. Meanwhile prices for food, housing, and clothing rose more than 10 percent, offsetting many of the wage increases. Some skilled workers, such as blacksmiths, machinists, and carpenters, earned $12 a week or more, but painters and wheelwrights earned much less. Male factory workers could earn a dollar a day, but female factory workers, many of whom toiled fourteen or more hours a day, earned barely $1 or $1.50 a week.

Few working class families could manage on one income. According to the *New York Tribune*, the minimum budget for a family of five in 1851 came to $10.37 per week. This figure included $3 for rent, $2 for clothing, $1.40 for meat (two pounds a day at 10 cents a pound), 50 cents for a half-bushel of potatoes, 14 cents for milk, and 62.5 cents for one-eighth barrel of flour. The only "frivolous" item included was 12 cents for newspapers. When asked if such a budget was too high, its compiler replied, "Where is the money to pay for the amusements, for ice-creams . . . to pay the doctor or apothecary, to pay for pew rent in the church, to purchase books or musical instruments?" No wonder then, that to accumulate enough for minimal subsistence, thousands of families depended on women and children to supplement the earnings of the household head. Peddling, scavenging, theft, and prostitution joined casual laboring, sewing, and domestic employment as the means by which women and children helped their families make ends meet.

The growth of urban inequality was castigated in literary accounts. Intellectuals like Ralph Waldo Emerson scorned the materialism and artificiality of urban life, and Nathaniel Hawthorne half seriously proposed that "all towns should be made capable of purification by fire, or of decay, within each half century." Much that was written about the American city in these years in sentimental and sensational novels, stories, and sketches portrayed it as a font of evil and wickedness. But popular nonfictional accounts of city life went beyond sensationalism to attempt a comprehensive description of the new urban society. Their central revelation was the increasing wealth and pretentiousness of the very rich and the simultaneous desperation of the very poor. It was not urbanization per se but the maldistribution of wealth and income that accounted for the disintegration of community; in New York City the geographical distance was minimal, but the economic divisions were enormous from Broadway's opulence and Wall Street's financial might to Five Points, the locus and symbol for the squalor and misery of the very poor.

The polarization between wealthy and poor was perhaps the most dramatic aspect of urban class structure, but the emergence of a middle class as a self-conscious group was an equally striking though perhaps less visible development in the antebellum city. The increase in small-scale retailers and investors and salaried clerks and managers placed a group of men and their families in between the working classes and the wealthy controllers of capital. The separation of retailing from production and wholesaling, along with the development of far-flung markets, facilitated the emergence of small-scale, specialized retail merchants, managers of larger retail outlets, male office and store clerks, and contractors, who now helped to define the distinction between "commercial pursuits" and "mechanical trades," white and blue collars. Given the era's economic instability, Americans could fall out of the middle class as rapidly as they rose into it. But increasingly recognizable characteristics came to define urban middle-class position. Middle-class Americans with rising incomes, expectations, and living standards provided a demand for consumer goods—carpeting, wallpaper, pianos, clothing, books, and magazines. They also responded strongly to the evangelical religious renewal known as the Second Great Awakening, joined new voluntary associations, and supported new codes of morality such as temperance, which they attempted to popularize among and ultimately to legally impose upon the working classes. But the most distinguishing characteristic of the new middle class was their family life. Home came to be defined by its distance from the public world. The urban middle classes were the most enthusiastic proponents of the work ethic, and family relationships were the template for new male and female personalities that expressed middle-class norms of respectability, hard work, and upwardly mobile striving for men, moral guardianship and sentimental nurturance for women.

Within middle-class families the everyday patterns of men's and women's lives were becoming more distinct. In towns and cities, male wage earning became tied to the external discipline of a clearly defined working day, while women continued to do the home-bound and less clearly differentiated tasks of food preparation, child rearing, and washing. Increasingly the home became idealized as a bastion of what were defined as feminine virtues—piety, morality, affection, and self-sacrifice—commodities absent from the public world ruled by male values of competition and aggression. In reality few women had a staff of servants to allow them to be completely separate from either home production or physical work. In addition, with white-collar incomes often precarious, women's maternal labors in keeping boarders, sewing, or opening schools in their homes provided the income that sustained the family's middle-class status.

The idealization of the home as spiritual refuge imbued household work and child care with new significance. Both middle-class men and women came increasingly to perceive the home as an institution presided over by women, inhabited by children, frequented by men. Although middle-class status was dependent on male-earned income and public roles, the elusive quality of "respectability" derived from the character of domesticity provided by women's efforts. Control over male sexual appetites was a battle fought with great vigor inside middle-class families. The smaller size and fewer children of the urban middle class was a critical factor by which "respectable" people measured their distance from farming and immigrant working-class families. Although national fertility rates fell after 1800, the most precipitous decline was among new middle-class families in towns and cities. Maternal nurture was critical to the success of middle-class children, and fewer children allowed families more resources to invest in their children's education and allowed mothers to devote more time to their children's upbringing and to instilling in them values that would enable the children to maintain a middle-class position. Paternal authority in the urban household was beginning to weaken as maternal affection became the driving force in family life.

Evangelical Protestantism bolstered the ideology of women's sphere. Christian virtues of humility, submissiveness, piety, and charity coincided with the new descriptions of female moral character. Although many men were converted in the evangelical revivals that swept the urbanizing northeast and made their way westward along the trail of settlement, women made up the majority of converts and the bulk of congregations thereafter.

By 1814, women outnumbered men in church and religious societies of bustling Utica, New York, and the most zealous activists of the early revivals were women of the new middle classes—wives and daughters of men who worked outside the home. Forming voluntary associations with evangelical goals extended the realm of domesticity outside the home. Middle-class women were formally excluded from business and politics, but, imbued with a positive sense of their roles and responsibilities as women and supported by ministers, they created a community of their peers and an associational life that claimed space for women in between the poles of domesticity and public life.

Even in the years of its greatest popularity the ideology of a separate women's sphere coexisted with exceptions to it. By midcentury, 10 percent of adult women, most of them in cities, worked for pay. Single women's superior moral qualities made them prime candidates to *leave* the home to fill the increasing number of teaching jobs, expanding with the spread of the common school. By 1860, one-fourth of the nation's teachers were women, but in heavily urbanized Massachusetts, almost four-fifths of the teaching force was female, and one out of five women had taught at some point in their lives, expanding the realm of domesticity at least as far as the schoolroom. For those largely unmarried women who produced textiles, men's clothing, and shoes in factories, constituting one-fourth of the labor force in manufacturing, the experience of living outside the family and earning wages did appear to have altered their future domestic lives. They married at later ages, married men who were more their equal in age, had fewer children, and settled disproportionately in cities and towns rather than the countryside. The crowds of poor women in cities, competing for miserably paid garment piecework, peddling hot sweet potatoes or scrub brushes for pennies on street corners to keep their families afloat, were excluded by definition from the culture of domesticity. In frontier towns like Santa Fe, San Antonio, Tucson, and Los Angeles the harshness of the frontier environment mediated against the sexual division of labor except in the wealthiest families.

Changes associated with the spread of commercialization extended into the most intimate corners of daily life. Until the expansion of the market economy and the emergence of merchant capitalism, most wage earners in cities had lived with their employers and had shared their private lives. Work, leisure, and domestic life had been acted out in the same place and by the same people. Now the hallmark of the employer's home was its separation from production, its private social life, and its withdrawal from patterns of shared sociability. Apprentices were no longer thought to be members of the master's family; rather, they were considered trainees in a business that was now often conducted outside the household. As master and journeymen saw themselves less as members of a common household, they viewed themselves more as employers and employees. Their interests were more separate and conflicting than they had been before, and they formed new class conscious organizations to protect those interests. Between 1786 and 1816 at least twelve major strikes by various craftsmen occurred—the first major strikes by employees against employers in American history.

As commercialization drew farms and cities into closer relations with each other, changes associated with the expansion of the market began to affect areas not usually identified as cities. The extension of improved transportation, post offices, and newspapers brought more people into contact with urban life. In Massachusetts in 1820 the nine print shops that had given colonial Boston a monopoly on news had given way to 120 print shops scattered throughout the state, publishing fifty-three daily and weekly newspapers for twenty-three different towns. Some 443 post offices blanketed the state, giving nearly every community access to the national communications system. Wherever population expanded and the number of men working as clerks, agents, and other nonmanual occupations increased, there was also a striking rise in the number of specialized voluntary associations such as charity organizations, libraries, fire-fighting societies, and masonry. Interest-group associations split the population into a series of exclusive cells, which sometimes overlapped and sometimes competed with prior loyalties to place, family, and church. A rich associational life in towns signified the expansion of social stratification and heterogeneity associated with urban experience.

Until the Civil War, America's major cities remained primarily mercantile in function. But by the 1840s economic and technological changes were beginning to launch the cities and the nation into an age of industrialization. The Revolution had loosened traditional restraints on incorporation, and the number of joint-stock and limited-liability corporations mushroomed, establishing banks, insurance companies, and manufacturing concerns, plus bridge, road, and canal companies. Expanded capital and commercial resources enabled regional railroad systems to grow big enough to deliver raw materials and distribute finished products cheaply and speedily. The 2800 miles of rail in America in 1840 grew to 30,600 miles by 1860, linking urban centers. At the same time, telegraph construction revolutionized communications and the ways in which business was done. No longer did merchants and manufacturers have to depend on ships and stagecoaches to bring them news about markets. Expanded use of steam engines and replacement of wood fuels by coal allowed factories to locate inside of larger cities and away from sources of water power. Production of interchangeable parts and development of the machine-tool industry aided the creation of mechanized factory production. The exhaustion of New England farming soil and the mass exodus from shifting economic and social conditions in Europe provided factory owners with a growing labor supply. The commercial development of the hinterlands and the new urban residents helped increase the size and number of domestic markets. The transportation revolution, with its wagons, steamboats, and railroads; the commercial revolution, with its corporate enterprises and expanded marketing and credit techniques, and the beginnings of the industrial revolution, with its factories and mass-produced goods, had ushered in a new era in urban life.

CONTESTED TERRAIN

Migration, population increase, and commercial and industrial transformation brought sweeping social changes to city life. Perhaps the most striking feature of early nineteenth-century cities was the heterogeneity of peoples and the fragmentation of earlier communal institutions that had attempted to bridge social divisions and provide social cohesion. New groups competed for the employment and housing the city had to offer and contended for political inclusion and social recognition in the urban community.

A free black community of institutional complexity was a new feature of urban life. Before the Revolution only a tiny fraction of the black population had been free, and those who were free were either the product of mixed racial unions or former slaves who were too old to undertake productive work for their masters. But in the war years and after, considerable numbers of slaves had been freed, in the North through statewide emancipation, and in the South, through individual manumissions or successful illegal flight from bondage. Free black people moved to cities in large numbers. While the free black population of Virginia more than doubled between 1790 and 1810, that of Richmond increased fourfold and that of Norfolk increased tenfold. By 1820 the largest free black community lived in Baltimore, but Boston, New York, Philadelphia, Cincinnati, Charleston, New Orleans, and Mobile also had sizable free black populations. In the early years of the nineteenth century, cities were the centers of free black life.

Ex-slaves were drawn to cities because of the opportunities for employment and because the concentration of free blacks offered a greater chance to find an acceptable marriage partner, establish a family, and participate in activities of black churches, schools, fraternal societies, and benevolent organizations. In northern seaports, most free black men worked as laborers or mariners, but a few managed to hold positions as artisans, particularly in trades identified with servile, dirty, or distasteful labor like butchering and barbering. A few were able to serve the black community as small proprietors, ministers, and teachers. In Charleston, free black men constituted 16 percent of the city's skilled male work force and 11 percent of the unskilled male laboring population. In Richmond and Lynchburg, Virginia, free black men were nearly 30 percent of the unskilled male work force. In most cities the majority of the free black population were women, most of whom worked as servants and washerwomen, although a few kept small shops and ran boarding houses. In Petersburg, Virginia, most free black women worked as domestics, but a few were nurses, midwives, store-keepers, and bakers, and free black women managed to accumulate half the property owned by blacks in the city.

Although most free blacks remained poor and propertyless, some rose to modest wealth and respectability, and slowly a black elite emerged in Boston, Philadelphia, Baltimore, Richmond, Savannah, and Charleston. Wealthier and better educated, urban black leaders petitioned Congress and state legislatures to abolish slavery and to grant full political rights to black citizens. They established community institutions where black people could pray, educate their children, entertain, and protect themselves. In Philadelphia, free blacks established their own church in the 1790s. By 1800, black communities from Boston to Savannah had their own churches, and in 1816, leading black churchmen from various parts of these regions joined together to form the first independent black denomination, the African Methodist Episcopal Church. From the beginning black people named their churches, schools, mutual assistance associations, and fraternal organizations African, to signify their own group identity and to distinguish themselves from white society. In Philadelphia the Angola Beneficial Society was established in 1808, the Africa Insurance Company in 1809, the Sons of Africa in 1810, and the African Female and Male Benevolent Societies in the following years. By the 1820s in Philadelphia, Afro-Americans had created an institutional life that was richer and more stable than that of the lower-income whites with whom they shared their neighborhoods. In Boston the African Society, founded in 1797, established the African School in 1798 and the African Meeting House in 1805. A black fraternal order of Masons had been organized in Boston in 1784. Their hard-won associational life also helped to shape new residential patterns for black urban dwellers. Although slaves were scattered throughout the city, free blacks tended to cluster in particular neighborhoods, attracted by cheaper housing and drawn by African churches and schools.

As the free black population in cities grew, white people used legislation to limit their economic opportunities and to restrict their political rights to vote and to testify in court. But the dense network of urban black institutions and a rich community life made it more possible in the cities than in the countryside for free blacks to try to protect themselves and even sometimes to confront racism.

Slaves were an indispensable part of the urban work force in southern cities. In Charleston, Richmond, and Lynchburg, slaves constituted from 50 to 60 percent of the workingmen; in Mobile, Baton Rouge, and Nashville, they constituted from 25 to 35 percent of the adult male working population. Nearly all slaves did manual labor of some sort, ranging from

African Meeting House, Boston   The African Meeting House was built in Smith Court, Boston, in 1806 by black laborers to serve as a center for black community life in Boston. This photograph was probably taken in the 1890s. *(The Society for the Preservation of New England Antiquities.)*

domestic duties to artisan trades and industrial labor. Throughout the urban South, merchants, professionals, and factory owners in factory towns like Richmond and Lynchburg remained the largest employers of slave labor, and for the most part, these employers required unskilled rather than skilled laborers. During the colonial period slaves had actively participated in almost all the artisanal trades, but by the mid-nineteenth century there were a significant number of slave artisans only in Charleston.

Skilled and unskilled, urban slaves were a considerable social presence in southern cities. By the 1850s, slave hiring, where masters hired out slaves to other employers, was commonplace and profitable to both masters and slaves. It provided slaveowners, particularly widowed women, a steady income, and it gave slaves experience with wage labor and the marketplace, a possibility of accumulating cash, and an added measure of control over their own lives. Urban slaves enjoyed greater mobility and cultural autonomy than did their counterparts in the countryside. Bondsmen on plantations lived in the slave quarters and saw only their masters' families and occasionally slaves from a nearby plantation. City slaves partook of a wider world. They had access (even when it was illegal) to food, drink, entertainment, and the common sociability of urban life. They sometimes ran their own churches, and they often sneaked away to talk and drink with fellow slaves, free black people, and even working-class whites in the back-alley groceries and grogshops scattered throughout every Southern city. Preferring to avoid costs of housing their slaves, some masters gave their slaves permission to live as well as work away. When slaves lived out, they often resided in rented rooms in working-class neighborhoods on the fringes of town that housed free blacks and poor whites.

These circumstances made it difficult for owners to supervise the activities of their bondsmen every minute of the day, and slaves who hired out and lived out challenged traditional patterns of control. In the fringe neighborhoods where free blacks, urban slaves, and working class whites lived, a fugitive slave might purchase a set of freedom papers; a Richmond newspaper complained in 1860 that "Not only free Negroes but low white people can be found who will secret a slave from his master." Cities responded with more stringent restrictions on the activities of all black people, slave and free. These black codes resulted in formal segregation—the exclusion of black people from most public accommodations. Black people were required to have licenses for certain occupations and were barred from others, were forbidden to assemble without a license, were prohibited from being taught to read and write, from testifying against white people. These codes were enforced with increasing vigor after the 1830s.

In these same years the number of slaves in the workforce of southern cities decreased relative to the numbers of immigrant laborers. In 1840 the total slave population of the ten largest southern cities was 67,755; in 1860 it was 68,013. Meanwhile the total white population of the same cities ballooned from 233,000 to 690,000. Only in Richmond, where slave manpower was essential to iron and tobacco processing, did a large proportion of slaves still persist in 1860. In New Orleans, on the other hand, the number of slaves dropped from 23,000 in 1840 to 13,000 in 1860. But in spite of the increase in restrictions and the decrease in slave population, free black people and urban slaves continued to assert their claim to a place of their own in city life.

The crowds of transient white men and women who filled the cities looking for work were also a new sight in the early nineteenth century. In manufacturing cities like Lowell and Lynn, farm sons and daughters worked in new textile factories and shoemaking workshops; and in commercial boom towns like Rochester, New York, predominantly male migrants were drawn from the countryside to work on canals and railroads. By the 1820s and 1830s a rising percentage of the populations of these cities were propertyless wage earners, without the customary stake in the community that property-holding represented. Many were first-generation wage laborers and factory workers, unaccustomed to the particular patterns of impersonal employment or the discipline of factory labor. As working-class streets and neighborhoods became distinct from middle-class areas, visibly separate patterns of sociability heightened the sense of distance between classes. These crowds of working people represented another new subgroup in urban life.

Immigrants, pushed out of Ireland, Germany, and England when their livelihoods were threatened by agricultural commercialization and competition from machine-made goods, were another new presence in nineteenth-century urban populations. By the 1850s more than half the residents of Boston and New York City were foreign born, and in Philadelphia 30 percent of household heads were born in Europe. By 1860, 40 percent of New Orleans's population was foreign born. Foreign-born workers, mostly from Ireland and Germany, constituted more than half of Charleston and Mobile's free adult workingmen's population, and between 40 and 50 percent of free adult male workingmen in Richmond, Nashville, and Baton Rouge. Major concentrations of Irish immigrants could be identified in New York, Boston, and Philadelphia, and strong German communities emerged in Cincinnati, Louisville, St. Louis, and Milwaukee. Irish and German immigrants brought their own cultural traditions to American cities, traditions of work and leisure, spirituality and sociability, which often came into conflict with those of native-born residents. Immigrant labor helped to build the growing cities, and immigrant cultural traditions would leave a permanent mark on city life as well (see Chapter 4).

This diversification of urban population took place in the context of broadened suffrage for male citizens, circumstances that reshaped political life. After the Revolution, electioneering and open competition for office had increased, and the number of contested elections and the turnover of legislative representatives had multiplied. Still, until the 1820s, and later in some states, property restrictions on suffrage continued to disenfranchise many men. Even for those granted the ballot, political interest and electoral turnout usually remained low. Many citizens appeared to have retreated from the extraordinary political demands of the Revolutionary period, instead deferring once again to the political leadership of the community's most distinguished men.

After 1820 the abandonment of restrictions on white male suffrage coincided with a reemergence of citizen interest in politics. Commercial transformation and ethnic, religious, and class tensions helped to spark a process by which community factions were institutionalized in the form of political parties. Local entrepreneurs were excited about the possi-

Election Day in Philadelphia, 1816 Men gather at the State House in Philadelphia to mobilize support for their candidates and parties. Note the few women on the fringes of the crowd, outside of the electoral activity. *(Library of Congress.)*

bilities of using government to tie localities to new markets and hoped to use city politics as a vehicle for raising revenue to expand urban commercial facilities. But citizens were deeply divided on the direction the economy ought to take and the role government ought to play, fearing the loss of local control over economic decisions. Evangelical Protestants hoped to use government to impose their convictions about proper moral behavior on the community, a goal opposed by older Protestant groups and new Catholic immigrants. Local political leaders linked these debates to the national parties and leaders, and the rise of workingmen's parties in urban areas seemed to spring from a similar set of questions and unease about the direction of commercial capitalism. Political organization provided a set pattern of responses to divisive questions, and raising problems to a national level partly defused potential community divisions. First Federalists and Republicans, then Whigs and Democrats created formal organizations at the town level. As early as 1810, political sectarianism was a durable feature of local politics, although especially in older settled towns, local politics sometimes returned to a search for consensual, nonpartisan solutions to community questions.

The growth of local political parties meant that political leadership by the men dominant in the community's social and economic life—bankers, commission merchants, and lawyers—was sometimes challenged by a new breed of professional politicians who assiduously courted newly enfranchised workingmen. Rarely were those in the lower three-fourths of the social order elected to city councils; elections at large provided a structure for those dominant in the social and economic life of the community to dominate in its formal political life as well. But political competition often set members of the business elite against each other, and the increasing numbers of working-class voters could sometimes check the ability of elites to exercise political power commensurate with their economic and social power.

No issue was as politically divisive in early nineteenth-century cities as temperance. Drinking had previously been assumed to be an inevitable aspect of the artisans' working day. According to historian Paul Johnson, "liquor was embedded in the patterns of irregular work and easy sociability sustained by the household economy," and public drinking traditions persisted in the interstices of the expanding commercial economy where these older economic forms held on.[3] But new standards of discipline within central shops and factories included abstinence from alcohol. Indeed in Massachusetts the manufacturers who were most technologically innovative were also those who turned most enthusiastically to temperance. For the new middle classes, sobriety became the key to economic growth, individual success, happy homes, and quiet streets. The new, more private homes, under the guidance of pious housewives, were now considered to be inappropriate places for all baser passions, including drunkenness. Factory owners were among the first to banish liquor from their workshops and from their own homes, and as they did so, whiskey marked the dividing line between middle-class respectability and working-class sociability. Drinking became the central prerogative of an autonomous working-class social life, even before Irish and German immigrants brought distinctive ethnic drinking traditions to American cities.

The first temperance reformers were wealthy Federalists, whose organizations hoped to encourage temperance by appealing to drinkers to cooperate with their betters in abstaining from alcohol. In the 1820s the success of evangelical revivals sparked a new wave of middle-class temperance organizations that were as hostile to the wealthy as to the poor, denouncing liquor retailers as trafficking in vice. In Rochester, hotel proprietors and tavern keepers whose trade depended on working-class drinking let their church memberships lapse, but manufacturers, merchants, lawyers, shopkeepers, master artisans, and skilled journeymen whose lives were changed for the better by the commercial revolution were the first and most enthusiastic supporters of the revivals and temperance. Progressing from tactics of moral suasion and conversion to firings, boycotts, and political campaigns to outlaw drink, by the 1830s the evangelical reformers converted thousands to new ideas about temperance and respectability.

It was not until the 1840s after severe economic collapse had shattered what remained of artisans' and workingmen's organizations that a genuine working-class temperance movement, the Washingtonian Society, arose. In Cincinnati the Washingtonian movement drew men who had resisted temperance in the 1830s, more likely to be Democrats than Whigs, into an altogether different style of temperance organization than those organized by evangelical Protestants. Noisily public and male-oriented rather than under the moral guardianship of women, Washingtonian societies recruited in streets and grogshops, gathered together supporters in picnics and parades rather than in prayer meetings, and dramatized alcohol's depths of degradation rather than the righteous fruits of abstinence. In Philadelphia in the 1840s, waves of working-class revivalism, often Methodist in character, reached working-class neighborhoods and sparked a working-class temperance movement, drawing in master craftsmen, journeymen, shopkeepers, and the most ambitious unskilled laborers.

In all cities the decision to abstain from alcohol was the key symbol of a new morality and a commitment to self-improvement. But in the 1840s, evangelical workingmen measured their own sobriety and discipline against the unreconstructed drinking habits of expanding Irish and German immigrant neighborhoods. The revivalism and temperance that bolstered the self-respect of native-born workers divided communities in new ways. While the Whig party drew church-going merchants, professionals, and master workmen to join together in a campaign for coercive temperance, nonevangelical Protestants, immigrant Catholic workingmen, and the grocers and petty retailers who served them found refuge in the antitemperance, anticoercion stand of the Democratic party. Native-born enthusiasm for temperance translated into passionate anti-Catholicism, sharply splitting the working classes along ethnic lines and turning neighborhoods into battlegrounds. Incidents like the destruction of Irish weavers' looms and houses by native-born weavers in Philadelphia's Kensington in 1844, the fierce fighting between Philadelphia native-born and Irish fire companies in the 1830s and 1840s, the riot that ensued from a collision between a native-born fire company and an Irish funeral procession on Broad Street in Boston in 1837 and other anti-Catholic and anti-Irish riots in Baltimore, St. Louis, and Louisville that occurred in this period need to be understood in this context.

Abolition vied with temperance as an incendiary issue lying below the surface of political debate, fought out largely in extra-legal battles in the 1830s. Between 1834 and 1835 the abolitionist organization, the American Anti-Slavery Society, became dramatically more visible. The number of local societies increased and their constituency of women, children, and free black people defied conventional notions of political participation. Using new penny postage and steam printing technology, the abolitionists increased their distribution of antislavery tracts ten times from 1834 to 1835, sending out 1.1 million pieces of abolitionist literature as tracts, newspapers, children's readers, even medals, emblems, bandannas, and chocolate wrappers. But in local communities, "gentlemen of property and standing"—prominent lawyers, bankers, merchants, doctors, and local political leaders of both the Democratic and Whig parties—acted to defend the status quo by mobilizing disruption of antislavery conventions, attacks on abolitionist leaders, and destruction of abolitionist meeting places and printing presses. In Utica in 1835, a Jacksonian congressman led a crowd that drove the New York Anti-Slavery Society out of town. Abolitionist leader William Lloyd Garrison was nearly lynched by a crowd of respectable Bostonians in 1835, and abolitionist Elijah Lovejoy was shot and killed while trying to defend a new printing press from a crowd of prominent citizens in Alton, Illinois, in 1837. In 1834, leading New Yorkers cheered on a crowd of butcher boys and day laborers who smashed and burned the home of Lewis Tappan, a prominent and wealthy local supporter of antislavery.

In other incidents in these years, crowds turned on free black communities. Here the rioters were often workingmen who expressed pent-up economic and social grievances through racial violence. In the summer of 1835 in Washington, D.C., an angry crowd of striking ship carpenters searched free black homes for abolitionist literature, destroying a black-owned restaurant and burning or stoning other free black businesses, schools, churches, and homes. The crowds of mechanics and artisans who terrorized free black communities in Cincinnati, Providence, and New York City in the 1830s and 1840s were not in direct competition with blacks for jobs but were fighting for urban turf, coming disproportionately from neighborhoods that bordered black residential areas.

Other instances of confrontation too explosive for established political channels took place on the streets of antebellum cities. When the Pennsylvania state legislature gave permission in 1839 for a railroad to extend track down the main street of Philadelphia's Kensington section, residents expressed their fears that burning coals and fast-moving trains would endanger their shops, homes, and children. When petitions to the state legislature proved futile and workmen began to tear up the street to build the railroad tracks, residents used the upturned paving stones to wage war on the proposed railroad and the laborers who were building it. Two years of sporadic street battles and noisy public demonstrations finally resulted in the state legislature's acceding to neighborhood demands and revoking the right of way. Similarly the limits of political action and legal recourse were tested in Baltimore in 1835, where citizens rioted when trustees and secret partners of the failed Bank of Maryland used various legal obstacles for over a year to avoid settlement of the bank's affairs. The kinds of concerns that drew the crowd into the streets could not be expressed through the ballot. The extraordinary press of diverse populations, new experience with heightened social and economic inequality, and fierce competition between groups contending for political power left antebellum cities deeply scarred and divided.

Conflict Over the Use of City Streets, 1839 This poster, circulated in Philadelphia in 1839, called on residents to stand firm against entrepreneurial incursions into local space. *(National Archives.)*

SERVICING THE CITY

Nearly a thousand people died in antebellum riots, revealing the inadequacy of constables, sheriffs, and night watchmen in keeping the peace. A sense that crime as well as disorder was on the increase prompted cities to establish permanent professional uniformed police forces, whom they could pay with revenues raised through taxing and borrowing provisions in new city charters. Most urban crime took place in the poorer sections of cities, where both criminals and victims were part of the lower classes, but the new mix of urban population, the rise of inequality, and the decline of older patterns of neighborhood authority led to an increase in crimes against property, especially burglary and arson. In St. Louis in the 1850s only fifty day constables had the responsibility for policing a population of one hundred thousand, and entrepreneurs were concerned that a reputation for lawlessness would hurt their city's attractiveness for commercial investment. A St. Louis newspaper editor spoke for local businessmen when he stressed that "the prosperity of our city, its increase in business, the enhancement in the value of its property . . . depend on the preservation of order."

By midcentury, fear of disorder had overcome fear of professional police in many cities. In 1838 the Massachusetts General Assembly enabled Boston to appoint salaried officers. New York obtained similar authority in 1844, Philadelphia in 1850, and Baltimore in 1857. In an industrial city like Lynn the impetus for a professional police force came from the city's shoe manufacturers who wanted better protection for their investments in buildings and machinery and who were concerned about the crowds of unsupervised and potentially disorderly strangers who congregated in the streets before and after work.

Residents of these cities soon discovered, however, that creation of a professional police force failed to solve old problems of law enforcement and even raised new ones. First, there were never enough policemen. Between 1845 and 1855 New York City's population grew from 250,000 to 630,000, while its police force was increased from 800 to less than 1200. Other cities suffered from similar shortages. In Lynn the largest number of police were on night duty patrolling the streets on the lookout for burglaries and fires, but even this commitment did not satisfy some wealthier businessmen who felt they needed to hire specially deputized police as night watchmen in their shops and factories. Because there were not enough officers to patrol an entire city, police protection was concentrated in commercial and affluent residential districts and was minimal in crowded, working-class neighborhoods, giving crime a spatial dimension. As newspapers published journalistic accounts of police activities and police reports were publicized, notions of what constituted criminal behavior broadened, and poor neighborhoods were labeled as criminal by definition, abandoned to poor residents now dismissed as "dangerous classes."

In addition, police forces could become embroiled in political conflicts. Historian Alan Dawley has argued that in Lynn the police force was a highly visible body of men responsible not to the community as a whole but to the party in public office who hired them and funded their salaries.[4] In an attempt to lift police appointments in New York City out of local corruption and party politics the New York General Assembly in 1857 created a state-controlled metropolitan police force. Mayor Fernando Wood resisted this imposition of state power over his Democratic regime and refused to disband the local police, with the result that the city was patrolled by two competing police forces. The U.S. Court of Appeals forced Wood to back down, and the metropolitan police remained in operation until the 1870s, even though it failed to improve law enforcement in the city. Yet the New York example sparked the subsequent creation of state-controlled municipal police in over a dozen large cities, from Baltimore to San Francisco, Detroit to New Orleans.

More important, the police as agents of law enforcement were buffeted between conflicting urban groups who held different notions of what the law was and how it should be enforced. There were, for example, people who demanded strict enforcement of vice, temperance, and fugitive-slave laws. Yet police action in these areas could antagonize others who saw no harm in a little gambling, whose cultural background included the use of wine or beer, and whose moral values condoned the protection of fugitive slaves. Furthermore, according to Roger Lane,[5] in earlier years police activity had been directed at individual offenders or at "a voiceless class of unfortunates," such as vagrants or drunks. With the establishment of more formal police, however, law enforcement could affect a much broader population—including those who considered themselves law abiding. In the late 1840s vigorous police activity in Boston resulted in the arrest of hundreds of people for failing to clear ice off their sidewalks and for keeping unlicensed dogs. Clearly a gap existed between society's idealistic intentions for criminal law, particularly its moral aspects, and individuals' actual desires for freedom of action. The police were buffers between these pressures, fulfilliing the felt need for law enforcement on the one hand, and easing the impact of the law by their action or inaction on the other. The achievement of the proper balance has always stymied urban Americans, because changes in living standards, ethnic and racial mix, technology, and morals have been too fast for government institutions to react to. City dwellers in the mid nineteenth century were just beginning to feel the forces and frustrations that perplex the modern age.

Reorganizations of fire departments duplicated the processes in the police department. Volunteer fire companies of artisans, who were able to leave their work to chase a fire and who enjoyed the battle with competing fire companies for access to water as much as the excitement of battling the fires themselves, were clearly inadequate to the task of protecting buildings, wharves, and machines now found in commercial cities. By the 1860s most cities had replaced hand pumps with steam engines, disbanded the volunteer fire companies, and in their place hired permanent full-time firefighters on alert in specially constructed fire stations.

With or without the professional reorganization of firefighters, communities were not really safe from fire until they had access to efficient and ample water. At an early date, fear of fire and disease had induced city officials to think more seriously about providing water for their citizens. In the 1790s yellow fever had ravaged the Northeast—particularly Philadelphia—causing several cities to become passionately convinced that cleanliness was the only way to prevent or minimize disease. This need for sanitation meant a more liberal use of water. Most urbanites drew their water from public or private wells, but the springs that fed these wells simply could not supply tens of thousands of people, and they were often polluted with seepage from privies and graves. Attention focused on nearby rivers and streams as sources of larger, cleaner supplies of .water. Who should undertake projects to tap these sources—the municipality or private corporations?

Under pressures resulting from the yellow fever epidemics, Philadelphia constructed the first major public waterworks in this country. In 1798 the Philadelphia City Council hired engineer and architect Benjamin Latrobe. He devised a system to pump water from the Schuylkill River to a high-ground reservoir called Centre Square, from where it could be pumped through wooden pipes to various parts of the city. Although it operated at a deficit—largely because people could not readily accept the idea of paying for water and because the steam pumps often broke down—the Centre Square waterworks won national admiration. The system eventually accustomed Philadelphians to consider water as a public utility. When the city outgrew the system, it constructed a larger public waterworks in 1811, raising water from the Schuylkill to reservoirs atop Fairmount Hill and distributing it through iron pipes.

But Philadelphia was the exception in these early years. Other large cities received water from private companies. The quality of service ranged from adequate in Baltimore, where the Baltimore Water Company was conscientious about its function, to intolerable in New York, where the Manhattan Company devoted most of its attention and capital to banking privileges granted by its charter. Private corporations were concerned about profits; few were willing to commit a huge amount of capital to the construction and maintenance of an elaborate water system. In addition they catered to paying customers and balked at extending service to lower-class districts that would furnish little revenue. Eventually, however, leaders of other cities, looking to the example set by Philadelphia, began to press for public waterworks. In 1835 New York voters solidly approved a project to bring water to the city through an aqueduct from the Croton River. In 1845 Bostonians accepted an act passed by the Massachusetts General Assembly enabling the city to construct its own water system. In 1857 the city of Baltimore purchased its private waterworks and began constructing an additional reservoir. In factory towns, industrialists pressured city officials to protect their property with municipal water systems that provided water piped through the business districts. By 1860 the country's sixteen largest cities had reasonably efficient water systems, only four of which were still privately owned.

Yet leaders who congratulated themselves for providing their cities with adequate water often became complacent. Abundance of water and higher standards of public health created new habits of consumption. Indoor plumbing, with tub and toilet, became a facility of city life, at least for the wealthy. Industrial use of water rose. But as population growth and industrialization quickened, the ability of public and private waterworks to meet local demand faltered. The obstacle was one of leadership more than of technology. As Sam Bass Warner, Jr., has noted, Philadelphia's Fairmount works made running water available for middle-class houses and street pumps, but public leaders were reluctant to require and offer running water where it was needed most—in the homes of the poor.[6] Industrialists in every city tapped water from public supplies because it was the cheapest and handiest coolant and waste-carrying agent; they had little concern for pollution or future shortages. This shortsightedness and the elevation of private needs over public welfare began to block the potential of public water systems.

Professional police, fire, and water services relieved some problems of commercial cities, but poverty, delinquency, mental illness, disease, and moral decay defied easy solutions. Colonial methods of warning out debtors, fining and whipping criminals, and farming out paupers and orphans to relatives and other townspeople or confining them in workhouses and almshouses were unfeasible in the nineteenth century. Cities grew too large for officials to keep track of all newcomers, and old forms of punishment and relief failed to stem increasing crime, sin, and poverty. Moreover, constant population migration churned the social structure of all cities, increasing anonymity and aggravating fears of anarchy and social breakdown.

To combat overcrowding, unemployment, and poverty on a scale previously unknown in American cities, middle-class evangelical reformers created programs that were shaped by their own gender, class, and ethnic prejudices. A characteristic response of antebellum reformers was to try to convert the poor and depraved, infuse them with Christian morality, and to establish new reforming institutions such as penitentiaries, asylums, and public schools that would inculcate values of order and restraint. Housed together, away from their families and the temptations of city life, the poor could be rehabilitated in a controlled environment that would teach them values of orderliness and industry. Between 1820 and 1840 scores of cities and towns opened almshouses and workhouses for the poor. These institutions won support as much because they removed the poor from the streets and were more economical than outdoor assistance as they did for their reforming functions. Nevertheless they signaled a new approach to relief.

The belief that deviant behavior was the product of social rather than individual failure was applied to the criminal, the insane, and the delinquent. Penitentiaries, asylums, and houses of correction were constructed to serve the same functions for these groups that the almshouses served for the poor—removing the criminal, the insane, and the delinquent from the city's temptations and restoring mental health and lawful behavior by exposure to an institutional life of regimentation and restraint. With the goal of returning the inmates to preurban social harmony, the institutions were located in rural settings, although the values of regimentation, punctuality, and obedience the institutions represented were more suited to life in the present than the past. The sentiment behind these institutions subsequently took two paths. On the one hand, the sense of community responsibility for the alleviation of social problems foreshadowed the Social Gospel movement that spread across the urban scene later in the nineteenth century. On the other hand, as David Rothman has shown, the ideal of confining deviants and dependents in order to reform them could easily harden into the objective of incarcerating these groups simply to isolate them from the rest of society.[7]

Almshouses, penitentiaries, and asylums could neither hold nor reform all the poor, however. A more inclusive institution was needed to destroy the growing cycle of poverty, a process whereby succeeding generations of the same families failed to escape indigence and became increasingly dependent upon public support. Beginning in the 1820s, urban leaders began to rally around state-supported free education as the instrument that would break the chain of destitution while restoring social order in the same fashion as other institutional reform.

In the 1820s and 1830s the most insistent voices for state-supported education were those of urban politicians, humanitarians, and educators who campaigned for educational reform as insurance against social upheaval. Horace Mann, a Boston lawyer, Henry Barnard, a leading citizen of Hartford, Connecticut, and Calvin Stowe, a professor of biblical literature at Cincinnati's Lane Theological Seminary, were among the most influential proponents of free public education. Schooling, they claimed, would instill habits of regularity and restraint in the lower classes and lift them from poverty into hard-working respectability. It would assimilate immigrants and teach all children to withstand temptations. As cities grew and social conflict became more threatening, the public-education movement gained momentum. Boston established free elementary schools in 1818, New York followed in 1832, and Philadelphia in 1836.

By the 1850s the majority of cities and states in the North and the West had some system of state-supported education. Moreover, schooling had become more uniform. Pupils were placed in grades according to age and ability, procedures for advancement from grade to grade were standardized, decisions about curriculum and textbooks were centralized, and teachers were required to meet certain professional qualifications. Control was more firmly consolidated in the hands of city and state bureaucracies.

Public schooling in diverse communities was now shaped by the political, economic, and cultural agendas of native Protestant political leaders, who intended the schools to train students in punctuality, cheerful obedience, honesty, and persistence. McGuffey's series of readers, which after 1836 became the basic reading textbook in countless schoolrooms, taught children to accept their position in the class hierarchy and strive for respectability rather than mobility or the trappings of wealth. The readers counseled that when the good little boy sees other children "riding on pretty horses, or in coaches, or walking with ladies and gentlemen, and having on very fine clothes, he does not envy them, nor wish to be like them." For he has been taught "that it is God who makes some poor and others rich; that the rich have troubles which we know nothing of; and that the poor, if they are good, may be very happy." The content of public education expressed values antagonistic to the cultures of Catholic, black, rural, southern, immigrant, and working-class peoples, the very groups who held out for local community control of schools in opposition to the reformers' vision of centralized, homogenized education. Not surprisingly these were also the groups least likely to be able to attend public schools. When Catholics in New York City lost their challenge to Protestant monopoly of public education, the Church decided to construct its own system of schools, an enormously costly program that took decades to complete. After Los Angeles was incorporated as a city in 1850, its Hispanic mayor, Antonio Franco Coronel, and city council, the majority of whom were Mexican, supported the establishment of public schools that were bilingual. When the school board failed to find teachers who could teach in both English and Spanish, the first public school opened with only English permitted for instruction.

The educational reformers' most visible accomplishment was the creation of the school systems themselves, represented by the uniformly designed school buildings proliferating in diverse urban neighborhoods. The expansion of urban schooling did not cause poverty to disappear. But the reformers succeeded in winning public support for enormous expenditures on education because politics in antebellum cities called for a literate and informed electorate, disorder and diversity in cities made bureaucratic organization and standardization appealing, and expanding commercial capitalism created a demand for well-trained workers and managers.

Despite the triumphs of educational reformers the reach of public schooling was still limited. In many cities, population increased faster than new schools could be built. As immigration accelerated in the 1840s, illiteracy rose instead of declined. More and more children were squeezed into existing classrooms. In 1850 Boston schools provided only one teacher for every fifty-five students. At the same time, school reformers attempting to bring all children into the school contended with officials and taxpayers determined to hold down public expenditures and with working-class and immigrant families insistent on resisting educators' intervention in family decisions about children's upbringing.

In the 1850s the attack on immigrant and working-class families implicit in calls for salvation through institutionalization in asylums and public schools was made more explicit in a new reform strategy. The male and female reformers active in the New York Children's Aid Society and the Association for Improving the Condition of the Poor initiated an ambitious campaign to eradicate poverty by clearing children and women from the streets and transforming working-class family life. The new ways in which the middle class perceived the work ethic and ideology of domesticity made traditional working-class street life, particularly the visible activities of children, seem especially dangerous and damaging. To middle-class humanitarians the enclosed, privatized, protected home and the clearly differentiated roles for men, women, and children on which it was based represented *the* critical social institution.

From this perspective the engagement of women and children in public wage work and social life rather than being sheltered in the enclave of the home became in itself evidence of parental neglect and family disintegration and the root cause of poverty. According to reformers, working-class households that sent women and children to find casual labor in the streets were not homes. In fact, some humanitarians viewed children on the streets as orphaned or abandoned, although in many cases they were neither. To "save" such children, New York reformer Charles Loring Brace established the Children's Aid Society (CAS) to remove poor children from their households, shipping boys off to vigorous farm labor with rural families in the countryside and teaching girls sewing, cooking, and housecleaning as preparation for a life of domesticity either as servants or as wives. Although the CAS solutions made no dent in urban poverty, its attempts to control the streets and shape the family life of the poor raised cultural antagonisms that would remain long after the reform societies abandoned their mission.

Migration, industrialization, and social change charged the first half of the nineteenth century with extraordinary activity, for all these movements fused in the cities. Although the United States was far from an urbanized nation on the eve of the Civil War, the three decades before the war witnessed the most intense growth of cities this country would ever experience. Between 1830 and 1840 the number of urban residents grew by 64 percent; between 1840 and 1850, by 92 percent; between 1850 and 1860, by 75 percent. By 1860, twenty-one cities had more than forty thousand inhabitants (see Table 2-2). These places and the activities they supported had helped bring the nation into a period of transition, suspended between preindustrial and industrial society, on the brink of still more major changes that lay ahead.

TABLE 2-2   Populations of Major Cities, 1830–60

	1830	1840	1850	1860
New York	202,589	312,700	515,500	813,600
Philadelphia	161,271	220,400	340,000	565,529
Brooklyn	15,396	36,230	96,838	266,660
Baltimore	80,620	102,300	169,600	212,418
Boston	61,392	93,380	136,880	177,840
New Orleans	46,082	102,190	116,375	168,675
Cincinnati	24,831	46,338	115,435	161,044
St. Louis	5,852	14,470	77,860	160,773
Chicago		4,470	29,963	109,260
Buffalo	8,653	18,213	42,260	81,130
Newark	10,953	17,290	38,890	71,940
Louisville	10,340	21,210	43,194	68,033
Albany	24,209	33,721	50,763	62,367
Washington	18,826	23,364	40,001	61,122
San Francisco			34,776	56,802
Providence	16,833	23,171	41,573	50,666
Pittsburgh	15,369	21,115	46,601	49,221
Rochester	9,207	20,191	36,403	48,204
Detroit	2,222	9,102	21,019	45,619
Milwaukee		1,712	20,061	45,246
Cleveland	1,076	6,071	17,034	43,417
Total urban population	1,127,000	1,845,000	3,544,000	6,217,000
Percentage of U.S. population that was urban	8.8	10.8	15.3	19.8
Percentage of increase in urban population		63.7	92.1	75.4

Sources: U.S. Censuses of 1850 and 1860; and Blake McKelvey, *American Urbanization: A Comparative History* (Glenview, Ill.: Scott, Foresman and Company, 1973), Table 3, p. 37.

BIBLIOGRAPHY

The historiography of urban America in the period between 1780 and 1860 has a number of branches. The growth of new cities in the West and South is examined by Richard C. Wade, *The Urban Frontier: 1790–1830* (Cambridge, Mass.: Harvard University Press, 1957); Bayard Still, "Patterns of Mid-Nineteenth Century Urbanization in the Middle West," *Mississippi Valley Historical Review*, 28(September 1941):187–206; Leonard P. Curry, "Urbanization and Urbanism in the Old South: A Comparative View," *Journal of Southern History* 40(February 1974):43–60; Blaine A. Brownell, "Urbanization in the South: A Unique Experience," *Mississippi Quarterly* 26(Spring 1973):105–20; David R. Goldfield, *Urban Growth in the Age of Sectionalism: Virginia, 1847–1861* (Baton Rouge: Louisiana State University Press, 1977); Gunther Barth, *Instant Cities: Urbanization and the Rise of San Francisco and Denver* (New York: Oxford

University Press, 1975); Robert M. Senkewicz, S.J., *Vigilantes in Gold Rush San Francisco* (Stanford, Calif.: Stanford University Press, 1985); and Kenneth W. Wheeler, *To Wear a City's Crown: The Beginnings of Urban Growth in Texas, 1832–1865* (Cambridge, Mass.: Harvard University Press, 1968). For cities in the East see Richard D. Brown, "The Emergence of Urban Society in Rural Massachusetts, 1760–1820," *Journal of American History* 61(June 1974): 29–51. For a discussion of the emergence of voluntary associations in a frontier town see Don Doyle, *The Social Order of a Frontier Community: Jacksonville, Illinois, 1825–1870* (Urbana: University of Illinois Press, 1978).

Several works have probed the development of urban rivalries. Among the most notable are Julius Rubin, *Canal or Railroad? Imitation and Innovation in the Response to the Erie Canal in Philadelphia, Baltimore, and Boston* (Philadelphia: American Philosophical Society, 1961); and Wyatt W. Belcher, *The Economic Rivalry Between St. Louis and Chicago, 1850–1880* (New York: Columbia University Press, 1947). The boosters who often spurred these rivalries are described in Daniel J. Boorstin, *The Americans: The National Experience* (New York: Random House, 1965).

For a discussion of the impact of commercialization in the countryside see Michael Merrill, "Cash Is Good To Eat: Self-Sufficiency and Exchange in the Rural Economy of the United States," *Radical History Review* 3(Fall, 1977):42–71; Christopher Clark, "The Household Economy, Market Exchange and the Rise of Capitalism in the Connecticut Valley, 1800–1860," *Journal of Social History* 13(Winter, 1979):169–89; the articles in Stephen Hahn and Jonathan Prude, eds., *The Countryside in the Age of Capitalist Transformation: Essays in the Social History of Rural America* (Chapel Hill: University of North Carolina Press, 1985). See also David Szatmary, *Shays' Rebellion: The Making of an American Insurrection* (Amherst: University of Massachusetts Press, 1980).

For a discussion of the transformation of the work process with the introduction of merchant capital, see Brian Palmer, "Social Formation and Class Formation in North America, 1800–1850," in *Proletarianization and Family History*, ed. David Levine (New York: Academic Press, 1984), 229–309; Paul Johnson, *A Shopkeeper's Millennium: Society and Revivals in Rochester, New York, 1815–1837* (New York: Hill and Wang, 1978); Paul Faler, *Mechanics and Manufacturers in the Early Industrial Revolution: Lynn, Massachusetts, 1780–1860* (Albany: State University of New York Press, 1981); Alan Dawley, *Class and Community: The Industrial Revolution in Lynn* (Cambridge, Mass.: Harvard University Press, 1977); Sean Wilentz, *Chants Democratic: New York City and the Rise of the American Working Class* (New York: Oxford University Press, 1984); Christine Stansell, *City of Women: The Female Laboring Poor in New York City, 1789–1860* (New York: Alfred A. Knopf, 1986); Bruce Laurie, *The Working People of Philadelphia, 1800–1850* (Philadelphia: Temple University Press, 1980); David Montgomery, "The Working Classes of the Pre-Industrial American City, 1780–1830," *Labor History* 9(Winter 1968):5–22. Sean Wilentz, "American Republican Festivals and the Rise of Class Conflict in New York City, 1788–1837," in *Working-Class America: Essays on Labor, Community and American Society*, eds. Michael Frisch and Daniel Walkowitz (Urbana: University of Illinois Press, 1983), 37–77. For discussion of the impact of industrialization see Christine Stansell, "The Origin of the Sweatshop: Women and Early Industrialization in New York City," in *Working-Class America*, 78–103; Susan Hirsch, *Roots of the American Working Class: The Industrialization of Crafts in Newark, 1800–1860* (Philadelphia: University of Pennsylvania Press, 1978); Thomas Dublin, *Women At Work: The Transformation of Work and Community in Lowell, Massachusetts, 1826–1860* (New York: Columbia University Press, 1979); Michael B. Katz, Michael J. Doucet, Mark J. Stern, *The Social Organization of Early Industrial Capitalism* (Cambridge, Mass.: Harvard University Press,

1982). The rise of a self-conscious middle class is discussed in Mary P. Ryan, *The Cradle of the Middle Class: The Family in Oneida County, New York, 1790–1865* (Cambridge, England: Cambridge University Press, 1981) and John S. Gilkeson, Jr., *Middle-Class Providence, 1820–1940* (Princeton, N.J.: Princeton University Press, 1986).

Some of the many works on early nineteenth century social structure include Betsy Blackmar, "Rewalking the 'Walking City': Property Relations in New York City, 1780–1840," *Radical History Review* 21(1980):131–48; Stuart Blumin, "The Hypothesis of Middle Class Formation in Nineteenth Century America: A Critique and Some Proposals," *American Historical Review* 90(April 1985):299–338; Blumin, "Explaining the New Metropolis: Perception, Depiction and Analysis in Mid-Nineteenth Century New York City," *Journal of Urban History* 11(November 1984):9–38; Stephan Thernstrom, *Poverty and Progress: Social Mobility in a Nineteenth Century City* (Cambridge, Mass.: Harvard University Press, 1964); Peter R. Knights, *The Plain People of Boston: A Study in City Growth* (New York: Oxford University Press, 1971); Edward Pessen, "The Egalitarian Myth and the American Social Reality: Wealth, Mobility, and Equality in the 'Era of the Common Man,' " *American Historical Review* 76(October 1971):989–1034, and "The Social Configuration of the Ante-Bellum City: An Historical and Theoretical Inquiry," *Journal of Urban History* 2(May 1976):267–306.

On women in antebellum cities see Stansell, *City of Women;* Stansell, "Women, Children and the Uses of the Streets: Class and Gender Conflict in New York City, 1850–1860," *Feminist Studies* 8(Summer 1982):309–336; Suzanne Lebsock, *The Free Women of Petersburg: Status and Culture in a Southern Town, 1784–1860* (New York: W.W. Norton & Co., 1984); Nancy Cott, *The Bonds of Womanhood: 'Women's Sphere' in New England, 1780–1835* (New Haven: Yale University Press, 1971); Faye Dudden, *Serving Women: Household Service in Nineteenth Century America* (Middletown, Conn.: Wesleyan University Press, 1983); Sharon Harley, "Northern Black Female Workers in the Jacksonian Era," in *The Afro-American Woman: Struggles and Images,* eds. Sharon Harley and Rosalyn Terborg-Penn (Port Washington, N.Y.: Kennikat Press, 1978); 5–16; Alice Kessler-Harris, *Out To Work: A History of Wage-Earning Women in America* (New York: Oxford University Press, 1982); Hasia Diner, *Erin's Daughters in America: Irish Immigrant Women in the Nineteenth Century* (Baltimore: Johns Hopkins University Press, 1983); Carol Groneman, "Working-Class Immigrant Women in Mid-Nineteenth Century New York: The Irish Woman's Experience," *Journal of Urban History* 4(May 1978):255–74.

For other materials on women and reform see Paula Baker, "The Domestication of Politics: Women in American Political Society, 1780–1920," *American Historical Review* 89(June 1984):620–47; Carroll Smith-Rosenberg, *Religion and The Rise of the City: The New York City Mission Movement, 1812–1870* (Ithaca, N.Y.: Cornell University Press, 1971); Smith-Rosenberg, "Beauty, the Beast and the Militant Woman," *American Quarterly* 23(Fall 1971):562–84; Barbara Berg, *The Remembered Gate: Origins of American feminism—the Woman and the City, 1800–1860* (New York: Oxford University Press, 1978); Nancy Hewitt, *Women's Activism and Social Change: Rochester, New York, 1822–1872* (Ithaca, N.Y.: Cornell University Press, 1984); Mary P. Ryan, "The Power of Women's Networks: A Case Study of Female Moral Reform in Antebellum America," *Feminist Studies* 5(Spring 1979):66–86; Susan P. Benson, "Business Heads and Sympathizing Hearts: The Women of the Providence Employment Society, 1837–1858," *Journal of Social History* 12(Winter 1978):301–12.

On blacks in cities before the Civil War see Gary Nash, "Forging Freedom: The Emancipation Experience in the Northern Seaport Cities, 1775–1820," in *Slavery and Freedom in the Age of the American Revolution,* eds. Ira Berlin and Ronald Hoffman (Charlottesville: University of Virginia Press, 1983), 3–48; Suzanne

Lebsock, "Free Black Women and the Question of Matriarchy: Petersburg, Virginia. 1784–1820," *Feminist Studies* 8(Summer 1982):271–87; James Oliver Horton, "Freedom's Yoke: Gender Conventions Among Antebellum Free Blacks," *Feminist Studies* 12(Spring 1986):51–76; Ira Berlin and Herbert Gutman, "Natives and Immigrants, Free Men and Slaves: Urban Workingmen in the Antebellum American South," *American Historical Review* 88(December 1983):1175–1200; Leonard P. Curry, *The Free Black in Urban America: The Shadow of a Dream* (Chicago: University of Chicago Press, 1986). See also Richard C. Wade, *Slavery in the Cities: The South, 1820–1860* (New York: Oxford University Press, 1964); Letitia Woods Brown, *Free Negroes in the District of Columbia, 1790–1846* (New York: Oxford University Press, 1972); Ira Berlin, *Slaves Without Masters; The Free Negro in the Antebellum South* (New York: Pantheon Books, 1974); and Claudia Dale Goldin, *Urban Slavery in the American South, 1820–1860: A Quantitative History* (Chicago: University of Chicago Press, 1976).

On antebellum immigrants, see Hasia Diner, *Erin's Daughters in America: Irish Immigrant Women in the Nineteenth Century* (Baltimore: Johns Hopkins University Press, 1983); Oscar Handlin, *Boston's Immigrants: A Study in Acculturation*, rev. ed. (Cambridge, Mass.: Harvard University Press, 1959); Earl F. Niehaus, *The Irish in New Orleans, 1800–1860* (Baton Rouge: Louisiana State University Press, 1965); Robert Ernst, *Immigrant Life in New York City, 1825–1863* (New York: King's Crown Press, 1949); Jay P. Dolan, *The Immigrant Church: New York: Irish and German Catholics, 1815–1865* (Baltimore: Johns Hopkins University Press, 1975); and Kathleen Neils Conzen, *Immigrant Milwaukee: 1836–1860* (Cambridge, Mass.: Harvard University Press, 1976).

On drinking traditions see Paul Faler, "Cultural Aspects of the Industrial Revolution: Lynn, Massachusetts, and Industrial Morality, 1826–1860," *Labor History* 15(Summer 1974):367–94; W.J. Rorabaugh, *The Alcoholic Republic: An American Tradition* (New York: Oxford University Press, 1979). On temperance movements see Ian Tyrell, *Sobering Up: From Temperance to Prohibition in Antebellum America, 1800–1860* (Westport, Conn.: Greenwood Press, 1979); Jed Dannenbaum, *Drink and Disorder: Temperance Reform in Cincinnati from the Washingtonian Revival to the WCTU* (Urbana: University of Illinois Press, 1984); Robert C. Harpel, *Temperance and Prohibition in Massachusetts, 1813–1852* (Ann Arbor: University of Michigan Research Press, 1982); Paul Johnson, *A Shopkeeper's Millennium: Society and Revivals in Rochester, N.Y., 1815–1837* (New York: Hill and Wang, 1978); Jill Siegel Dodd, "The Working Classes and the Temperance Movement in Antebellum Boston," *Labor History* 19(Fall 1978):510–531.

On riots in Jacksonian cities see Leonard Richards, *Gentlemen of Property and Standing: Anti-Abolition Mobs in Jacksonian America* (New York: Oxford University Press, 1970); David Montgomery, "The Shuttle and the Cross: Weavers and Artisans in the Kensington Riots of 1844," *Journal of Social History* (Summer 1972):411–46; Michael Feldberg, *The Turbulent Era: Riot and Disorder in Jacksonian America* (New York: Oxford University Press, 1980); Feldberg, *The Philadelphia Riots of 1844: A Study in Ethnic Conflict* (Westport, Conn.: Greenwood Press, 1975); Bruce Laurie, "Fire Companies and Gangs in Southwark: the 1840s," in *The Peoples of Philadelphia*, eds. Allen F. Davis and Mark H. Haller (Philadelphia: Temple University Press, 1973), 71–86; David Grimsted, "Rioting in Its Jacksonian Setting," *American Historical Review* 77(April 1972):361–97; Theodore M. Hammett, "Two Mobs of Jacksonian Boston: Ideology and Interest," *American Historical Review* (March 1976):845–868.

The development of city services has received considerable attention in such works as Nelson Manfred Blake, *Water for the Cities: A History of the Urban Water*

Supply Problem in the United States (Syracuse, N.Y.: Syracuse University Press, 1958); Roger Lane, *Policing the City: Boston, 1822–1885* (Cambridge, Mass.: Harvard University Press, 1967); James F. Richardson, *The New York Police: Colonial Times to 1901* (New York: Oxford University Press, 1970), and *Urban Police in the United States* (Port Washington, N.Y.: Kennikat Press, 1974); David Johnson, *Policing the Urban Underworld: The Impact of Crime on the Development of the American Police, 1800–1887* (Philadelphia: Temple University Press, 1979); Charles E. Rosenberg, *The Cholera Years: The United States in 1832, 1849 and 1866* (Chicago: University of Chicago Press, 1962); Raymond A. Mohl, *Poverty in New York, 1783–1825* (New York: Oxford University Press, 1971); David J. Rothman, *The Discovery of the Asylum: Social Order and Disorder in the New Republic* (Boston: Little, Brown, 1971); Stanley K. Schultz, *The Culture Factory: Boston Public Schools, 1789–1860* (New York: Oxford University Press, 1973); Michael Katz, *The Irony of Early School Reform: Educational Innovation in Mid-Nineteenth Century Massachusetts* (Cambridge, Mass.: Harvard University Press, 1968); Carl F. Kaestle, *The Evolution of an Urban School System: New York, 1750–1850* (Cambridge, Mass.: Harvard University Press, 1973); and Kaestle, *Pillars of the Republic: Common Schools and American Society, 1780–1860* (New York: Hill and Wang, 1983).

For the interplay among population and economic growth, the need for services, and the impact of change upon the urban community, see Sam Bass Warner, Jr., *The Private City: Philadelphia in Three Periods of Its Growth* (Philadelphia: University of Pennsylvania Press, 1968); Michael Frisch, *Town Into City: Springfield, Massachusetts, and the Meaning of Community, 1840–1880* (Cambridge, Mass.: Harvard University Press, 1972); Stuart M. Blumin, *The Urban Threshold: Growth and Change in a Nineteenth Century American Community* (Chicago: University of Chicago Press, 1976); Thomas Bender, *Toward an Urban Vision: Ideas and Institutions in Nineteenth Century America* (Lexington: University of Kentucky Press, 1975); Paul Boyer, *Urban Masses and Moral Order in America, 1820–1920* (Cambridge, Mass.: Harvard University Press, 1978); Roger W. Lotchin, *San Francisco, 1846–1856: From Hamlet to City* (New York: Oxford University Press, 1974).

ENDNOTES

[1]Richard C. Wade, *The Urban Frontier, 1790–1830* (Cambridge, Mass.: Harvard University Press, 1959).

[2]Bruce Laurie, *The Working People of Philadelphia, 1800–1850* (Philadelphia: Temple University Press, 1980), 15–27.

[3]Paul Johnson, *A Shopkeeper's Millennium: Society and Revivals in Rochester, N.Y., 1815–1837* (New York: Hill and Wang, 1978), 56–7.

[4]Alan Dawley, *Class and Community: The Industrial Revolution in Lynn* (Cambridge, Mass.: Harvard University Press, 1977), 110.

[5]Roger Lane, *Policing the City: Boston, 1822–1865* (Cambridge, Mass.: Harvard University Press, 1967), 89. For additional elaboration, see David Johnson, *Policing the Urban Underworld: The Impact of Crime on the Development of American Police, 1800–1887* (Philadelphia: Temple University Press, 1979).

[6]Sam Bass Warner, Jr., *The Private City: Philadelphia in Three Periods of Its Growth* (Philadelphia: University of Pennsylvania Press, 1968), 109.

[7]David J. Rothman, *The Discovery of the Asylum: Social Order and Disorder in the New Republic* (Boston: Little, Brown, 1971).

3

Industrialization and the Transformation of Urban Space, 1850–1920

THE WALKING CITY

Until the 1850s almost all American cities could be characterized by their compactness. Located near harbors or river junctions, they focused their activities on the waterfront. Here wharves, warehouses, mercantile offices, and manufacturing establishments (usually processing operations or commerce-related industry such as shipbuilding or ropewalks) were built, because access to water transportation was of principal importance. Public buildings, churches, hotels, and a few shops clustered nearby. The homes of prominent families often were interspersed among these structures or, as in Cincinnati, Providence, and St. Louis, were located on a hill overlooking the port. Around these cores and in the valleys between hills were the residential areas of craftsmen, storekeepers, and laborers. The two- and three-story buildings in these districts contained shops and workshops on the bottom floors and residential quarters in back or above. Certain businesses needing water supplies—mills, tanneries, slaughterhouses, breweries—grouped along nearby streams. As the nineteenth century progressed, some heavy industry, particularly base metals, grew in the outskirts near railroad connections. Most business establishments, however, remained dispersed throughout the settled areas of town.

Wagons, carriages, horses, mules, and pedestrians jammed the central streets. Neither public officers nor mechanical signals regulated the speed and direction of traffic. People seldom observed any custom of keeping to one side of the street or the other, and right of way at intersections went to the boldest—or most reckless. Cobblestones or gravel paved only a

The Walking City This extraordinary daguerreotype is one of a series taken of Cincinnati in 1848. The view shows the concentration of settlements, and businesses along the waterfront and the substantial homes perched on the hills overlooking the city. *(The Public Library of Cincinnati and Hamilton County.)*

fraction of urban thoroughfares; most retained their original dirt surfaces, which nature and traffic turned into choking dust or slogging mud.

The heaviest users of streets were not wheels or hoofs, but human feet. In the early American city the vast majority of people walked to their destinations, and it was this form of transportation that determined the city's size and shape. Studies of commuting and intracity traffic, from the early nineteenth century down to the present motor age, indicate that few people travel more than thirty or forty minutes to work, shop, or visit. Until the 1850s the settled areas of even the largest cities, such as New York, Boston, and Philadelphia, rarely extended beyond two miles from the city center—the average distance a person can walk in half an hour. Thus historians have labeled this early urban configuration the *walking city* because of its size and major mode of conveyance. No specific policies or legislation limited the area of any city; it was simply more convenient for people to locate businesses and residences on available sites that had easy access to most business, work, and social activities.

The limitations of walking largely contributed to the compactness of the premodern city, a compactness with several important features. First, land use was mixed—commercial, storage, residential, and industrial buildings mingled together. There were few distinct districts; even waterfront property had various uses. As cities grew, their business districts became more defined, but here too residences and primitive factories remained interspersed with the stores, banks, and offices.

Second, mixed, intensive land use meant that city dwellers were relatively integrated. Short distances separated poor from rich, immigrant from native, black from white, proximity that may have sparked some of the conflicts over turf discussed in Chapter 2. Factory owners often built their residences next to their factories and within sight of workingmen's homes, and laborers often lived along alleys in blocks where the more well-to-do lived on the main street. In southern cities such as Charleston and New Orleans, black slaves inhabited compounds behind their masters' houses. Row housing, the characteristic urban style in early nineteenth-century cities, accentuated the appearance of homogeneity, making inequalities of wealth less visible. Moreover, people lived not only near one another but also near, or at, their places of work. Those who worked away from their residences walked to and from their jobs. It has been difficult to uncover exactly why city dwellers lived where they did, but it seems likely that proximity to place of work was not a primary consideration because most places of employment were accessible by foot from any part of town.

As time passed and populations increased, enclaves did form. In Boston, newly arrived Irish filled the North End and the neighborhood along the wharves. In Philadelphia, blacks clustered in the southern wards. Residential districts of free blacks and living-out slaves grew on or outside the edges of Charleston and Richmond. Still, however, the relatively small areas of all cities left all groups of people physically close together.

Historian Samuel Hays has argued that urban political leadership reflected circumstances of the integrated community. City councils were usually elected in a town meeting to represent the city as a whole. Invariably they were composed of men dominant in the community's social and economic elite—bankers, commission merchants, lawyers. Rarely were those in the lower three-quarters of the social order elected. Elections at large gave an opportunity for those dominant in the city's social and economic life to be dominant in its formal political life as well. Without distinctive geographical enclaves that corresponded to social class, the capacity of the lower classes to develop and effectively express a clear political view was limited.[1]

The necessity of walking confined the horizontal expansion of premodern cities. Technological limitations prevented vertical expansion. Only after the 1850s did the invention of the elevator and the use of iron, rather than masonry, for structural support enable the construction of buildings more than a few stories in height. The skyscraper, with its steel frame and electric elevators, did not appear until the 1880s. Until then the major type of physical development occurred when builders covered remaining empty property within the walking city or reclaimed land by leveling hills, draining marshes, or filling in coves and bays. As cities filled up and vacant lots disappeared, land values soared, especially in comparison with construction costs. Now more than just speculation and boosterism inflated urban land values; rising demand and diminishing supply became ever important. In Chicago, for example, the total valuation for land within a one-mile radius of the central business district increased from $810,000 in 1842 to $50,750,000 in 1856, a 6000-percent gain.

Meanwhile many cities were practically bursting at their seams. It has been common for Americans to consider urban crowding a consequence of industrialization and mass immigration during the late nineteenth and early twentieth centuries. Yet at no time in the country's history were total urban densities as high as they were in the mid-nineteenth century. Chapter 2 noted that these years witnessed the greatest proportionate growth of urban populations this country has ever experienced. An almost annual excess of new arrivals over those departing doubled and tripled the populations of St. Louis, Pittsburgh, and Cincinnati between 1840 and 1850. Densities in settled areas swelled. By 1850 there were 135.6 persons per acre in New York, 82.7 in Boston, 80.0 in Philadelphia, and 68.4 in Pittsburgh. In Providence at mid-century an average of two families occupied every dwelling, a much larger figure than in similar-sized towns in Europe, or even in fast-growing regions of England. Inner-city wards in most big cities would become even more densely populated in the latter half of the century, but because urban areas were smaller at mid-century, crowding spread to a larger proportion of their districts.

In the 1820s and 1830s ferries and bridges opened up new areas for development. Smaller towns adjacent to and often dependent upon a major city had existed since colonial days, but now many more neighboring regions became accessible. Areas of new settlement included the Jersey shore across the Hudson River from Manhattan, and Brooklyn across the East River; South Boston, Roxbury, Cambridge, and Charlestown near Boston; and land across the Schuylkill River at Philadelphia, across the Allegheny and Monongahela at Pittsburgh, the Cuyahoga at Cleveland, and the New Buffalo Creek at Buffalo. Populations in these places doubled and tripled in a single decade. Regular steam service from Brooklyn Heights to New York City began in 1814. By 1860, various East River ferries carried 33 million passengers per year; Brooklyn contained more people than Boston and was the third most populous city in the country.

Most of these newly developed areas had their own economies and retained their political independence, preferring only to purchase services such as water and gas from the nearby city. Historian Henry Binford has argued that Boston's first suburbs grew out of a fringe economy that flourished between 1815 and 1840, housing those who processed goods for city use, linking urban and rural economies by supplying milk and produce, and creating industries producing such urban necessities as bricks and glass. Few communities as yet served as residential areas for large numbers of commuters who left in the morning and returned at night. In the Boston area the new suburbs would gain over ten thousand commuters between 1845 and 1860. The commuters would reshape the fringe communities as domestic retreats, building homes, schools, and churches to be free from "vicious associates," and these would eventually crowd out the "scattered centers of craft and processing" that had characterized the earlier settlements.[2] Even initially, however, the bridges and ferries gave big-city merchants links to new local markets and enabled some of the wealthiest families to escape the crowded walking city and to live in more attractive surroundings.

THE GROWTH OF MASS TRANSIT

By the middle of the nineteenth century three accelerating forces were breaking apart the walking city. The rise and spread of mass transportation, the application of technological and economic innovations to industrial production, and foreign and internal migration refashioned the contour and character of urban America and created the modern industrial city. The three developments are closely interrelated, but for the sake of simplicity, migration and immigration will be discussed in the next chapter. The remainder of this chapter will focus on mass transit and industrialization and their consequences.

Professor Richard C. Wade has written, "No incendiary ever looked so poorly suited to the task of creating such far-reaching change as [the] awkward object moving down Broadway in 1829."[3] This object was an omnibus, a large, horse-drawn coach designed to transport the urban public over fixed routes for fixed fares. The omnibus combined the functions of two traditional types of public transportation: the hackney, an early version of the taxicab, which carried passengers where they wished; and the stagecoach, which operated over long-distance routes at scheduled times. The idea originated in France and first appeared in this country in 1827 when Abraham Brower ran a stagecoach up and down Broadway in downtown Manhattan, picking up and discharging passengers at their request for a flat fee of one shilling (12½ cents) per ride. In 1829 Brower added another vehicle to the route. This coach contained seats running lengthwise, instead of across, and an entrance at the top of an iron stairway at the rear. About the same time, Ephraim Dodge initiated mass transportation in Boston by driving a hack on a regular schedule between Boston and South Boston. The schemes of Brower and Dodge spread quickly. By 1833 some eighty omnibuses operated on the streets of New York, and by the middle of the decade transportation companies had appeared in Boston, Philadelphia, New Orleans, Washington, D.C., and Brooklyn.

An omnibus drawn by two horses normally seated twelve people, but when traffic was heavy, several more riders could be packed inside. In the winter some operators replaced their wheels with runners for easier conveyance over the snow. At first a boy was employed to collect fares at the rear, but eventually his job was eliminated by a fare box located next to the driver's platform. Most omnibuses were individually owned, often by men who had previously engaged in some aspect of horse-drawn transportation: carriage making, blacksmithing, or hauling. The owners were entrepreneurs, small businessmen whose objective was to make as much money as they could. Seldom, if at all, did they consider their operation a public service. Thus they ran their vehicles only on those streets that promised the most riders. Almost all stretched their routes between two important centers of activity—usually a wharf, railroad depot, or suburb at one end and a focal point of the business district at the other.

Although there was often keen competition between operators for favorable routes, the rapid proliferation of omnibus companies and vehicles attests to their success. New York City alone granted licenses to 108 omnibuses in 1837, 260 in 1847, and 683 in 1853. One observer claimed that one coach coming from each direction crossed a particular intersection on lower Broadway every fifteen seconds. By mid-century the omnibus had become essential to transportation in other cities as well: Boston, Philadelphia, Washington, Baltimore, Pittsburgh, and St. Louis. In several areas coach traffic clogged thoroughfares and endangered human life. Congestion and reckless driving provoked local governments to require the relocation of some omnibus routes and to fine drivers who failed to operate their vehicles safely. In spite of increasing regulations the citizenry constantly complained that drivers intentionally ran down pedestrians and private carriages.

Inside a crowded coach the situation was no better than outside. The seats were usually primitive benches, and construction was such that there was never enough ventilation in summer and always too much in winter. A bumpy, noisy journey of twenty people in a space intended for twelve strained human patience. The *New York Herald* described the situation vividly, if a bit overdramatically, in 1864:

Modern martyrdom may be succinctly defined as riding in a New York omnibus. The discomforts, inconveniences, and annoyances of a trip on one of these vehicles are almost intolerable. From the beginning to the end of the journey a constant quarrel is progressing. The driver quarrels with the passengers, and the passengers quarrel with the driver. There are quarrels about getting out and quarrels about getting in. There are quarrels about change and quarrels about the ticket swindle. The driver swears at the passengers and the passengers harangue the driver through the strap hole—a position in which even Demosthenes could not be eloquent. Respectable clergymen in white chokers are obliged to listen to loud oaths. Ladies are disgusted, frightened, and insulted. Children are alarmed and lift up their voices and weep. Indignant gentlemen rise to remonstrate with the irate Jehu and are suddenly bumped back into their seats, twice as indignant as before, besides being involved in supplementary quarrels with those other passengers upon whose corns they have accidentally trodden. Thus the omnibus rolls along, a perfect Bedlam on Wheels.

Such mayhem did not discourage people from riding, however. An 1853 New York guidebook advertised that some 120,000 passengers rode the city's omnibuses daily.

In spite of its wide use, mass transportation remained a luxury. Early urban transit never met the expectations of those who believed omnibuses would erase class lines by bringing all types of people together. In 1841 an optimistic writer for *Godey's Ladies Journal* had proclaimed, "The statesman and politician, . . . the greasy citizen who votes against him and the zealots of different sectaries, dismounted of their several doxies, are compelled to ride cheek by jowl, with one another. Such is the leveling and democratic Omnibus." But economic realities prevented most "greasy citizens" from riding vehicles of mass transit. In the 1840s, 1850s, and 1860s the ordinary wage earner received little more than a dollar a day and rarely more than two. The fares on most omnibus lines ranged from six to twelve and a half cents per ride. Few laborers could afford twelve to twenty-five cents a day for transportation.

Although it was used mainly by the middle and upper classes, the omnibus altered urban life-styles in several important ways. It made wheeled transportation available to more people than did hackneys and carriages, and it carried people over a set route for a standard price on a reasonably predictable schedule. It facilitated intracity communications in an age when economic specialization was making such communications increasingly necessary. Probably most important, the omnibus created the commuter—enabling the affluent to escape the crowded walking city and live in outlying regions. And, as historian Glen Holt has suggested, the omnibus's rapid expansion and growing numbers of customers helped city dwellers develop a "riding habit," a disposition few had ever had before.[4]

While omnibuses began rumbling down city streets, steam-powered trains were beginning to travel between cities. Although originally intended to carry freight and passengers over long distances, several early railroads also engaged in short-distance commuter services. By mid-century nearly all the trains leaving Boston made commuter stops within fifteen miles of the city, and railroads based in New York and Philadelphia ran several trains daily to and from nearby towns. Over the next decade such service spread into the Midwest. A person living outside the city could now take the train into town and then ride an omnibus, which stopped at the railroad depot, to his or her ultimate destination.

The commuter railroad, even more than the omnibus, was a convenience for the wealthy. A one-way ticket cost fifteen to twenty-five cents, too high for most working people. Cheaper rides could be obtained by purchasing season tickets, but few people could afford ten to thirty dollars for three- or six-month passes. But like the omnibus, the commuter railroad opened outlying areas for settlement. In 1854, for example, the Chicago and Milwaukee Railroad (later renamed the Chicago and Northwestern) built a depot in

Evanston, Illinois, and helped populate—and popularize—that northern suburb of Chicago. By 1859 forty trains were running daily between Philadelphia and Germantown, almost all their passengers commuters.

The New York and Harlem Railroad pioneered the next major development in urban mass transportation. In 1832 John Mason, one of the New York and Harlem's promoters, decided to combine the technologies of the omnibus and the railroad. By running horse-drawn coaches over rails instead of cobblestones, he could offer faster, smoother rides and enable the horses to pull larger, heavier cars. Over the next two years Mason laid four miles of track in lower Manhattan and thus began the first street, or horse, railway. By 1860 street-railway companies were operating in at least eight other major cities, and there were 142 miles of track in New York and 155 in Philadelphia. The cars held two or three times as many passengers as omnibuses and could travel faster, while utilizing the same number of horses. In addition, because horsecars moved on rails only down the middle of the street, they interfered less with other traffic than did the omnibuses.

Horse railways had several social and political consequences. Rails made mass-transit routes completely fixed and predictable. This certainty combined with the new emphasis on the structuring of time, a product of incipient industrialization, to give people more regimented lives: daily routes and routines came to be dictated by working hours and transit schedules. And because the equipment and construction of horse railways were so much more expensive than they were for omnibuses, company owners had to be even more concerned with laying track and running cars along the most profitable routes. Although horse railways spread people into outlying areas, they also provided limited service, often operating along the same streets that omnibuses traveled. Because transit owners built track only where it appeared that settlement would be most dense and because subdividers and builders located their real-estate projects near mass-transit lines, outward expansion proceeded unevenly. In St. Louis, for example, mass transportation stretched the built-up area far to the northwest, but land to the southwest long remained underdeveloped because it lacked transit service. And in Boston the early street railways extended real-estate development in the same directions as omnibus lines. Only slowly did they fill in the vacant districts between existing fingers of settlement.

Finally, the issue of control became more pressing. Early omnibuses had evoked few public regulations. Local governments established little more than licensing taxes, vehicle inspection, and speeding restrictions. But the laying of track and the capitalization of horse-railway companies complicated the relations between mass-transit companies and public authority. Incorporation of the company required a charter from the state, and construction of track on city streets necessitated permission from the local government. Beginning in the 1850s such permission was usually obtained in the form of a franchise that enabled a company to operate over a specific route for a limited, though renewable period. Most early franchises granted monopolistic or semimonopolistic privileges, often for terms of fifty to one hundred years. Although the contracts generally stipulated maximum fares, usually five cents, the privilege of an exclusive franchise, plus almost certain population growth—and therefore increasing numbers of passengers—assured recipients of high profits.

With several street-railway and omnibus companies contesting for such grants, mass transportation inevitably became involved in local politics. The problem was that city councils seldom granted franchises on purely objective bases. Besides mass transit, utilities such as street lighting and water were provided by private companies who sought franchises. Some local officials were so intent upon securing these services for their community that they paid little heed to the consequences of generous franchises. In their anxiety they gave transit and other companies long-term, exclusive contracts that included low tax rates on their property and revenues, low fees paid to the city, no responsibility to repair torn-up streets, and other advantages. More often these favors were obtained by political manipulation and corruption. The granting of public franchises in scores of cities in the latter half of the nineteenth century lured city officials and businessmen into collusions that included bribes, kickbacks, illegal transfers of stock, and other influence-buying activities. The use of public land by private companies, a major proportion of them operating horse railways and mechanically powered mass transit, helped to create unsavory connections between business and politics—connections that would become objects of municipal reform in succeeding generations.

The next major breakthrough in urban mass transportation occurred in the last quarter of the nineteenth century when innovators applied mechanical power to their vehicles. Aspiring entrepreneurs tried a variety of devices of propulsion, including steam engines and large springs—the latter method was akin to running a streetcar with a rubber band—but the first successful effort was the cable car. Cleaner and faster than horses, the cable car was introduced in San Francisco by Andrew S. Hallidie in 1873. Hallidie, a wire manufacturer, had known that the English miners hauled coal cars along large cables, and he decided to try the idea on San Francisco's steep hills, where horsecars could not operate. His system utilized a moving, underground wire rope driven by a steam engine. Each cable car ran along track and had a clamp that extended through a slot in the pavement. The clamp attached to, or detached from, the cable at the will of the vehicle's operator. Brakes, similar to those on horsecars, could halt the vehicle after the grip had been released from the cable. The scheme was so impressive that a company headed by California railroad magnates Leland Stanford, Mark Hopkins, and Collis P. Huntington applied for one of the first franchises.

Although the cable car has remained a historic relic of San Francisco, its widest use occurred in Chicago. Here cable-car lines spread rapidly in the 1880s, particularly to the city's South Side, and by 1894 Chicago had 86 miles of cable track and over 1500 grip and trailer cars. Initial costs of construction and equipment were very high, but cable cars were generally more economical to operate than horsecars, mainly because horses required higher maintenance costs. Cable cars had their drawbacks, however. A break in the cable halted all traffic, the intricate mechanical equipment suffered frequent breakdowns, and operating a car required considerable skill. Nevertheless cable lines existed for varying periods of time in Washington, D.C., Baltimore, Philadelphia, New York, Providence, Cleveland, St. Louis, Kansas City, Omaha, Denver, Oakland, and Seattle.

The cable car era lasted less than two decades. By the beginning of the twentieth century electric trolleys had almost completely replaced horse railways and cable cars as the major means of urban transportation. Since the 1830s inventors in Europe and America had been experimenting with electricity to power vehicles, but it was not until 1886 that someone harnessed electric energy to propel a city-wide system of transportation. The previous year James Gaboury, a leading promoter of mass transit in the South, had hired Charles J. Van Doeple, a Belgian engineer, to construct an electric railway in Montgomery, Alabama. Service began in the spring of 1886. The vehicles resembled those pulled by horses but contained a motor on the front platform. A chain running from the motor to the wheels powered the vehicle, and a cable from an overhead wire to the motor transmitted electrical power. During the same time a young electrician, Frank Sprague, built a similar system in Richmond, Virginia. It utilized a four-wheeled vehicle pulled along the overhead wires that transferred electricity to it. This device was called a *troller* due to the manner in which it was pulled. According to John Anderson Miller, a corruption of the word produced *trolley,* the term used for electric streetcars.[5] In 1888 Sprague allayed all doubts about electrified mass transit when he successfully demonstrated that his cars could conquer the steep grades of Richmond and that electrical generators could provide enough power to operate several cars concentrated on a short stretch of track.

During the 1880s and 1890s nearly every large city in the country granted franchises to trolley companies. In 1890 when the federal government first surveyed the nation's street railways, it found about 5700 miles of track for vehicles operated by animal power, 500 miles of track for cable cars, and 1260 miles of electrified track. By 1902 the total of electrified track had swelled to 22,000 miles, while that of horse railways had dwindled to 250 miles.

At the turn of the century companies in some of the largest, most congested cities raised part of their track onto stilts, giving their vehicles unrestricted right of way and freeing them from the interference of pedestrians and animal-powered vehicles. These were the electric elevated railways—the *els*—and they became most prominent in New York, Chicago,

Boston, Philadelphia, Brooklyn, and Kansas City. Although New York had had a successful steam-powered elevated since the 1870s, the noise, vibration, dirt, and danger to traffic below made other cities unwilling to risk an el. Thus it appeared in only a few places, even after Frank Sprague had designed a mechanism that enabled steam elevateds to be electrified.

Sprague's device, a master control that operated the motor and control on each car of the train, could be used for railways below, as well as above, ground. The subway originated in London in the 1860s when coal-burning locomotives began pulling mass-transit cars through tunnels beneath the city. Promoters raised the idea in America, particularly in New York, but fears of smoke and tunnel cave-ins, plus heavy opposition from street-railway companies, prevented construction. Electrification and the success of the London experiment removed some of the objections, and in Boston Henry M. Whitney, who had consolidated most of the city's transit lines under his ownership, obtained permission to construct tunnels for his trains. At a cost of $4,350,000, he built a subway one and two-third miles in length underneath Tremont Street. In 1897, its first year of operation, the service handled more than fifty million passengers, running as many as four hundred cars in each direction at peak periods and still reducing travel time in the downtown area. This success prompted the revival of interest in building subways in New York, and in 1904 that city's first subway opened. The extraordinary costs of subway construction and its disruption of above-ground activity limited expansion, however. With the exception of a combined el-subway that appeared in Philadelphia in 1908 no additional underground projects occurred until the 1930s, when one began in Chicago.

Subways and elevateds were the only means of *rapid* transit that American city dwellers were to have, and in only a very few cities did schemes, which were many, materialize. Mass transportation was almost always considered a private business, not a public utility, so profitability was the chief criterion for the construction of any system. At first omnibus and street-railway companies made huge profits from a population eager for urban expansion and anxious to cut down traveling time—or at least to travel farther in the same amount of time. There were other beneficiaries too. Land values along streetcar lines soared, and real-estate developers scrambled to buy up property along projected routes. The screeching wheels and unnerving vibration of els eventually drove the wealthy classes away, but land adjacent to elevated track remained lucrative for tenement and commercial investment. Technological advances made mass transit more efficient and convenient, but they also raised costs of construction and maintenance. Because elevateds, subways, and street railways required heavy outlays of capital, mass transportation in many cities quickly became the domain of just one or two large-scale operations. As early as the 1880s shrewd businessmen were consolidating independent companies under their aegis. Colorful personalities such as Henry M. Whitney of Boston and

Charles Tyson Yerkes of Chicgo deftly and ruthlessly established city-wide railway systems and huge personal fortunes.

Systems such as those of Whitney and Yerkes brought several benefits to their riders. The increased scale of operations enabled companies to preserve the five-cent fare, and the constant quest for new riders pushed track into new districts. Equally important, the merger of several lines produced free transfers from one route to another, enabling passengers to travel farther for a single fare. Yet also the combined functions of public service and private profit loaded transit companies with nagging predicaments. The limits of a five-cent fare, whether self-imposed or legislated by government, forced traction companies to seek higher revenues by increasing their passengers. But if they laid track into newer districts, they risked overextension and fewer riders than anticipated. If they restricted operations to densely settled areas, they faced public charges of inadequate and discriminatory service. In addition the huge capitalization necessary for construction often invited stock watering and nonlocal investors. The result was that managers, intent on profits rather than on service, directed company policies toward producing dividends for anxious stockholders.

The riding public understandably had little sympathy. According to Professor Holt, traction companies too often cited their financial plight as an excuse for failure to improve service, and they used their indispensability to force local governments to grant additional privileges, such as renewed franchises or lighter taxes.[6] Moreover as reformers sought to regulate public transportation, they encountered growing collusion between traction interests and local politicians, an alliance that, as noted earlier, included graft and boodling. Indignation at such activities often pulled reformers together, and they translated their revulsion into a move for governmental reform, including municipal ownership of mass transit. New York in the early 1890s and Chicago in 1907 established municipal authority to build or buy public transit systems. As scores of companies went bankrupt during and after World War I, in many cities public ownership became the only way to sustain mass transit. But public assumption of mass transportation responsibilities occurred just when the private automobile began to replace the streetcar as the major mode of conveyance. The American hunger for speed and convenience had outgrown mass transit, but not until the omnibus and all its descendants had made their mark on urban life.

SPATIAL SEGREGATION AND THE BEGINNING OF URBAN SPRAWL

Mass transportation revised the social and economic fabric of the American city in three fundamental ways. It catalyzed physical expansion, it sorted out people and land uses, and it accelerated the inherent instability of urban life. By opening vast areas of unoccupied land for residential expansion, the omnibuses, horse railways, commuter trains, and electric trolleys pulled set-tled regions outward two, three, and four times more distant from city cen-ters than they were in the premodern era. In 1850, for example, the borders of Boston lay scarcely two miles from the old business district; by the turn of the century the radius extended ten miles. Now those who could afford it could live far removed from the old walking city and still commute there for work, shopping, and entertainment. The new accessibility of peripheral land sparked an explosion of real-estate development and fueled what we now know as urban sprawl. Between 1890 and 1920, for example, some 250,000 new residential lots were recorded within the borders of Chicago, most of them in outlying areas. Over the same period another 550,000 were plotted outside the city limits but within the metropolitan area. Anxious to take advantage of the possibilities of commuting, real-estate developers added 800,000 potential building sites to the Chicago region in just thirty years—lots that could have housed five to six million people.

Of course, many lots were never occupied; there was always a huge surplus of subdivided, but vacant, land around Chicago and other cities. This excess underscores a feature of residential expansion related to the growth of mass transportation: urban sprawl was essentially unplanned. It was carried out by thousands of small investors who paid little heed to coordinated land use or to future land users. Those who purchased and prepared land for residential purposes, particularly land in subdivisions near or outside city borders where transit lines and middle-class inhabitants were anticipated, did so to create demand as much as, if not more than, to respond to it. Chicago is a prime example of this process. The Great Fire of 1871 sparked a building boom, amplified by real-estate subdivision proceed-ing even faster than the growing population, which tripled between 1860 and 1900. The new lots reflected the booster spirit that had characterized the city's history. It was a spirit that represented the transformation of anticipation into reality. This belief led the *Chicago Times* to decree:

> Chicago, as most people are aware, is situated on an open prairie, skirted on the east by the lake. In the latter direction, therefore, the enterprising real estate developers meets with some difficulty in disposing of water lots, but westward there is an unlimited space, bounded only by the swamps of the Calumet, the Mississippi, the British Provinces, and the imagination. Some day the Queen's dominions will be annexed, and then there will be no limit to Chicago's enterprise.

A profound side effect of mass transit and constant expansion of city limits in the last half of the nineteenth century was heightened spatial specialization. Various urban areas became sharply differentiated. Down-town areas took on more distinct characteristics. People who could afford to move from the center established new residential communities and a new suburban life-style on the periphery. Immigrants and working-class labor-ers settled in new industrial districts adjacent to but distinct from the city's older districts. The physical growth of cities in this period was deeply implicated in the process of unmasking social differentiation; new subcommunities generated more varied cultures, and cities became more fragmented and decentralized.

The downtown took a characteristic shape as it developed to house a variety of mercantile endeavors, financial institutions, and cultural attractions. The new volume and complexities of trade required specialization, particularly the division of wholesale, retail, and credit functions. Retail activities were particularly transformed with the appearance of department stores. In New York, A. T. Stewart's magnificent Marble Palace, opened in 1846, sold only dry goods, but it was the prototype of the grand downtown department stores to come, such as Macy's, Bloomingdale's, and Lord and Taylor's in New York, Wanamaker's in Philadelphia, Marshall Field's and Carson Pirie Scott in Chicago, Jordan Marsh and Filene's in Boston, Rich's in Atlanta, Hutzler's in Baltimore, Bullock's in Los Angeles, and I. Magnin's in San Francisco. The department store's contribution would be to display the abundant fruits of mass production, its magnificence shining through large plate-glass windows, bestowing its aura on the surrounding sidewalks. The financial institutions, banks, brokerage firms, and insurance companies, which serviced the concentration of capital in urban places, were other downtown landmarks increasingly likely to be housed in the new multistory office buildings that shaped the city skyline.

As demand for urban real estate encroached on public open space and as open land disappeared in cities, urban leaders began to argue for the preservation of green areas explicitly designated as parks. Town commons and greens had existed since the seventeenth century, and ornamental squares since the late eighteenth century, but the public park specifically designed for recreation emerged in this period. Its antecedents were the rural cemeteries, such as Mount Auburn Cemetery (1831) in Cambridge and Laurel Hill Cemetery (1836) in Philadelphia, designed as instructional institutions and inculcators of morality by exposing the living to the contemplation of a constructed rural landscape. The most important development in the urban-park campaign occurred in New York. Here public figures, such as landscape architect Andrew Jackson Downing and poet William Cullen Bryant, succeeded in convincing the state legislature to reserve over 600 acres of Manhattan Island for a public park. The park advocates had high hopes for the social impact of such open spaces. As Downing wrote in 1848, "[Parks] will be better preachers of temperance than temperance societies, better refiners of national manners than dancing schools, and better promoters of general good-feeling than any lectures on the philosophy of happiness." A state-appointed commission sponsored a competition to determine the best design for the park. They awarded the prize to a young landscaper and journalist, Frederick Law Olmsted, destined to become one of the most influential figures in American urban and landscape design.

As superintendent of the Central Park project, Olmsted attempted to bring what he believed to be the physical and social enjoyment of rural beauty to city dwellers. Olmsted thought that the quiet contemplation of a park's rural scenery would calm "the rough element of the city" and "divert men from unwholesome, vicious, destructive methods and habits of seeking recreation." This objective involved Olmsted and his associate Calvert Vaux in two kinds of designing. First, they tried to create a pastoral effect by improving upon nature in different ways to suit different tastes. Thus their design included a series of distinct vistas, some rough in terrain, others more formal. They also built sunken roadways to conceal city traffic and planted trees strategically to screen out abutting buildings. Second, they inserted special facilties to meet different needs. They laid 114 miles of pipe to feed and drain ponds for boating and skating, provided trails for riding and hiking, and designed a mall for social gatherings and concerts. The park was an instant success, attracting twenty-five thousand visitors a day even before it was completed. By 1879, Olmsted boasted that "no one who has closely observed the conduct of the people who visit Central Park can doubt that it exercises a distinctly harmonizing and refining influence upon the most unfortunate and lawless classes of the city—an influence favorable to courtesy, self-control, and temperance." Although plagued by political squabbles over park control and declining public commitment to its maintenance, Olmsted remained as superintendent until 1878 and constantly studied the use and misuse of the park in order to try to preserve his vision of its purpose.

Central Park inspired similar projects throughout urban America— many of them undertaken by Olmsted and Vaux or by their equally influential contemporary H. W. S. Cleveland. In eastern cities where space was at a premium, park planners sometimes tried to exclude what they called the "boisterous fun and rough sports" of the working classes. Their parks were designed for small groups to contemplate nature, not for a rowdy, exuberant, collective style of play. The clash between what environmental historian J. B. Jackson called "two distinct and conflicting definitions of the park"—"the upper-class definition with its emphasis on cultural enlightenment and greater refinement of manners, and a lower-class definition emphasizing fun and games"—characterized the history of park evolution in many communities.[7] Boston park design centered on its plan for an "emerald necklace" of interconnected parks and roadways, a multipart green space corridor stretching far out to the city's suburban reaches. Chicago and Kansas City built metropolitan park systems, Chicago's ultimately covering over 59,500 acres. Many parks were located at excursion distance from the built-up parts of their cities, dependent on mass transit to bring the crowds. Everywhere the establishment of recreational parks signified the new specialization of urban space.

Commercial amusements demonstrated a similar pattern of specialization in the second half of the nineteenth century. Amusements in the walking city had paralleled contemporary social life and were part of an informal public life with little segregation by class or sex. In Richmond, Virginia, taverns near the capitol served all classes except blacks, and exhibitions, circuses, and theaters enjoyed the patronage of heterogeneous groups. After 1830, however, and especially after 1850, this pattern began to change. Tavern patrons became more exclusively male, lower class, and foreign. As the middle and upper classes became preoccupied with womanly restraint and decorum, "good" women were increasingly insulated from a more rowdy public life. Men might still pursue informal pleasures in the semipublic milieu of the saloon or dance hall, but these were clearly separate from the institutions of respectable society.

The same process of specialization was apparent in the theaters of New York City. The early melodramatic stage had produced a variety of performances housed under one roof, so that audiences in the 1830s might see drama, circus, opera, and dance on the same bill. In New York's Park Theatre, each class had its own section of seats, but all attended; mechanics in the pit, upper classes and women in the boxes, and prostitutes, lower-class men, and blacks in the gallery. Prostitutes occupied a special section, the third tier, because respectable women refused to attend institutions where they came into contact with prostitutes. After 1850, theaters were increasingly differentiated by class and function, and the legitimate theater and concert hall, appropriate for women and the genteel upper classes, distinguished themselves from the popular stage of minstrelsy, variety, and burlesque. These popular entertainments were often tied to the saloon, a lower-class and male preserve that offered liquor, food, sports talk, boxing, politics, and sometimes dancing and singing. The origins of the public dance hall probably also lay primarily in the nineteenth-century saloon. The segregation of red-light districts, such as New York's Bowery and Tenderloin, San Francisco's Barbary Coast, Chicago's South Side, and the New Orleans French Quarter, containing saloons, dance halls, and sporting houses, separated vice from respectable neighborhoods at the same time as providing men relief from Victorian standards of formality and restraint.

The most striking spatial specialization in this period was the suburb, which institutionalized the division between work and home and recast the residential ideal. Prior to the development of mass transit, only the wealthiest merchants and professionals, who could afford leisurely trips to town in their own horse-drawn carriages or on expensive commuter railroad lines, had been able to buy a "box in the country," as Bostonian Harrison Gray Otis described his house in Watertown. But after 1870, horse-drawn streetcars and trolleys opened up whole new residential areas. Streetcar suburbs offered the opportunity for a wide range of people with middle-class occupations and income to escape the crowding, dirt, noise, and crime of the central city. They could afford homes (if not to build or buy, then to rent) as well as the fares to commute to and from work every day. So they moved into the rings of residential areas that were forming outside the old urban cores.

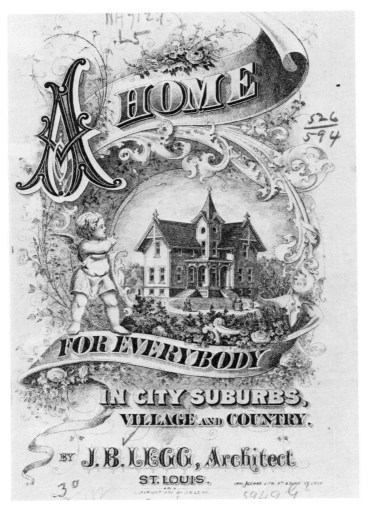

The Suburban Dream   This illustrated title page from an architecture book published in 1876 suggests the pastoral and romantic qualities of the suburban ideal. *(Library of Congress.)*

Here they could fulfill a dream of a rural-like private life in a single-family dwelling, secure in an economically homogeneous community. When suburban builders advertised through brochures and newspapers, they promised an escape from the problems of poor health, social unrest, and vice associated with urban life. A private dwelling in a safe residential neighborhood would protect especially women and children from the dan-

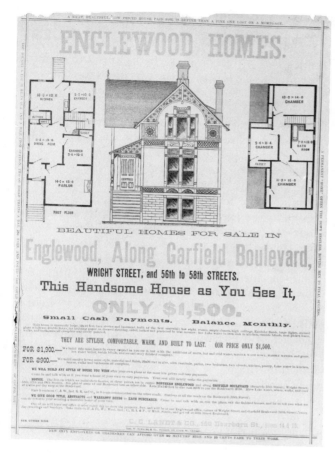

The Surburban Reality A newspaper advertisement for actual middle-class housing built in Chicago during the construction boom of the 1880s promised more prosaic virtues such as durability and affordability. *(Courtesy Chicago Historical Society.)*

gers of the city; suburbanites could redeem their own families, if not the nation as a whole. Greenery and fresh air would invigorate spirits deadened by urban drabness, and porches and yards would facilitate social contacts within the boundaries of family privacy to substitute for the uncontrollable sociability of urban streets. Promoters tried to identify their projects with the more exclusive picturesque retreats for the wealthy, but they were aiming for a different market. Subdivisions of small- or moderate-sized lots, near transit lines, were intended to attract the families of salesmen, schoolteachers, clerks, and carpenters.

Suburban builders promised a combination of urban comforts and rustic simplicity, made possible by technological innovation. Availability of land, improvements in building techniques, and mass production of construction materials enabled construction of houses with larger and more rooms than in homes of earlier eras. In the eighteenth century only the wealthy could afford homes with three or more bedrooms and separate living and dining areas. By the 1880s, however, such facilities were possible for a much larger segment of the urban population. The specialization of space inside the home, creating distinct zones for different activities, with formal social space, kitchen work space, and private upstairs rooms, paralleled the specialization of urban space the suburbs themselves helped to create.

City outskirts became places of detached houses, private yards, and tree-lined streets. Historian Sam Bass Warner, Jr., has estimated that half or more of Bostonians found some level of suburban living within their reach.[8] Families with a single wage earner with steady employment could move out along a particular streetcar line, but families dependent on two or more wage earners to pay the mortgage or rent had to locate themselves near lines with cross-town connections so that working family members could each get to work. Statistics for Boston, like those for other cities, show that many suburbanites rented their homes. Only a quarter of the suburban households owned their own homes, and half of these were actually held by mortgage-financing institutions. Building and loan associations that financed mortgages for families of modest means adamantly preferred suburban sites to urban row houses. But the difference between owning or renting was less important than the move to the suburbs itself; the suburban home, how it was furnished, and the family life the wife created there contributed to the definition of "middle class" as much as the family income.

Suburban development was not uniform. The Chicago suburb Riverside, designed by Olmsted and Vaux, and Chestnut Hill, near Philadelphia, were some of the more luxurious communities inhabited by wealthy suburbanites; Chicago's Ravenswood and Normal Park, Boston's Roxbury and Dorchester, much of New York's Queens, and Milwaukee's Humboldt and Wauwatosa offered inexpensive lots to families of more modest means. Site plans of affluent suburbs, featuring curving paths and English garden landscaping, differed dramatically from the gridiron plots that facilitated subdivision of less expensive suburbs. Still, within a given development, mass-production techniques in the building industry and an unspoken consensus encouraged builders to erect houses similar in style and size to those that surrounded them. Most of the new communities tended to be segregated by income and ethnic group.

The growth of suburbs had a profound effect on urban centers. As early as 1873, nearly one hundred suburbs with a combined population of more than fifty thousand surrounded Chicago. Los Angeles, a city largely composed of discrete suburban developments, expanded from six thousand in 1870 to nearly one-hundred thousand by 1887, housing its new residents in sixty new communities spawned outside prior city boundaries. Smaller cities like Richmond, Memphis, and San Francisco were also surrounded by suburbs. Municipalities preferred to annex new suburban areas as a way of holding on to the tax base and spreading the cost of city services. In 1854, Philadelphia's annexation of Philadelphia County allowed the city to expand from 2 to 130 square miles. In 1889, Chicago annexed 133 square miles of suburban territory, including the communities of Hyde Park, Woodlawn, South Chicago, and Pullman. In 1898 New York City grew from 44 to 299 square miles with the consolidation of Manhattan, Brooklyn, Queens, Staten Island, and the Bronx. Early Boston suburbanites were confident enough of their ability to exercise political clout to agree to annexation in exchange for the provision of services, and the annexation of streetcar suburbs Roxbury, West Roxbury, and Dorchester added 20 square miles to the city, but Brookline's refusal to annex in 1873 marked the beginning of a trend of suburban insistence on political independence, sparking a more antagonistic relationship between city centers and suburbs.

The new suburban developments changed common perceptions of urban space and particularly the use of streets. Older urban architectural styles placed housing close to the street, and street space served vital neighborhood and family social uses as routes for pushcart vendors, meeting place for adults, and playspace for children. Historian Clay McShane has argued that late nineteenth-century urban residents expressed their commitment to this use of the streets by opposing pavement changes that facilitated the high-speed movement of vehicles.[9] By controlling street paving, residents of older, more densely packed sections could prevent local government from turning their only open social and recreational spaces into "arteries" whose sole function was to carry people and goods out of the city. By the 1890s, the consensus had swung in favor of smooth street paving that used new more easily drained surfaces and that reoriented city streets to high-speed travel. Supported as public works by socialists as well as machine politicians, lobbied for by municipal engineers and public-health experts who argued that smoothly paved streets would be easier to clean, and demanded by residents in outlying districts whose concern was for fast travel, asphalt and concrete streets literally paved the way for the automobile, whose wheels then destroyed whatever was left of the old pavements. A suburban interpretation of street use for high-speed travel rather than as neighborhood social space was powerfully pervasive even before automobile use confirmed this reorientation of urban geography.

Another significant effect of residential sprawl was the decentralization of economic functions. The increased concentration of people living at the city periphery and traveling on mass-transit lines turned outlying transfer points, such as streetcar intersections and elevated railway stations, into natural business centers. The result was a multinuclear development of

A Secondary Business Center   The intersection of Milwaukee Avenue and Chicago Avenue in Chicago became one of many nodes of retail activity that grew around intersections of important arteries and streetcar routes. *(Courtesy Chicago Historical Society.)*

commercial districts. That is, as consumers moved outward, businesses followed them. Groceries, drugstores, specialty shops, and saloons developed along traffic centers in newer regions of settlement. There they were joined by chain stores, banks, and theaters that had branched out from the main business district. These secondary business centers quickly became important focuses for neighborhood life.

The same forces that fueled peripheral growth also altered the center of cities. What had once been the entire walking city now became the zone of work, crammed with offices, stores, and warehouses. As middle-class residents departed, immigrants took their places, doubling and tripling up in old houses or filling tenements after single-family structures had been razed (this turnover is discussed in more detail in Chapter 4). Tenements and row housing encircled the factories now located downtown near rail and water outlets, creating vast and crowded working-class districts, such as the back-of-the-yards neighborhood in Chicago, which housed the meat-packing workforce near the factories and the eastern edge of Birmingham, Alabama, where steelworkers' housing clustered around the mills. Frequently commercial buildings replaced residential structures, creating genuine business districts, such as the Loop in Chicago and Lower Manhattan in New York. More than ever before downtown districts contained an extraordinary concentration of economic and cultural functions. Chicago's Loop was the ultimate central business district. One official described it as follows in 1910:

The Emergence of Downtown   State Street in downtown Chicago around 1870 was beginning to become a major business center, but it was still unpaved, and its sidewalks were wooden. After the Great Chicago Fire in 1871, it was rebuilt and became one of the most famous streets of urban America. *(Courtesy Chicago Historical Society.)*

Within an area of less than a square mile there are found the railway terminals and business offices, the big retail stores, the wholesale and jobbing businesses, the financial center, the main offices of the chief firms of the city, a considerable proportion of the medical and dental professions, the legal profession, the city and county governments, the post office, the courts, the leading social and political clubs, the hotels, theaters, Art Institute, principal libraries, labor headquarters, and a great number of lesser factors of city life.

Thus in pushing city borders outward and creating separate social and economic districts, mass transit was simultaneously a centripetal and centrifugal force. On the one hand, most of the city's important economic activities remained centralized within the old core, and commuters streamed inward each day on the trolleys and els to work and to shop. "Downtown" acquired a clear image: a place where stores and offices formed canyon walls surrounding streets clogged with human and vehicular traffic. On the other hand, the streetcars launched people (or the half of the population that could afford it) into the urban periphery, and the people dragged with them many economic institutions that began small-scale operations in the outskirts. Transportation also enabled new industrial plants, shut out from the crowded core, to build on vacant land outside the city. The growth of industry in these areas pumped life into many suburbs and created new boom

A Nineteenth-Century Traffic Jam   This congestion of people, animals, and vehicles on a Philadelphia cobblestone street in 1897 combines nearly all early forms of urban transport—pedestrians, horse-drawn wagons and carriages, and an electric trolley car. *(U.S. Bureau of Public Roads, The National Archives.)*

towns, such as Cambridge and Somerville near Boston, and Cicero, Aurora, and Elgin near Chicago. Freight and commuter railroads shuttled between these places and the big city nearby. The expansion of transportation spread companies and people into regions far removed from the old walking city, while also drawing new areas into the city's orbit.

But there were social costs involved in the outward sprawl and sorting out of people and districts. Nearly half the urban population could not afford the new way of living. Families whose breadwinners earned only a dollar or two a day and whose children worked in mills and sweatshops to help feed their brothers and sisters could dream of escaping their crowded quarters and filthy street, but for many of them the goal was elusive. The exodus of the middle class intensified the problems that urban population growth had always bred. Those with resources fled and left the discomforts, disease, and decay to those least endowed to cope with them.

Eventually (often within the span of one generation) some lower-income families could and did escape, usually first to the *zone of emergence*—the ring between the slums and the areas of new houses—and then to the outer neighborhoods. But in many cases their outward migration destroyed the ideal that suburban and peripheral development had sought to achieve. When lower-income groups sought homes in neighborhoods beyond the slums, they could afford only modest payments for mortgages or rents. Moreover, most were young families who needed four- or five-room cottages, not the six- or eight-room houses that had been built for larger, more affluent households. Thus some newcomers had to double up in dwellings originally built to house one family. Even when a family could afford to live alone in a house, it seldom had enough money to maintain the structure at the standards of repair that were originally intended. Those who moved from cramped flats and tenements into the single and divided houses of the outer neighborhoods undoubtedly improved their living conditions. But they also brought with them the accompaniments of more intensive land use—not just more *people* per acre, but more businesses, more traffic, more garbage, more noise. The unplanned nature of outward growth, which had ignored future land uses and architectural needs, quickly began to haunt the modern city. Those who had enough money, or who scraped together enough, kept moving farther away—a flight that has continued unabated to the present—but the specter of decay was always close behind.

Besides physical expansion and land-use differentiation a third consequence of mass transportation was its effect on population mobility. Trains and trolleys enabled people to travel farther and faster. Speed and punctuality became urban habits. The new urban sprawl, made possible by mass transit, reinforced the migratory tendency that had always marked American life. The numbers of people moving from one home to another throughout the nineteenth century and into the twentieth clearly reveal that there is nothing new about our present transient society and that residential mobility has been one of the most dynamic and pervasive features of American history. There are three kinds of population movement that affect cities: in-migration, out-migration, and intraurban migration. The first two are part of the process to be discussed in the next chapter. The third type, change of residence within the same city, was (and is) one of the most constant characteristics of city life. It affected practically every family, every neighborhood. It made the ideal of a stable community a fantasy, and it became an available path for those who sought a way to higher socioeconomic status.

Today social analysts note with wonder that each year one in five Americans changes residence. Yet evidence suggests that decades ago residential mobility was as frequent as—if not more frequent than—it is presently. A study of Omaha, Nebraska, at the end of the nineteenth century and the beginning of the twentieth revealed that less than 25 percent of the city's young and middle-aged famliy heads lived in one place for as long as five years; only 3 percent failed to move in twenty years. Of those who remained in the city for as long as fourteen years, over half had lived in three or more places over that time span; of those who remained for twenty years, one third had occupied four or more dwellings. Not every group shifted with the same frequency: foreign-born moved less often than native-born, white-collar workers moved less often than blue-collar.[10] However, the differences between groups were slight; more important was the entire population's remarkable impermanence, an impermanence that characterized almost every city.

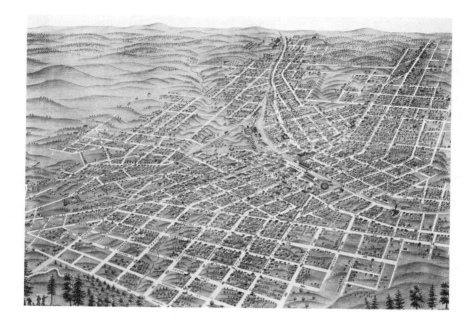

A Blossoming City of the New South   Two similar aerial drawings of Atlanta, one in 1871 and the other in 1892, vividly reveal the process of geographical development and expansion. Top: A. Ruger *(Library of Congress.)* Bottom: August Koch *(Library of Congress.)*

Certainly some of those who skipped from one home to another within a city never improved their condition; they were fleeing delinquent rent payments or were seeking new quarters because their old residences were to be torn down. So they moved to a house or tenement down the street or around the corner. Yet it appears that many more people did better themselves by changing residence. In Boston, Atlanta, Omaha, and a host of other cities, thousands of families followed the streetcar lines into the newer neighborhoods, where housing was roomier and yards were greener. A family's most common residential pattern involved a series of moves, usually radiating outward from the center of the city toward the periphery or suburbs. The frequency of movement often frustrated reformers who sought to order society by creating stable communities. "I want to arouse neighborhood interest and neighborhood pride," pleaded Jacob Riis in 1901, "to link the neighborhood to one spot that will hold them [*sic*] long enough to take root and stop them from moving. Something of the kind must be done or we perish." Such a goal ran counter to the dynamics of urban life. Quests for more space, more convenience, and better facilites uprooted families and overturned neighborhoods. In the half-century after the Civil War these urges were as strong as before the war. Only now the new forces of urban growth and opportunity—outward sprawl, real-estate booms, and mass-transit construction—spread people into new and more numerous directions.

THE QUICKENING PACE OF INDUSTRIALIZATION

The rise of streetcars and els furnishes but one example of the interrelationship between urban growth and technological advance. While mass transit was changing the face, pace, and space of American cities, the larger force of industrialization was increasingly guiding the course of urbanization. If we define industrialization as the coordinated development of economic specialization, mass mechanized production, mass consumption, and mass distribution of goods and services, it is important to emphasize that this phenomenon did not occur on a large scale until the last third of the nineteenth century. The construction of railroads and canals, the increased use of water power and steam engines, and the introduction of the factory system in the Northeast by 1850 has laid the foundations for industrial growth. But the real burst came after the Civil War, when transcontinental transportation links and the proliferation of urban sites created a mass, national market for goods and services and when new applications of science and new inventions radically altered business, employment, and living styles.

During the 1860s and 1870s four transcontinental railroads pushed westward to the Pacific, triggering urban growth at many points along their routes. Indeed the railroads helped to complete the national urban network, whose framework was laid in the first half of the century. Between 1860 and 1910 the number of cities with populations of over 100,000 swelled from 9 to 50; the number with 25,000 to 100,00 grew from 26 to 178; and those with 10,000 to 25,000 increased from 58 to 369. A list of the most prominent new cities boosted by the railroads contains nearly the entire urban West: Albuquerque, Butte, Cheyenne, Dallas, El Paso, Fort Worth, Kansas City, Los Angeles, Minneapolis, Oklahoma City, Omaha, Portland, Reno, St. Paul, Salt Lake City, San Antonio, San Diego, San Francisco, Santa Fe, Seattle, Spokane, and Tacoma. In cities like Los Angeles, San Diego, and Santa Barbara the dramatic growth of the Anglo population began a process that shifted the local economy and shut out Chicanos, lowering their status, residentially segregating them in barrios, and reconstituting them as an unskilled and semiskilled working class. Desert cities like Albuquerque, El Paso, Phoenix, and Tucson stagnated until the coming of the railroad transformed them into focal transit points for surrounding farms, ranches, and mines. The coming of four railroad connections to El Paso dramatically expanded its population from less than one thousand to over ten thousand in the space of the decade from 1880 to 1890. By 1887, El Paso was a genuine city, granting franchises for gas, electricity, and telephone companies, supporting streetcar systems, fire companies, police agencies, fraternal lodges, churches, and schools. Railroads brought a new kind of urban growth to the South as well, fostering the growth of a more complex industrial base in cities such as Atlanta and Birmingham, and wider commercial and industrial exchange possibilities in cities such as Memphis and Nashville.

Most of the towns that the railroads helped boost to cities had become centers of commerce before any track had been laid. Omaha, for example, was an important outfitting center for settlers crossing the Missouri River, and Seattle served as a lumber port and intermediary transfer point between San Francisco and northwestern Canada. These places became natural locations for terminals once the railroads began construction. However, the iron horse could turn a regional trading post into a boom town, and competition for railroad connections amplified the urban imperialism that was so characteristic of American economic expansion. Omaha subscribed money to build a bridge across the Missouri; leaders of Kansas City offered generous subsidies and land grants; and citizens of Seattle laid their own stretch of track—all to lure the railroads to their front doors. Cities, therefore, built railroads as much as railroads built cities.

Meanwhile, the major components of industrialization were converging—new sources of raw materials and energy, new machines and modes of production, new supplies of labor and skills. During the 1860s inventors in France and America developed methods of producing high-quality steel from iron and carbon, thereby providing the basic staple of industry. Over the next generation technicians harnessed electrical energy to furnish almost unlimited power for operating huge machines or for lighting streets and buildings. At the same time, the refinement of petroleum, the production of high explosives, and the creation of new alloys (such as aluminum) opened new possibilities for the application of physics and chemistry to industrial concerns. The development of successful new products and processes heartened would-be investors to deluge the U.S. Patent Office with ideas, prompted academic institutions to expand programs for training scientists and engineers, and inspired large businesses to establish their own laboratories or to subsidize research in technological colleges. The demands for capital made by expanding industry encouraged widespread adoption of corporate organization with its stocks, bonds, limited stockholder liability for company debts, and bureaucratic management of operations. Increased scales of production, the use of more mechanically

A Streetcar Subdivision   This 1883 newspaper advertisement heralds a new suburban tract just north of Chicago (it was annexed to the city in 1889). Note how transit plays a central role in the ad. *(Courtesy Chicago Historical Society.)*

powered devices, and the adoption of interchangeable parts as a means of standardizing products paved the way for assembly-line production and created a huge demand for labor—unskilled workers to run the machines, specialized and supervisory personnel to fix the machines and oversee the workers, and clerical and managerial employees to fill the business bureaucracy. These developments generated a *pull* factor of employment opportunities that attracted people from Europe to America and from one place to another inside the country's borders (see Chapter Four).

As the place that centralized resources, labor, transportation, and communications, the city became the chief arena of industrial growth. By the end of the nineteenth century urban factories were responsible for nine-tenths of America's industrial output. The types of industrial cities responsible for this production were quite varied. Some cities utilized unskilled immigrant labor and new, easier techniques of production to furnish goods for mass consumption. Thus the shoe industry became prominent in Rochester and Philadelphia, the clothing industry in New York, and textiles in Lawrence, Lowell, and Fall River. Other cities exploited and processed products of their agricultural hinterlands: flour in Minneapolis; cottonseed oil in Memphis; meat and butter in Omaha; beer in Milwaukee. Others grew by extracting and utilizing other nearby resources: minerals in Denver; fish and lumber in Portland and Seattle; coal and iron in Cleveland, Pittsburgh, and Birmingham; oil in Dallas, Houston, Los Angeles, and Oklahoma City.

There were other variants, other industries—such as Detroit's automobiles, Akron's tires, and Dayton's cash registers—but in each case industrialization involved several common requisites. First, cities needed the traditional ingredients of economic growth: land, labor, entrepreneurship,

Industrialization   Silk warping and skein winding to spools at the Royal Weaving Company, Pawtucket, Rhode Island, about 1910. Machines and female operatives extend almost endlessly into the background. *(Courtesy of The Rhode Island Historical Society.)*

transportation, market demand (a population of consumers), and specialization (some principal product or function that could be exported for profit). These elements had existed in American cities in one degree or another since the late seventeenth century. But by the late nineteenth century large amounts of available capital and increasing technological innovation appeared and mixed with the old factors to feed the process of industrial change. That is, industrialization proceeded most strongly in those cities where successful commercial activities produced capital for industrial investment. All the western cities and most of the eastern ones were founded on a speculative and commercial base. Their commercial functions—attracting and distributing raw materials, wholesaling and retailing goods and services—remained integral to their industrial development and their economic viability, because they created capital for investment and because they generated the "multiplier effect" of spiraling growth. Only when their economies filled out with a complete range of business and consumer services could one-industry towns reach the stage of maturity that qualified them as genuine regional metropolises—nodes connecting and controlling a large surrounding area. To be sure, in the closing decades of the nineteenth century, manufacturing, rather than trade, provided the major impetus to urban growth, but still no city could exist without its commerce.

The growing importance of industrialization in cities meant that factory-owners' decisions to cut wages or lengthen workdays had an enormous impact on many city dwellers, both inside and outside the factories. Historian Herbert Gutman has argued that the political and social power of the new industrialists was often contested, especially in smaller and medium-sized industrial cities.[11] Values oppositional to the managerial patterns of factory discipline were sustained by vital subcultures among immigrant and native-born poor as well as among craftsmen and artisans. Many property owners and professionals shared more common values and social connections with factory workers than with factory owners. The huge concentration of working-class people in industrial districts helped different groups of workers to sympathize with each other's causes. In 1877, factory workers, wives, and even local merchants aided railroad strikers in stopping railroad traffic in cities along the railroad lines, from Baltimore to Philadelphia to Pittsburgh, eventually all the way to Chicago and St. Louis. Between 1885 and 1889, labor coalitions contended for political power in cities diverse as Jacksonville, Boston, Baltimore, New Bedford, Detroit, Cincinnati, and Akron and reported electoral victories in cities like Milwaukee, Richmond, Harrisburg, Lynn, Chicago, and Dubuque. Industrialization sharpened new divisions between urban residents at the same time that it generated new alliances among them.

In summary, urbanization and industrialization were not the same process. Cities had grown long before modern manufacturing was possible, and factories could and did develop outside of urban areas. But by the onset of the Civil War, urban and industrial growth were bound tightly together. The commercial cities and transportation revolution of the early nineteenth century bred the manufacturing cities and industrial revolution of the late nineteenth century. The twin forces of urbanization and industrialization now fed upon each other: each reinforced and modified the course of the other. Together they induced unprecedented economic change and freed the United States from reliance upon European products and capital. Imports and foreign investments still flowed into the country, but increasingly cities and their factories transformed the United States from an agricultural, debtor nation into a manufacturing and financial power.

BIBLIOGRAPHY

The walking city is discussed in Sam Bass Warner, Jr., *The Urban Wilderness: A History of the American City* (New York: Harper & Row, Publishers, 1972); Richard C. Wade, "Urbanization," in *The Comparative Approach to American History*, ed. C. Vann Woodward (New York: Basic Books, 1969); and Samuel P. Hays, "The Changing Political Structure of the City in Industrial America," *Journal of Urban History* 1 (November 1974):6–38.

For a discussion of the form of early suburban communities see Henry Binford, *The First Suburbs: Residential Communities on the Boston Periphery, 1815–1860* (Chicago: University of Chicago Press, 1985); Kenneth T. Jackson, *Crabgrass Frontier: The Suburbanization of the United States* (New York: Oxford University Press, 1985). On suburban development after 1850 see also Sam Bass Warner, Jr., *Streetcar Suburb: The Process of Growth in Boston, 1870–1900* (Cambridge, Mass.: Harvard University Press, 1962); Mathew Edel, Elliot D. Sclar, and Daniel Luria, *Shakey Palaces: Home Ownership and Social Mobility in Boston's Suburbanization* (New York: Columbia University Press, 1984); Jon Teaford, *City and Suburb: The Political Fragmentation of Metropolitan America, 1850–1970* (Baltimore: Johns Hopkins University Press, 1979). On roads and pavements, see Clay McShane, "Transforming the Use of Urban Space: A Look at the Revolution in Street Pavements, 1880–1924," *Journal of Urban History* 5(May 1979):279–307.

Studies of the development and consequences of mass transportation include George R. Taylor, "The Beginnings of Mass Transportation in Urban America," *The Smithsonian Journal of History*, 1(Summer 1966):35–50 and (Autumn 1966):35–54; Glen E. Holt, "The Changing Perception of Urban Pathology: An Essay on the Development of Mass Transit in the United States," in *Cities in American History*, eds. Kenneth T. Jackson and Stanley K. Schultz (New York: Alfred A. Knopf, 1972), 324–43; Joel A. Tarr, "From City to Suburb: The 'Moral' Influence of Transportation Technology," in *American Urban History: An Interpretive Reader with Commentaries*, 2d ed., ed. Alexander B. Callow, Jr. (New York: Oxford University Press, 1973), 202–12; Tarr, *Transportation Innovation and Changing Spatial Patterns: Pittsburgh, 1850–1910* (Pittsburgh: Carnegie Mellon University, 1972); Clay McShane, *Technology and Reform: Street Railways and the Growth of Milwaukee, 1887–1900* (Madison: State Historical Society of Wisconsin, 1974); Charles W. Cheape, *Moving the Masses: Urban Public Transit in New York, Boston, and Philadelphia, 1880–1912* (Cambridge, Mass.: Harvard University Press, 1980). On the expansion of city services, see Roger D. Simon, *The City Building Process: Housing and Services in New*

Milwaukee Neighborhoods, 1880–1910 (Philadelphia: Temple University Press, 1978), and Harold L. Platt, *City Building in the New South: The Growth of Public Services in Houston, Texas, 1830–1910* (Philadelphia: Temple University Press, 1983). See also John B. Stilgoe, *Metropolitan Corridor: Railroads and the American Scene* (New Haven, Conn.: Yale University Press, 1985).

On architecture and technology see Leo Marx, *The Machine in the Garden: Technology and the Pastoral Ideal in America* (New York: Oxford University Press, 1964); Christopher Tunnard and Henry Hope Reed, *American Skyline* (Boston: Little, Brown, 1955); John Coolidge, *Mill and Mansion: A Study of Architecture and Society in Lowell, Massachusetts* (New York: Columbia University Press, 1942); Gwendolyn Wright, *Building the Dream: A Social History of Housing in America* (Cambridge, Mass.: MIT Press, 1983).

On early department stores see Neil Harris, "Museums, Merchandising, and Popular Taste: The Struggle for Influence," in *Material Culture and the Study of American Life,* ed. Ian M. G. Quimby (New York: W. W. Norton & Co., 1978), 140–74; Gunther Barth, *City People: The Rise of Modern City Culture in Nineteenth Century America* (New York: Oxford University Press, 1980), 110–47.

On rural cemeteries see Stanley French, "The Cemetery as Cultural Institution: The Establishment of Mount Auburn and the 'Rural Cemetery' Movement," *American Quarterly* 26(March 1974):37–59. On parks see John A. Peterson, "The Evolution of Public Open Space in American Cities: A Review Essay," *Journal of Urban History* 12(November 1985):75–88; Roy Rozenzweig, "The Parks and the People: Social History and Urban Parks," *Journal of Social History* 18 (Winter 1984):289–96; Galen Crantz, *The Politics of Park Design: A History of Urban Parks in America* (Cambridge, Mass.: MIT Press, 1982); Cynthia Zaitzevsky, *Frederick Law Olmsted and the Boston Park System* (Cambridge, Mass.: Harvard University Press, 1982). For a discussion of parks as contested space see Roy Rozenzweig, *Eight Hours for What We Will: Workers and Leisure in an Industrial City, 1880–1920* (New York: Cambridge University Press, 1983). For a discussion of the change from park reform to commercial amusement see John B. Kasson, *Amusing the Million: Coney Island at the Turn of the Century* (New York: Hill and Wang, 1978).

On popular amusements in the walking city see David Grimsted, *Melodrama Unveiled: American Theater and Culture 1800–1850* (Chicago: University of Chicago Press, 1968); Claudia Johnson, "That Guilty Third Tier: Prostitution in Nineteenth Century Theaters," *American Quarterly* 27(December 1975):575–84. On Victorian amusements see also Robert C. Toll, *Blacking Up: The Minstrel Show in Nineteenth Century America* (New York: Oxford University Press, 1974); Jon Kingsdale, "The Poor Man's Club: Social Functions of the Urban Working Class Saloon," *American Quarterly* 25(October 1973):472–89; Perry Duis, *The Saloon: Public Drinking in Chicago and Boston, 1880–1920* (Urbana: University of Illinois Press, 1983); Albert F. McLean, Jr., *American Vaudeville As Ritual* (Lexington: University of Kentucky Press, 1965). For a discussion of the changing presentation of culture in the nineteenth century see Lawrence W. Levine, "William Shakespeare and the American People: A Study in Cultural Transformation," *American Historical Review* 89(February 1984):34–66; Susan G. Davis, *Parades and Power: Street Theater in Nineteenth Century Philadelphia* (Philadelphia: Temple University Press, 1986).

On industrial cities see David Gordon, "Capitalist development and the History of American Cities," in *Marxism and the Metropolis,* eds. William K. Tabb and Larry Sawers (New York: Oxford University Press, 1978), 25–63; Herbert Gutman, "The Workers' Search for Power: Labor in the Gilded Age," in *The Gilded Age: A Reappraisal,* ed. H. Wayne Morgan (Syracuse, N.Y.: Syracuse University Press, 1963), 38–68; Morgan, *Work, Culture, and Society in Industrializing America: Essays in*

American Working-Class and Social History (New York: Alfred A. Knopf, 1976); Daniel J. Walkowitz, *Worker City, Company Town: Iron and Cotton Worker Protest in Troy and Cohoes, New York, 1855–1884* (Urbana: University of Illinois Press, 1978); Alan Dawley, *Class and Community: The Industrial Revolution in Lynn* (Cambridge, Mass.: Harvard University Press, 1977); John T. Cumbler, *Working-Class Community in Industrial America: Work, Leisure and Struggle in Two Industrial Cities, 1860–1930* (Westport, Conn.: Greenwood Press, 1979); Leon Fink, *Workingmen's Democracy: The Knights of Labor and American Politics* (Urbana: University of Illinois Press, 1983); Francis Couvares, *The Remaking of Pittsburgh: Class and Culture in an Industrializing City, 1877–1919* (Albany: State University of New York Press, 1984); Roy Rosenzweig, *Eight Hours for What We Will: Workers and Leisure in an Industrial City, 1870–1920* (Cambridge, England, and New York: Cambridge University Press, 1983); Steven J. Ross, *Workers on the Edge: Work, Leisure and Politics in Industrializing Cincinnati* (New York: Columbia University Press, 1985); Ross, "The Politicization of the Working Class: Production, Ideology, Culture and Politics in late Nineteenth Century Cincinnati," *Social History* 11(1986):171–96.

ENDNOTES

[1]Samuel P. Hays, "The Changing Political Structure of the City in Industrial America," *Journal of Urban History* 1(November 1974):6–38, esp. 8–9.

[2]Henry Binford, *The First Suburbs: Residential Communities on the Boston Periphery, 1815–1860* (Chicago: University of Chicago Press, 1985).

[3]Richard C. Wade, "Urbanization," in *The Comparative Approach to American History*, ed. C. Van Woodward (New York: Basic Books, 1969), 191.

[4]Glen E. Holt, "Changing Perceptions of Urban Pathology: An Essay on the Development of Mass Transit in the United States," in *Cities in American History*, eds. Kenneth T. Jackson and Stanley K. Schultz (New York: Alfred A. Knopf, 1972), 327.

[5]John Anderson Miller, *Fares Please! From Horsecars to Streamliners* (New York: Appleton-Century-Crofts, 1941), 62.

[6]Holt, *op. cit.*, 335.

[7]John B. Jackson, *American Space: The Centennial Years, 1865–1876* (New York: W. W. Norton & Co., 1972), 214–15.

[8]Sam Bass Warner, Jr., *Streetcar Suburbs: The Process of Growth in Boston, 1870–1900* (Cambridge, Mass.: Harvard University Press, 1962).

[9]Clay McShane, "Transforming the Use of Urban Space: A Look at the Revolution in Street Pavements, 1880–1924," *Journal of Urban History* 5(May 1979):279–307.

[10]Howard P. Chudacoff, *Mobile Americans: Residential and Social Mobility in Omaha, 1880–1920* (New York: Oxford University Press, 1972).

[11]Herbert Gutman, *Work, Culture and Society in Industrializing America* (New York: Alfred A. Knopf, 1976).

4

Newcomers and the Urban Core, 1850–1920

MIGRATION, OLD AND NEW

Today the American metropolis is a dichotomy, a population center separated into inner and outer parts. The division is a legacy from the social, economic, and technological changes that advanced from the middle of the nineteenth century onward, setting in motion centrifugal waves of settlement. But while the middle classes accompanied the trolley lines into the periphery and suburbs, working-class immigrants squeezed into the older districts and transformed the walking city into the urban core. To those on the outside the residential rings that surrounded business and manufacturing districts embodied the worst of American urban life because of the problems they bred—slums, crime, disease. Yet the inner city served necessary functions for those who lived there. It provided shelter and jobs. It created opportunities for social contact and group activity. It eased uprooted peasants into a new, urban-industrial world. And it blended millions of foreigners into pluralistic, American society.

Between 1860 and 1920 the number of people living in American cities of eight thousand or more inhabitants mushroomed from 6.2 to 54.3 million (see Table 4.1). Although an excess of births over deaths accounted for some of this population growth, the bulk of the increase consisted of newcomers—people from American rural areas, a foreign country, or another American town or city. This migration resulted from two forces: a push and a pull. A variety of pressures drove young people and whole families from their farms in America and from their villages in Europe. Prices for agricultural products were increasingly affected by the development of national markets; manufactured goods were sold in the countryside

TABLE 4-1 Population Composition of Major Cities, 1910

	TOTAL	FOREIGN-BORN WHITE		NATIVE-BORN OF FOREIGN OR MIXED PARENTAGE		BLACK	
		NUMBER	%	NUMBER	%	NUMBER	%
New York	4,766,883	1,927,703	40.4	1,820,141	38.2	91,709	1.9
Chicago	2,185,283	781,217	35.7	912,701	41.8	44,103	2.0
Philadelphia	1,549,008	382,578	24.7	496,785	32.1	84,459	5.5
St. Louis	687,029	125,706	18.3	246,946	40.0	43,960	6.4
Boston	670,535	240,722	35.9	257,104	38.3	13,564	2.0
Cleveland	560,663	195,703	34.9	223,908	39.9	8,448	1.5
Baltimore	558,485	77,043	13.8	134,870	24.1	84,749	15.2
Pittsburgh	533,905	140,436	26.3	191,483	35.9	25,623	4.8
Detroit	465,766	156,565	33.6	188,255	40.4	5,741	1.2
Buffalo	423,715	118,444	30.0	183,673	40.4	1,773	0.4
San Francisco	416,912	130,874	31.4	153,781	36.9	1,642	0.4
Milwaukee	373,857	111,456	29.8	182,530	48.8	980	0.3
Cincinnati	363,591	56,792	15.6	132,190	36.4	19,639	5.4
Newark	347,469	110,655	31.8	132,350	38.1	9,475	2.7
New Orleans	339,075	27,686	8.2	74,244	21.9	89,262	26.3
Washington	331,069	24,351	7.4	45,066	13.6	94,446	28.5

Source: 1910 U.S. Census.

and competed with the handiwork of artisans, and more land was being bought and sold and hence turned into a commodity. Migration was directly connected to the development of communications, markets, commerce, and capital—themselves the signposts of economic change. Roads and railways, canals and steamships, post offices and telegraphs, banks, and travel agencies were the products of those forces that were transforming the American and European countryside as well as the means that migrants used in beginning their personal journeys in search of expanded opportunities. Local impetus for migration came from declining prices for crops, rising prices for provisions, high taxes and rents, eviction from customary farm lands, drought, hard winters, insect plagues, and crowded local economies.

But migrants left because there was somewhere else to go. Widening horizons in American cities amidst the awareness of the unalterable course of change at home prompted rural villagers to travel in search of the means to survive and prosper. "America appealed to me very much," one immigrant remembered. "The whole country seemed to be at the roof of the world." Cities, with their promise of money and jobs, beckoned to rural Americans and to Europeans. Here is where national forces bore down upon the city to produce the dynamics of urbanization. The commercial revolution of the eighteenth and early nineteenth centuries, the transition through merchant capitalism of the early and middle nineteenth century, and then the industrial revolution created the jobs and other opportunities that charged cities with magnetism. Moreover, the cities themselves generated labor opportunities. In the second half of the nineteenth century and the first decades of the twentieth practically every major city constructed or enlarged its basic facilities, all with the help of unskilled immigrant labor and most with public funds. Streets, bridges, water and gas systems, sewers, schools, and government buildings were built by and for the new city dwellers.

Who were these newcomers? Exactly where did they come from? Many came from the American countryside. Although the number of farms in this country almost tripled between 1860 and 1900 and mechanization boosted productivity, foreign competition increased and supplies exceeded national and worldwide demand for agricultural products, so prices for staple crops dropped steadily. Meanwhile transportation, storage, and commission fees remained high, and the cost of seed, fertilizer, manufactured goods, taxes, and mortgage interest drove many families deeper in debt. Farmers were caught in a cycle in which, given a contracted currency, the more they produced, the more prices fell. The future of farming belonged to large producers who could make use of expensive machinery, crop specialization, and economies of scale. The impact of mechanization, the consolidation of land holdings, and the rise in farm tenantry was to push thousands of young people off the farm toward the manufacturing cities of the Northeast and Midwest. Rural areas of several states, including New Hampshire, Vermont, New York, Maryland, Ohio, and Illinois suffered absolute as well as relative declines in population in the 1880s.

Movement off the farms and into the cities changed the patterns of life in the countryside, particularly in the Old Northwest—Ohio, Indiana, Illinois, Michigan, and Wisconsin. In the last half of the nineteenth century urban migration boosted the growth not only of Detroit, Cleveland, Chicago, and Milwaukee but also of a host of secondary cities which shortened distances between the rural markets and the nearest social centers. Dayton, Toledo, Indianapolis, Fort Wayne, South Bend, Grand Rapids, Kalamazoo, Peoria, Rockford, La Crosse, Oshkosh, and many more cities brought the amenities of urban life closer to the farmers. Rural Free Delivery brought farmers letters, newspapers, advertisements, and catalogues after 1896, and parcel post brought deliveries from big city mail-order department stores such as Sears and Montgomery Ward after 1913. Still rural emigrants streamed inward; regional centers such as Atlanta, Los Angeles, San Francisco, and Seattle swelled, and upstart places such as Birmingham, Houston, Kansas City, and Albuquerque matched their growth rates. By 1900, 80 percent of Memphis's population came from the adjacent Mississippi or Tennessee countryside.

Equally significant sources of immigration were from the European, Asian, and Mexican countrysides. Together the three major migrant groups that peopled American cities—native whites, foreigners, and native blacks—sowed the seeds of modern American urban culture, to which each group made important contributions. Cities nurtured rich cultural variety: American folk music and literature, Italian and Mexican cuisine, Irish comedy, Yiddish theatre, Afro-American jazz and dance, and much more. Like their predecessors, newcomers in the nineteenth century changed the urban environment as much as they were changed by it. Ethnicity and religious identification, key components of our modern urban culture, have derived from the immigrant experience in American cities during the past 150 years. Certainly in the half-century that followed the Civil War foreign immigrants living in the urban cores provided the focuses of most social and political issues.

European immigration to the United States is traditionally split into two major waves: one beginning in the 1840s, peaking in the 1880s, and ebbing thereafter; and the other beginning in the 1880s, peaking between 1900 and 1910, and declining in the 1920s when federal legislation closed the doors to the unrestricted influx of foreigners. The first wave of immigrants consisted of five main groups: Irish Catholics, German Catholics, German Protestants, English Protestants, and Scandinavian Protestants. Most entered through one of the large eastern ports. Settled newcomers then built chains of migration, across which traveled relatives and friends from the Old World to join fellow countrymen in the New.

Many immigrants were too poor to go farther than their port of arrival or they found ready use for whatever skills they had. These immigrants remained in the eastern ports of Boston, New York, Philadelphia, and Baltimore, or they ventured only a short distance away to growing secondary towns such as Providence, Paterson, Newark, and Reading. Others plunged almost immediately into the hinterland. From the 1850s onward, Germans, Swedes, and Norwegians took up farming in the states of the Old Northwest and the Plains. English, Welsh, and Scottish immigrants traveled inland to work in the coal mines of Pennsylvania, West Virginia, Ohio, and Illinois. Many newcomers followed the rivers and railroads into the new, growing cities of the West, settling in ports along the Ohio and Mississippi rivers or around the Great Lakes. Some moved on even farther, adding a foreign flavor to newer places such as Minneapolis, Des Moines, Omaha, Denver, Kansas City, and Los Angeles. By the late 1860s, Mexican influence in western and southwestern cities including Los Angeles, San Antonio, and Santa Barbara began to fade. Before 1870 the Spanish surname population constituted the majority group in many western cities, but a series of natural disasters, droughts, and floods, coupled with the large influx of native and European-born migrants, dramatically altered the status of the native Mexican population. By 1870 the Irish were the largest foreign-born group in California. Often the migrants settled in these cities for no other reason than that their funds ran out, and they suffered the pangs of poverty as much in the West as their counterparts did in the East. But the western towns offered opportunities for people with skills and resources, and many immigrants achieved nominal success—Scandinavians in construction trades, Germans in brewing, English and Irish in jobbing and retailing. The commercial elites of many western cities often included foreign-born members.

These "old" immigrants, as they came to be called, brought with them new and different traits that modified the American urban environment—dialects, dress, culinary and drinking habits (wine, ale, and beer now competed wtih traditional American rum and whiskey), and social institutions. The most consequential of the new features was religion. Between 1840 and 1890 7.5 million Irish and German immigrants arrived in America; of these, 5.5 million were Catholics. These groups transformed the United States from a Protestant to a Protestant-Catholic nation. By 1870, 40 percent of all churchgoers in this country were Catholics. Although American Catholicism lacked internal unity because of its ethnic diversity and the semiautonomous nature of local parishes, external forces imposed a kind of unity upon Catholics by emphasizing their difference from Protestantism. A latent fear of "popery," inherited from England in colonial times, surfaced and joined with a growing nativist sentiment in the 1830s, 1840s, and 1850s to intensify criticism, prejudice, and violence. Anti-Catholic sermons and pamphlets plus the nativist Know-Nothing party spread into several cities, raising emotions to a fever pitch. As one fearful editor wrote,

> Have we not reason to believe that now while popery is losing ground in Europe, that this land presents to the Pope a fine field of operations, and that he is endeavoring by every means in his power, to establish his falling throne, and that he is now sending out his minions to accomplish his fiendlike purpose, to prepare the way before him, that he may make a grand and triumphant entree [*sic*] into this country, when he shall be hurled from his tyrannous and polluted throne in Europe?

Occasionally, bloody clashes erupted, particularly sparked by tense competition for employment and the threat of immigrant political mobilization. In 1834 a mob burned and sacked an Ursuline convent near Boston. In 1844 Protestants and Irish Catholics fought in Philadelphia, and thirteen were killed. In 1855 twenty died in a battle between Germans and nativists in Louisville. In other cities churches were burned and homes were looted. Other foreign religious groups would make their mark, though less emphatically—Jews from Germany and Lutherans from Denmark, Sweden, and Germany. But the native-Protestant/foreign-Catholic dichotomy, fashioned primarily in the cities during the first period of mass immigration, has remained one of the most decisive factors in party politics, educational debates, and family organization to this day.

The second wave of immigration both resembled and contrasted with the first. Like their predecessors, most of the new immigrants were poor and of peasant origins. But they were much more numerous. Between 1840 and 1880 the average influx per decade numbered about 2.4 million, with a high of 2.8 million in the 1870s. In the 1880s over 5.2 million immigrants arrived; 8.8 million came between 1900 and 1910. Although the English, Irish, Germans, and Scandinavians continued to come in large contingents, they were far outnumbered by four new groups: Catholics from eastern Europe, Catholics from Italy, Jews from Russian and eastern Europe, and Catholics from Canada. Smaller sources included Greece, Syria, Mexico, and Japan. By 1910, arrivals from Mexico were beginning to outnumber arrivals from Ireland, and a large number of Japanese had moved to the west coast. A higher percentage of later immigrants settled in cities. The Dillingham Commission of 1907–1911, which in large part was responsible for perpetuating artificial distinctions between "new" immigrants and "old," reported that in 1920, 78.6 percent of those born in eastern and southern Europe lived in urban areas, compared with 68.3 percent of those born in northern Europe and the British Isles. Less skilled than the old immigrants, those arriving from new areas brought only their willingness to work. As one Italian immigrant woman explained, "I never have a lot of money, but I have my hands." These newcomers worked in the sweatshops and factories of larger cities and in the mills, slaughterhouses, construction gangs, and dock crews of most cities outside the South. Although many of these groups concentrated in eastern centers (particularly New York), they spread across the continent quite rapidly. By 1920 Poles were the largest foreign-born group in Detroit and Toledo, Czechs in Omaha, Italians in Youngstown, and Hungarians in Akron. Indeed immigrants, together with their American-born children, dominated many cities. By 1890 three-fourths of St. Paul's population and four-fifths of Milwaukee's population were either foreign-born or native born of foreign parents. Most southern cities in this period tended to attract more rural emigrants than foreign born. Although Memphis's population had been 37 percent foreign born in 1860, the foreign-born part of the population dropped to 15 percent by 1900. Still, in Birmingham one out of four white industrial workers was of foreign stock.

The arrival of millions from Italy, Russia, Hungary, Romania, and what later became Czechoslovakia, Yugoslavia, and Poland completed the formation of America's white religio-cultural mosaic. Newly arrived Catholics moved into industrial centers along the Northeast coast and in many cities constituted at least half the population. As they moved westward, they joined the Irish and Germans to raise Catholic proportions in Buffalo, Cleveland, Chicago, and Milwaukee to 40 or 50 percent. As before, the Church lacked uniformity, primarily as a result of its very catholicism. Traditionally the hierarchy centralized the Church, and geography determined parish boundaries. This system was derived from Europe, where most parishes

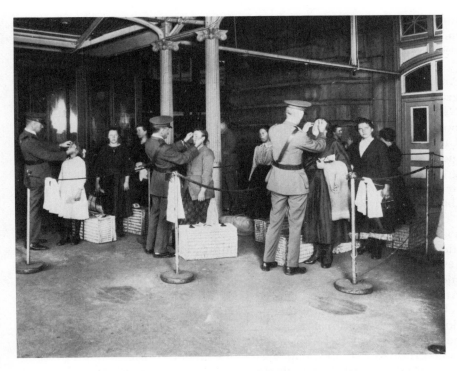

Trauma of Immigration   Foreigners entering this country through the port of New York first had to stop at Ellis Island in the harbor where they underwent close scrutiny for disease. Photo by Sy Seidman *(Records of the Public Health Service, National Archives.)*

contained only one nationality. But in American cities Catholics of different ethnic origins were in close contact with one another, and friction was inevitable. In several cities Italian, Polish, and French-Canadian Catholics clashed with Irish and German bishops over demands for parish priests of the same nationality as themselves. Newer immigrants struggled to retain, for themselves and their children, familiar ethnic and religious rituals and to make them meaningful in their new environment. However, some of the younger generation, descendants of the earlier Catholic immigrants, disavowed this kind of protection. They were willing to Americanize the Church because they believed that as long as doubts existed about their own and their fellow Catholics' loyalties the Church would never be accepted in America. A group of Catholics led by Cardinal James Gibbons of Baltimore, Archbishop John Ireland of St. Paul, and Bishop John L. Spalding of Peoria worked to minimize points of conflict, such as language and parochial education, between Catholics and other Americans. The task proved difficult, however. Prejudice and bigotry continued to confront Catholics, particularly during hard times when social tensions were most acute. Moreover, increasing Catholic immigration after the turn of the century only sharpened the dialogue between retentionists and accommodationists.

Jews also wrestled to retain their consciousness while adjusting to American urban life. They were probably the most urbanized of all immigrant groups—in 1910 close to 85 percent of Russian Jews lived in cities. New York City alone contained 1.5 million Jews, one of the largest Jewish populations in the world. Unlike their European ancestors Jews in the United States no longer lived in forced isolation: the law gave them religious freedom, civic equality, and political privileges. Yet like other immigrants, they sought self-identification. Like the Catholics, children of earlier Jewish immigrants developed an accommodationist sentiment. Many of them adopted Reform Judaism, a movement originated in the 1840s by German intellectuals who wished to conciliate Judaism with middle-class society. To many liberal Jews in America, the Reform movement seemed ideally suited to ease problems of cultural difference that occured when Jews attempted to find their place in diversified urban society. Leaders such as Rabbi Isaac Mayer Wise of Cincinnati reformed the prayer book, Anglicized the service, and loosened the rigors of ritual in an attempt to use religion as an Americanizing instrument. The movement reached full flower in Pittsburgh in 1885 with adoption of a platform that rejected the national character of Judaism and stressed the position of Jews as a religious group that should adapt itself to the modern world.

At this time, however, disruption of the eastern European land system and brutal pogroms broke apart Jewish communities and sent waves of immigrants to America from Romania and Russia. These Jews, poverty-stricken and often illiterate, crowded into the cities, where they soon outnumbered their coreligionists whose ancestors had arrived earlier. Like their Catholic counterparts, these newcomers tried to anchor their lives with religious ways of the past. They recoiled from Reform Judaism, seeking instead to re-create the orthodox, ritualistic Judaism of eastern Europe. Although forms of religious expression continued to split the two major Jewish groups, a philanthropic concern for the plights of their coreligionists at home and abroad gradually bound the two together. As the second generation of eastern European immigrants matured, some of them developed a new branch of Judaism, the Conservative movement. Led by Rabbi Sabato Morais, founder of the Jewish Theological Seminary in New York, and then by Solomon Schechter, this group retained much of the old ritual as well as Hebrew prayers and readings, but it dropped outmoded customs—such as segregating women from men in the synagogue—and eased English into the service. Like Reformism, Conservatism grew out of the junction between the immigration experience and the American urban environment.

Despite differences in origin, skills, and religion, most of the foreigners who came to American cities between 1840 and 1920 shared several characteristics. First, they were a long way from home. Although the immigrants brought some of their "cultural baggage" with them, the journey across land and sea left behind old ways of life—village communalism and activities directed by the changing seasons. Meanwhile their new urban surroundings confounded their lives with polyglot streets, a regulated workday, the uncertainties of housing and employment. Their own disorientation plus external pressures, including native disdain and bigotry, forced the immigrants back upon themselves into a search for self-identity. The search inevitably led them to their origins. Regional loyalties coexisted with newly constructed national self-definitions. People from County Galway and County Cork became Irishmen; those from Mecklenburg and Württemberg became Germans; and those from Calabria and Campania became Italians. Provincial loyalties underlay a rich associational life, and regional rivalries persisted, but all Germans could read the same foreign-language newspapers, and Italians from different villages could take communion together. Moreover, native Americans nearly always grouped immigrants by their nationality (or, in the case of Jews, by their culture)—a tendency resulting from innocent classification and vicious stereotyping.

Second, nearly all who came to America during the years of mass immigration were lured by the promise of economic opportunity. The dream of land drove many, but more were attracted by the hope of jobs in the growing cities, for jobs meant money, and money meant security, something rare to the European peasant. Overall migration from Europe was sensitive to the American economy, rising in times of job surplus, falling in times of recession. Many immigrants were advised by prior migrants as to specific employment opportunities in specific cities. For example, from the 1890s to the 1930s a steady stream of Italians from the village of Ateleta, Abruzzi, came to the Bloomfield section of Pittsburgh to work in the pipe construction department of the Equitable Gas Company. Many immigrants came to this country with no intention of remaining. Once here, however, the vast majority never realized their schemes of working for a while and returning home in affluence. "After six months," said an Italian who arrived in 1907, "I wanted to go back. What held me was that I didn't have enough money to go back." Still there was an often ignored current of migration from the eastern ports back to Europe. Although government statistics concerning this movement were not kept until after 1908, there is some evidence that many foreigners remigrated, especially during hard times. Some even shuttled back and forth across the Atlantic to take advantage of seasonal wage differences. Return migration became especially feasible from the 1870s onward, when steamships rendered ocean passage safer and faster and made more European ports accessible to America. It has been estimated that for every 100 aliens who entered the United States between 1820 and 1870, 10 to 20 left the country. The figures for 1870 to 1900 and 1900 to 1914 are 24 per 100 and 33 to 40 per 100, respectively.

A third characteristic common to both the "old" and "new" immigrants was their propensity to live initially in the older, inner districts of a city. The Irish and Germans began to arrive just as the transportation and industrial revolutions were creating the modern city with its expanded residential area and segregation of social groups. This urban transformation left almost all cheap housing in the city cores. Especially after 1850 the concentration of urban employment in industrial districts strongly influenced the location and characteristics of the residential areas of new immigrants, most of whom sought low-cost housing close to their places of employment. Heavy concentrations of foreigners appeared in New York's Lower East Side, Boston's North End, Chicago's West Side, Los Angeles's East Side barrio, and the inner wards of Pittsburgh, Cincinnati, St. Louis, Buffalo, and San Francisco. Immigrant enclaves, composed of Italians from the same province, Japanese from the same island district, or Russian Jews from the same *shtetl* (village) were part of working-class wards. The neighborhoods provided fertile ground for ethnic businesses, churches, mutual aid societies, fraternal associations, and newspapers. These ethnic institutions, as well as friendship and kinship relationships in the crowded neighborhoods, reinforced identification with common origins. Neighborhood businesses also provided more accessible economic opportunities for members of the same ethnic group.

At the end of the nineteenth century a third population movement began—the migration of blacks from the rural South to the urban North and West. These people were native born, but their impact upon cities became just as important as that of the flood of foreign immigration. As of 1890 well over 90 percent of blacks lived in the South. But that year migration to the North began to accelerate. Trapped in rural debt peonage, southern-born black people moved in gradually wider and wider circles to earn supplemental wages. Many moved in search of work first to southern cities. Between 1880 and 1900 the black population of Memphis tripled and that of Chattanooga grew by 600 percent. More blacks, however, followed rail and water routes into expanding commercial and industrial centers in the North. Once they had reached their destination, they too encouraged relatives and friends to join them, supplying them with information about wage rates and job selection. In 1900 there were thirty-two cities with more than ten thousand black inhabitants, and of all blacks who lived in the North and West 70 percent could be found in urban areas. In 1910 Washington, D.C., had the largest black population of any city in the country. New York was close behind, Philadelphia fifth, and Chicago eighth. By 1920 New York, Philadelphia, and Chicago ranked first, second, and fourth. Moreover, newer cities such as Denver, Oklahoma City, and Los Angeles experienced phenomenal increases in their black population.

Although blacks resembled foreign migrants in their peasant backgrounds, their urban destinations, and their economic motivations, several factors distinguished them. Because they were generally excluded from factory work and thus could not utilize kin to help them get industrial jobs, blacks in cities had to rely on their own resources if they wanted to improve their circumstances. Education provided what appeared to be the best path to such improvement, and blacks expressed their self-reliance and hopes for their children through strikingly high school-attendance rates. By 1920 in Pennsylvania, 84.5 percent of black males aged fourteen and fifteen enrolled in school compared to only 72 percent of adolescent males of foreign-born parents. Black adolescent girls were more likely to be in school in their midteens than immigrant girls. In New York and New Jersey black attendance rates also exceeded those of immigrant children. Blacks also had distinctive employment patterns and living arrangements. Whereas young males tended to be overrepresented in foreign groups, black women outnumbered black men in New York, Philadelphia, southern cities, and border cities around the rim of the South. As growing factory and clerical jobs attracted white women away from domestic service, black women were the only people available to take their places. Thus, at least at this time, there was a greater demand for black female labor than for black male labor in these cities. As a result a much larger proportion of black women than white held jobs. In 1900 although only one-fourth of all women in the eleven largest cities of the North worked, 46.3 percent of the black women were classified as wage earners. In New York the proportion reached 55 percent. Of all male and female blacks employed in the cities, two-thirds were engaged in what was classified as "domestic and personal service." In northern and midwestern cities the institutional structures of racism, which excluded black workers from many avenues of employment, and competition from immigrant labor concentrated black migrants in menial occupations. In Cleveland 32% of the black labor force had been engaged in skilled trades in 1870, but only 11 percent were so employed by 1910. Southern black males had a stronger grip on skilled trades than their northern brothers, owing to the relative absence of immigrant competition. In New Orleans, blacks remained strong in the building trades well into the twentieth century, and in Savannah they doubled their representation in several trades betwen 1870 and 1880. But in Boston, New York, Philadelphia, and Chicago, studies by social reformers identified the characteristics so common to black urban experience in northern and midwestern cities: higher infant mortality than for whites, higher rents for inferior quarters, and lower wages for the lowest jobs. The persistence of racial barriers in employment stymied urban migrants' hopes for advancement.

Black urban newcomers moved into black neighborhoods, which in nineteenth-century cities were characteristically scattered in several different locations. In Washington, D.C., many migrants moved into houses facing on alleys that formed into self-sufficient neighborhoods interlaced with ties of kinship and friendship. Historian Howard Rabinowitz has argued that in Atlanta, Montgomery, Nashville, Raleigh, and Richmond, patterns of segregation emerged in the period of Reconstruction as a way of protecting black institutions in the face of white racial animosity.[1] Black community organizations of men and women honeycombed the neighborhoods, providing churches, Sunday schools, adult night schools, social activities, and mutual-benefit societies to provide a cushion for sickness, death, or unemployment. By the early 1870s Richmond supported over four hundred such societies. Boston black migrants between 1870 and 1890 joined veterans' organizations, social clubs, women's clubs, music clubs, lodges, literary associations, churches, political clubs, and protest organizations. These associations proved to be critical in extending the resources of family and kin to protect migrants from the harsh racial discrimination of urban life.

It was the white evacuation of the urban core between 1890 and 1920 that led to the consolidation of black enclaves into larger areas of black-only residence. Ghettos as we know them today emerged in the early twentieth century, consolidating nineteenth-century patterns of segregation and freezing their boundaries. These teeming, densely packed residential districts, with housing decaying from years of landlords' neglect, became the womb of black urban culture. Within the ghetto, black Protestantism assumed its distinctive character. Each city had a few large black congregations of Methodists and Baptists, but numerous informal storefront churches, outgrowths of the southern experience, sprouted everywhere and became fixtures of ghetto life. In several cities an indigenous black elite arose, consisting of clergymen, small-business men, educators, lower public officials, doctors, and vice operators. These people, all men, had achieved minor success and were torn between hopes of raising their community within the larger white society and the reality of the rigid segregation imposed by that society. Though there were strong differences, in some ways this ambivalence resembled the struggle between self-identification and accommodation that occurred among immigrant Catholics and Jews.

More important than its religious institutions or the leadership it developed was the way in which the ghetto became the cultural center for all blacks. The contrast between bright store windows and ill-kept tenements on ghetto streets embodied the tensions between the promise of urban life and the barriers to black advancement, breeding frustration and despair, but the streets also offered the social and physical outlets of informal camaraderie and impromptu athletic events. Ghetto saloons offered escape into alcohol, but they also nurtured the musical expression of the black soul.

HOUSING AND HEALTH

Where to live? All migrants face this predicament, but only recently has it become a concern of public-policy makers. The requisites of housing evaded public control since this country's beginning. Thus cities made no provisions for housing the millions of newcomers who arrived in the decades that followed the Civil War. As native and foreign migrants streamed into the inner regions of northern cities, they pressed private housing markets beyond their capacities. In the late nineteenth century three out of every four city dwellers lived in rented quarters; in working-class districts the proportion was much higher. Increases in population and rising land values drove up rents and tempted landlords to squeeze every penny from their tenants. Thus inner-city rents became high, given the amount of services and space a family received for its money. The middle and upper classes could avoid this plight by buying or building houses in the outskirts, where land was cheaper. Lower-class families had to find a different solution. They frequently lacked resources to reduce costs per area. But they could reduce cost per capita by sharing their space—and their rents—with others. Countless families took in lodgers, and often two or three families occupied a single three- or four-room flat.

Builders and property owners developed several types of multiple-family structures from city to city, and the extent of crowding varied. But everywhere the private market fit supply to demand on a makeshift basis, with no assistance and little direction from public authority. Since the eighteenth century, row houses had been the most common form of housing in central Philadelphia, and after the Civil War, builders made them smaller and packed more people into them. The new-style row house was only sixteen feet wide, but a two-story building held four to six families. The same pattern appeared in Baltimore. In New England the predominant style was the three-decker—a long, narrow frame building consisting of three stories and a loft. Pleasant-looking, substantial three-deckers housed one family to a floor and often appeared in middle-class neighborhoods. But because they were among the least expensive types of housing to construct, three-deckers more frequently were located in working-class districts of Boston, Providence, Worcester, and other industrial cities. Here they housed two and three families to a floor and one each in the loft and cellar. In Chicago and St. Louis two- and three-story wooden buildings, and later brick tenements, squeezed against each other. In Detroit, Milwaukee, Memphis, and Seattle, lower-class immigrants crowded into converted warehouses, and into single-family dwellings split up for multiple-family occupancy.

New York City was unique in its acute crowding and degenerate housing. But the development of mass housing there is important because it influenced construction patterns in other cities and prompted the first

Immigrant Neighborhood Life   This photograph of a group of immigrants gathered behind a tenement in the Italian neighborhood in Providence, Rhode Island, in 1912, was taken by documentary photographer and reformer Lewis Hine. Hine's own caption for the photograph, "Housing Conditions, Rear of Republic Street," probably meant to protest a back alley strewn with trash, festooned with laundry, and packed with people. *(Courtesy Slater Mill Historic Site.)*

concerted effort for housing reform. The city plan of 1811 set a standard lot size of 25 by 100 feet over most of Manhattan Island. Thereafter these measurements rigidly determined the exchange of land and the size of buildings. In the early 1800s one of these lots might have contained a single row house or cottage inhabited by one or two families. Because the lot was so narrow the house may have abutted adjacent buildings, leaving no room for side windows. But there was light in front and behind, and enough space to accommodate four to six people. By the middle of the century population growth increase, demand, and temptation for profit may have encouraged the house's owner to convert it into a four-family unit, with two or three families living on the ground floor and one each in the attic and cellar. Because the house occupied only 40 or 50 feet of the length of the lot, there would have been room to build another house in the back yard. This dwelling could hold four families in a fashion similar to the one in the front. By the 1860s the 25-by-100-foot lot, originally plotted to hold one family, now housed eight. As this process of transformation spread across the city, the growth of slums accelerated.

But the crowding had only begun to approach its limits. Property owners met population pressure from immigration in the 1860s and 1870s by razing the old houses and replacing them with four- and six-story tenements. These buildings were usually 80 feet long and contained four apartments to a floor. Each building could hold a minimum of 16 to 24 families. Usually, however, tenants shared or sublet rooms within their apartments, so a single building would often house nearly 150 people. A 200-by-1,000-foot block filled with these buildings might contain 2,500 families. The population density of such neighborhoods was rarely equaled in even the most crowded European cities. Inside the structures living conditions were abominable. Rooms were miniscule, some barely 8 feet wide. Only those few rooms facing the front or rear had direct light and ventilation. Indoor plumbing was almost nonexistent; privies were located in cellars or along the alleys. There were no kitchens and no heat. A wood-burning stove was the only appliance, and it was usually provided by the tenants.

These conditions evoked the first concerted efforts at housing reform. Certainly not all inner neighborhoods were so squalid, and certainly New Yorkers had been concerned about the poorest areas well before the mid-nineteenth century. But the crowding, disease, vice, and crime of the inner city that seemed to multiply as immigration increased wounded the middle-class urge for propriety and clouded visions of a well-ordered, conflict-free society. In 1876, for example, the *New York Times* reported, "Young girls are found sleeping on the floor in rooms where are crowded men, women, youths, and children. Delicacy is never known, purity is lost before its meaning is understood." Beginning in the 1850s a mixed sense of alarm and optimism prodded humanitarians to seek ways of controlling the threat posed by these neighborhoods. Their alarm led reformers to investigate the facts of inner-city life and to support measures that would regulate the practices of builders and landlords. Their optimism led them to expect that better conditions would result from heightened public consciousness and enlightened capitalism.

Housing reform originated in New York City. In 1864 the Council of Hygiene of the New York Citizen's Association launched a campaign to create a new health department for the city. When the Tammany machine of Boss Tweed stymied its efforts, the council undertook an investigation of the city's housing and sanitary conditions to alert the public to the dangers of crowding and filth. Directed by Dr. Stephen Smith, a prominent physician who was a leading figure in the nation's public-health movement, the council's investigation produced an indictment of slum housing. The report raised enough publicity that when a cholera epidemic threatened in 1866, the New York General Assembly created a Metropolitan Board of Health and gave it authority to regulate housing and sanitary conditions through provisions of the Tenement House Law of 1867. This law required landlords to furnish minimum facilities for fire escape, for ventilation to interior rooms, and for indoor plumbing. The provisions were very weak (one privy per twenty inhabitants and one water tap per building satisfied the legal requirements), and enforcement was difficult, but the law had symbolic value. It imposed public regulation on a landlord's property rights, and it established a precedent for stronger codes in the future.

Before the Council of Hygiene had begun its activities, other reformers were trying to reconcile housing improvement with the aims of capitalism. Beginning in the 1850s the New York Association for Improving the Conditions of the Poor (AICP) advanced the idea of a model tenement, a type of housing in which private investors would accept lower profits for the sake of safer, healthier facilities and philanthropic service to the poor. To set an example the AICP constructed its own model tenement in 1854. Although the project failed, the idea continued to dominate housing-reform attitudes for the rest of the century because it left the provisions concerning housing to private builders.

In fact the model-tenement idea was responsible for the notorious *dumbbell* tenement that spread across New York after 1879. The dumbbell, named for its shape rather than its designer, was fashioned to meet provisions of the New York Tenement House Law of 1879, which required that every room in new tenements have a window. (The 1867 law required only that every room have *access* to a window.) An indentation on each side of the building gave it the shape of a dumbbell. The indentation, when combined with that of the adjoining building, created an air shaft five feet wide. Each tenement was five or six stories high. Each floor contained fourteen rooms, in two three-room and two four-room apartments, and two water closets in the hallway. Ten of the fourteen rooms had windows bordering the air shafts.

That the dumbbell tenement was an example of housing *reform*—it was the winning entry in a contest to determine the best mass-housing design that could fit a 25-by-100-foot lot—dramatizes the tragic state of low-income housing in New York. The largest room in any dumbbell apartment measured only 10 by 11 feet. The narrow air shaft, originally designed to provide light and air, acted as a receptacle for garbage, a breeding place for vermin and insects, and a duct for fire and noise. The major consequence of the dumbbell was not comfort, but more crowding. Between 1880 and 1893 the density of New York's tenth ward, the heart of the immigrant-filled Lower East Side, increased from 432 to 702 persons per acre. By 1893 most of the ward's 75,000 inhabitants were packed into twelve hundred tenements.

The dumbbell's rapid spread across Manhattan to Brooklyn, and to other cities, had two additional effects. One was the permanent association of the term *tenement* with working-class housing. Originally the word had applied simply to any multistory rental building housing more than three families. Now it became a term of discredit. Second, continuing deterioration of inner-city housing conditions ignited new reform crusades, not the least of which was a move to end the abuses created by dumbbell tenements.

Airshaft of a Dumbbell Tenement   This view, taken from the roof of a New York apartment house around 1900, shows how narrow the air shaft between the two dumbbell tenements actually was. Such openings could hardly provide the light and ventilation that housing reformers sought. *(Public Housing Administration, The National Archives.)*

Led by Lawrence Veiller, the nation's first full-time professional housing reformer, new investigations and outcries resulted in passage of the New York Tenement Housing Law of 1901, which revised the existing regulations. The new code replaced the dumbbell's air shaft with a longer, more open court. It also required a separate water closet for each apartment, and it provided stronger fire-protection measures. Significantly, however, these regulations applied only to *new* buildings. The law included a few weak provisions directed at improving light, ventilation, plumbing, and fireproofing in existing tenements (such as requiring landlords to install windows in windowless rooms), but it could not effectively remedy the eighty thousand tenements that covered the five boroughs of New York City.

What happened in New York occurred in other cities on a diminished and less acute scale. Multistory tenements, dumbbell or otherwise, did not appear to any great extent until the end of the century, but dilapidated shanties and cellar dwellings multiplied everywhere as swelling populations flooded the housing markets. The situation was particularly severe in Chicago, where rear tenements blighted the inner city. These were flimsy shacks constructed in the space between an alley and the rear of the building that fronted the street. Rear tenements probably constituted the worst of all inner-city housing in Chicago and New York, but they were often overlooked by reformers more concerned with larger structures. In the South much of the only housing available to blacks consisted of old, converted slave quarters that remained in yards and alleyways behind white homes. New Orleans and Charleston had their own kind of housing crisis, ignored by white humanitarians.

The successes of Veiller and New York journalists Jacob Riis and Richard W. Gilder in investigating inner-city crowding, in arousing public concern, and in prompting legislation generated similar movements in other cities. Civic organizations sponsored investigations and exhibits, and they lobbied succesfully for the establishment of housing commissions and regulatory codes in cities such as Baltimore, St. Louis, Chicago, Kansas City, San Francisco, Philadelphia, New Orleans, Los Angeles, and Washington, D.C. In some places reformers added a third scheme to their goals for building regulations and model housing. This was decentralization, the removal of poor families from high-density central cities to less congested, more inexpensive land on the urban fringe. Reformers unconsciously assumed that their vision of the appropriate residential setting was inherently superior to inner-city residents' patterns of work, family life, and sociability. Reformers hoped that new planned communities could grow up around industries that were locating outside city limits, and some applauded George Pullman's planned model factory town that opened in 1880 outside of Chicago. Located on Lake Calumet, Pullman, Illinois, included rows of brick houses situated on tree-lined streets interspersed with churches, schools, and a hotel, all within walking distance of the sleeping-car factory, and, like the factory, owned by Pullman. However, worker dissatisfaction with Pullman's control over their rents and politics as well as their jobs provided the fuel for the railroad strike of 1894. Sparked by Pullman's cutting wages in the shops while holding rents and prices steady, the strike, although eventually lost, contributed to the town's decline. Thereafter large corporations generally shied away from building decentralized new towns. Planning and housing were returned to private real-estate speculators. Schemes to build towns on the model of Ebenezer Howard's English "garden cities" fizzled from lack of capital. The new small projects that were begun, such as the Russell Sage Foundation's Forest Hills Garden in Queens, New York, in 1911, could not reduce costs enough to attract working-class inhabitants. Decentralization, like housing codes and model tenements, never met the expectations of its proponents.

Efforts by reformers to improve housing conditions for low-income people often reflected middle-class values and in doing so raised opposition among urban dwellers who held different values. Many could not afford rents for rooms in improved buildings, and tighter housing codes only made their situations more difficult. Because their buildings were cheap to buy and provided high rates of return, some tenement dwellers saw themselves as potential tenement owners. Costly improvements required by re-form codes discouraged investors from purchasing tenements and blocked an avenue of economic mobility for some lower-class individuals. More-over, reform efforts to lessen crowding within buildings by limiting the number of people who could live in one apartment threatened the institu-tion of boarding, one of the most pervasive and important forms of inner-city habitation.

The strongest restraint on housing reform was the privatism that governed prevailing attitudes toward property. Americans have always con-sidered the management and disposal of land and buildings as a sacred civil right. Any interference with this right came to constitute a threat to a cultural inheritance. Thus not only did landlords resist and evade housing codes (which tended to be poorly enforced anyway), but also humanitarian reformers avoided any interference with the housing market. Public agen-cies could neither demolish dilapidated and dangerous buildings nor con-struct adequate housing for low-income citizens. Eventually, by expanding their police powers and their privileges of eminent domain, governments did begin to assume greater responsibilities for furnishing public housing. As later chapters will suggest, many of these efforts were clumsy, costly, and even detrimental. Nevertheless government initiative was a generally necessary, though late, improvement. During the nineteenth century pri-vate builders and speculators had assumed by default the responsibility for housing urban immigrants. Their profit motives dictated maximizing reve-nues and minimizing expenditures. The results were crowding, filth, and disease for the half of the population least capable of improving its lot. Genuine humanitarianism, coupled with fear of disorder, spawned reform crusades. Although these efforts met with at best partial success, they at least established greater public responsibility for the health and safety of all a city's inhabitants.

Although housing reforms improved life in inner-city neighbor-hoods only slightly, public health professionals and municipal engineers made cities safer and healthier. Concern over housing and public health had much in common. Countless surveys revealed that death rates in slum areas were two to three times those in other urban districts. Congestion and poorly constructed housing amplified all the problems of urban life: ventila-tion, fire prevention, sewage disposal, water purification, personal hygiene, and control of disease. Advances in engineering and medicine reduced dangers in almost all these areas, and legislative bodies were willing to use public police power to control and to prevent threats to public safety. Sig-nificantly, these advances occurred most readily in cities because only cities had the resources and institutions that could make their implementation feasible.

Discoveries by the European scientists Koch, Lister, and Pasteur con-vinced most of the western world that tiny organisms called bacteria caused specific diseases, such as cholera, typhoid, diphtheria, and tuberculosis. This evidence strengthened the link between sanitation and public health. Since colonial times sanitarians and boards of health had emphasized the need for personal and public cleanliness. Support for sanitation intensified as slum areas spread in the 1860s and 1870s. Efforts of men like Dr. Edwin Snow of Providence and George E. Waring, Jr., of New York, who crusaded for public hygiene and for improved sewer systems, succeeded in reducing mortality rates in American cities even more after bacteriology won wide acceptance. As knowledge of the germ theory became more common in the 1880s and 1890s, the stature of the medical profession rose, and state and municipal boards of health (many of which had been established in the aftermath of cholera, typhoid, and yellow-fever epidemics that had ravaged scores of cities during the nineteenth century) could apply scientific certainty to the enforcement of cleanliness regulations.

Increasing knowledge about the origins of diseases also fostered public activities in the field of preventive medicine. Beginning in the 1890s a number of cities established diagnostic laboratories in order to analyze the incidence of certain diseases and to try to avert their spread. Meat and milk inspections were tightened. Local and state health departments sponsored education programs to alert the public to the causes and prevention of disease. Newspapers, pamphlets, lectures, and school programs explained contagion, personal hygiene, and proper diets. Around the turn of the century various clinics and dispensaries were opened. They provided information on baby care and dental hygiene, and they offered assistance to those suffering from tuberculosis, venereal disease, and minor injuries. Although they brought needed services to many neighborhoods, especially in New York, the clinics and dispensaries functioned mainly as charity institutions. Restoring the health of the poor would save tax dollars by helping to maintain the labor force and might keep the epidemic diseases of poor districts from spreading to well-to-do neighborhoods.

In addition to medical advances, improvements in fire protection and in other utilities increased public safety. The Great Chicago Fire, which consumed nearly 1,700 acres and destroyed over $200 million in property in 1871, and the huge conflagration that swept Boston in 1872 were evidence that fire remained the principal threat to urban safety. New building codes, architectural developments, and more professional fire-fighting forces began to lessen this danger. New buildings increasingly included fire walls, fire barriers, and steel-frame, fire-resistant construction (however, most of these buildings were too expensive for the poor). Much of the drive for better fire protection was spearheaded by the National Board of Fire Underwriters, organized in 1866. The NBFU adopted a nationwide policy of drawing local maps, examining ordinances, and inspecting fire-fighting equipment as determinants of local insurance rates. This practice stirred cities to upgrade their building codes and fire departments. City governments began to purchase steam engines and pumping machinery and to install electric fire-alarm boxes, as well as to expand their fire-fighting personnel. In addition to fire protection, electricity (especially its use for lighting) and sewer construction promised new benefits in urban health and safety.

By the early twentieth century the United States had achieved the highest standards of mass urban living in the world. But neither the benefits nor the facilities reached all city dwellers evenly. By the 1870s most municipalities had assumed responsibilities for constructing water and sewerage systems and for insuring public health. But public responsibility virtually ended at the borders of private property. Landlords and builders who wanted water and sewers had to pay for connections between their buildings and the water main and trunk-line sewer. Owners of newly developed property were assessed for public improvements according to the amount of their land that abutted a street. Those who could afford such facilities, or whose tenants could absorb the costs in their rent, readily installed modern plumbing, heating, and lighting. But for those forced into high-density, low-quality dwellings modern amenities were much scarcer. Inner-city landlords, eager to maximize profits, tried to avoid expensive improvements. And governments remained reluctant to enter the sanctum of housing construction and property management. Thus inner-city residents, most of them newcomers and most of them poor, were at the mercy of the housing market. Over time some of the improvements in sanitation and housing construction trickled down to the poorest neighborhoods. For most people, however, the best solution was to escape, to somehow acquire a home beyond the inner core, or to pack up and take a chance that things would be better elsewhere.

SOCIAL CONFIGURATIONS OF INNER CITY LIFE

People, crowded into too little space, created the problems in housing, health, and safety outlined above. But on the other hand the urban cores themselves transformed the everyday lives of their inhabitants. The congestion, the streets and neighborhoods, the housing and job markets—all necessitated personal, family, and community adjustments. Some were easy and salutary. They were part of the socialization process that enabled American cities to absorb a variety of peoples and cultures without too much trauma. Other adjustments left scars.

Unlike the residents of the periphery or suburbs, whose environment consisted of detached single-family houses, slum dwellers seldom knew privacy. Blocks with tenements jammed together, buildings housing a score of families, and apartments inhabited by a dozen people determined personal behavior and development. People had to endure the ways of others who lived so close by. Toleration was not always easy; the terrible strain from inadequate space and facilities tried tempers and created frequent opportunities for misunderstandings. Domestic squabbles and neighborhood fights were common. The shared spaces that helped generate sociability also created the conditions for quarrels. Observers from the middle class, accustomed to spacious surroundings and little public scrutiny, rarely understood how the circumstances of neighborhood life bred strong emotions that included shouting and fighting as a part of working-class culture.

Crowding also complicated modes of living outside the tenements. In many areas each apartment building covered almost the entire lot on which it was built, leaving no room for recreational activity. Housing reformers urged that at least 35 percent of each residential lot be left open, but they could not undo the past and their guidelines were usually ignored. Yards, vacant lots, and playgrounds remained scarce. Children were forced either into the streets, where traffic interrupted their play and threatened their safety, or onto the roofs, where they found privacy but faced more danger. Adults who wished to escape the tenements went to the neighborhood saloon, a custom that unnerved middle-class reformers. Yet by providing not only liquor but also newspapers, cards, singing, free lunch, drinking water, and public toilets, the saloon served inner-city men's needs more than any other institution. In working-class neighborhoods, bars were places where men relaxed, traded information, gossiped, and organized everything from political campaigns to labor unions to funerals. Many workingmen used the saloon as a mailing address, as a place to leave and pick up messages and meet friends, and as a bank, depositing money, cashing checks, or borrowing from the saloon keeper. In spite of the drunkenness and occasional violence that it fostered, the neighborhood saloon proved to be one of the most durable features of the urban environment.

To obtain minimal food and shelter, working-class families pieced together an income from the labor of all family members. Urban women found that their household work had an increased economic value; without gardens, the cost of feeding a family depended on women's skills in bargaining with grocers, fishmongers, and butchers. When the rent was due would depend on women's skills at cajoling landlords. Women and children also exploited whatever opportunities presented themselves for generating income, such as cooking and cleaning for boarders and lodgers, mopping the steps and halls of tenements, washing laundry, peddling food, and helping out in neighborhood shops. Women and children worked alongside men in tenement sweatshops, where whole families would be engaged in the production of clothing, cigars, artificial flowers, or foodstuffs, working long hours for low wages. Where it was available, women and children also did industrial manufacturing at home, finishing pants, carding snaps, linking chains, shelling nuts, stringing rosary beads, pulling lace threads for pennies an hour. One investigator found three- and four-year-olds aiding a cigar-making operation by straightening tobacco leaves and putting lids on boxes. Reformers were always horrified to find women and children working at home both because of the obvious exploitation and because such labor violated their norms of appropriate family life. Earning money while at the same time tending their ongoing responsibilities for cooking and child rearing exhausted homeworkers, but working together as a family at home was part of how working-class families taught their children to survive. As one immigrant remembered, doing homework was part of how she and her siblings "were raised to work every minute."

Certainly the housing and work patterns of the inner-city influenced household composition and family relationships. Residence in a single-family house rather than in quarters shared with others has been a traditional American value. Historians have only begun to uncover the household patterns of past eras, but it seems quite clear that this norm seldom occurred in the urban cores. The great majority of *families* (kin grouping) were nuclear in structure, consisting only of the head of the household, spouse, and children all living in one place. But a large number of inner-city *households* (including *all* the people inhabiting one residential unit) contained lodgers and boarders. Evidence has revealed that at any point in time about one-fourth of all urban households contained nonfamily residents. Countless city dwellers—perhaps the majority—boarded or lodged with others for at least a few years during their lives. The most common pattern was for young people, usually unmarried migrants who had left their parents' households, to board with an older family whose children were grown. Sometimes, however, whole families boarded. Lodgers frequently stayed until they could obtain quarters of their own, but a number of individuals spent most of their adulthood living with others, either lodging in one place for a long time or shifting from board to board, city to city. Lodging houses and boardinghouses were also common in most cities. Middle-class and working-class families frequently took in boarders to help pay the rent. European immigrants and black migrants often lodged newly arrived relatives and fellow villagers until they could establish themselves. Boarders were often also related to people in the households that lodged them, which meant that alleys and tenements that appeared to reformers as crowded horrors of social disorganization and chaos were more likely to be complex webs of kinship and friendship. Creating networks of mutual assistance by turning kin into neighbors was one of the ways that migrants shaped their residential space and added to their resources as families.

Housing reformers charged that boarding caused overcrowding and loss of privacy. Yet for those who boarded, the practice was highly useful. As one immigrant woman recalled:

> We had four boarders and I had to cook for them. When I first came here I didn't want to do this because everybody want to have their own house. Well,

I change my mind because everybody was doing this thing. That time some
of the people that came from the other side didn't have no place to stay and
we took some of the people in the house that we knew. . . . This is the way
that everybody used to do it that time.

Boarding was a transitional stage, providing boarders with a quasi-family
environment until they set up their own households, easing migrants' struggle with anonymity in a strange city. And it gave the household flexibility,
bringing in extra income to meet its needs.

Approximately 15 or 20 percent of households included extended
family members, parents, siblings, aunts, uncles, and cousins, who lived as
quasi boarders. Often a family would take in a widow or unmarried sister or
brother who would otherwise have had to live alone. Immigrants and migrants often doubled up with family who had preceded them to a city
during the months or years while they were in the process of getting settled.
Even when relatives did not live in the same household, they often lived
nearby. The kind of triple-decker housing commonly built as migrants
crowded into cities was particularly well-suited to the exchange of services
such as shopping, child care, advice, and consolation. Women migrants
particularly benefited from this exchange of assistance.

The obligations of kinship, however, were not always welcome or
even helpful. Immigrant families often put pressure on last-born children
to stay at home and care for aging parents, a practice that could stifle
opportunities for education, marriage, and economic independence. As an
aging Italian-American father confessed, "One of our daughters is an old
maid [and] causes plenty of troubles. . . . It may be my fault because I
always wished her to remain at home and not to marry for she was of great
financial help." Tensions also developed when one relative felt that another
was not helping out enough. One woman, for example, complained that
her brother-in-law "resented the fact that I saved my money in a bank
instead of handing it over to him." Nevertheless, kinship, for better or for
worse, provided migrant families with an important set of resources for
coping with the demands of urban industrial life. Urbanization, industrialization, and migration did not crack the resilience of family life.

Although the city actually reinforced or augmented family life in
several ways, the pressures of poverty and inner-city housing still threatened family solidarity. When they entered the urban job market, most
migrant men and women took manual employment that was both dangerous and physically wearing. Long hours of work in poor lighting and poor
ventilation induced mental lapses that had harmful results. The incidence
of industrial accidents was high in many cities, and there was no compensation to support families whose breadwinners or other members were killed
or incapacitated. Moreover, men or women who worked eighty or ninety
hours a week without proper rest and nourishment fell easy prey to tubercu-

losis, pneumonia, and other diseases. The death of the father of a working-class family at the age of thirty or thirty-five was a common occurrence. Widowhood among black and immigrant groups was more than a stereotype; it was a reality.

Migration, city life, and poverty also touched children. The need for supplementary family income pressed many children into the labor market at early ages. Others, who did not have jobs but whose parents worked twelve to fourteen hours a day, roamed the streets away from adult supervision. Some of them became *street Arabs,* homeless youths who slept in stairwells and begged in the streets. Older youths joined gangs, formal groupings of both boys and girls that cultivated peer-group solidarity but that also harassed merchants, antagonized police, and frightened neighborhoods with their defiant activities. But the child laborers, the vagrant boys, and the gangs were minorities. By the end of the nineteenth century most inner-city children went to public schools. Yet here too problems arose, especially among immigrant generations. Children of foreign-born (or even of native-born rural) parents were caught between two worlds. Although the public schools taught values of independence and self-made opportunity, parents often demanded that their children remain obedient and useful family members who would set aside self-fulfillment in favor of working for the benefit of the entire family. Those who chose the schools assimilated more easily into the native middle-class cultural mainstream. Those who held on to their parents' values remained within their ethnic social structure and were generally less upwardly mobile, although there were important exceptions in the areas of politics and crime.

Immigrant and black mothers had special responsibilities for carrying on ethnic and religious cultural traditions, maintaining family responsibilities in caring for kin, and contributing to a family economy. Mothers' rates of labor-force participation varied by race, ethnicity, husband's income, resources for caring for children at home, and urban occupational structure. In all cities black women left their homes to work as domestics, and in some cities Irish and Polish wives toiled outside their homes as domestics or in factories. Italian wives in Buffalo worked with their children as family crews in vineyards and in canning factories, and Mexican-American women worked with their families as farm laborers and in food-processing plants. Most unmarried daughters had opportunities for a wider range of jobs (as sales clerks, for example) than did their mothers, who were more confined by maternal responsibilities and community norms. In some cities at least two out of three young women had worked before marriage. Rates of labor-force participation after marriage were more varied, depending on class, ethnic group, and local economies.

Several demographic and social factors bonded family members closer to each other than they are today. First, parents had more children—often four to six, compared with two or three today. Thus there were more

Women's Work in the City   The spread of mass production techniques meant that many women, such as these workers at National Cash Register Company in Dayton, Ohio, photographed in 1902, had expanded opportunities for wage work outside the home by the early twentieth century. *(Library of Congress.)*

siblings spread along the age continuum, which enabled older children to tend to the needs of younger brothers and sisters. Moreover, women's childbearing spans were much longer than they are currently: in the nineteenth century women began to bear children in their early or mid twenties and often did not have their last child until they were in their late thirties or early forties. Thus childbearing lasted for twelve to fifteen years, compared with five or so more recently. This long span meant that at least some children were growing up and living at home when their parents were in their late fifties and early sixties, and thus that parental responsibilities consumed almost all the adult lives of married men and women. When a parent died young, it was not unusual, particularly in an immigrant household, to find a thirty-five or forty-year-old unmarried son or daughter living at home with the widow or widower.

Today lower fertility and shorter childbearing spans have magnified age differences between parents and children, and people depend on social security and other government institutions in their old age, but a century ago both culture and demography narrowed the gap between generations and linked siblings to each other. Emotional ties within the family may not have been stronger; indeed the sacrifices that people had to make to fulfill family obligations may have engendered resentment. Nevertheless the urban family was a much different institution in size and organization than it would become in the twentieth century.

Movement to and residence within the inner city influenced social and cultural groups consisting of many individuals, many families. How much cultural baggage did immigrants bring with them? How much did life in the city change long-held cultural patterns? Certainly immigrants, particularly those from abroad, sought anchors of familiarity upon arriving in American cities. They often tried to live near friends and relatives. Whole villages were transferred from the Italian or East European countryside to New York, Philadelphia, and Chicago. Chinese migrants from the Panyu district dominated the Chinatown in Hanford, California, and the Teng (or Ong) clan from Kaiping settled in Phoenix, Arizona. The perpetuation of institutions, feasts, and pageants helped sustain memories of the homeland. Reformers, concerned with the poverty of immigrants, often overlooked the richness of group life that many immigrants sustained.

This group solidarity affected the larger urban society as well as daily life in the inner city. In factories immigrants often segregated themselves in individual departments, perpetuating their separation by recruiting fellow ethnics into similar jobs. In the steel mills of Steelton, Pennsylvania, in 1910, for example, native-born Americans plus Irish and Germans concentrated in the most skilled, highest paying jobs while blacks, Croats, and Serbs clustered in the lowest paying and most dangerous departments. On the job, wage earners of all types had similar interests in opposing exploitation by owners and managers and in obtaining better wages and safer and more secure working conditions. Off the job, immigrants withdrew into their own social organizations, neighborhood saloons, and churches. The American Federation of Labor, the main form of labor organization in the late nineteenth and early twentieth centuries, was not interested in organizing unskilled workers, which in practice meant black and immigrant male and female labor. There were moments when groups of workers outside of mainstream union organization crossed ethnic lines to work together in a strike: steelworkers in McKees Rocks, Pennsylvania, in 1909; textile workers in Lawrence, Massachusetts, in 1912; copper miners in southeast Arizona in 1915, all built coalitions that crossed ethnic lines to demand recognition of workers' prerogatives. But in other circumstances, ethnic loyalties precluded cooperation, and corporate use of Asian and black workers as strikebreakers seemed to confirm unions' racist exclusion. Ethnic and racial difference has been a part of the legacy of the American labor movement that has distinguished it from its European counterparts.

Yet no group could live in isolation. Socially complex cities fostered contact and exchange between people. They altered old customs and spawned new institutions. The necessity of learning the English language, Americanization campaigns, new patterns of employment, and the bustle of the streets all undermined attempts to re-create an unchanged Old World culture. The voluntary nature of churchgoing in America tended to foster democratization and sectarianism among all religious groups, diluting dogma and elevating personal religious experience. Larger workplaces, the Democratic party, and public schools drew urban people together across ethnic boundaries. Commercial amusements like baseball, vaudeville, and movies gave disparate ethnic groups common exposure to American mass culture, although different audiences responded to the experience in ways that reflected their various cultural traditions. As they could afford them, immigrants filled their homes with mass-produced buffets and sideboards that substituted for traditional dowry chests, and plush upholstered Grand Rapids furniture and voluminous draping that replaced hand-crafted ornamentation. Chosen furnishings were part of immigrants' and their children's attempts to come to terms with American ways, to claim the good life that America promised, to assert that they were at home in urban America.

For over a century many Americans have viewed the ethnic neighborhood as one of the strongest institutions of inner-city life. The urge for familiarity and cultural identity drove immigrants to seek out their own kind. Very quickly colonies of distinct nationalities formed, most noticeably in cities at or near ports of entry, but also in interior cities from Cleveland to Chicago to Denver. There were Little Italys, Bohemiantowns, Jewish sections, Greek districts, and other "ghettos," as these colonies came to be called. The ghettos softened the shock of migration and prepared immigrants for merger into American culture. Yet most of them were neither as stable nor as monolithic as most people thought, because the high incidence of residential mobility kept them in constant flux. Only rarely did one immigrant group constitute a majority of residents in an area one-half to one square mile in size. Little Italy and Polish Town might have contained a plurality of Italians and Poles, but seldom a majority. Moreover rapid residential mobility scattered residents of these districts to other parts of the city or to other cities, so even the most homogeneous neighborhoods experienced rapid turnover. They appeared stable only because people moving in were of the same nationality as those moving out. A 1915 survey of Italian and Polish districts in Chicago revealed that nearly half the residents moved each year. And a study of Omaha at the turn of the century has shown that members of all ethnic groups who remained in the city fanned out from the central city into many outlying districts well within the span of one generation.

Thus for most immigrant families residence in a particular ghetto was not a lasting experience. In some cities, principally New York and the congested industrial cities of the Northeast, pockets of single groups did

A Market on the Lower East Side Warren Dickerson's view of Hester Street in New York around 1900 scans a street lined with Jewish shops and peddlers. This photograph reveals the vitality of immigrant life in the city, an informality that is often viewed with nostalgia today. *(History Division, Natural History Museum of Los Angeles County.)*

form, and when the immigrants moved, they transferred their whole colony to another district. But generally, residential experiences of immigrants involved dispersion into a number of ethnically mixed neighborhoods. The ghetto's major importance was cultural. In most places an area's institutions and enterprises, more than the people who actually lived there, identified it as an ethnic neighborhood. A certain part of town, familiar and accessible to a particular group, became the location of its churches, clubs, bakeries, meat markets, and other establishments. Some members of the group lived nearby, while others lived farther away but could travel there on streetcars or on foot. Thus some of the secondary business centers that formed at the intersections of mass-transit routes became locations of ethnic business and social activity. A Bohemian town, for example, received its name because it was the location of Swoboda's Bakery, Cermak's Drug Store, Cecha's Jewelry, Knezacek's Meats, St. Wenceslaus Church, and the Bohemian Benevolent Association. Such institutions gave a district an ethnic identity even though the surrounding neighborhoods were mixed and in flux.

If the term *ghetto* is defined as a place of enforced residence from which escape is at best difficult, only nonwhites in this era had a true ghetto experience. Wherever Asians and Mexicans immigrated, they encountered discrimination in housing, occupations, and other areas of public life. Though these groups often preferred to remain separate in Chinatowns and *barrios,* white Americans made every effort to keep them confined. In the 1880s the city of San Francisco tried to prohibit Chinese laundries from locating in most neighborhoods, and in 1906 its school board tried to isolate Japanese children in special schools. Restrictive covenants kept blacks, Asians, and Chicanos from buying property in various areas. Chinese were refused service in barber shops, hotels, and restaurants. Chicanos were restricted to certain schools and specially designated sections of movie theaters.

Prejudice and discrimination not only trapped blacks at the bottom of the occupational ladder but also operated in housing markets to limit their residential opportunities. Whites organized protective associations that pledged not to sell homes in white neighborhoods to blacks and occasionally used violent harassment to scare away black families who did move in. Such efforts seldom worked. Whites who lived on the edges of black neighborhoods often fled, leaving their homes and apartments to be sold and rented to black occupants. In almost every city, totally black residential districts expanded while native white and ethnic neighborhoods dissolved. By 1920 ten Chicago census tracts were over three-fourths black. In Detroit, Cleveland, Los Angeles, and Washington, D.C., two-thirds or more of the total black population lived in only two or three wards. Within these districts, blacks nurtured distinct cultural institutions that reinforced racial unity. Some individuals and organizations sounded a new note of militance after 1890. Activities ranged from boycotts against segregated streetcars in the South to support for black entrepreneurship and retaliation against white violence in the North. But the ghettos also bred frustration, stunted opportunity, and perpetuated racial bigotry. Color, more than any other factor, made the urban experiences of blacks different from those of whites. Color was not cultural baggage; it was an indelible legacy.

PATTERNS OF SOCIAL MOBILITY

If immigrants came off the farms and from abroad seeking security and an improvement in their life-styles, what were the chances that these hopes would be fulfilled? At the end of the nineteenth century beliefs remained strong that there was an open road from the bottom of society to the top, or at least to the middle. The century's expanding industrial economy spun off new jobs, new markets, new areas for investment. Although hard times punctured the booms with unprecedented frequency—there were serious, though temporary, declines in each of the four decades preceding World War I—the euphoria of expansion soothed harsh memories.

Yet dark clouds persisted. By the late nineteenth century the spread of slum decay, the power and impersonality of giant factories, and the ever widening gulf between rich and poor withered the dreams of many. In addition the social complexity, churning neighborhoods, and competition for space and jobs so common to city life fanned hostilities between newcomers and those who considered themselves guardians of the "American Way." Many people came to fear that immigrants were displacing native workers, driving down wage rates, deteriorating residential districts, subverting traditional morality, and threatening political order. Newspapers and even some "scientific" theories reinforced vicious stereotypes of Italians as swarthy and stupid, Irish as lazy and drunkardly, Jews as greedy and cunning. In the 1880s influential reformers such as Charles Loring Brace and Josiah Strong voiced strong fears that heightened waves of foreign newcomers would bring down American civilization. After the turn of the century Madison Grant, a trustee of the New York Museum of Natural History, warned that among the new immigrants were

> a large and increasing number of the weak, the broken and the mentally crippled of all races drawn from the lowest stratum of the Mediterranean basin of the Balkans, together with the hordes of the wretched, submerged populations of the Polish ghettos. Our jails, insane asylums and almshouses are filled with this human flotsam and the whole tone of American life, social, moral, and political, has been lowered and vulgarized by them.

These beliefs plus the activities of nativist organizations, such as the American Protective Association and the American Patriotic League, impeded immigrants' (particularly Catholics') chances for betterment. In addition racism stifled the opportunities of blacks in southern and northern cities and pinned them to the very bottom of urban society.

The major purpose of migration has been to seek the road to a better future. Basically there were three ways a person could get ahead: occupational advancement (and the higher income that accompanied it), property acquisition (and the potential for greater wealth it represented), and migration to an area of better conditions and greater opportunity. These options were open chiefly to white men. Although many women worked, owned property, and migrated, their social standing was usually defined by the men in their lives—their husbands, fathers, or other kin. Many women did improve their economic status by marrying men with wealth or potential, but other avenues were mostly closed. Men and women who were Afro-American, American Indian, Hispanic-American, or Asian-American had even fewer opportunities for success. Disadvantaged by institutional structures of racism, these groups were expected to accept their inherited station.

To a large number of people, however, the urban and industrial expansion of the late nineteenth century should have offered broad opportunity for occupational mobility. Thousands of small businesses were needed to supply goods and services to burgeoning urban populations. As corporations grew larger and centralized their operations, they required new managerial personnel. Although capital for a large business was hard

Commerce Comes to a Residential Street   Peddlers display household goods for housewives' inspection and children's curiosity in Somerville, Massachusetts, a primarily working-class community near Boston, in 1905. *(The Boston Public Library.)*

to obtain, a person could open a saloon or small store for only $200 to $300. And knowledge of accounting or typing could qualify one for a number of white-collar jobs that sometimes paid better and were more secure employment than manual labor. Thus nonmanual work and the higher social status that tended to accompany it were possible.

Such advancement occurred often. To be sure, only a few traveled the rags-to-riches path that men like Andrew Carnegie and Henry Ford had discovered. Studies of the era's wealthiest businessmen have shown that the vast majority started their careers with distinct advantages: American birth, Protestant religion, better-than-average education, and relatively affluent parents. Yet considerable movement occurred along the path from rags to moderate success as men climbed from manual to nonmanual jobs or saw their children do so. Thus personal successes like that of Meyer Grossman, a Russian immigrant to Omaha, Nebraska, who worked as a teamster before saving enough to open a successful furniture store, were common.

Rates of occupational mobility in late nineteenth- and early twentieth-century American communities were slow but steady. Constant economic change and growth vitalized urban job markets, especially for skilled and white-collar labor. To be sure, mechanization and new products pushed some callings into obsolescence, but the expansion of other areas more than compensated for the contraction. In new, fast-growing cities such as Atlanta, Los Angeles, and Omaha, approximately one in five manual workers rose to white-collar or owner's positions within ten years—provided they stayed in the city that long. In older northeastern cities like Boston and Newburyport, upward mobility averaged closer to one in six in ten years. Some people slipped from a higher to a lower rung of the occupational ladder, but rates of upward movement were almost always double the downward rates. Although patterns were far from consistent, immigrants generally experienced lower rates of upward mobility and higher rates of downward mobility than natives did. Still, regardless of birthplace, the chances for a white male to rise occupationally over the course of his career or to have a higher-status job than his father had were relatively good. This trend was reinforced by the influx of unskilled newcomers—immigrants in northern cities, blacks in southern cities—who filled the lower ranks of the labor force and formed a base on which others could climb.

It must be remembered, however, that what constitutes a better job depends on an individual's definition of improvement and desires. Many an immigrant artisan, such as a German carpenter or an Italian shoemaker, would have considered an accountant's job demeaning and unproductive. People with long traditions of pride in manual labor neither wanted nonmanual jobs nor encouraged their children to seek them. As one Italian tailor explained, "I learned the tailoring business in the old country. Over here, in America, I never have trouble finding a job because I know my business from the other side[Italy]. . . . I want that my oldest boy learn my trade because I tell him that you could always make at least enough for the family."

Moreover, business ownership entailed risks. Rates of failure were high among shopkeepers, saloon owners, and the like because business was so uncertain. Thus many manual workers sought security rather than mobility, preferring a steady job to the risks of ownership. A Sicilian who lived in Bridgeport, Connecticut, observed that "the people that come here they afraid to get in business because they don't know how that business goes. In Italy these people don't know much about these things because most of them work on farms or in [their] trade."

In addition to or instead of advancing occupationally a person could achieve social mobility by acquiring property. But property was not easy to acquire in turn-of-the-century America. Banks and savings institutions were far stricter in their lending practices than they would become after the 1930s, when the federal government began to insure real-estate financing. Mortgage loans carried relatively high interest rates and short repayment periods. Thus renting, even of single-family houses, was common, especially in big cities. Nevertheless a general rise in wage rates enabled many families to build savings accounts, which could be used as down payments on property. Particularly in northeastern cities, small building and loan associations financed home ownership for working-class families. Philadelphia had four hundred of these associations by the 1870s. Among working-class families who stayed in Newburyport for as long as ten years a third to a half managed to accumulate some property; two-thirds did so within twenty years. In 1900, 36.3 percent of urban families owned their homes. There were significant ethnic variations. In Pittsburgh, for example, homeowners included over 30 percent of foreign-born whites, nearly 24 percent of native-born whites, and only 8.4 percent of black households.

Finally, each year millions of families tried to improve their living conditions by packing up and moving elsewhere. As early as 1847 a foreign visitor, amazed by American transiency, wrote, "If God were to suddenly call the world to judgement He would surprise two-thirds of the American population on the road like ants." The urge to move affected every region, every city. From Boston to San Francisco, from Minneapolis to San Antonio, no more than half the families residing in a city at any one time could be found there ten years later (see Table 4-2).

Some evidence suggests that many people who left one place for another, particularly unskilled workers, did not improve their status. They were probably moving in response to patterns of layoff and unemployment, exchanging one low-paying job for another. Others, however, did

A Product of Geographical Mobility Budding frontier towns such as Helena, Montana—photographed below in 1870—sprouted all over the West as migrants sought their fortunes in urban as well as rural communities. *(Geological Survey, The National Archives.)*

TABLE 4-2 Percentage of Residents at Beginning of Decade Who Had Left by End of Decade

DECADE	CITY	PERCENTAGE WHO HAD LEFT
1870–80	Atlanta	56
	Poughkeepsie, N.Y.	50
	San Francisco	52
1880–90	Boston	36
	Mobile	62
	Omaha	60
	San Francisco	50
1900–1910	Omaha	59
1910–20	Boston	59
	Norristown, Penn.	41

Source: Derived from Table 9.1 in Stephan Thernstrom, *The Other Bostonians: Poverty and Progress in the American Metropolis, 1880–1970* (Cambridge, Mass.: Harvard University Press, 1973), pp. 222–23.

find greener pastures. Studies of turn-of-the-century Boston, Omaha, Atlanta, and other cities have revealed that most of the men who rose occupationally had migrated from somewhere else. Thus although cities frustrated the hopes of some, they offered opportunities to others.

In addition to population movement between cities, extraordinary numbers of people moved from one residence to another within the same city. In American communities today one in every five families moves in a given year. A hundred years ago the proportion was closer to one in four, or even one in three. In Omaha between 1880 and 1920, for example, nearly 60 percent of the families who remained in the city for as long as fourteen years had lived at three or more addresses during that span of time. Population turnover affected almost every neighborhood, every white ethnic and occupational group.

What were some of the consequences of the movement that did occur? For one thing social mobility did *not* eliminate poverty. Economic freedom and mobility produced greater distinctions between rich and poor, rather than more equality. Although few members of the middle class fell into the lower class, downward mobility did occur within the lower ranks, with somber results. Unemployment frequently ran high in the industrial cities, and a breadwinner's loss of job or physical incapacitation could plunge his or her family into destitution. Additionally, huge numbers of people entered urban society at the lowest levels and never rose. Thus the absolute numbers of urban poor constantly expanded in spite of the opportunities that the American economy promised.

As cases of dependency multiplied, public attitudes toward the poor hardened. Economy-minded officials and their middle-class supporters began to attack forms of outdoor relief. Believing direct grants of money and provisions encouraged pauperism, several city governments abolished out-door relief by 1900, and others made such grants only in return for work. Poverty relief increasingly depended on institutions—poorhouses, alms-houses, juvenile homes, and special homes for the blind, deaf, mentally ill, and physically handicapped. The trend was for states to assume manage-ment of these institutions, but efforts by state boards to administer "scientifi-cally" (that is, to change the poor into productive citizens) usually fizzled. Increasing destitution and dependence exacerbated the trends that had developed before the Civil War. The public was more anxious to remove undesirables from society than it was to help such people become produc-tive citizens. Rehabilitation, costly and demanding, lapsed into the confin-ing and isolating of social undesirables from the outside world.

Reflecting the larger trend toward efficient, scientific administration of all forms of organized activity at the end of the nineteenth century, private social-welfare organizations emphasized coordinated, systematic ef-forts to relieve poverty. By the 1890s many major cities contained a Charity Organization Society (COS) that organized communications among local charities, established agencies to find jobs for the unemployed, and sent employees to ascertain that every dependent was truly needy. These activi-ties reflected the long-standing moralistic attitudes toward poverty: the belief that individual weaknesses, such as drunkenness, and laziness, caused poverty. Yet the emphasis on investigation and close supervision of the poor stressed by the COS induced the conclusion that low incomes, low-quality housing, and inadequate sanitation, rather than individual failure, were responsible for dependence. The investigations led welfare agencies to support reforms that sought to relieve the environmental problems af-flicting the poor. These efforts slightly improved slum and factory condi-tions, but the public resisted large-scale change. According to Raymond Mohl, "reformers suffered in the long run from the constraints imposed by a society that was unprepared and indisposed to accept responsibility for those who were unable to survive in a competitive system." Both the down-wardly mobile and those immobilized at the bottom still had to fend for themselves.

The kinds of hardship that were so common in the inner cities of industrial America produced two sets of reactions: pessimism and resigna-tion born of despair, and unrest and violence born of frustration. Urban areas in the half-century following the Civil War suffered from crime and civil discontent. Several cities experienced labor violence in the 1870s and 1880s. New Orleans witnessed a race riot in 1866 and an anti-Italian riot in 1891. Over fifty people were killed in Cincinnati in 1884 as a result of a three-day riot that burst out after an attempted lynching. There were race riots in Wilmington in 1898, Atlanta in 1906, and in Springfield, Illinois, in 1908 and flare-ups of harassment against Chinese and Mexican immigrants in southwest and Pacific Coast cities.

But the extent of these incidents was much smaller than conditions should have warranted, because various factors—"safety valves"—relieved the pressures of social unrest. First, geographical mobility left open a means of escape. America is not only a nation of immigrants, but a nation of migrants. If life was unsatisfactory in one place, the grass was always greener somewhere else. More important, nearly everyone could—and countless people did—seek greener grass in the cities. Migration patterns reversed Frederick Jackson Turner's theory that open land in the West calmed urban tensions by drawing away the discontented. Instead, cities attracted those disappointed with farm life and those fed up with life in another city. To be sure, many dreams were wistful, and many migrants found only more of the same at their destination. But how was improvement to be measured? The man who moved from the textile mills of Manchester, New Hampshire, to the grain mills of Minneapolis may not have increased his income, but he may have moved his family from a three-room dormitory apartment to a four-room rented house, and he may have paid a penny for a loaf of bread instead of two cents. Each city had its attractions, mythical and real. It took over a thousand dollars to start a farm but only a few dollars to buy a railroad ticket to Chicago or Kansas City. New York was the place of glamour and excitement, the home of millionaires. Why not go? Life there couldn't be worse.

Second, the existence and hope of upward mobility soothed the sores of urban dissatisfaction. As Stephan Thernstrom has written, "It is not equality of *condition* but equality of *opportunity* that Americans have celebrated."[2] In spite of the widening gap between the rich and the poor, the American economy left room for upward movement: if not at the top, then in the middle; if not for new entrepreneurs and industrialists, then for workers in new trades and services and for white-collar laborers in the new commercial, industrial, and public bureaucracies. Even if there seemed to be no hope of individual improvement, things might be better for the next generation. Often they were. The big success story, the rise from bottom to top, was usually a myth. But improving one's status by taking a new job, acquiring some real estate, or buying a horse and wagon was altogether possible.

Thus mobility—whether geographical or socioeconomic—may have dampened class conflict in American cities. The ability of people to edge upward within or, occasionally, out of lower- or working-class ranks meant that urban workers' expectations often were satisfied: for a poverty-stricken immigrant a weekly wage check and a home for the family represented a genuine improvement over life in the old country. Such conditions gave many a feeling that they were part of the American dream, not outside of it. Even when strikes were organized, many workers could not afford to stay off the job for long and deprive their families of sustenance. Although working-class protest existed in American cities, it proved difficult to organize, as many socialists painfully discovered. Yet one kind of organization within urban cores was very successful, because it often addressed the experiences of inner-city life. The institution was the political machine.

BIBLIOGRAPHY

For an excellent discussion of the forces that led to migration, see Frank Thistle-thwaite, "Migration from Europe Overseas in the Nineteenth and Twentieth Centuries," in *New Perspectives on the American Past, 1877–Present,* eds. Stanley Katz and Stanley Kutler (Boston: Little, Brown, 1969), 75–78; Joseph Barton, *Peasants and Strangers: Italians, Romanians, and Slovaks in an American City, 1900–1950* (Cambridge, Mass.: Harvard University Press, 1975); John Briggs, *An Italian Passage: Immigrants to Three American Cities, 1890–1920* (New Haven, Conn.: Yale University Press, 1978); John Bodnar, *The Transplanted: A History of Immigrants in Urban America* (Bloomington: University of Indiana Press, 1985). Other sources on immigration, family, and residential patterns include Marcus Lee Hanson, *The Atlantic Migration, 1670–1860* (Cambridge, Mass.: Harvard University Press, 1940); Hanson, *The Immigrant in American History* (Cambridge, Mass.: Harvard University Press, 1940); Oscar Handlin, *Boston's Immigrants: A Study in Acculturation,* rev. ed. (Cambridge, Mass.: Harvard University Press, 1959); Handlin, *The Uprooted* (Cambridge, Mass.: Harvard University Press, 1954); Dennis Clark, *The Irish in Philadelphia: Ten Generations of Irish Experience* (Philadelphia: Temple University Press, 1974); JoEllen Vinyard, *The Irish on the Urban Frontier: Nineteenth Century Detroit* (New York: Arno Press, 1976); Hasia Diner, *Erin's Daughters in America: Irish Immigrant Women in the Nineteenth Century* (Baltimore: Johns Hopkins University Press, 1983); R. A. Burchell, *The San Francisco Irish, 1848–1880* (Berkeley: University of California Press, 1981); Moses Rischin, *The Promised City: New York City's Jews, 1870–1914* (Cambridge, Mass.: Harvard University Press, 1962); Irving Howe, *The World of Our Fathers* (New York: Harcourt Brace Jovanovich, 1976); Steven Hertzberg, *Strangers Within the Gate City: The Jews of Atlanta, 1845–1915* (Philadelphia: Jewish Publication Society of America, 1978); Judith E. Smith, *Family Connections: A History of Italian and Jewish Immigrant Lives in Providence, Rhode island, 1900–1940* (Albany: State University of New York Press, 1985); Elizabeth Ewen, *Immigrant Women in the Land of Dollars: Life and Culture on the Lower East Side, 1890–1925* (New York: Monthly Review Press, 1985); Rudolph J. Vecoli, "Contadini in Chicago: A Critique of *The Uprooted,*" *Journal of American History* 51(September 1964):404–17; Virginia Yans-McLaughlin, *Family and Community: Italian Immigrants in Buffalo, 1880–1920* (Ithaca, N.Y.: Cornell University Press, 1978); Donna R. Gabaccia, *From Sicily to Elizabeth Street: Housing and Social Change Among Italian Immigrants, 1880–1930* (Albany: State University of New York Press, 1983); Dino Cinel, *From Italy to San Francisco: The Immigrant Experience* (Stanford, Calif.: Stanford University Press, 1982); Robert Orsi, *The Madonna of 115th Street: Faith and Community in East Harlem, 1880–1950* (New Haven, Conn.: Yale University Press, 1986); Gary Mormino, *Immigrants on the Hill: Italian Immigrants in St. Louis, 1882–1982* (Urbana: University of Illinois Press, 1986); Nicaela DeLeonardo, *Varieties of Ethnic Experience: Kinship, Class, and Gender Among California Italian-Americans* (Ithaca, N.Y.: Cornell University Press, 1984); Gary R. Mormino and George E. Pozzetta, *The Immigrant World of Ybor City: Italians and Their Latin Neighbors, 1885–1985* (Urbana: University of Illinois, 1987); John Bodnar, Roger Simon, and Michael Weber, *Lives of Their Own: Blacks, Italians and Poles in Pittsburgh, 1900–1960* (Urbana: University of Illinois Press, 1982); Eva Morawska,

For Bread with Butter: Life Worlds of East Central Europeans in Johnstown, Pa., 1890–1940 (New York: Cambridge University Press, 1986); Olivier Zunz, *The Changing Face of Inequality: Urbanization, Industrialization and Immigrants in Detroit, 1880–1920* (Chicago: University of Chicago Press, 1982); Caroline Golab, *Immigrant Destinations* (Philadelphia: Temple University Press, 1977); Tamara Hareven, *Family Time and Industrial Time* (Cambridge, England, and New York: Cambridge University Press, 1982). See also Virginia E. Sanchez, *From Colonia to Community: The History of Puerto Ricans in New York, 1917–1948* (Westport, Conn.: Greenwood Press, 1983); Mario T. Garcia, *Desert Immigrants: The Mexicans of El Paso, 1880–1920* (New Haven: Yale University Press, 1981); Ricardo Romo, *East Los Angeles: History of a Barrio* (Austin: University of Texas Press, 1983); Albert Camarillo, *Chicanos in a Changing Society: From Mexican Pueblos to American Barrios in Santa Barbara and Southern California, 1848–1930* (Cambridge, Mass.: Harvard University Press, 1979); Richard Griswold Del Castillo, *The L.A. Barrio, 1850–1890: A Social History* (Berkeley: University of California Press, 1980); Del Castillo, *La Famiglia: Chicano Families in the Urban Southwest, 1848 to the Present* (Notre Dame, Ind.: University of Notre Dame Press, 1984); John Modell, *The Economics and Politics of Racial Accommodations: The Japanese of Los Angeles, 1900–1942* (Urbana: University of Illinois Press, 1977); Evelyn Nakano Glenn, *Issei, Nisei, War Bride: Three Generations of Japanese American Women in Domestic Service* (Philadelphia: Temple University Press, 1986); Stanford M. Lyman, *Chinese Americans* (New York: Random House, 1974); W.L. Tung, *The Chinese in America, 1820–1973* (Dobbs Ferry, N.Y.: Oceana Publications, 1974).

The nativist reaction is best examined by John Higham, *Strangers in the Land: Patterns of American Nativism, 1860–1925* (New Brunswick, N.J.: Rutgers University Press, 1955); Stuart C. Miller, *The Unwelcome Immigrant: The American Image of the Chinese, 1785–1882* (Berkeley: University of California Press, 1969); Alexander Saxton, *The Indispensable Enemy: Labor and the Anti-Chinese Movement in California* (Berkeley: University of California Press, 1971); and Roger Daniels, *The Politics of Prejudice* (Berkeley: University of California Press, 1962).

Important studies of black migration, family and residential patterns, include Claude Kiser, *Sea Island to City: A Study of St. Helena Islanders in Harlem and Other Urban Centers* (New York: Columbia University Press, 1932); St. Clair Drake and Horace Cayton, *Black Metropolis* (New York: Harcourt, Brace and Company, 1945); Gilbert Osofsky, *Harlem: The Making of a Ghetto* (New York: Harper & Row, Publishers, 1966); Allan H. Spear, *Black Chicago: The Making of a Negro Ghetto* (Chicago: University of Chicago Press, 1967); David Katzman, *Before the Ghetto: Black Detroit in the Nineteenth Century* (Urbana: University of Illinois Press, 1973); John Blassingame, *Black New Orleans, 1860–1880* (Chicago: University of Chicago Press, 1973); Kenneth Kusmer, *A Ghetto Takes Shape: Black Cleveland, 1870–1930* (Urbana: University of Illinois Press, 1976); Howard Rabinowitz, *Race Relations in the Urban South, 1865–1890* (New York: Oxford University Press, 1978); Elizabeth H. Pleck, *Black Migration and Poverty: Boston 1865–1900* (New York: Academic Press, 1979); James Borchert, *Alley Life in Washington: Family, Community, Religion and Folklore in the City. 1850–1970* (Urbana: University of Illinois Press, 1980); Peter Gottlieb, *Making Their Own Way: Southern Blacks' Migration to Pittsburgh* (Urbana: University of Illinois Press, 1987); Peter Rachleff, *Black Labor in the South: Richmond, Virginia, 1865–1890* (Philadelphia: Temple University Press, 1984); Janice L. Reiff, Michael R. Dahlin, and Daniel Scott Smith, "Rural Push and Urban Pull: Work and Family Experiences of Older Black Women in Southern Cities, 1880–1900," *Journal of Social History* 16(Summer 1983)39–48; Daniel M. Johnson and Rex Campbell, *Black Migration in America: A Social and Demographic History* (Durham, N.C.: Duke University Press, 1981); Jacqueline Jones, *Labor of Love, Labor of Sorrow: Black Women, Work* *and the Family from Slavery to the Present* (New York: Basic Books, 1985). Black and immigrant experience are compared in John Bodnar, Roger Simon, and Michael Weber, *Lives of Their Own: Blacks, Italians and Poles in Pittsburgh, 1900–1960* (Urbana: University of Illinois Press, 1982); Elizabeth H. Pleck, *Black Migration and Poverty: Boston: 1865–1900* *New York: Academic Press, 1979); Olivier Zunz, *The Changing Face of Inequality: Urbanization Industrialization and Immigrants in Detroit 1880–1920* (Chicago: University of Chicago Press, 1982); Stanley Lieberson, *A Piece of the Pie: Blacks and White Immigrants Since 1880* (Berkeley: University of California Press, 1980); and Thomas J. Philpott, *The Slum and the Ghetto: Neighborhood Deterioration and Middle-Class Reform, Chicago, 1880–1930* (New York: Oxford University Press, 1978).

Changing patterns of ethnic and religious identity are discussed in Nathan Glazer and Daniel Patrick Moynihan, *Beyond the Melting Pot: The Negroes, Puerto Ricans, Jews, Italians, and Irish of New York City*, 2d ed. (Cambridge, Mass.: MIT Press, 1970); Milton Gordon, *Assimilation in American Life: The Role of Race, Religion and National Origins* (New York: Oxford University Press, 1964); Abner Cohen, ed., *Urban Ethnicity* (London: Tavistock, 1977); Timothy L. Smith, "Religion and Ethnicity in America," *American Historical Review* 83(December 1978):1155–85; Harold J. Abramson, *Ethnic Diversity in Catholic America* (New York: John Wiley & Sons, 1973); Henry F. May, *Protestant Churches in Industrial America* (New York: Harper & Row, Publishers, 1949); Deborah Dash Moore, *At Home in America: Second Generation New York Jews* (New York: Columbia University Press, 1981); William Toll, *The Making of an Ethnic Middle Class: Portland Jewry Over Four Generations* (Albany: State University of New York Press, 1982); Randall M. Miller and Thomas D. Marzik, eds., *Immigrants and Religion in Urban America* (Philadelphia: Temple University Press, 1977); John Higham, ed., *Ethnic Leadership in America* (Baltimore: Johns Hopkins University Press, 1978); Victor P. Greene, *For God and Country: The Rise of Polish and Lithuanian Ethnic Consciousness in America, 1860–1910* (Madison: State Historical Society of Wisconsin, 1975); Timothy Meagher, " 'Irish All The Time': Ethnic Consciousness Among Irish-Americans in Worcester, Massachusetts, 1880–1905," *Journal of Social History* 19(December 1985):273–303. Two recent considerations of these questions include William L. Yancey, Eugene Ericksen, and Richard Juliani, "Emergent Ethnicity: A Review and a Reformulation," *American Sociological Review* 41(June 1976):391–403; Kathleen Neils Conzen, "Immigrants, Immigrant Neighborhoods and Ethnic Identity: Historical Issues," *Journal of American History* 66(December 1979):603–15.

On housing reform, public health, and city services, see Roy Lubove, *The Progressive and the Slums: Tenement House Reform in New York City, 1890–1917* (Pittsburgh: University of Pittsburgh Press, 1962); Thomas J. Philpott, *The Slum and the Ghetto: Neighborhood Deterioration and Middle-Class Reform, Chicago 1880–1930* (New York: Oxford University Press, 1978); James Cassedy, *Charles V. Chapin and the Public Health Movement* (Cambridge, Mass.: Harvard University Press, 1962); Barbara G. Rosenkrantz, *Public Health and the State: Changing Views in Massachusetts, 1842–1936* (Cambridge, Mass.: Harvard University Press, 1972); Judith Walzer Leavitt, *The Healthiest City: Milwaukee and the Politics of Health Reform* (Princeton, N.J.: Princeton University Press, 1982); Clayton R. Koppes and William P. Norris, "Ethnicity, Class, and Mortality in the Industrial City: A Case Study of Typhoid Fever in Pittsburgh, 1890–1910," *Journal of Urban History* 11(May 1985):259–279; Martin V. Melosi, ed., *Pollution and Reform in American Cities, 1870–1930* (Austin: University of Texas Press, 1980); Melosi, *Garbage in the Cities: Refuse, Reform, and the Environment, 1880–1980* (College Station, Tex.: Texas A&M University Press, 1981); Roger Lane, *Violent Death in the City: Suicide, Accident and Murder in Nineteenth Century*

Philadelphia (Cambridge, Mass.: Harvard University Press, 1979); John C. Schneider, *Detroit: The Problem of Order, 1830–1880* (Lincoln: Univ of Nebraska Press, 1980); Eric H. Monkkonen, *The Dangerous Class: Crime and Poverty in Columbus, Ohio, 1860–65* (Cambridge, Mass.: Harvard University Press, 1975); Monkkonen, *Police in Urban America, 1860–1920* (Cambridge, England, and New York: Cambridge University Press, 1981); James F. Richardson, *Urban Police in the United States* (Port Washington, N.Y.: Kennikat Press, 1974); Robert M. Fogelson, *Big-City Police* (Cambridge, Mass.: Harvard University Press, 1977). See also Christine Rosen, *The Limits of Growth: Great Fires and the Process of City Growth in America* (New York: Cambridge University Press, 1986).

For analysis of the connections between migrant residential patterns and family and community life see John Modell and Tamara Hareven, "Urbanization and the Malleable Household: An Examination of Boarding and Lodging in American families," *Journal of Marriage and the Family* 35(August 1973):299–314; John Bodnar, Michael Weber, and Roger Simon, "Migration, Kinship, and Urban Adjustment: Blacks and Poles in Pittsburgh, 1900–1930," *Journal of American History* 66(December 1979):548–65; James Borchert, "Urban Neighborhood and Community: Informal Group Life, 1850–1970," *Journal of Interdisciplinary History* 11(Spring 1981):607–31; Donna Gabaccia, "Sicilians in Space: Environmental Change and Family Geography," *Journal of Social History* 16(Winter 1982):53–66; Lizabeth A. Cohen, "Embellishing a Life of Labor: An Interpretation of American Working Class Homes, 1885–1915," *Journal of American Culture* 3(Winter 1980):752–775; Judith E. Smith, "The Transformation of Family and Community Culture in Immigrant Neighborhoods, 1900–1940," in *The New England Working Class and the New Labor History*, eds. Herbert Gutman and Donald Bell (Urbana: University of Illinois Press, 1986), pp. 159–83.

On urban women see Susan J. Kleinberg, "Technology and Women's Work: The Lives of Working Class Women in Pittsburgh, 1870–1900," *Labor History* 17(Winter 1976)58–72; Kleinberg, "The Systematic Study of Urban Women," in *Class, Sex, and the Woman Worker*, eds. Milton Cantor and Bruce Laurie (Westport, Conn.: Greenwood Press, 1977), 20–42; Barbara Klacynska, "Why Women Work: A Comparison of Various Groups—Philadelphia, 1910–1930," *Labor History* 17(Winter 1976):73–87; Carol Groneman, "She Earns as a Child, She Pays as A Man: Women Workers in a Mid-Nineteenth Century New York City Community," in *Class, Sex and the Woman Worker;* Miriam Cohen, "Italian-American Women in New York City, 1900–1950: Work and School," in *Class, Sex and the Woman Worker;* Elizabeth H. Pleck, "A Mother's Wages: Income Earning Among Married Italian and Black Women, 1896–1911," in *The American Family in Socio-Historical Perspective*, 2d ed., Michael Gordon (New York: St. Martin's Press, 1978); Gary P. Mormino and George E. Pozzetta, "Immigrant Women in Tampa: the Italian Experience, 1890–1930," *Florida Historical Quarterly* 61(January 1983):296–312. See also Alice Kessler-Harris, *Out to Work: A History of Wage-Earning Women in America* (New York: Oxford University Press, 1982) and Jacqueline Jones, *Labor of Love, Labor of Sorrow: Black Women, Work and the Family from Slavery to the Present* (New York: Basic Books, 1985).

Residential experiences and social mobility are examined in Stephan Thernstrom, *The Other Bostonians: Poverty and Progress in an American Metropolis, 1880–1970* (Cambridge, Mass.: Harvard University Press, 1973); Howard P. Chudacoff, *Mobile Americans: Residential and Social Mobility in Omaha, 1880–1920* (New York: Oxford University Press, 1972); Chudacoff, "A New Look at Ethnic Neighborhoods: Residential Disperson and the Concept of Visibility in a Medium-Sized City," *Journal of American History* 60(June 1973):76–93: Clyde Griffen and Sally Griffen, *Natives and Newcomers: The Ordering of Opportunity in Mid-Nineteenth Century Poughkeepsie* (Cambridge, Mass.: Harvard University Press, 1977); Dean R. Esslinger, *Immigrants and the City: Ethnicity and Mobility in a Nineteenth Century Midwestern Community* (Port Washington, N.Y.: Kennikat Press, 1975); Thomas Kessner, *The Golden Door: Italian and Jewish Immigrant Mobility in New York City, 1880–1915* (New York: Oxford University Press, 1977); Peter Decker, *Fortunes and Failures: White Collar Mobility in Nineteenth Century San Francisco* (Cambridge, Mass.: Harvard University Press, 1978); Gordon W. Kirk, Jr., *The Promise of American Life: Social Mobility in a Nineteenth Century Immigrant Community, Holland, Michigan, 1847–1894* (Philadelphia: American Philosophical Soiety, 1978); and Theodore Hershberg, ed., *Philadelphia: Work, Space, Family and Group Experience in the Nineteenth Century* (New York: Oxford University Press, 1981).

ENDNOTES

[1]Howard Rabinowitz, *Race Relations in the Old South, 1865–1980* (New York: Oxford University Press, 1978).

[2]Stephan Thernstrom, *The Other Bostonians; Poverty and Progress in the American metropolis, 1880–1970* (Cambridge, Mass.: Harvard University Press, 1973), 256.

5

City Politics in the Era of Transformation

ORIGINS OF THE MACHINE

Huge increases in migration and immigration, which created an ethnically stratified urban population; acceleration of industrialization, commercial expansion, and technological change, which recast social structure and reshaped economic relationships; and the expansion and specialization of urban space—these conditions generated unprecedented challenges for urban governments between 1870 and 1900. Tensions between workers and their new corporate employers that exploded in violent strikes in the 1870s, 1880s, and 1890s, confrontations between natives and immigrants, and overcrowding, ill health, poverty, substandard housing, and crime in tenement neighborhoods fomented what some have termed a crisis of public order. Between 1870 and 1900 many cities enlarged their boundaries by thousands of acres, and the myriad new households and businesses strained existing services and created an urgent need for water, gas, street lighting, and sewer systems, more police officers, firefighters, and teachers, and more streets, schools, and government buildings. How would these improvements be financed? Who among contending groups would determine public priorities?

The governmental forms that had evolved during the urbanization of the early nineteenth century seemed to generate political chaos rather than effective governing strategies. After 1820 most city governments had copied the federal form of government: two legislative councils elected from districts (wards) and an executive (mayor) elected at large (citywide). Before 1850 most mayors could exert only limited control over municipal policy. Many mayors had ceremonial powers that entitled them to hand out keys to the city and cut ribbons, but they took only a minor role in the selection and supervision of municipal officials, and many lacked the power to veto council ordinances. Mayors were often unable to overcome the particular interests of councilmen, and both branches constantly fought with state governments over the exercise of power. As the creators of cities, states jealously guarded their prerogatives to determine their cities' needs and to control finances by limiting local taxing and bonding powers. Consequently most cities had to expand their functions in piecemeal fashion by petitioning the statehouse for charter amendments. Also, as new needs called for new officials, a confusing array of boards and commissions piled on top of each other. Some were appointed by the governor, some by the mayor, some by the city council, and some were popularly elected. Jersey City's charter was amended ninety-one times in forty years, and at one time thirty separate boards administered public functions in Philadelphia.

Governmental confusion and economic change tended to fragment political leadership. By the middle of the nineteenth century many local entrepreneurs—merchants, manufacturers, contractors, and real-estate operators—vied for political control in order to steer public policy in directions suited to their own interests, sometimes in concert with and sometimes in competition with the older political leadership that had drawn from mercantile and professional elites. At the same time, other businessmen whose concerns focused on interurban and interregional networks of transportation, finance, and communications withdrew from active involvement with local affairs. Expansion of the franchise after 1820 created a new electorate with their own political goals and leadership. The independent political parties—the Free Soil, Know-Nothing, and numerous workingmen's parties—emerging out of deep divisions over labor, temperance, and land confounded heads of the major parties. New kinds of political leaders, frequently self-made men whose careers were based on close attention to the concerns of their constituents, emerged from the newly enfranchised electorate. Political power once based on more general social deference, came to be based on party organization and mass partisan loyalty.

The emergence of career politicians, the abandonment of the caucus system for nominating candidates, and the function of ward organization both to get out the vote and structure partisan loyalties came to be common aspects of local political activity. The less affluent career politicians who were replacing the wealthy in office boasted of the benefits they brought to their constituents. As the ward became the basic unit of political life, both career politicians and patrician leaders depended on these benefits to justify their claim to office and for reelection. Career politicians, however, lacked the personal resources of patricians; as a consequence, when politicians provided for constituents, they did so from the city budget. To succeed, however, they had to associate themselves with others who shared their goals. By the 1860s and 1870s what insiders called "the organization" and what outsiders disparaged as "the machine" shaped politics in most large cities.

Irish immigrants were particularly well situated to machine politics. In the 1820s Daniel O'Connell's Catholic Association had introduced Irish peasants to modern techniques of mass political organization, and during the 1830s entire districts had become intensely involved in campaigns against the British government. Voters as well as nonvoters turned out to encourage their candidate and to intimidate political opponents. In America the rising tide of Irish immigration coincided with expansion of the franchise to propertyless males after 1820. The power of the Irish vote increased with the growth of more geographically distinct neighborhoods that could be exploited politically. The personal reciprocal relationship on which the power of the political machine was based and the respect for seniority and service that characterized the hierarchical structure of machine politics also harkened back to Ireland.

As political associations distinct from established government agencies, machines flourished because they were able to barter among diverse groups by centralizing political power and material resources. By taking advantage of mass suffrage, they "delivered" the ethnic vote for selected candidates in the immigrant wards. Machines distributed important material benefits; they provided jobs and favors for their constituency, and utility franchises, contracts, tax adjustments, and favorable legislation for selected members of the business community. Machine politicians used these resources both to raise money and to build a personal political following. By resourcefully distributing patronage and material benefits, machine politicians also built strong centralized party organizations that overcame the fragmentation of authority characteristic of the formal governmental structure of the times. The machines acted as brokers among contending political interests; they supplied material and symbolic rewards to immigrant and working-class residents who otherwise lacked resources, and by centralizing political authority, they brought some semblance of social and political order to the cities.

STRUCTURE AND FUNCTIONS OF THE MACHINE

Critics depicted political machines as monolithic mobs and bosses as despots who dictated every act, every crime. The images were seldom true. Like most other political organizations, machines were coalitions. They appeared homogeneous only because their leaders kept the parts well oiled, preventing friction and dissolution. Most big-city machines were federations, consisting of smaller machines organized at the levels of ward, precinct, and even block. The bosses who became the subjects of muckrakers' exposés were not autocrats who ruled their domains with iron fists. Rather, they were executives, chairmen of boards, and brokers who coordinated whole hierarchies of smaller bosses.

Ward and precinct bosses derived power directly from the neighborhoods. They were the ones who mustered numbers and utilized votes as a marketable commodity. To offer their constituents more, smaller bosses allied into a large organization under the aegis of a city-wide boss. It was the city boss's job to keep order within this organization, but often unity proved impossible. For example, throughout much of its early history Chicago changed so rapidly and spawned so many diverse power bases that a single city-wide machine could not be formed until well into the twentieth century. On the other hand the establishment and growth of Tammany Hall in New York in the early 1800s provided a framework within which lower-class political interests could combine. In most instances an agent who could weld the various local organizations into a more powerful machine could promise unprecedented benefits to all. Such promises gave city bosses their power.

Yet bosses held their positions as leaders of coalitions only by the support and good will of others. Their power was not absolute; it was checked by the lower bosses who operated the gears of the machine. Moreover the entire system was based on neighborhood support. Corruption and chicanery gave bosses influence and leverage, but bosses sustained their power only because they provided services that many people wanted and needed. Although machines thrived on the vulnerability and manipulation of the needy and ignorant, bosses could not lead their constituents where they did not want to go. Bosses who forgot these limitations fell.

The specific functions of boss politics flowed in two directions. In return for votes, machines personalized government for immigrants and other constituents. In return for material gratuities, machines granted privileges to segments of the business community. Both sets of functions reinforced American traditions of competitive individualism, entrepreneurial success, and private property.

Immigrants looked to politics not as the fulfillment of some abstract ideal but as an extension of the family and communal economy. The boss based his power on values most working-class immigrants had learned at home: reciprocity and mutual assistance. Supplying work, charity, and personal service, bosses met immigrants' daily needs, but in doing so they diminished the ability of immigrant voters to use politics as a tool for redressing economic grievances. In the 1880s, independent labor political initiatives directly challenged machine candidates. In 1886, in one of the most famous contests, Henry George, running on the United Labor party ticket, narrowly lost the New York City mayoralty to the Tammany Democrat and iron manufacturer Abram Hewitt, coming in far ahead of the third place candidate, Republican Theodore Roosevelt. But the collapse of labor politics by the mid 1890s left workers with little alternative to the major parties. In many circumstances, machines were actively antagonistic to the collective orientation of the labor movement, which threatened both the machine's electoral base and its business constituency. The rise of the machine was connected with a growing tendency in American political agitation to separate workplace concerns, relegated to unions, from community issues, abandoned to an electoral fate.

Bosses were often immigrants or sons of immigrants; they knew the inner city and its needs firsthand. Building their constituencies by providing jobs, bosses needed to control governmental offices as a means of influencing employment. The enormous extent of public and private construction within cities in the late nineteenth century meant that many jobs fell formally or informally within the reach of public officials. Local officials on public-works boards and in inspectors' offices could easily convince contractors and other employers to hire men faithful to the machine. Bosses and their associates could also provide constituents with jobs on the expanding public payroll. Men who received work and wages as a result of machine influence were always reminded where their jobs came from. Some were required to express their appreciation by making a contribution to machine coffers. This was especially true for public employees—policemen, firemen, teachers, clerks, and janitors. All were expected to remember the machine on election day.

However, there were always many more people who wanted favors than there were jobs to be distributed. Consequently bosses maintained their popularity by offering forms of public benevolence. Through control of city officials, they appropriated funds for neighborhood improvements such as parks, playgrounds, and bathhouses. They often took neighborhood children on summer picnics and sponsored free days at the amusement park, and they distributed turkeys and other food on Easter, Thanksgiving, and Christmas. Each boss had his own style. James Michael Curley, mayor and boss of Boston in the early twentieth century, wrote of how he would approach an old, bent woman who was plodding down the street by saying, "A woman should have three attributes. She should have beauty, intelligence, and money." As he handed her a silver dollar he would add, "Now you have all three." Reformers objected to these forms of what they called "mass bribery." Yet no one else was interested in providing welfare to the poor in such a personal way.

Machines also rendered intangible services that aided immigrants in a bewildering world. Bosses installed themselves as buffers between inner-city residents and the law and were increasingly expected to smooth over difficulties and to obtain exemptions from the law. The boss could convince authorities to look the other way when a neighborhood saloon wanted to stay open after hours or on Sundays, or he could prevent police harassment of a gambling house or other vice establishment. Most important, the boss intervened when one of his constituents ran afoul of the law. When an immigrant was arrested for intoxication, vagrancy, robbery, or assault, the boss would be the only person who could provide assurance, counsel, and, in many cases, bail. When a youth was brought in for disturbing the peace, the boss could go to the station house, talk to the officers, convince them that the young man came from an upstanding family, and secure his release. This kind of intervention gave neighborhood residents a sense of importance, confidence that someone was on their side, a feeling that they were getting a break in an otherwise oppressive system.

Bosses cultivated a mass following by making their power visible and accessible. They were joiners and boosters, card-carrying members of a host of ethnic and neighborhood associations. They set up their own clubs, often in a corner saloon, where a person could go to get help. Bosses held open house in these informal offices, distributing jobs and food and calling constituents by their first names. They appeared at wakes and weddings, and they readily offered cash to defray funeral expenses or to start a pair of newlyweds on the right foot. No wonder a boss's achievements, including the appearance of his name in the newspapers, reflected the glory of the neighborhood. The immigrants accepted the boss as one of their own. He spoke for them. National political issues were unimportant. A boss who became too interested in the tariff, public-land policy, or the amount of silver in national currency soon lost his neighborhood following. In the streets and tenements only local and personal issues counted—bathhouses, extra jobs, Mrs. Kelly's boy Tim. Here the success of a politician was measured by two canons: "He gets things done" and "He keeps his word." James Michael Curley's own jail term as punishment for taking a civil service examination for someone else was transformed into a badge of honor with an interpretation based on neighborhood values: "he did it for a friend."

The jobs, handouts, and personal relationships humanized politics for the working classes. More than the industrial machine, the political machine required constant attention. As George Washington Plunkitt preached, "[The boss] plays politics every day and night in the year, and his headquarters bear the inscription 'Never Closed.' " Bosses knew what happened in the streets and alleys, tenements and taverns, as well as what happened in government and business offices. They knew the needs of inner-city residents, and they tried to fill these needs when few others seemed to care. Charities and government agencies also tried to help, but they were obsessed with determining the worthiness of welfare recipients. Bosses asked no questions.

Martin Lomasney, boss of Boston's South End, once told Lincoln Steffens, "There's got to be somebody in every ward that any bloke can come to—no matter what he's done—and get help. Help, you understand, none of your law and justice, but help." Help was the ideology of boss politics: positive government, the belief that the government existed to help people. Bosses transformed politics into a full-time professionalized service. As a result the people served by bosses came to expect government to attend to the personal problems of everyday life. As early as the depression years of the 1850s, working-class voters pushed machine politicians in New York, Boston, Baltimore, and Philadelphia to provide public-works programs and public relief. Before the advent of social security, unemployment insurance, medicare, food stamps, and the aid to families with dependent children program, bosses and machines made meaningful attempts to distribute relief and welfare. Many people even in the poorest circumstances never used these services, but they knew they could receive help if they needed it.

Of course, not all immigrant groups were represented in party machines. In most cities the Irish initially dominated machine politics, and they frequently attempted to defend their political and social organizations from infiltration by outsiders, such as newer immigrant groups or black migrants. In Boston, New Haven, and New York the Irish took a disproportionate share of the patronage jobs, holding on with particular strength to the police force. In New York, Chicago, New Orleans, and Detroit, Irish-dominated machines ignored Italians and Poles for many years, and few machines offered any favors or concessions to blacks. These outsiders were the truly disadvantaged, for they were excluded from whatever helpful services machines could render. But there were important limits to the help the machines could offer even its favored sons. The number of jobs available to even loyal voters never came close to meeting peoples' needs and were in any case menial low-paying jobs unlikely to offer future advancement.

Machines did not depend on goodwill alone to ensure success at the polls. There were few legal constraints on the election process; most cities would not adopt voter-registration laws or the secret ballot until the twentieth century. Repeat voting, false counting, stuffed ballot boxes, and other kinds of voting fraud were common occurrences on election day. Politicians bought votes and used intimidation and violence to be sure of results. Kansas City boss Tom Pendergast used a combination of bribery, fraud, and violence to produce the majorities for a proposed railway franchise. The famous Chicago ward boss Johnny Powers intimidated voters by threatening landlords, merchants, and other businessmen with loss of licenses unless they supported him in his campaign for alderman. This form of coercion was the underside of machine politics.

Neighborhood constituents formed one special-interest group served by political machines; the business community was the other. The urban boom that spread across the country after the Civil War unleashed torrents of construction and commercial activity. Population growth and geographical sprawl forced cities into a frenzy of physical expansion. The increased need for municipal services resulted in an expansion of public agencies to administer them. By securing public offices and the patronage attached to them, machines could distribute political favors to their advantage. They could control the letting of contracts for public works, such as streets, sewers, and government buildings. They could influence the granting of streetcar, gas, telephone, and electricity franchises. They could juggle tax assessments for favored property owners. They could select printers, banks, and other firms who would receive city business. These privileges had their price: favored businessmen were expected to pay the machines for their contracts and franchises. Outsiders called the practice bribery. Bosses called it gratitude. Often the politicians padded public contracts so that the chosen firms could easily kick back huge sums to the bosses and their treasuries. Outsiders called this graft. Bosses doctored the ledger to hide it.

There were two kinds of graft. *Honest graft*, or *boodle*, was simply investment capitalism—only the kind that maximized profits while eliminating risk. From their positions within government machine politicians had an advantageous view of where lucrative instruments in real estate and utility companies could be made. Moreover, they could set policies that would assure the success of such investments. George Washington Plunkitt, a New York ward boss, illustrated this kind of graft with an example:

> My party's in power in the city, and it's goin' to undertake a lot of public improvements. Well, I'm tipped off, say, that they're going to lay out a new park at a certain place.

> I see an opportunity and I take it. I go to that place and I buy up all the land I can in the neighborhood. Then the board of this or that makes its plan public, and there is a rush to get my land, which nobody cared particular for before.

> Ain't it perfectly honest to charge a good price and make a profit on my investment and foresight? Of course it is. Well, that's honest graft.

Dishonest graft derived from participation in explicitly criminal operations. It usually consisted of shakedowns and payoffs from vice operations in return for protection from police harassment. This was the most sordid activity of boss politics, but it was difficult to avoid. Bosses were specialists in gaining exemptions from the law, and the line between who was to receive such favors and who would not seldom was drawn. Payoffs from gambling, prostitution, and illegal liquor trading were the most accessible revenues for machines. Many bosses operated vice establishments themselves, and many entered politics from backgrounds in illicit activities.

In addition to functioning as service agencies and dispensaries of political favors, machines provided important avenues of social mobility to immigrants. Politics posed few barriers of discrimination. Any man who commanded enough votes could attain office. Moreover, because machines transformed politics into a profession that reflected the glory of the neighborhoods, membership in the machine elevated an individual and opened opportunities to him. Every boss needed henchmen to carry out various operations. It was usually easy for an underling to grab a little of the honest or dishonest graft as it floated by. And there was usually room at the top for the energetic, bright young man.

Participation in politics seemed particularly attractive to second-generation immigrants. As Oscar Handlin has related, the sons of immigrants were a restless generation. A number of them recognized that their lack of skills, education, and capital frustrated their desires to move ahead in a supposed land of opportunity. They often felt the lash of discrimination and the chains of poverty. Yet their schoolbooks told them that government existed for the people, and machines offered them the opportunity to serve—and be rewarded for their service. So they entered politics because the machine promised that the organization's success would also mean personal achievement.[1] The magnetic force was the prestige that the machine could bestow, not only to the individual but to his family and his neighborhood. Prestige, service, loyalty, accomplishment—these were what the machine offered inner-city residents, and these were what enabled the boss system to withstand heated attacks for so many years.

SOME NOTABLE CASES

The essence of boss politics is best described by example. Each organization had unique features and personalities. Functions remained relatively constant, however. Sometimes the boss exerted power from an elected office. More frequently he pulled strings from backstage, attaching public officials to him by bonds of loyalty and patronage. Bosses could operate within the Republican as well as the Democratic party, although most machines developed as Democratic because of that party's attraction for workingmen and immigrants. Yet Democratic bosses felt no discomfort working out contracts and deals with Republican businessmen. All bosses pursued power and advantage, but some showed genuine concern for their constituents whereas others devoted more attention to dishonest graft and self-serving. Still all bosses used politics as a vehicle for personalized service, and they dispensed political favors on a cash-and-carry basis.

Modern urban bossism was reared in New York's Tammany Hall. The Society of St. Tammany evolved from an Anti-Federalist social club in the 1790s into a political organization that courted the expanded working-class vote by supporting popular issues of the 1830s. During the depression that followed the Panic of 1837 the Tammany Club distributed food, fuel, and clothing to the city's poor. It continued its relief services into the 1840s, paying particular heed to the increasing numbers of Irish immigrants. By this time Tammany had become a powerful wing of the Democratic Party in New York, and it used its charitable activities to win votes for its candidates. As the club acquired power, it exercised increasing control over local patronage. Party leaders consulted Tammany in the choice of candidates, and elected officials followed Tammany dictates in the distribution of government jobs, rewarding loyal members who worked for the cause of the club and the party.

William Marcy Tweed was the first man to use Tammany Hall as a powerful political organ. This achievement enabled him and his organization to run the entire city of New York and to milk its treasury of some $200 million in about six or seven years. Unlike later bosses Tweed did not emerge from a background of poverty. His father was a middle-class craftsman and former treasurer of the Tammany Society. Tweed became leader of a neighborhood gang, later of a volunteer fire company. His strength and popularity caught the attention of Tammany leaders, and Tweed was elected to the New York City Council at age twenty-eight and to the U.S. House of Representatives at thirty. The debates of Congress bored Tweed, and he did not seek reelection. Instead, he returned to New York and resumed his rise within the Tammany machine.

By the late 1860s Tweed had combined cunning and luck to win control of the entire city administration and part of the state legislature. He maneuvered his way into the chairmanship of Tammany and consolidated his power by boosting associates into public office through election or appointment. Once in command this crew became known as the Tweed Ring. The top echelon consisted of Tweed and four men. George Barnard, a graduate of gambling houses and minstrel troops, became city recorder and was elevated to the state supreme court. Richard B. "Slippery Dick" Connolly, an Irish immigrant, was city comptroller. Peter "Brains" Sweeney, was city chamberlain and had the task of depositing city funds in selected banks. Abraham Oakey Hall, actor, poet, and dandy, was district attorney and later Mayor of New York.

Tweed and his men worked daily to maintain their positions, but the machine was in full flower at election time. To insure victory it perfected three kinds of voting fraud. First, repeaters, supplied with names that had already been falsely registered, were hustled around to several polling places to cast their ballots. Second, Tammany-appointed election officials bought off Republican counterparts and manipulated vote tallies (following the proverb coined later in the century that "a vote on the tally sheet is worth two in the box"). Third, the machine made special efforts to naturalize immigrants so they could vote. It established neighborhood naturalization committees, paid fees, expedited paper work, and provided witnesses for prospective citizens who pledged to vote for the Democratic Party and Tammany candidates. Judge Barnard was usually listless on the bench, but he became a frenzied worker the month before an election. In October, 1868 he naturalized an average of 718 future Democrats a day. It was estimated that one sixth of the votes cast in New York City that year were fraudulent.

With his henchmen entrenched in office Tweed was ready to start his notorious assault on the public treasury. In 1870 he used his influence over the state general assembly to obtain a new charter for New York City. Among other things, the charter gave the mayor greater powers of appointment and created a board of audit that would handle all bills paid by the city and county. The charter cost Tweed $600,000 in bribes, but it was worth it. With the mayor's office and board of audit in the hands of Tweed men, contracts could be padded and kickbacks demanded. One of the richest bonanzas was the construction of a new county courthouse. By the time the Tweed Ring had finished inflating appropriations, the building had cost a total of $12,500,000, including $7,500 for thermometers, $190 apiece for cuspidors, $404,347 for safes, $41,190 for brooms and other "articles," and $2 million for plastering. In contrast, a similar courthouse was built in Brooklyn at the same time for $800,000.

In 1871 at age forty-seven Bill Tweed, bald and weighing over 300 pounds, reputedly was worth $12 million. He had a Fifth Avenue mansion, a Connecticut estate, a steam yacht, a well-stocked stable, and a blond mistress. But he always had enough money for others. In 1870 he spent $50,000 on the poor of the Seventh Ward. He reportedly raised a million and a half dollars for the Catholic Church. And his wallet was always open to Tammany candidates in need of campaign funds. Tweed clearly recognized that in industrial America power and money were inseparable. He did not set the standards of his day. He merely embellished those established by the rising business powers. As one writer has remarked, "Property and cash were the gods of America, to be stolen and spent, multiplied and glorified." Both politicians and businessmen participated in the ritual.

Tweed's career climaxed early in 1871 when an investigating committee found him innocent of misusing city funds in the 1870 elections. Then on July 18 the *New York Times,* acting on information divulged by a disaffected sheriff, printed "reliable and incontrovertible evidence of numerous, gigantic frauds on the part of the rulers of the city." The exposés of boodling, bribery, and embezzlement continued for over a month. A committee of seventy community leaders, headed by Samuel J. Tilden, investigated and publicized the extent of wrongdoing. As a result Judge Barnard was impeached, Mayor Hall was indicted, and several other Tammany lieutenants fled to Paris. After a frenzied attempt to cover his tracks, Tweed was arrested. He eventually was convicted on 104 counts of fraud and bribery and sentenced to twelve years in prison.

Tweed's jailors allowed him to make periodic visits to his family while he served his term. While eating dinner at his son's home one evening Tweed excused himself and went upstairs. No one saw him again until several days later, when he was picked up in Spain and shipped back to New York. Back in jail, Tweed offered to make a full confession in return for freedom to return to his family. Samuel Tilden, now governor, refused the request, but Tilden's successor, Lucius Robinson, agreed. Tweed confessed, but Robinson reneged, saying Tweed would be released only when he had paid back the state $6 million. Tweed refused, and instead donated huge sums to charity. He died of pnuemonia in prison in 1878.

The Tweed Ring left confusion and debt in its wake. Between 1867 and 1871 New York City's debt soared from $300 to $900 million and its account books were left in chaos. Yet all the sordid stories tell only a part of Tweed's impact on the city. Whatever his motives, Tweed saw that important things were accomplished. New York City was growing too fast for existing institutions to meet its needs. Tweed's regime by-passed traditional forms of administration. In doing so it extended streets, granted franchises to transit and utilities companies, developed Central Park, and generally oversaw the physical expansion of the city. It also secured revision of the city's antiquated government with charter reforms that, at least in theory, increased local efficiency. Amidst all this improvement the boss and his henchmen lined their pockets at public expense.

The Tweed Ring's power rested on personalities and on bribery; it was not a fully developed political machine that tightly controlled policy making and electoral decision. Bill Tweed was a personal boss, not an organization leader like those who followed him. Tweed's accomplishments outdistanced those of all the leaders who had preceded him in New York. He succeeded by coordinating physical growth with an organized, though expensive, political plan. He used numbers and votes, however fraudulently, to build his power, and he played the role of broker between business and government with optimal skill. Most important, to the poverty-stricken worker who received a free meal and a couple of dollars on election day or whose family received a basket of food at Christmas, Tweed was a hero, someone who cared.

The demise of William Marcy Tweed did not signal the end of Tammany Hall. "Honest" John Kelly succeeded him as head of the machine and molded Tammany into a more efficient organization by centralizing decision making and by appointing a more party-oriented breed of henchmen. After a brief hiatus Tammany candidates moved back into positions of power. In some ways Tammany Hall and similar machines elsewhere changed after 1880. Their graft and corruption became less flagrant, and they used the expanding municipal bureaucracy and the ever pressing need for services to cement their influence. But machines still based their existence on numbers, jobs, and favors.

Richard Croker was typical of the late-nineteenth-century boss. Born in Ireland in 1843, he sailed to the United States with his parents at the age of three. He grew up in the slums of Lower Manhattan, dropped out of school when he was thirteen, and joined the Fourth Avenue Tunnel Gang. Here he learned the lessons that prepared him for his political career: discipline through loyalty, reputation through results, and leadership through strength. Using his forceful personality and uncanny pugilistic skill, Croker became the gang's leader and was recruited into Tammany Hall in the 1860s. Starting as an attendant to Judge Barnard, Croker worked his way up through the machine until he became Tammany's—and the city's—boss in the late 1880s.

Croker was a very able politician. He could win a point with affable charm or with vicious attack; he also knew when to compromise. His candor often won the respect of his enemies. Reformer Lincoln Steffens wrote, "Richard Croker never said anything to me that was not true, unless it was a statement for publication." The reverence that the city's populace paid him was enormous. When he took his annual European vacation, thousands saw him off. He attended the opera annually on Thomas Jefferson's birthday, and the orchestra played "Hail to the Chief" while he took his seat.

Unlike Tweed, Croker did not steal outright from the public treasury. Rather, he perfected the use of honest graft. By using his control over city purchases and contracts, Croker could convince favored businessmen to grant stock in their companies to the boss and his associates or to offer tips on promising investments. Croker distributed his profits around the organization but also kept some for himself. By the early 1890s he owned a farm stocked with thoroughbred horses, a private Pullman car, and seven homes—even though he had no visible means of support after retiring from the public payroll in 1890. At first most of Croker's supporters took pride in this affluence: Dick Croker was one of them, a man who rose from the slums, a man who kept his word and got things done. Why shouldn't he reap the rewards of advantage?

Honest graft could not sustain the whole machine, however. Croker welded his underlings to him by permitting them to participate in dirty graft. He generally overlooked the activities of his ninety thousand precinct workers—many of them policemen, firemen, and other civil servants—as long as they carried their districts for Tammany candidates on election day.

Croker had many friends but also some enemies. In 1894 these opponents managed to dent Tammany's power for the first time since Tweed's demise. At the instigation of Thomas Platt, U.S. Senator and chairman of the Republican State Committee, a committee under the chairmanship of State Senator Clarence Lexow began an investigation of police corruption in New York City. The Lexow Committee's hearings—six thousand pages of testimony—detailed an extraordinary degree of police graft and accomplished just what Platt desired—disenchantment with the machine. But Croker stayed one step ahead. He sensed the public mood and resigned as Tammany's chairman so as not to be linked to an electoral defeat. In the mayoral election of 1894 the reformers' candidate, Republican merchant William Strong, won by forty-five thousand votes. After the election Croker sailed to England for a three-year vacation.

Mayor Strong and his police commissioner Theodore Roosevelt managed a few reforms, but their strict enforcement of the law made many people long for the looser Tammany days. In September, 1897, with the Lexow revelations buried, Croker returned to New York and reestablished his control over Tammany. He was just in time. The state legislature had given the city a new charter that on January 1, 1898 would consolidate Brooklyn, Queens, Staten Island, and the Bronx with Manhattan. The winner of the 1897 mayoral election would administer a Greater New York City of over three million people. Reformers entered Seth Low, president of Columbia University and former mayor of Brooklyn, as their candidate. Croker and the Democrats selected a political unknown, Judge Robert Van Wyck, and frankly aimed their campaign at the tenement districts, where reform crackdowns had been heaviest. Their slogan was "To Hell with Reform!" The strategy worked. The close election was decided by a Democratic landslide in the inner wards. Croker and Tammany again ruled the city.

Croker's triumphant return damaged his political savvy, for he began to make mistakes, something bosses could not afford. First, he divorced his wife and moved into the Democratic Club on Fifth Avenue. Here he kept a court, forcing lieutenants to visit him in their best dress and to remain standing at dinner until the boss was seated. Then Croker tried unsuccessfully to lead his machine into state and national politics. He pressured his organization to run a Tammany candidate against Teddy Roosevelt for governor in 1898, and he backed William Jennings Bryan for president in 1900. In both instances Croker's ignorance of larger issues and his antagonistic speeches hurt him and his candidates. In addition, reformers revived public disaffection with the machine in New York City. An investigation led by Assemblyman Robert Mazet exposed Croker's connections with a firm that furnished most of the city's ice and that was planning to double its prices to consumers. Croker's participation in the scheme was still honest graft, but it was the kind that directly drained the pockets of ordinary, working-class families. Moreover exposés revealed that dirty graft had again spread throughout the city. These occurrences loosened Croker's grip on his machine. When Seth Low defeated the Tammany candidate for mayor in 1901, Croker again sailed for England.

Croker had presided over some thirty-five district leaders. The career of one of these smaller bosses, Timothy D. Sullivan, illustrates how the city boss was a broker and how his power could be checked. "Big Tim" Sullivan was a second-generation immigrant, born in the Bowery and raised by his widowed Irish mother. Like Tweed and Croker he left school at an early age and became the leader of a gang. His savvy and brawn gave him ready entry into Tammany Hall. He became a political prodigy and

New York's "King Richard" Tammany boss Richard Croker, with top hat and boutonniere, ruled the city from the driver's seat of a well-oiled political machine. He had no reservations about his motives. When once he was asked if he was working for his own interests, Croker retorted, "All the time—the same as you." *(Brown Brothers.)*

was elected to the state legislature in 1886 when he was twenty-three years old. He later served a term in the U.S. House of Representatives, but like Tweed he could not stomach life in Washington and returned to New York after two years.

Back in New York, Sullivan secured control over the Lower East Side and Bowery districts by learning Yiddish and soliciting support from the Jewish immigrants who were replacing some of the Irish residents. He used his political leverage to place his supporters on public payrolls and to open a string of profitable gambling halls. He also cultivated his personal appeal with consummate skill. He arranged bails, sent food and medicine to the sick and feeble, gave shoes to needy schoolchildren, and sponsored annual summer picnics. His Timothy D. Sullivan Association was a poor man's social club that operated out of neighborhood saloons. The Sullivan club-houses became distributing centers for those who needed jobs, food, and other services, as well as for political intrigue. Sullivan built his machine on trust and loyalty—he was a man who kept his word. It was said that he was so well-liked that his portrait hung in nearly every building in his district.

Like other district bosses Sullivan generally stood behind Boss Croker. But Big Tim had such a loyal following that he could assert his independence if he so desired. On one occasion Sullivan threatened to withhold the huge payments that his gambling and prostitution ring made to Tammany Hall unless Croker would restore an ousted police chief to power. Later Sullivan touted his own aldermanic candidate over an incumbent who was a loyal Croker ally. When Sullivan's candidate won, the district boss reputedly boasted, "Croker ain't the whole thing." Yet after Croker's fall Sullivan shirked the opportunity to become city boss, preferring to influence the policies of city hall from his own district and to look after his multimillion-dollar vice operations. He kept his independence until 1912, when he became ill and was committed to an insane asylum. He escaped shortly but was apparently struck by a freight train and was found dead in a railroad yard. His funeral attracted over twenty-five thousand mourners.

New York City provides the most colorful showcase for the examination of machine politics, but bossism flourished in many other cities as well. Moreover machines were not peculiar to the Democratic Party. Philadel-

The Ward Machine in Action   This photograph depicts one of many gatherings of the Timothy D. Sullivan Association (see banner at left), the political club run by ward boss "Big Tim" Sullivan from New York. Note that a political outing was generally an all-male event. *(Brown Brothers.)*

phia had "King" James McManes, a Republican who controlled the city's fiscal policies and electoral politics from the late 1860s until 1881. McManes achieved and exercised his power by becoming the leading figure on a municipal board that superintended the city's gas utility. Using his authority over the distribution of jobs and letting of contracts, McManes spread his influence to other city departments. He required city employees to kick back a portion of their salaries to his organization, and he manipulated elections for his own benefit. Like other bosses McManes took care of himself. During his reign he reputedly earned two and a half million dollars, mostly from payoffs from favored contractors. Also like other bosses, McManes alarmed opponents by his lavish expenditures of public funds. Between 1860 and 1880 Philadelphia's municipal debt swelled by 350 percent. Although much of the money facilitated the city's physical expansion, a number of Republican businessmen became outraged. They formed the Committee of One Hundred and fused with local Democrats to defeat machine candidates in the 1881 elections. McManes retired to enjoy his private fortune, but bossism returned to Philadelphia later in the decade.

Chicago had its own brand of machine politics. Practically every ward boss was an independent entrepreneur, each courting his constituency in his own style. Johnny Powers of the Nineteenth Ward was known as "The Chief Mourner" because of his attendance record at funerals. Michael "Hinky Dink" Kenna of the First Ward served free lunches in his saloon. His partner, "Bathhouse John" Coughlin, received his nickname for the kind of services he sponsored. "King" Michael McDonald offered open gambling houses. "Blond Boss" William Lorimer worked to remove prejudices against Jews and other immigrants on Chicago's West Side. Although all but Lorimer were Democrats, no individual was able to construct one city-wide machine. Carter Harrison and his son Carter II held the mayoralty off and on through three and a half decades and cultivated faithful support among immigrants by championing "personal liberty"—meaning toleration of drinking and gambling. But neither Harrison could overcome the independence of the ward bosses.

Still, machine politics in Chicago contained familiar features. Political power derived from numbers and favors. City employees paid part of their salaries to the boss who got them their jobs. Boodling and graft were common. Powers maintained a mutually profitable relationship with streetcar companies, particularly with traction magnate Charles Tyson Yerkes. Roger Sullivan, one of the most powerful bosses of early-twentieth-century Chicago, specialized in granting favors to—and receiving gratuities from—banks and gas companies. The lack of a strong city boss, however, produced two extremes of instability. On one hand, it was somewhat easier for reformers to gain a foothold in Chicago politics because they did not have to battle a single, entrenched machine. Yet on the other hand, because there were so many bosses, so many enemies, reformers found it difficult to

Two Chicago Ward Bosses   Michael "Hinky Dink" Kenna and "Bathhouse John" Coughlin were bosses of Chicago's First Ward, the notorious "levee" district. *(Courtesy Chicago Historical Society.)*

mount a unified attack against every boss, and their footholds quickly eroded.

It is important to note that bossism was not confined to the very large cities. Small cities also needed leaders who could coordinate political power, mediate between immigrants and their new environment, and organize physical expansion. In Omaha Tom Dennison built an inner-city Democratic machine that influenced local politics for nearly three decades after the turn of the century. Dennison used politics to protect his multimillion-dollar vice business. By appealing to immigrant voters of the inner wards (Dennison's saloons would often be the only places where immigrant workers could cash their paychecks) Dennison could place his lieutenants in high offices and through them act as a broker between the city government and the business community. As in other cities the boss accumulated boodle from firms receiving city business. Dennison remained in power from the early 1900s to the late 1920s, with only a brief hiatus between 1918 and 1921, and retired to California a wealthy man.

Practically every major city experienced a period of boss rule some time after 1880. In Pittsburgh Christopher Magee supervised a Republican machine that lasted for half a century. In San Francisco Abe Ruef, whose Jewish ancestry and college training distinguished him from other city bosses, operated from within the Union Labor Party to acquire control in the early twentieth century. Martin Behrman of New Orleans directed most local affairs between 1900 and 1920 from his posts as mayor and as leader of the Democratic Choctaw Club. The Pendergast brothers, Jim and Tom, spread their influence from Kansas City's river wards to the entire city. The reigns of Jim and, later, Tom lasted from the late 1880s to the late 1930s. Edward H. Crump rose to power in Memphis around 1910 and did not lose control until the 1940s. In Jersey City Frank Hague ruled from 1917 to 1947 under the slogan, "I am the law." Like all the others these men were coordinators, not dictators. They presided over federations, not over autocracies. They directed their attention to a full range of services—from Thanksgiving turkeys to business franchises to gambling dens.

BOSSES AND THEIR OPPONENTS: POLITICAL POWER AND URBAN RULE

As early as 1860 the lines in many cities were drawn in what would become the characteristic political contest in the late nineteenth century: boss politics and the machine opposed by a relatively small elite minority organized under the banner of municipal reform. Although commentators at the time often claimed that "the better elements" had abandoned the city to "low-bred" Irish saloon keepers, actual political accommodations were much more complex. Reformers battled bosses in Philadelphia, Baltimore, Milwaukee, Boston, Pittsburgh, and Cincinnati, as well as in New York, and used many different strategies in their attempts to mold urban government to their vision of how cities should be run.

Bosses and machines that seemed invincible rarely had total control over a city's political apparatus. Historian Jon Teaford has argued that in many cases machines were fragile coalitions, makeshift alliances, torn by internal rivalry and competition, and periodically weakened by successful opposition mounted from outside the party.[2] Bosses rarely held important political office themselves, and their power was constrained by their limited ability to exercise the formal authority of the chief municipal offices. Instead bosses often found themselves compromising with the political independence of elected officials.

The city council or board of aldermen was the staging ground for ethnic political power as it emanated from the wards proliferating in late nineteenth-century cities. Prior to 1850 the ward system had begun to replace citywide representation, and most councilors and aldermen were elected by the voters of a certain ward. Ward representation had changed the type of men chosen as aldermen. By 1900 the typical ward-elected councilman was a modest saloon keeper, contractor, retailer, clerk, skilled artisan, or unskilled laborer who customarily lived and worked in the ward. Professionals and downtown businessmen were greatly outnumbered. Residential patterns guaranteed that some wards would be dominated by working-class Irish, others by Italians, and others by native-born Protestants. First Irish and German, then Italian, Polish, Czech, and black representatives were seated on city councils in New York, Boston, Chicago, St. Louis, Cincinnati, Philadelphia, and Baltimore. The ward system was also the vehicle through which labor and workingmen's slates and later socialist tickets won representation on city councils. The council served as the voice of the neighborhoods, the channel through which constituents won exemptions or licenses and neighborhoods obtained pavements, sewers, and water mains. By 1900, American cities included a mass of disparate neighborhoods with different social and ethnic orientations and diverse transportation, paving, and drainage needs, and city councils were the forum for debate over urban physical expansion and its implications.

During the late nineteenth century, urban elites recognized the emerging power of ethnic and working-class wards as they observed immigrants and their representatives gaining ground in city councils and party organizations. To counter erosion of their authority, downtown business and professional leaders organized themselves to be in a position to intervene in the political process. Through chambers of commerce, boards of trade, and specially constituted good government and municipal reform leagues these citizens sought to restore urban rule to the "better elements." Chambers of commerce were particularly active in promoting changes they felt would make the atmosphere of the city good for business and that would enable economic benefits to trickle down to the working classes. Momentary political alliances of well-known merchants, lawyers, and journalists, arguing that they were acting in the name of civic interest, organized themselves as the Committee of Seventy in New York and the Committee of One Hundred in Philadelphia and offered reform slates for municipal office that succeeded in ousting the Tweed Ring in New York in 1871 and the McManes machine in Philadelphia in 1881, at least temporarily. These reformers blamed bosses and machines for wasting taxpayers' money and polluting the American system. They wanted to cleanse politics by restricting the voting franchise with property qualifications and literary tests to ensure that only men like themselves, wealthy and refined, should have responsibility for urban government. These short-lived and temporary alliances were replaced by municipal leagues with paid executives that were organized explicitly to compete with party resources in promoting what were considered to be appropriate candidates. All these associations actively campaigned for cuts in expenditures and tax rates, drafted legislation and charter revision, and endorsed reform candidates for office.

Acting in concert with state legislatures often dominated by rural interests, municipal reformers also set their sights on transforming urban governance in the long run by shifting authority from ward to city-wide representatives and from elected to appointed officials. Just at the time when foreign-born representatives of working-class wards came to enjoy a prominent voice on the city council, the authority of the council itself was circumscribed. Before the 1860s and 1870s the city council had directly supervised municipal functions, determining appointments, hiring city employees, fixing policy, and even deciding administrative details. By the 1880s and 1890s the supervisory role of the council had declined sharply, particularly in terms of city appointments and finances. New municipal charters, lobbied for by elite members of chambers of commerce or reform leagues, shifted authority to expert commissions and executive departments either appointed or elected by a city-wide constituency that favored downtown business or professional interests. New York City's charter of 1873, Brooklyn's charter of 1882, Boston's charter of 1885, Baltimore's charter of 1898 all sharply limited aldermanic authority over public works, budgets, and police expenditures by substituting appointed commissions composed of specialists and experts.

In the same years in which councils lost authority to special independent commissions, mayors gained power through broadened use of the veto and expanded powers of appointment. Mayors became the ones to initiate policy and with their appointees to implement programs. Elected on a citywide basis, mayors were more likely to be successful downtown businessmen or professionals, drawn from the ranks of bankers, manufacturers, wholesale merchants, large-scale real-estate developers, and lawyers with old-stock social-register pedigrees. Mayors were not likely to be drawn from the city's wealthiest men, nor were multimillionaire robber barons likely to be elected. But big-city mayors were usually members of what Victorians would call the "better class" of citizens. Downtown businessmen were also likely to hold the crucial post of city comptroller, where their business orientation guided the auditing of city accounts and preparation of municipal budgets. Independent commissions that governed municipal parks, libraries, and police departments tended to draw their membership from the same social strata. Most commissioners held long terms of office and were increasingly likely to be independent from elected officials, and some commissions were formed as self-perpetuating boards of trustees.

Furthermore the importance of elected officials as policy makers paled in the face of a new group of urban professionals, civil engineers, landscape architects, public health officials, and school administrators who generated permanent urban bureaucracies to build and operate waterworks, design and run the parks, guard public health and safety, and oversee the education of millions of urban school children. Even before the effective application of civil-service laws, mayors and commissioners deferred to the judgment and expertise of these professionals. Steeped in a professional rather than local orientation, committed to centralized decision making, loyal to the perpetuation of their own departments, protected behind a fortress of expertise, municipal professionals by the end of the century were securing a place of permanent authority in city government. Together the downtown businessmen and professionals, who called themselves municipal reformers, and the new municipal experts claimed that their vision of the city constituted the public interest.

Despite the hopes and efforts of municipal reformers, bosses and machines did not disappear from cities. Croker's lieutenant George Washington Plunkitt claimed that reformers were "mornin' glories—looked lovely in the morning but withered up in a short time," but reform associations also proved to be enduring. In the twentieth century the lines between bosses and reformers would become blurred as successful reformers built up organizations that bore a striking resemblance to machines in their attempts to stay in power, and bosses found themselves joining reform coalitions around certain issues (see Chapter 6). Both would confront the implications of entrenched urban bureaucracies as they took part in the national debate on the consequences of industrialization under the banner of urban reform.

BIBLIOGRAPHY

For analysis of the early origins of machine politics see Amy Bridges, *A City in the Republic: Antebellum New York and the Origins of Machine Politics* (New York: Cambridge University Press, 1984). Jon C. Teaford has called for a major revision of urban history writing on late nineteenth century cities that recasts the contest between bosses and reformers; see his article, "Finis for Tweed and Steffens: Rewriting the History of Urban Rule," *Reviews in American History* 10(December 1982):133–49, and *The Unheralded Triumph: City Government in America, 1870–1900* (Baltimore: Johns Hopkins University Press, 1984). For other interpretations see Richard C. Wade, "Urbanization," in *The Comparative Approach to American History*, ed. C. Vann Woodward (New York: Basic Books, 1968); Robert K. Merton, "Latent Functions of the Machine," *Social Theory and Social Structure*, rev. ed. (New York: Free Press, 1949), 71–82; Elmer J. Cornwell, Jr., "Bosses, Machines, and Ethnic Groups," in *City Bosses and Political Machines*, ed. Lee S. Greene, Vol. 353 of *The Annals of the American Academy of Political and Social Science* (Philadelphia: American Academy of Political and Social Science, 1946), 28–34; and Eric McKitrick, "The Study of Corruption," *Political Science Quarterly,* 72(December 1957): 502–14. Anthologies and group studies include Blaine A. Brownell and Warren E. Stickle, eds., *Bosses and Reformers: Urban Politics in America, 1880–1920* (Boston: Houghton Mifflin, 1973); Bruce M. Stave, ed., *Urban Bosses, Machines, and Progressive Reformers* (Lexington, Mass.: D.C. Heath & Co., 1972); Harold Zink, *City Bosses in the United States: A Study of Twenty Municipal Bosses* (Durham, N.C.: Duke University Press, 1930); Alexander B. Callow, Jr., ed., *The City Boss in America: An Interpretive Reader* (New York: Oxford University Press, 1976); John M. Allswang, *Bosses, Machines, and Urban Voters: An American Symbiosis* (Port Washington, N.Y.: Kennikat Press, 1977); Bruce Stave and Sondra Stave, eds., *Urban Bosses, Machines, and Progressive Reformers*, 2nd rev. ed. (Malabar, Fla.: Robert E. Krieger, 1984).

On independent labor politics in this period, see Leon Fink, *Workingmen's Democracy: The Knights of Labor and American Politics* (Urbana: University of Illinois Press, 1983); Fink, "The Uses of Political Power: Toward a Theory of the Labor Movement in the Era of the Knights of Labor," in *Working-Class America: Essays on Labor, Community, and Working-Class Society*, ed. by Michael H. Frisch and Daniel J.

Walkowitz (Urbana: University of Illinois Press, 1983); Steven J. Ross, *Workers on the Edge: Work, Leisure, and Politics in Industrializing Cincinnati, 1788–1890* (New York: Columbia University Press, 1985); Ross, "The Politicization of the Working Class: Production, Ideology, Culture and Politics in Late Nineteenth Century Cincinnati," *Social History* 8(May, 1986):171–96; David Scobey, "Boycotting the Politics Factory: Labor Radicalism and the New York City Mayoral Election of 1884," *Radical History Review* 28–30(September 1984)280–325.

　　Among individual machines, Tammany Hall has received the most attention from historians, most notably from Jerome Mushkat, *Tammany: The Evolution of a Political Machine, 1789–1865* (Syracuse, N.Y.: Syracuse University Press, 1971); Seymour Mandlebaum, *Boss Tweed's New York* (New York: John Wiley & Sons, 1965); Alexander B. Callow, Jr., *The Tweed Ring* (New York: Oxford University Press, 1966); and Leo Hershkowitz, *Tweed's New York: Another Look* (Garden City, N.Y.: Doubleday, Anchor Press, 1977). Alfred Connable and Edward Silberfarb, *Tigers of Tammany: Nine Men Who Ran New York* (New York: Holt, Rinehart & Winston, 1967) is a lively, popular account. William L. Riordon, *Plunkett of Tammany Hall* (New York: Dutton, 1963) is a delightful memoir of a boss and includes a perceptive introduction by Arthur Mann. Also useful is Theodore F. Lowi, *At the Pleasure of the Mayor: Patronage and Power in New York City, 1898–1958* (New York: Free Press, 1964). For works on Chicago see Joel A. Tarr, *A Study in Boss Politics: William Lorimer of Chicago* (Urbana, Ill.: University of Illinois Press, 1971); Harold F. Gosnell, *Machine Politics: The Chicago Model* (Chicago: University of Chicago Press, 1937); Lloyd Wendt and Herman Kogan, *Lords of the Levee: The Story of Bathhouse John and Hinky Dink* (Indianapolis: Bobbs-Merrill, 1943); and Edward R. Kantowicz, *Polish-American Politics in Chicago, 1888–1914* (Chicago: University of Chicago Press, 1975). Mike Royko, *Boss: Richard J. Daley of Chicago* (New York: Dutton, 1971) is a popular account of a well-known modern boss.

　　Other important studies are Zane L. Miller, *Boss Cox's Cincinnati: Urban Politics in the Progressive Era* (New York: Oxford University Press, 1968); Lyle W. Dorsett, *The Pendergast Machine* (New York: Oxford University Press, 1968); Joy J. Jackson, *New Orleans in the Gilded Age: Politics and Urban Progress, 1860–1896* (Baton Rouge: Louisiana State University Press, 1969); William D. Miller, *Mr. Crump of Memphis* (Baton Rouge: Louisiana State University Press, 1964), and *Memphis During the Progressive Era, 1900–1917* (Memphis: Memphis State University Press, 1957); Eugene J. Watts, *The Social Basis of City Politics: Atlanta, 1865–1903* (Westport, Conn.: Greenwood Press, 1978); and William A. Bullough, *The Blind Boss and His City: Christopher Augustine Buckley and Nineteenth Century San Francisco* (Berkeley and Los Angeles: University of California Press, 1979); Walton Bean, *Boss Rueff's San Francisco: The Story of the Union Labor Party, Big Business, and the Graft Prosecution* (Berkeley: University of California Press, 1952). For a provocative analysis of what happened to bosses and machines during and after the 1930s see Bruce M. Stave, *The New Deal and the Last Hurrah: Pittsburgh Machine Politics* (Pittsburgh: University of Pittsburgh Press, 1970). A valuable and revisionist interpretation of bosses' relations with the reform movement can be found in John D. Buenker, *Urban Liberalism and Progressive Reform* (New York: Scribner's, 1973).

ENDNOTES

[1] Oscar Handlin, *The Uprooted* (New York: Grosset and Dunlap, 1951), 209.

[2] Jon Teaford, *The Unheralded Triumph: City Government in America, 1870–1900* (Baltimore: Johns Hopkins University Press, 1984), 175–84.

6

The Dispositions of Urban Reform, 1880–1920

THE IMPETUS TOWARD URBAN REFORM

In the closing years of the nineteenth century and dawning years of the twentieth, city dwellers debated the consequences of industrialization with new urgency. What caused the rising concern? The sudden ascendancy of finance capitalism—highly visible in the great merger wave between 1889 and 1903, producing such corporate giants as U.S. Steel Corporation, financed by J.P. Morgan, Amalgamated Copper, and American Tobacco Company—made it seemingly responsible for the nation's most severe depression, poverty, and labor unrest. Now ordinary urban residents came to experience their own powerlessness firsthand and in a daily way in the face of streetcar, gas, and electricity monopolies. Whatever the reasons, a variety of issues related to changing economic and social conditions inflamed the passions of city people and shaped diverse and shifting reform coalitions.

Urban-reform agitation emerged in a changing political context. Party loyalties began to erode with antiboss legislation, which tightened registration laws, made it easier to vote a split ticket, and instituted secret ballots and direct primaries. These measures, in combination with legal disenfranchisement of blacks and many poor whites in the South, led to a decline in voting. The political arena was now opening to extra-party pressure groups, such as manufacturers' associations, labor lobbies, civic leagues, women's clubs, and professional associations, making politics more fragmented, political combinations more fluid, and campaigns more issue oriented. Lobbying and coalition building supplanted older party channels, and reformers used new methods of trying to create and mobilize public opinion, such as sensationalistic journalism, celebrity picket lines, witness-calling investigations, referendum campaigns, and social-science surveys. Occasionally, maverick candidates could win political office and reform coalitions could reorient the direction of urban politics. In this context, radical groups found greater opportunity to express their views. American socialists vigorously denounced urban inequality, poverty, and lack of welfare services, proposing their own strategies for ameliorating urban conditions, which ranged from expanded public responsibility to employ the unemployed to municipal ownership of utilities and transportation. Municipal socialists were particularly visible in cities like Milwaukee, Reading, Schenectady, and Bridgeport where socialist mayors were elected to office, and in 1912 socialists held over twelve hundred public offices in 340 cities and towns across the country.

But nationally, men's allegiance to political parties waned, and the male political culture, which was the most striking characteristic of nineteenth-century political life, lost its vitality. As upper- and middle-class men left partisan politics to the working class and ethnic machines and turned their interest to single-issue reform tactics, they found themselves in the territory that women's voluntary reform associations had long occupied. As reformers turned to government to secure legislation to redress social problems by increasing the government's role in social welfare and economic life, men and women found themselves joining on common goals. The concerns of politics and the home came much closer together, and these new ideas about government's broader social responsibility resonated with women's social concerns. Not surprisingly, then, women social activists played a major role in the articulation of urban reform, prior to their own direct participation as voters.

The orientation of urban reform activities was deeply influenced by larger changes within the whole of American society. Businessmen within crucial sectors of the economy began to shift their orientation from competition to stability. Their concern was to rationalize their economic environment with policies that would reduce waste and inefficiency, applying centralized, bureaucratic control to financial, commercial, and industrial organization. As historian Daniel Rodgers has observed, businessmen in this period felt convinced that the new rationalized organizational mode of the corporation was also *the* appropriate model for city governance.[1] Thus in the newly fluid, issue-focused political contests of the period, the organizational resources commanded by corporations gave them a considerable advantage in shaping reform initiatives.

MUNICIPAL GOVERNANCE

Josiah Strong, a Congregationalist minister from Cincinnati, expressed the concerns of many when he wrote in 1885, "The city is the nerve center of our civilization. It is also the storm center. . . . [It] has become a serious threat to our civilization." Many middle- and upper-class people who inhabited the urban outskirts continued to identify boss politics as the eye of the storm. Largely native-born and Protestant, these people viewed what was happening in inner-city districts with rising apprehension. They feared immigrant-dominated political machines and offered various proposals to dismantle the power of bosses under the rubric of civic, or municipal, reform.

In their attempt to dismantle party machinery, some civic reformers discussed attempting to limit suffrage. The Tilden Commission, appointed in New York to investigate the Tweed Ring scandals, recommended in 1878 that the vote be restricted to those who owned property. A leader in a campaign for municipal reform in Newport, Rhode Island, made the case in 1907 that the current system failed to give property owners political power commensurate with their economic power: "The present system," he charged, "has excluded in large degree the representation of those who have the city's well-being most at heart." Rather than a government by "the least educated," which he claimed were also the "least interested class of citizens," he proposed a system that gave majority representation to the city's substantial citizens. As he put it, "It stands to reason that a man paying $5,000 taxes in a town is more interested in the well-being and development of his town than the man who pays no taxes." Civic reformers claimed that expanding the representation of propertied voters would be more "truly democratic" than current governments. Although municipal reformers looked with keen interest at legislation that had disenfranchised black and poor white voters in southern states, regulations that actually revoked immigrant voting rights never seemed politically feasible in cities. Democratic principles and universal white male suffrage were too deeply entrenched.

Instead, municipal reformers turned to political strategies that would lessen the impact of immigrant and working-class voters without actually interfering with voting rights. Several of these strategies were designed to regulate elections and to make nominations and election procedures more accessible to the public. By 1905 voter-registration laws were on the books everywhere, and in the next fifteen years, localities set up election boards, tightened laws making it illegal to vote more than once, and tried to define legitimate use of campaign funds.

But more important than electoral reform were strategies designed to weaken party machines and to remove party politics from municipal administrations. Because machines were based in ethnic neighborhoods and supported by party identification, reformers tried to institute at-large elections and nonpartisan ballots (no candidate could run for office under a party label) as a way of attacking the machines. Having to appeal to a large citywide electorate rather than one neighborhood or ethnic group would diminish the ability of candidates from ethnic and working class districts to gain office. Large organizations such as civic leagues and business groups would have an advantage in influencing citywide elections and electing business candidates because they had access to the funds required to reach a large and diverse electorate.

Nonpartisan ballots symbolized the reformers' claim that there was only one urban public interest, which businessmen best understood. Parties were not needed for public services to be provided as cheaply and efficiently as possible and for the city to be run as much like a corporation as possible. Civic reformers contended that a city did not need a Democrat or a Republican to build a school or lay a sewer; responsible local government was no place for party politics. Removing the party label from election ballots, supposedly to encourage civic loyalties rather than bloc voting, also would have the effect of depriving working-class and ethnic candidates of party resources for campaigning and party employment. Few machine politicians could have started or stayed in politics without the organization's help. Nonpartisan elections favored those who did not need party organization—men of wealth and social standing—who would once again be able to dominate political office holding.

Municipal reformers usually campaigned for civil service along with at-large elections and nonpartisan ballots. Aimed at the heart of boss politics, the machine's ability to provide employment to its foot soldiers, civil service was a system that provided presumably objective standards for hiring municipal employees, using written and oral examinations as the basis for hiring rather than party affiliation.

Between 1900 and 1920, nonpartisanship, at-large elections, and civil service were successfully implemented in cities throughout the nation. Municipal reform was less likely to be successful in large cities with complex electorates, where middle- and upper-class voters did not constitute an electoral majority; but smaller cities and new cities, usually in the Midwest and West, usually adopted reform programs in their charters. Sometimes annexations of outlying districts shifted the electoral balance toward municipal reform. But even in some big cities, reformers succeeded in getting nonpartisan at-large elections adopted; Los Angeles in 1908, Boston in 1909, Akron in 1915, and Detroit in 1918.

Municipal reform campaigns did change patterns of representation. The switch from ward to citywide electoral districts, which was consistently opposed by machines, ethnic politicians, socialists, and labor parties, made it much more difficult for ethnic and working-class wards and black neighborhoods without an absolute majority of the city's population to gain representation. Socialists in Dayton, Ohio, won 25 percent of the vote in 1909 and elected two aldermen and three assessors, but after the change to citywide elections, they failed to elect a single candidate even though their share of the total vote increased to 44 percent. The change to citywide representation in Los Angeles prevented black and Hispanic citizens from electing a city council representative until the most recent period. The change to citywide elections in Pittsburgh in 1911 meant that upper-class businessmen and professionals replaced lower and middle-class representatives on the city council and school committee.

The business orientation of most civic reformers was reflected in their commitment to applying principles of business management to cities. Trying to make the structure of urban governance match the model of the corporation, reformers proposed reorganizing cities to separate policy-making from administration either through a commission or city-manager form of government. The first city to be run on the business model was Galveston, Texas, where business and professional leaders had already secured a charter amendment from the state legislature replacing ward with citywide elections. Businessmen on the council continued to be outvoted by a nonbusiness faction, but then in 1900 emergency circumstances following a hurricane and flood that ravaged the city enabled the state legislature to replace Galveston's city council with a commission of local businessmen, each of whom administered a different branch of municipal affairs. The city then adopted the commission form permanently and elected seven commissioners on a nonpartisan at-large basis. In Nashville, Boss Hilary Howse's attempts to spend lavish amounts of public funds to improve the health, education, and welfare of ethnic and racial minorities who supported him provoked conservative business and Democratic party leaders to try to take power away from the ward bosses who were the backbone of his political base. Charter reforms, establishing a commission government in 1913, led to Howse's ouster two years later. With its aims to streamline government and facilitate the contributions of businessmen to government service, the city commission was an attractive organizational plan around which reformers could rally to challenge urban party bosses. Within ten years, more than one hundred communities, mostly small cities where ward organization had been weak, adopted commission plans, and by 1915 there were 456 cities under commission governance.

The city-manager form of government grew out of business reverence for expertise. In 1908 the city of Staunton, Virginia, hired a city manager to administer local affairs in the place of a politically elected mayor. The idea spread slowly at first. But in Dayton, Ohio, the president of National Cash Register, working with the chamber of commerce and a newly organized Bureau of Municipal Research, began a campaign for charter reform that was enacted, finally, as a consequence of a disastrous flood. Eventually a city-manager plan was tried in such larger cities as Cleveland, Cincinnati, and Kansas City. This plan created a new separation of power. It usually provided for a small city council elected on a nonpartisan ballot that would determine general policy and pass ordinances. The council would then appoint or hire a city manager, chosen for his administrative and technical skills, who would implement council policies and determine budgets. In some cases the mayor was retained and given mainly titular functions. By 1920 more than 150 cities had city managers. Business interests consistently led the campaign for this reform. For example, the *Dallas News* promoted the plan in 1930 by asking, "Why not run Dallas itself on a business schedule by business methods under businessmen? . . . The city manager is the executive of a corporation under a board of directors. Dallas is the corporation. It is as simple as that. Vote for it."

The efficiency argument also produced another, though more controversial, type of reform—municipal ownership of public utilities. Some reformers believed that regardless of the form of government, bribery and corruption would always fester as long as politicians could collude with big business at public expense. These reformers thought they could destroy bosses' financial resources and provide better services by replacing private franchises with publicly owned operations. City-owned water systems had been common since the mid-nineteenth century. Now a number of reformers began to advocate public gas, electric, and transportation systems. Although by 1910 several hundred cities, including Cleveland, Detroit, and Chicago, had experimented with this reform, public ownership succeeded mainly in smaller cities, where profits for private companies were more limited. Also, public ownership, supported by socialists, frightened many municipal leaders, and businessmen were not of one mind about it. Expenditures on public harbors, roads, docks, and sewers won general acceptance because they stimulated private enterprise. But when advocates of public projects tried to supplant private operations, they frequently met strong opposition. Nevertheless most city dwellers eventually accepted some form of public regulation of utility rates and services, even if public ownership proved unacceptable.

Some bosses were able to adjust to new structures of city governance and even use them for their own purposes. When a city-commission government threatened to subvert Omaha boss Tom Dennison's control of the city in 1912, the boss did not fight public sentiment. He merely entered his own slate of candidates for the commission, who then dominated that body for the machine's benefit. Boss Ed Crump solidified his grip on Memphis in the same way when a new city charter established a commission form of government in 1909. James Michael Curley was able to use new citywide elections in Boston as a way of undermining the ward-based political leadership whom he was contesting for control of the city. Flexibility and pragmatism in response to changing government structures characterized the bosses who were able to retain political power in twentieth-century cities, but the municipal structures they inherited from the civic reformers who were trying to oust them were intended to be unresponsive to popular concerns and perhaps explain the roots of bureaucratic rigidity in cities today.

The lines between bosses and reformers blurred in late nineteenth- and early twentieth-century cities, because bosses supported civic reforms they thought they could make use of and because bosses were pushed by their constituents to support reform campaigns such as public ownership of utilities and laws to improve working conditions for laborers that promised to help neighborhood residents. Even Big Tim Sullivan once dashed to the Statehouse in Albany to cast a decisive vote in favor of a bill limiting working hours for women to a fifty-four-hour week. (He later explained, "I had seen me sister go out to work when she was only fourteen and I know we ought to help these gals by giving 'em a law which will prevent 'em from being broken down while they're still young.") Republican Boss George B. Cox of Cincinnati was pushed by the suburban allies to whom he owed his initial election to support campaigns for the secret ballot and voter registration, usually anathema to a boss. Similarly, municipal reformers who hoped to intervene politically to solve problems of urban decay and poverty found themselves acting like bosses by using the prerogatives of centralized executive power and building political organizations to help them stay in office. Several big city reform mayors who responded to ethnic and working-class constituencies and moved beyond their initial goals of eliminating corruption and inefficiency to effecting social change that aimed to create social and economic equality have been labeled by historians as "reform bosses." The mayoral careers of Hazen S. Pingree of Detroit, Samuel M. Jones of Toledo, and Thomas L. Johnson of Cleveland illustrate this pattern.

Hazen Pingree was the first reformer to build his own political organization and the first politician to work explicitly for social reform. Pingree was a Detroit shoe manufacturer who was drafted into the 1889 mayoral election by the Michigan Club, an influential group of Republican businessmen who wanted to rid Detroit of corruption. Pingree won the election by appealing to the city's German, Polish, and Irish voters. He immediately began to apply business principles of prudence and efficiency to government operations, and his success won him reelection in 1891. Pingree's struggles to limit the rates and franchise privileges of street-railway, gas, electric, and telephone companies awakened him to the dangers of such monopolistic enterprises and sharpened his concern for the public who paid for these services. When the depression of 1893–94 brought suffering to tens of thousands of Detroiters, Pingree focused his administration directly on the welfare of the working classes. He bolstered relief agencies, authorized public works for unemployment relief, and cajoled businessmen to keep prices low and to not lay off workers. Pingree's passion for the poor influenced administrations in other cities to assume greater social responsibilities, and his constant battles with utilities companies furnished other reformers with strong arguments for municipal ownership. Although Pingree did succeed in reducing gas rates and in building a publicly owned electric plant, his efforts to bring down streetcar fares were continually frustrated. In 1896 he transferred his crusade to the state level and successfully ran for governor. There his battles with a reactionary legislature afforded him few victories, but he was able to raise issues that eventually became part of progressive reform.

Pingree was one of the few reform mayors to work for more than economy and efficiency in government. During his four terms as mayor he not only ended corruption but also built parks and schools, instituted a more equitable tax structure, established work-relief programs for the poor, reduced utility rates, and spoke out for a graduated income tax and municipal ownership. Moreover he ignored efforts to impose middle-class Yankee norms on others. He refused to enforce Sunday-closing laws applying to saloons, and he tolerated gambling and prostitution. His administration became a model for reform mayors in other cities.

Samuel "Golden Rule" Jones served as mayor of Toledo from 1897 until his death in 1904, and Tom Johnson was mayor of Cleveland from 1901 until a narrow election defeat in 1909. Like Pingree, Jones and Johnson were successful businessmen who became social reformers as politicians. Both actively supported municipal ownership of utilities, and both stressed the need for social justice and equality. Both also included a number of intellectuals in their administrations. Brand Whitlock, novelist and lawyer, was prominent among Jones's advisers and later succeeded him as mayor of Toledo. Frederick C. Howe, Newton Baker, and Edward Bemis were among Johnson's closest associates. Johnson was also influenced by the ideas of Henry George, whose book *Progress and Poverty* (1879) had made considerable impact upon reform thought around the turn of the century. George's proposal to eliminate social inequality by taxing profits that property owners unfairly received from the unearned increment of their land inspired Johnson and others like him to work for social and economic reform. Many of the programs supported by Jones and Johnson bordered on socialism and alienated their business allies. Yet, like Pingree, both mayors and the men who surrounded them sought only to preserve what they believed to be the American tradition, not to change it. Their popular appeal and social-welfare projects extended well beyond ordinary economy and efficiency, yet they envisioned their goals as the fulfillment of the American dream. As Whitlock wrote, "The ills from which our cities suffer are not the ills incident to democracy; they are the ills incident to a lack of democracy."

Pingree, Jones, and Johnson were the exceptions. Most civic reformers aimed only to "throw the rascals out," and when successful, their "clean governments" fizzled because they could not match the functions performed by political machines. Although civic reformers called for honesty and efficiency in government, they rarely mentioned social welfare. Behind their proposals was the notion that the purpose of city government was to provide a climate for profit making and profit taking through the provision of efficient public services. The city-as-a-business orientation provided a sharp contrast with socialist, social reform, and working-class ethnic demands that intended to redefine the public interest to include social programs aimed at improving the health, welfare, and living conditions of inner-city residents by extending public authority to restructure tax burdens, attempting to secure favorable utility rates, and expanding housing, recreational, and public-works programs. Protesting that "a city is more than a business corporation" and that "good health is more important than a low tax rate," social reformers' proposals were founded on the conception that government should expand its reach to improve the lives of those who suffered from poverty and unemployment.

Civic reformers' self-righteousness and obsessive budget cutting failed to touch common needs of jobs, housing, and health. Even their attempts to apply business principles to politics usually revealed insensitivity to the complexities of business and political administration. A reformer, said Mr. Dooley, the fictional Irish commentator created by newspaper columnist Finley Peter Dunne,

> thinks business an' honesty is th' same thing. . . . He's got them mixed because they dhress alike. His idea is that all he has to do to make a business administhration is to keep honest men ar-round him. Wrong, I'm not sayin', mind ye, that a man can't do good work an' be honest at th' same time. But whin I hire a la-ad, I find out first whether he is onto his job, an' after a few years I begin to suspect he is honest too. . . . A man ought to be honest to start with an' afther that he ought to be crafty. A pollytician who's on'y honest is jus' th' same as bein' out in a winther storm without anny clothes on.

Thus civic reformers may have succeeded in improving the general quality of municipal administration by reducing corruption, lowering taxes, and shoring up local control. But their tendency to view urban society only in business and moralistic terms ignored long-term political and social policy and posed no substitute for the welfare functions of political machines.

THE REMEDIES OF SOCIAL REFORM

The liberal creed of the early nineteenth century had been *laissez faire*, the belief that the natural order of things ensured equilibrium. But by the end of the century that faith had begun to break down. A broad phalanx of reformers, ranging from wide-eyed humanitarians to calculating special interests, marched under a banner of public and private intervention to remove injustices from urban society. The counterforce to individual self-interest was community responsibility—the extension of public functions to promote the welfare of all. Daniel Rodgers has described a shared language of social reform, one characteristic of which was a conception of social

A Settlement House Sewing Class, 1912   In this photograph, taken at Sprague House, Providence, Rhode Island, documentary photographer Lewis Hine pictures the remedies of social reform, with well-dressed immigrant daughters learning domestic skills and the director of the settlement caring for a recently deserted baby. *(Courtesy The Slater Mill Historic Site.)*

bonds that challenged older notions that poverty and success depended on strengths of individual character, that the economy was the product of individual calculations, and that governance was a matter of empowering the best men. This focus on public responsibility was expressed in a new interest in the social and physical environment, the discovery of what Rodgers termed "new forms of social sinning and corresponding new measures of social control," and an intense concern with community cohesion.[2] Social reformers also concerned themselves with protecting those they saw as victims of industrialization, such as women and child laborers, those injured by industrial accidents, and unemployment people, and they committed their efforts to goals of industrial peace and cooperation.

Like civic reform, social reform grew out of changing economic and social conditions. Indeed, some social reformers were also civic reformers. It was based largely in what historian Robert Wiebe has called the "new middle class."[3] Its membership consisted basically of men and women who were becoming specialists in expanding areas of law, medicine, education, social work, and other professions, as well as new-breed professionals in fields of business, labor, and agriculture. Their awakening professional consciousness encouraged them to apply their expertise to their environments. More important, it led them to support and to undertake "scientific" investigations of urban problems. From the 1870s onward a number of different groups, mostly private and voluntary, sponsored examinations of aspects of urban life. These activities included surveys of public health and housing, studies of the incidence and location of poverty, and investigations of local corruption. One of the most striking aspects of the early development of social science was the way in which the field tied science to women's traditional community concerns. Agencies and organizations that were committed to social-science methods provided women reformers with quasi-professional positions as investigators from which they carried domestic and social concerns into far corners of the city. By the turn of the century the methods and language of social science and women's role as social investigators had become institutionalized components of reform strategy.

The emphasis on investigation had two objectives. First, the middle-class reformers were an inquiring generation: they felt a strong urge to know all the facts. Many of them believed they had temporarily lost their ability to understand fast-growing, ever-changing urban society. Only by restoring that understanding could they soothe their sense of crisis and begin to formulate plans to improve present conditions. Second, and more important, reformers from new middle-class ranks had a strong faith in knowledge and conscience as reforming agents. Many believed that if the general public could be kept well informed and if the major problems could be identified and exposed, an enlightened citizenry would rally behind programs to destroy injustice.

A new kind of journalism—the journalism of exposure—became a central vehicle in the drive for information. For nearly a century after the Revolution few city newspapers gave more than a passing glance to local affairs. In the early nineteenth century most newspapers had limited circulations and acted as organs for a political party, focusing mainly on state, national, and international issues. But the decades following the Civil War witnessed an extraordinary popularization and proliferation of newspapers and magazines. The invention of the steam press, which could print copies much faster than the old hand presses, and the increasing use of paper made of wood pulp instead of rags and linen enabled printers to produce copy much more cheaply and voluminously. The telegraph and telephone quickened the pace of communications and made information more accessible than ever before. To sell more newspapers publishers began to replace political prose with news and features. Journalists now created news as well as reported it. Circulation-hungry publishers such as Joseph Pulitzer, who bought the *New York World* in 1883, and William Randolph Hearst, who acquired the *San Francisco Call* in 1887 and the *New York Journal* in 1896, filled their front pages with screaming headlines, sensational stories, and dramatic photographs. At the same time, the old literary magazines began to give way to more popular, cheaper periodicals, such as *Cosmopolitan, McClure's,* and *Everybody's,* whose circulations grew to hundreds of thousands.

A large number of newspapers and magazines tried to attract readers by publishing articles that exposed the scandals and injustices of contemporary society. Some articles were lurid and ill informed, but many others were based on careful investigation—a major standard of social science—and were designed to alert the middle-class public to the need for reform. A leading spokesman for this journalism was Jacob Riis, a Danish immigrant who worked for twenty years as a police reporter for the *New York Tribune* and later the *Evening Sun.* Riis rose to national prominence in 1890 with the publication of his *How the Other Half Lives,* an intimate, vivid portrayal of poor people in New York. In a tone that was alternately sympathetic and indignant, Riis tried to describe "what the tenements are and how they grew to what they are." The book was illustrated with photographs, most of them taken by the author—he was one of the first to use the camera as an instrument of reform. But Riis wanted to do more than describe conditions: his goal was to inform and arouse his readers to the plights of the "other half."

Other journalists stirred public attention with their investigations of political abuses. Probably the most well-known reporter was Lincoln Steffens, whose seven articles on urban corruption in *McClure's* in 1902–3 were combined in a book titled *The Shame of the Cities,* published in 1904. Steffens was particularly incensed by the unfair privileges that he saw pervading modern American society. Through exposure of the misrule that he observed in St. Louis, Pittsburgh, Minneapolis, and Philadelphia and through his review of the partial success of reform in Chicago and New York, Steffens appealed to mass sentiments of responsibility, indignation, and guilt. He carefully constructed his articles to achieve dramatic impact for the sake of sounding the alarm and enlightening the public. Steffens and other journalists wrote their exposés to arouse the popular will and to revive democracy. As Steffens wrote in his introduction to *The Shame of the Cities,* "These articles, if they have proved nothing else, have demonstrated beyond doubt that we can stand the truth; that there is pride in the character of American citizenship; and that this pride may be a power in the land." The irony was that in the name of democracy the realism of the magazines threatened to deepen the passivity of the readers by overwhelming them with the complexity of events and then reassuring them with the counsel of the experts. As critic Christopher Wilson has observed, instead of promoting participation, the magazines elevated "seeing"; instead of encouraging readers' criticism, the editors interpreted for them and told readers simply to "stay informed."[4]

Certainly not all reform-bent journalists—they received the epithet of "muckrakers" from Theodore Roosevelt in 1906—focused exclusively on urban problems. Many writers attacked the malpractices of big business and national politics. Ida Tarbell and Henry Demarest Lloyd exposed the abusive power of the Standard Oil Company. Charles Edward Russell's *Greatest Trust in the World* assaulted the beef industry. Burton J. Hendrick's *Story of Life Insurance* examined the frauds of that business. David Graham Phillip's *The Treason of the Senate*, originally written for *Cosmopolitan*, accused many senators of being servants to big business. Yet because urban problems were so stark and because many middle-class reformers felt threatened and outraged by the problems arising from urbanization, most reform-oriented journalists and other writers directed their attention to the cities.

Attempts at reform also pervaded fictional writing. In their search for "realism" novelists probed the impact of urban life on human character. The impersonal quest for power and wealth was depicted by Theodore Dreiser in *The Financier* and by Winston S. Churchill in *Coniston*. Stephen Crane's *Maggie, A Girl of the Streets* and Upton Sinclair's *The Jungle* explored the depths of urban poverty. Sinclair's novel also exposed the loathsome practices of the meat-packing industry and shocked Congress into passing a federal meat-inspection law in 1906. Women's victimization in the city was poignantly treated by David Graham Phillips in *Susan Lenox, Her Fall and Rise* and by Dreiser in *Sister Carrie* and *Jenny Gerhardt*.

In 1907–8, investigative social science and journalism combined to produce the most extensive catalog of modern urban life yet collected. Under the direction of Paul U. Kellogg, a professional social worker, and sponsored by the Russell Sage Foundation, the six-volume *Pittsburgh Survey* detailed the economic progress of the city and the social costs of industrialization. It particularly showed how political corruption and irresponsible business practices had contributed to the city's problems of poverty, pollution, and inequitable tax practices. Kellogg and many like him in other cities were almost obsessed with the potential of reason and information as reforming instruments. They invested their strongest faith in the outrage of an informed public. This faith reflected the new middle-class reformers' strength and also their shortcomings.

The activities of these reformers included a multitude of causes, ranging from the religious humanizing of the Social Gospel movement to the "breadbasket" issues of labor organizations. Such a variety of concerns does not fit a generalized interpretation that can categorize every program and personality. From an urban point of view one of the most salient aspects of the reform movement was the attempt by middle-class individuals and groups to control and mitigate the problems of inner-cities, where conditions seemed most menacing. In addition to the concerns with housing and health discussed in Chapter 4, social reformers' efforts in the inner city took four major focuses: moral and religious responsibility for social betterment, epitomized by the Social Gospel; the civic and cultural enlightenment of inner-city dwellers sponsored by educational reformers; the settlement-house movement's drive to bridge cultural gaps and improve neighborhood life; and the promise of aesthetic invigoration from city planning.

Religious and Moral Reform

During the 1870s and 1880s a few clergymen of older Protestant sects reacted to the social crises and labor struggles resulting from urbanization and industrialization by espousing a new interpretation of their religious mission. The Social Gospel, as this ethic came to be called, emphasized the social aspects of Christianity. According to the Social Gospel the salvation of society replaced the salvation of an individual soul as the principal religious goal. Before the Civil War, Unitarian ministers such as William Ellery Channing and Theodore Parker had stressed the duty of good Christians to attend to the needs of the "degenerate" classes. As problems of urbanization heightened after the war, this attitude spread and leaders of other Protestant sects tried to make their churches instruments of reform.

The leading figure of the Social Gospel movement was Washington Gladden, a Congregationalist minister in Columbus, Ohio. Gladden preached that modern Christians should seek salvation by attempting to realize the Kingdom of God on earth rather than worrying about the afterlife of their individual soul. Gladden, Walter Rauschenbusch, a Baptist minister and professor at the Rochester (New York) Theological Seminary, Josiah Strong, pastor of the Central Congregational Church of Cincinnati, Shaler Mathews of the University of Chicago Divinity School, and R. Heber Newton, a New York Episcopalian, stressed the social responsibilities of Christianity through good works and social betterment. Gladden mediated between labor unions and employers, and he supported arbitration as a means of achieving industrial peace. Rauschenbusch worked with Jacob Riis to obtain better living conditions for the poor. Other clergymen sponsored investigations and worked to alleviate poverty and decay in slum districts.

Several socially conscious congregations, with the help of contributions from wealthy members, established institutional churches in poor neighborhoods. These churches offered programs such as nurseries, kindergartens, clinics and dispensaries, employment agencies, recreation centers, and adult-education classes. The goal of all activities was service. As Josiah Strong wrote in *The Challenge of the City*, "Inasmuch as Christ came not to be ministered unto but to minister, the open and institutional church, filled and moved by his spirit of ministering love, seeks to become the center and source of all beneficent and philanthropic effort, and to take the leading part in every movement which has for its end the alleviation of human suffering, the elevation of man, and the betterment of the world."

The Social Gospel was particularly influential in advancing the environmental explanation of urban social ills. Men like Gladden and Rauschenbusch believed that people were not intrinsically bad; rather the conditions in which people lived corrupted them. Social Gospelers believed that by reforming the environment they could create a moral society. Dismayed by the greed and banality of industrial capitalism, they poured their energies into the inner city, and through investigations, missions, and institutional churches they awakened a host of sensitive men and women to the needs and methods of social reform. A few Social Gospelers took radical approaches to the solution of urban problems. Boston's W. D. P. Bliss, for example, became a socialist and helped found the Society of Christian Socialists in 1889. But the majority were moderates—clergymen who felt guilty about their own and their churches' neglect of social problems and who reacted by trying to reorient the gospel into a more secular direction. The Social Gospel influenced some Catholics and Jews as well, and it also reached rural areas. But for the most part it evolved from the impact of urban problems on modern Protestantism.

One specific crusade that many Social Gospelers joined was the drive to close down saloons. The temperance movement was not new to late-nineteenth-century urban America. But after the Civil War the movement gathered fresh momentum, spurred by activists who believed they could improve conditions of the laboring classes by destroying the centers of immorality and political corruption. Temperance reformers were convinced that inner-city neighborhoods contained too many saloons. (They may have been right—by the 1890s many city districts had one saloon for every fifteen or twenty adult men.) Because competition was so keen, reformers theorized, an establishment could survive only by staying open after hours or by offering extra services such as gambling and prostitution. Such temptations, plus the addictive effect of liquor, weakened family life and caused men and women to squander their wages. Moreover saloons were the bunkers of boss politics. Destroy the saloon and you remove the boss's base of operations.

The post–Civil War temperance movement was particularly fueled by the energies of native-born Protestant women. These women were attracted to temperance because it addressed the real problems of women victimized by their dependence on alcoholic men and because as a social problem the issue of drink fell within women's traditional domestic concerns. Women's first activities were to stage marches, rallies, and prayer vigils to try to close saloons. Then temperance activism took organizational shape in the Women's Christian Temperance Union, the largest single women's organization, with 245,000 members by 1911. Under Frances Willard's leadership, local chapters organized departments in areas such as labor, health, social purity, peace, education, and eventually, suffrage, all under the banner of "home protection." The WCTU taught women how to expand domestic imperatives into wider social concern and political action, and locals were directly involved in electoral politics. The pressure group tactics of organizations like the Anti-Saloon League, which ultimately resulted in state and national prohibition laws, shared a great deal with the reform strategies engineered by the WCTU.

Although temperance and prohibition attracted large numbers of rural enthusiasts who feared the evil ways of the big city, much of the leadership and financial support of these crusades came from city dwellers, largely native white Protestants who inhabited the outer wards. Some temperance advocates were willing to abandon quests for total prohibition in favor of more pragmatic goals. They worked for enforcement of licensing and closing laws, and they used pamphlets and public-school programs to emphasize the dangers of liquor and the virtues of abstinence. In a few cities temperance reformers helped to establish local-option rules that permitted individual wards or precincts to vote themselves dry. The greatest successes occurred in Chicago, where by 1908 almost half of the city was dry—mostly in the outer districts.

In the minds of many moral reformers it was a short step from the bottle to other temptations. Thus crusades against saloons often spread to gambling and prostitution. Most big cities tolerated unofficial segregation of gambling dens and brothels in red-light districts. Chicago's "levee" district, New York's Tenderloin and New Orleans's Bourbon Street were well-known centers of vice and were generally safe from police raids. But what Victorians had regarded as a "necessary evil" was regarded by reformers as *the* "social evil," a moral problem and a national menace. According to historian Ruth Rosen, middle-class reformers saw prostitution as a cultural symbol of the ways in which modern industrial culture allowed the cold, impersonal values of the marketplace to invade the most private areas of peoples' lives.[5] The terms of the reformers' writings about prostitution reflected their anxieties over unrestricted immigration, the anonymity of the city, the evils of liquor, the growth of what seemed to be an urban working-class culture far outside their control, and the changing role of women in society. The presence of women in public life had blurred the nineteenth-century distinction between "public" women, almost always synonymous with fallen women, and respectable wives and mothers. Women reformers saw prostitution somewhat differently, focusing much more on it as the symbol of sexual and economic exploitation of women. They blamed prostitution on the impossibility of survival on the pitifully low wages paid for "women's work" and identified prostitutes as the most victimized female labor. They hoped that eradication of prostitution would elevate the status of all women.

In Cleveland, St. Louis, and a few other cities the response to prostitution was to experiment with police registration and medical inspection of prostitutes rather than trying to abolish their profession. But most of the outcry about the "white slave trade" triggered efforts to abolish prostitution altogether. In the early 1900s reformers in several cities established vice commissions to investigate prostitution and gambling and to recommend legislation. They wanted crackdowns on saloons, bordellos, cheap hotels, dance halls, and red-light districts. Reformers recommended four measures as remedies: (1) labor legislation to improve working conditions for women so that they would not be lured by adversity into prostitution; (2) education campaigns to alert the public to the dangers of venereal disease; (3) neighborhood recreational facilities to replace vice centers; and (4) nuisance and abatement laws by which private citizens could obtain court orders to close down offensive establishments.

By the 1920s, however, technology enabled vice operators to circumvent most repressive legislation. The automobile enabled gambling and prostitution to flourish in roadhouses outside city borders away from the law, and the telephone created the bookie and the call girl. In addition, the effect of legal crackdowns on prostitution was not to root out the "social evil" but to force prostitutes from the relative security of public brothels to the riskier but less visible act of streetwalking. Control of prostitution shifted from madams and prostitutes themselves to pimps and organized crime syndicates. Such changes meant new types of "protection" for prostitutes but also that prostitutes faced new kinds of brutality from the police and from their "new employers."

Educational Reform

Reformers had high hopes for using the public schools as an agent of social reform. Public education could be the key to instilling the urban masses with reformers' standards of citizenship and democracy. However, late nineteenth-century critics of urban school systems charged that schools were disorganized, overcrowded, too vulnerable to political pressures from neighborhood and ward interests, not effective enough in reaching immigrant children, and not really relevant to the needs of modern industrial life. In many cities seldom more than two thirds of school-age children attended classes—often because immigrant and working-class families could not afford to withhold their children from the labor market.

An initial response to the problem of school attendance was the enactment of compulsory attendance laws, with truant officers mandated to enforce them. Such laws passed in the 1870s and 1880s, in combination with increasing populations, began to swell enrollments, confronting cities with new problems of inadequate buildings and teacher shortages. New schools accounted for large increases in bonded indebtedness in many cities during the last decade of the nineteenth century. Between 1860 and 1890 the number of normal (teacher-training) schools quadrupled, but they still could not meet the demand for teachers. Significantly the increased demand opened up the profession to women, who now outnumbered men in the common schools. By paying women only half as much as they paid men (salaries of $600 to $700 per year for female teachers as opposed to $900 to $1,200 for males), school committees could increase teaching staffs without straining budgets. The pressures on public-school facilities and personnel would have been worse had it not been for the expansion of parochial education. Responding to the needs of growing numbers of Catholic immigrants, the Third Plenary Council, meeting in Baltimore in 1884, urged that each parish provide schools for its children. By the end of the century nearly a million children were enrolled in Catholic elementary schools and several dioceses had established parochial high schools. Between 1870 and 1910 public school enrollments rose from 6.9 million to 17.8 million, and the number of public high schools swelled from five hundred to ten thousand. By 1920, parochial schools enrolled between 20 and 40 percent of school-age children in cities with large immigrant Catholic populations like New York, Boston, Philadelphia, Chicago, and St. Louis.

Social reformers saw the problems of schools as extending beyond issues of enrollment to more basic questions of school organization and educational content. Reformers' commitment to scientific efficiency led them to fight to establish centralized rather than ward-based school districts and to appoint professional rather than politically based administrators. A leader in administrative innovation was William T. Harris, superintendent of St. Louis public schools from 1867 to 1880. Harris believed that urban education should conform to new patterns of economic organization— meaning the factory—and he constantly stressed the need for regularity in school administration and pupil discipline. He supported reforms such as graded schools, centralized policy making, standardized curricula, and even uniform architecture. In an 1885 report on American urban schools, John Philbrick of Boston wrote, "The history of city systems of schools makes it evident that in the matter of administration the tendency is toward greater centralization and permanence of authority, and that the tendency is in the direction of progress and improvement."

To expand the reach of the schools into the burgeoning immigrant neighborhoods, school systems experimented with kindergarten programs for very young children, modeled on the educational program of German educator F. W. A. Froebel, and with evening schools to teach English and civics to immigrant adults. Kindergarten programs stressed the importance of pleasant surroundings, self-activity, and physical training as a means of developing learning capacities, and according to the editor of *Century Magazine*, they also provided "the earliest opportunity to catch the little Russian, the little Italian, the little German, Pole, Syrian and the rest and begin to make good American citizens of them." Increasingly support for kindergartens was based on the claim that they would "furnish a happy transition from those homes and the unwholesome influences of street life to the healthful schoolroom surroundings." Proponents of evening schools claimed that their manual training programs would enhance social mobility and economic efficiency and that their classes in English instruction could Americanize immigrants and maybe even elevate their taste from moving picture houses and vaudeville theatres to "good literature." Some localities even attempted to make evening instruction compulsory for immigrants, so convinced were they of the necessity of extending the public school's outreach beyond the daytime classroom.

One of the most important educational innovations proposed by reformers was vocational education. By the early 1900s, scores of cities had established trade schools and vocational education programs to train children in industrial skills, and a 1910 survey located industrial education programs in twenty-nine states, mostly in urban schools. Proponents of vocational education claimed that it would link students with manual discipline taken for granted in the past and make schooling more relevant to everyday life. Philosopher John Dewey believed that vocational training would restore what industrial progress had eroded. "The invention of machinery, the institution of the factory system, and the division of labor have changed the home from a workshop into a simple dwelling place," he wrote. "While need of the more formal intellectual training in the school has decreased, there arises an urgent demand for the introduction of methods of manual and industrial discipline that shall give the child what he formerly obtained in his home and social life." But increasingly vocational education, soon accompanied by programs of vocational guidance, functioned to track working-class and immigrant children into manual work and in practice to redefine the mission of education. As Boston's superintendent of schools argued in 1910, "until recently they [schools] have offered equal opportunity for all to receive one kind of education, but what will make them truly democratic is to provide opportunity for all to receive such education as will fit them equally well for their particular life work." Family, ethnic, and class background tended to be the basis of the measures used to determine which program would best fit a child "for his future position in life."

By the 1910s, expectations for what urban education could accomplish were extraordinarily high. According to Robert Wiebe, education reform reflected a belief that "the schools would facilitate the arrival of Social Rationality, preparing the nation for a higher civilization."[6] Even those reforms directed at the middle class—establishment of high schools, for example—revealed a strong belief in formal schooling as the best instrument for shaping American culture and for bringing order to heterogeneous urban society.

Settlements

The settlement-house movement was one of the most influential branches of urban reform. The idea originated in England, where a group of young intellectuals established themselves in a residence called Toynbee Hall in the London slums in 1884. These men and women sought to improve living conditions for lower-class laborers by bringing them education and appreciation for the arts. At the same time, the residents of Toynbee Hall believed they could learn something about life from the people they hoped to serve. Their objective was to bridge the gap between classes. Toynbee Hall inspired a number of young Americans who were visiting or studying in England, and several of them organized settlement houses when they returned to the United States. Stanton Coit started the Neighborhood Guild (renamed University Settlement) in a New York tenement apartment in 1886. Over the next few years Vida Scudder and Lillian Wald started other settlements in New York, Jane Addams and Ellen Gates Starr founded Hull House in Chicago, Graham Taylor opened Chicago Commons in that city, and Robert A. Woods founded Andover House in Boston. By 1897 there were seventy-four settlements in the United States, and by 1910 over four hundred.

Most participants in early settlements were young, middle-class, well-educated, religious-minded, and idealistic men and women who were disturbed by the social barriers between classes and frustrated by their own apparent uselessness in a society that cried for reform. As Allen Davis has noted, settlement workers had a strong desire to help, to apply their ideas of service (influenced by the Social Gospel) to the challenges of the city. They also had a strong investigative impulse, an urge to find out for themselves what urban society's problems were like. Women particularly found new opportunities in settlements. Settlement work resolved the problem of the young, college-educated woman who had no purposeful way to participate in "life," no outlet to apply her training. Replacing what Jane Addams referred to as "the family claim" with a larger, public one, settlement work fused an activist social role with conventional female concerns. Combining traditional charity with intellectual challenge, settlements also provided a supportive environment for women who chose social activism as an alternative to marriage. The women's communities established in urban settlement houses created social and political networks that propelled settlement workers into leadership roles in early twentieth-century social and political reform agitation.

As residents of the inner city, settlement workers viewed problems of poverty firsthand, and they actively sought to improve living conditions for immigrants and other poor people. The settlement house itself became an instrument of reform, acting as an educational center, information clearing house, and forum for debate. Settlement workers organized English and civics classes, amateur concerts and theatrical productions, and kindergartens. Jane Addams, Robert A. Woods, and Lillian Wald joined other educational reformers in lobbying for public adoption of kindergartens, vocational training, school nurses, and playgrounds. Because one of their major goals was revitalization of inner-city neighborhoods, settlement workers strongly backed housing reforms and worked closely with individuals such as Jacob Riis, Lawrence Veiller, and Robert W. DeForest in support of regulatory legislation. In the cause of labor reform, settlements offered rooms for union meetings and settlement leaders Florence Kelly, Mary McDowell, Jane Addams, and Mary Simkhovitch spoke out in support of workers' rights. Inevitably settlement workers were drawn into the politics of reform. They often fought local bosses on the ward level, and they moved into larger arenas of city-wide reform in order to achieve their objectives.

The importance of the settlement movement lay in its flexibility and influence. Although settlement workers were occasionally romantic and naive (one program tried to teach destitute immigrant women how to serve tea from a silver service), their eagerness to learn enabled them to adjust and to help the inner-city poor. They could not always erase attitudes of condescension and paternalism toward immigrants, and they kept facilities for blacks separate from those for whites for fear of driving whites away. But they also poured energy and compassion into the slums, and they invested faith in a pluralistic, urban society. They believed that immigrants did not have to shed their cultural backgrounds to become good Americans and that middle-class Americans could learn from immigrants as well as teach them. Settlements were based, remarked Jane Addams, "on the theory that the dependence of classes on each other is reciprocal."

Eventually the settlement movement succumbed to professionalization. After World War I the houses lost their attractiveness and their functions were assumed by trained social workers, who brought more expertise to the slums but also more bureaucratic impersonality. As a result the poor came to be viewed as clients rather than as partners in the thrust against poverty and decay. Yet for a full generation settlements provided hundreds of sensitive women and men with training and experience in social reform.

City Planning

During the middle and late nineteenth century, efforts to create large, landscaped city parks had awakened people to the possibilities of determining the mode and direction of future urban growth. By 1890 landscaping had merged with the new professions of architecture and engineering to create the City Beautiful movement, an attempt to improve life within cities by enhancing civic design. The City Beautiful blossomed at the

World's Columbian Exposition in Chicago in 1893–94. This was the largest of a score of fairs that were held in American cities during the last quarter of the nineteenth century and early years of the twentieth. Heralded as commemorative expositions, these extravaganzas were usually organized to advertise a city's progress and opportunities. The 1893 fair marked the tercentennial of Columbia's voyage to the New World, and Congress had chosen Chicago as the site because the city had made a remarkable recovery from its devastating fire of 1871. The fair's impressive exhibits of agricultural and industrial technology, plus its fantastic entertainments (the Midway offered everything from a Cairo street to a Hawaiian volcano), lured spectators into an idealized future and a romanticized past.

More important, the Chicago exposition showed what planners could do if they had the chance. Daniel Burnham, a prominent architect and the fair's supervisor, mustered a battery of notables—including landscaper Frederick Law Olmsted and maverick architect Louis Sullivan—to plan a totally new city in Jackson Park, on Chicago's southern lakefront. Over seven thousand workers (seventeen of whom died in the frenzy of activity to complete the project by opening day) built a "White City," complete with neoclassical buildings, streets, sewers, a water system, and other services, all coordinated to a preconceived master design. The spacious, orderly, monumental character of the exposition in no way resembled the gray, smoky, teeming streets of most inner cities. Yet the "White City" captured the imaginations of civic leaders and inspired them to beautify

The Aftermath of the Great Chicago Fire, 1871

A View of the World's Columbian Exposition, Chicago, 1893.   Although these two photographs do not show the same area of the city, they do contrast the extraordinary destruction that Chicagoans experienced in 1871 with the buoyant optimism that they exhibited in 1893. The Great Fire leveled some seventeen hundred acres and destroyed $200 million worth of property. The 1893 fair, the epitome of the City Beautiful, cost $19 million to construct and impressed millions of visitors, including novelist Hamlin Garland, who wrote his parents on their Dakota farm, "Sell the cook stove if necessary and come. You *must* see this fair." *(Both photographs courtesy Chicago Historical Society.)*

their own communities. Most commonly the City Beautiful was translated into the construction of new public buildings and civic centers. Burnham, Olmsted's son Frederick Jr., Charles M. Robinson (an architect from Rochester whose many publications made him the spokesman of the City Beautiful), and other planners were hired by cities to draw plans for new courthouses, libraries, and government centers.

In a few instances the City Beautiful movement generated projects that addressed the city as a whole, not just one part. In 1900 several planners who had been active in the Chicago fair were commissioned to prepare a plan for the beautification of Washington, D.C. Their efforts left the city with a mall between the Capitol and the Potomac River, a number of new monuments, and Rock Creek Park. In 1906 the Commercial Club of Chicago engaged Burnham and his associates to devise a comprehensive plan for the city. Their scheme, submitted in 1909 and accepted by the city council in 1910, shaped Chicago's development for the next five decades and became one of the most influential documents in the history of city planning. The Burnham Plan sought to create a "well-ordered, convenient, and unified city." In practical terms this meant improved transportation, accessible areas for public recreation, and provisions to control subsequent growth. The plan specified a new railroad terminal, an east-west boulevard, a civic center, the development of lakefront parks and beaches along the full length of Chicago's shoreline, and large forest preserves around the city's borders. The project was expensive, and several of its more elaborate schemes had to be abandoned. Yet most of it was eventually realized, and its scope and innovation aroused nationwide fascination.

Burnham's motto was "Make no little plans. . . . Make big plans; aim high in hope and work." Yet few other cities could reproduce Chicago's accomplishments. In most places City Beautiful projects were attempts to make commercial districts more attractive and profitable for business and government personnel who lived on the urban fringe. Problems of poverty and social inequality were not the primary concerns addressed by these projects. Burnham, Robinson, and others were not oblivious to social problems, but they claimed that improvements such as parks and sanitation would correct imbalances. Their uncritical optimism—plus a faithfulness to the needs of private investment—limited the accomplishments of early planning. By the time of the St. Louis Exposition of 1904 the City Beautiful movement began to split, with some planners continuing to advocate aesthetics as the answer to urban problems and others involving themselves in planning that froze the divisions between uptown and downtown, center and suburbs, through the institutionalization of zoning and metropolitan and regional plans (see Chapter 7).

Unlike the agrarian reformers, whose crusades against big business, hard money, and the railroads dominated social protest in the 1880s and 1890s, urban middle-class social reformers accepted, even embraced, the city. They believed that within the city lay the potential for human progress. As Frederick Howe wrote in 1905, "The ready responsiveness of democracy, under the close association which the city involves, forecasts a movement for the improvement of human society more hopeful than anything the world has ever known." But this faith often betrayed a failure to accept the pluralism of modern urban society. Although social reformers felt a responsibility to help the masses, many also wanted to restore what they wished were traditional values of social deference and cultural purity. The spirit of service, sacrifice, and love could easily be refashioned into condescension and paternalism. Thus moral idealism allowed some reformers to support prohibition, immigration restriction, and separate and unequal facilities for blacks. Moreover, service-minded middle-class humanitarians often misunderstood human nature. As Mr. Dooley candidly observed,

> [T]is a gr-reat mistake to think that annywan ra-ally wants to rayform. Ye niver heerd of a man rayformin' himself. He'll rayform other people gladly. He likes to do it. But a healthy man'll niver rayform while he has th' strenth. . . . But a rayformer don't see it. . . . [He] spinds th' rest iv his life tellin' us where we are wrong. He's good at that. On'y he don't unherstand that people wud rather be wrong an' comfortable thin right in jail.

What was service to some was meddling to others. Yet in spite of their limitations, civic and social reform together brought many changes to urban America. Perhaps more important, they provided the foundation for the Progressive Era.

REFORM BECOMES PROGRESSIVISM

The twentieth century brought with it the progressive era, a period between 1895 and 1920 when reform activism spread through almost all facets of American life. Progressivism was not a single movement; it involved shifting coalitions of varied reformers operating on a number of fronts. Some progressive reforms, particularly those involving government reorganization and railroad regulation, were adopted from the Populist movement of the 1890s. Most Populist causes, however, grew out of rural economic distress and were centered in the Midwest and South. In contrast, progressive issues were national in scope and focused on urban problems. In fact the progressive era culminated three decades of urban reform. In

Downtown Norfolk, Virginia, in 1915 This photograph of Granby Street from the corner of City Hall Avenue shows both men and women making use of downtown streets. *(Library of Congress.)*

this respect the issues of the period were not new; they had been the concerns of civic and social reformers for some time. What was new was the combination of like-minded reformers from different cities into national organizations.

Nationwide reform activism was the product of several ingredients. In large part it grew from reformers' basic optimism in their causes. No problem seemed too complex; no geographical area was too large. Failure and frustration on the local level had not dampened reform ardor; they only made national programs more imperative. National organization was also derived from the new middle-class expertise, with its impulse for standardization and professionalization. And certainly faster and easier communications by mail, rail, telegraph, and telephone aided intercity contacts, just as they had facilitated the growth of economic systems that stretched between regions. Whatever the origins, a large number of urban reformers now carried their particular causes to the national level and provided progressive movements with their intellectual and organizational bases.

One of the earliest of these organizations was the National Municipal League, organized in Philadelphia in 1894 by the First Annual Conference for Good City Government. The league attracted a number of civic reformers, and it included 180 affiliated societies by 1895. At first members favored the types of elitist reforms that business and professional groups had supported in the 1870s and 1880s—civil service, stronger vice laws, tighter governmental fiscal policies. But, the depression of the mid 1890s catalyzed broader concerns about the social and economic problems of urban society and prompted organizations such as the National Municipal League to consider more comprehensive programs for reform. In 1899 the league consolidated its various governmental proposals into a model city charter that provided for home rule, a strong mayor, civil service, and ceilings on taxing and bonding powers. In 1916 members drew a revised model charter that included a combined commission-manager plan, nonpartisan elections, and shorter ballots. Also some, though not all, league members became strong advocates of municipally owned city services. The model charters, support for municipal ownership, and other programs signaled the league's recognition that strong tools were needed to break the bonds between bosses and big business and to reconstruct democratic government. Electing the "best men" and passing "good laws" were no longer enough. Civic reform needed a plan, a plan that could be formulated and supported nationally. Although no city adopted a model charter verbatim, the league's recommendations had considerable influence on local charter committees for the next several decades. To aid the planning process, bureaus of municipal research, often supported by self-interested corporate donors, provided important information and lobbying services to public officials and municipal reformers.

The desire for coordinated programs also characterized other national reform organizations. The National Civic Federation, founded by business liberals in 1900, organized local branches and enlisted prominent leaders such as Seth Low of New York City and Senator Mark Hanna of Ohio to mediate in labor disputes. The federation also campaigned nationally for a moderate version of workmen's compensation and other forms of social insurance. In 1904 Florence Kelly and other middle-class social reformers launched the National Child Labor Committee, which campaigned to passage and enforcement of laws restricting child labor. Such restrictions had long been the goal of local reformers concerned about the welfare of working-class children and the conditions of tenement sweatshops. The Child Labor Committee also drafted a bill prohibiting child labor, which passed Congress in 1916, only to be overturned by the Supreme Court. The formation of the Federal Council of Churches of Christ in 1905 climaxed the Social Gospel movement. At its first annual conference in 1908 the council adopted a platform calling for better housing, educational reform, government-sponsored poverty relief, better working conditions in factories, unemployment insurance, minimum wages for manual workers, and equal rights for all.

In 1910 Lawrence Veiller succeeded in combining the various housing-reform groups when he convinced the Russell Sage Foundation to finance organization of the National Housing Association. Settlement workers had helped to found the National Child Labor Committee and the National Playground Association of America, and in 1911 they organized their own National Association of Settlements. In 1909 a number of architects, engineers, and housing reformers concerned with urban congestion and city planning formed the National Association of City Planning, the forerunner of the American City Planning Institute (today called the American Planning Association), founded in 1917. In 1906 the various proponents of vocational training organized the National Society for the Progress of Industrial Education, whose board of managers included efficiency expert Frederick W. Taylor, settlement-house leaders Jane Addams and Robert A. Woods, the president of American Telephone and Telegraph Company, and the head of the Union of Electrical Workers. After 1900, municipal employees formed specialized associations of the National Associations of Port Authorities, the Municipal Finance Officers Association, the American Association of Park Superintendents, and the National Conference of Mayors and Conference of City Managers. This complex national network of specialized organizations helped to develop a coherent reform agenda and a communications and lobbying network that financed and organized reform on a national scale.

As a result of national organization, by the early twentieth century reform programs revealed a detached, pragmatic approach to social and political problems. Their tone was less indignant and less moralistic than that of earlier reformers of the 1870s and 1880s. At the same time, the character of reform shifted from elitist paternalism—the idea that the best men should rule—to bureaucratic control—the idea that experts and specialized agencies should determine social, political, and economic policies. This organizational emphasis was the modern era's legacy from the reform movement.

Most urban progressives believed that trained professionals could best define the public interest and execute proper policies in that interest through specialized, independent agencies. This faith in scientific management blinded reformers to the contradictions between disinterested (nonpolitical and uncorruptible) social engineering and democratic self-determinism. Thus they could advocate more trust in the people and more popular involvement on the one hand while they worked for centralized power and impersonal bureaucratic administration on the other. Moreover they confused the independence of experts and bureaucrats with neutrality, when in fact bureaucracies became as self-serving as the machines that reformers wished to replace. Finally attempts by progressive reformers to transfer their own achievement-oriented values to all of urban society neglected working-class cultures and institutions as socializing agents. Family life among immigrants and blacks was considerably stronger than educational and humanitarian reformers suspected, and saloons provided more important functions than mere escapism or political connivance. The impersonality of bureaucratic management of social problems and the inability to accept the complexities of urban society with its multiplicity of groups and overlapping interests limited the accomplishments of urban reform movements. Yet progressive-era reformers accepted the difficult challenge of grappling with the problems of modern mass society. They realized that the future of American civilization was in its cities, and they tried to prepare for that future while easing the strains of the past and present.

THE RISE OF URBAN LIBERALISM

Although many reform movements evolved from outer-city concerns over conditions in the urban core, the inner regions also organized to improve conditions and to serve working-class interests. Political machines, which were generally inimical to reform, tended to provide inner-city residents with the most accessible means of protecting their interests. But, as J. Joseph Huthmacher and John D. Buenker have shown, reform included a strong working-class component, and bosses themselves were often responsive to reform goals.[7] In fact immigrant-stock working classes, in conjunction with middle-class reformers, provided much of the foundation for the development of "urban liberalism," the ideology of intervention by the government to ensure the safety and promote the welfare of its citizens.

"Urban liberalism," writes Professor Buenker, "was a product of the American urban experience in an industrial age, a growing realization that the power of government could be used to ameliorate the kind of conditions every urban lawmaker had encountered first hand."[8] During the late nineteenth and early twentieth centuries a number of politicians emerged from immigrant working-class districts to take seats in Congress and in state legislatures. These were men who had worked their way up, usually through the Democratic party, and who were beginning to assume positions of influence by the second decade of the twentieth century. Although their numbers remained too small for them to wield legislative power alone, these urban new-stock immigrant-descended lawmakers were frequently able to coalesce with reform-minded colleagues to produce some of the progressive era's most important measures, involving labor and welfare issues, regulation of big business, home rule, and electoral reform.

From the beginning of the post-Civil War period urban workingmen had rallied behind legislation promising better conditions in factories and sweatshops. In 1869 Boston laboring groups succeeded in convincing the Massachusetts General Assembly to establish the Massachusetts State Labor Bureau to protect the interests of workers. The bureau's investigations and statistical reports aided the passage of reform legislation dealing with factory safety and workmen's compensation. These activities set important precedents for the creation of similar bureaus in other states, particularly in the industrialized Northeast. By the end of the century laboring classes, often led by immigrant-based machine politicians, were pressing for housing and health reforms as well as for breadbasket issues such as higher wages, shorter hours, and more comfortable working conditions.

During the progressive era representatives of new-stock working classes helped to sponsor reform measures such as widows' pensions, wages and hours legislation, limitations on women's and children's labor, workmen's compensation, factory-safety legislation, and tenement regulation. In New York many of these laws grew out of the Factory Investigation Commission hearings instituted after the tragic Triangle Shirtwaist Company fire in New York City in 1911 in which 145 women workers were killed. Robert F. Wagner and Alfred E. Smith, graduates of Tammany Hall politics, chaired this commission, and they and their fellow Democrats introduced nearly all of the fifty-six welfare laws passed as a result of the commission's recommendations. In New Jersey Irish-American Democrats from Jersey City and Newark gave strong support to workmen's-compensation and factory-safety bills in the state legislature. Cleveland's immigrant-based Democrats pushed for welfare legislation in the Ohio legislature. And new-stock delegations supported similar issues in other northern and midwestern states. Their efforts were not always fruitful, and they achieved legislative success only when they worked in cooperation with other groups sympathetic to workers' concerns. But in each instance new-stock representatives exerted considerable force in guiding the course of reform legislation.

These same lawmakers also backed, though less successfully, measures to strengthen unions, to regulate big business, and to equalize tax burdens. Urban Democratic leaders often rose out of the ranks of organized labor and became strong advocates for the rights of unions to organize, bargain, and strike. In 1911, for example, Boston representatives to the Massachusetts Senate supported a bill permitting strikers to picket. Urban lawmakers generally favored government regulation of big business rather than breaking up trusts, because workers believed regulation was the surest means of stabilizing economic conditions and ensuring job protection. New-stock Democrats particularly favored government control over the rates and services of public utilities, upon which working classes depended. Many of them supported municipal ownership of utilities and streetcar companies. For example, Edward F. Dunne, Democratic mayor of Chicago and governor of Illinois in the early twentieth century, backed measures to provide for municipal ownership of several utilities in Chicago. Though these measures were defeated, Dunne was able to create a public-utilities regulatory commission in 1913. Urban legislators also worked to shift tax burdens to those most able to pay by supporting inheritance taxes, stronger enforcement of intangible-property taxes, and, most of all, a graduated federal income tax. In New York, Massachusetts, New Jersey, Ohio, and other states urban Democrats backed the Sixteenth Amendment to the Constitution, which established congressional power to levy an income tax, because they viewed it, in Robert Wagner's words, as "a tax on plenty instead of necessity. It will lighten the burdens of the poor."

Finally, lawmakers rising from working-class and immigrant constituencies occasionally promoted political changes that promised to bolster popular control of government. They seldom could agree with most civic reformers, who sought to purify and to centralize government by instituting nonpartisan elections, civil service, short ballots, and at-large candidates. But working-class interests often did favor broadening participation in government by establishing initiatives and referendums, recalls of appointed officials and judges, women's suffrage, and direct election of U.S. senators. In Massachusetts and New York, urban delegations favored initiatives, referendums, and direct election of senators as a means to temper control of their states by hostile rural representatives. Although urban machines initially opposed giving women the right to vote ("You can't trust these women," asserted Boston's Martin Lomasney. "They are apt to blab everything they know."), by the 1910s many inner-city leaders, including those of Tammany Hall, were backing women's suffrage in hopes of luring women into the Democratic party once they were enfranchised. And new-stock working classes also could lend support to measures such as city commissions and direct primaries when it proved politically profitable to do so.

Working classes of inner cities were more than just a social problem: their interests often complemented the goals of progressive reform. Representatives of these interests were not the sole instigators of reform. In fact they often fought key aspects of the middle-class drive to improve society, particularly moral reforms such as prohibition, Sunday blue laws, and other attempts to control personal liberty. But such resistance, as Professor Huthmacher has contended, actually fit modern notions of cultural pluralism, the idea that in a heterogeneous society differing groups have a right to maintain their own values.[9] Moreover the types of measures that new-stock urban lawmakers did favor—those directed toward opening up political and economic opportunities and establishing government responsibility for ensuring social welfare—have become the principal components of national reform from the progressive era to the present.

BIBLIOGRAPHY

Two particularly important essays that shed light on the impetus toward urban reform are Daniel Rodgers, "In Search of Progressivism," *Reviews in American History* 10(December 1982):113–32; and John D. Buenker, "Essay on Progressivism," in *Progressivism*, eds. John D. Buenker, John C. Burnham, and Robert M. Crunden (Cambridge, Mass.: Schenkman, 1977), 31–69. Other important studies include J. Joseph Huthmacher, "Urban Liberalism and the Age of Reform," *Journal of American History* 49 (September 1962):31–41; John D. Buenker, *Urban Liberalism and Progressive Reform* (New York: Scribner's, 1973); Samuel P. Hays, "The Politics of Reform in Municipal Government in the Progressive Era," *Pacific Northwest Quarterly,* 55 (October 1964), 157–69; Blake McKelvey, *The Rise of Urban America, 1865–1915* (New Brunswick, N.J.: Rutgers University Press, 1963); and Michael Ebner and Eugene Tobin, eds., *The Age of Urban Reform: New Perspectives on the Progressive Era* (Port Washington, N.Y.: Kennikat Press, 1977).

Contemporary works by reformers themselves provide useful insights into the motivations of the reform movement. Especially enlightening are Joseph Lincoln Steffens, *The Shame of the Cities* (New York: McClure, Phillips & Son, 1904); and *The Autobiography of Lincoln Steffens* (New York: Harcourt Brace, 1931); Jacob Riis, *How the Other Half Lives* (New York: Scribner's, 1890); Jane Addams, *Twenty Years at Hull House* (New York: Macmillan Publishing Co., 1910); and Frederick C. Howe, *Confessions of a Reformer* (New York: Scribner's, 1925); Tom Johnson, *My Story* (New York: B. W. Huebsch, 1911). See also James B. Lane, *Jacob Riis and the American City* (Port Washington, N.Y.: Kennikat Press, 1975); and Allen F. Davis, *American Heroine: The Life and Legend of Jane Addams* (New York: Oxford University Press, 1973).

There are numerous specialized studies on the topics discussed in this chapter. For works on politics and government see Melvin G. Holli, *Reform in Detroit: Hazen S. Pingree and Urban Politics* (New York: Oxford University Press, 1969); Zane L. Miller, *Boss Cox's Cincinnati: Urban Politics in the Progressive Era* (New York: Oxford University Press, 1968); Roy Lubove, *Twentieth Century Pittsburgh: Government, Business and Environmental Change* (New York: John Wiley & Sons, 1969); James B. Crooks, *Politics and Progress: The Rise of Urban Progressivism in Baltimore, 1895–1911* (Baton Rouge: Louisiana State University Press, 1968); Bradley R. Rice, *Progressive Cities: The Commission Government Movement in America, 1901–1920* (Austin: University of Texas Press, 1977); Kenneth Fox, *Better City Government: Innovation in American Urban Politics, 1850–1937* (Philadelphia: Temple University Press, 1977); Martin J. Schiesl, *The Politics of Efficiency: Municipal Administration and Reform in America, 1880–1920* (Berkeley: University of California Press, 1977); and Ernest Griffith, *A History of American City Government: The Progressive Years and Their Aftermath, 1900–1920.* See also Carl V. Harris, *Political Power in Birmingham, 1871–1921* (Knoxville: University of Tennessee Press, 1977); Don Doyle, *Nashville in the New South, 1880–1930* (Knoxville: University of Tennessee Press, 1985); William Issel and Robert W. Cherny, *San Francisco, 1865–1932: Politics, Power and Urban Development* (Berkeley: University of California Press, 1986); A. Theodore Brown and Lyle W. Dorsett, *A History of Kansas City, Missouri* (Boulder, Colo.: Pruett Publishing Co., 1978); David C. Hammack, *Power and Society: Greater New York at the Turn of the Century* (New York: Russell Sage Foundation, 1982); Frederick Cople Jaher, *The Urban Establishment: Upper Strata in Boston, New York, Charlestown, Chicago, and Los Angeles* (Urbana: University of Illinois Press, 1982). For a general discussion of policy see James T. Patterson, *America's Struggle Against Poverty, 1900–1980* (Cambridge, Mass.: Harvard University Press, 1981); and Michael B. Katz, ed., *Poverty and Policy in American History* (New York: Academic Press, 1983). Studies discussing urban socialism include Bruce Stave, ed., *Socialism in the Cities* (Port Washington, N.Y.: Kennikat Press, 1975); James Weinstein, *The Decline of Socialism in the United States, 1912–1925,* rev. ed. (New Brunswick, N.J.: Rutgers University Press, 1984); Mari Jo Buhle, *Women and American Socialism, 1870–1920* (Urbana: University of Illinois Press, 1981); Sally M. Miller, *Victor Berger and the Promise of Constructive Socialism, 1910–1920* (Westport, Conn.: Greenwood Press, 1973).

On women as the architects of reform see Paula Baker, "The Domestication of Politics: Women and American Political Society, 1780–1920," *American Historical Review* 89(June 1984):620–47, esp. pp. 632–47; Anne F. Scott, "On Seeing and Not Seeing: A Case of Historical Invisibility," *Journal of American History* 71(June 1984):13–17; Kathryn Kish Sklar, "Hull House in the 1890s: A Community of Women Reformers," *Signs* 10(Summer 1985):658–677.

On moral reform see Thomas J. Noel, *The City and the Saloon: Denver, 1858–1916* (Lincoln: University of Nebraska Press, 1982); James Timberlake, *Prohibition and the Progressive Movement, 1900–1920* (Cambridge, Mass.: Harvard University Press, 1963); Perry Duis, *The Saloon: Public Drinking in Chicago and Boston, 1880–1920* (Urbana: University of Illinois Press, 1983); David J. Pivar, *Purity Crusade: Sexual Morality and Social Control, 1868–1900* (Westport, Conn.: Greenwood Press, 1973); Mark Thomas Connelly, *The Response to Prostitution in the Progressive Era* (Chapel Hill: University of North Carolina Press, 1980); Ruth Rosen, *The Lost Sisterhood: Prostitution in America, 1900–1918* (Baltimore: Johns Hopkins University Press, 1982); Joan Brumberg, " 'Ruined Girls': Changing Community Responses to Illegitimacy in Upstate New York, 1890–1920," *Journal of Social History* 18(Winter 1984):247–72. See also Dominick Cavallo, *Muscles and Morals: Organized Playgrounds and Urban Reform, 1880–1920* (Philadelphia: Temple University Press, 1981); David Nasaw, *Children of the City: At Work and At Play* (New York: Doubleday, 1985).

For educational reform see Marvin Lazerson, *Origins of the Urban School: Public Education in Massachusetts, 1870–1915* (Cambridge, Mass.: Harvard University Press, 1971); Selwyn K. Troen, *The Public and the Schools: Shaping the St. Louis System, 1838–1920* (Columbia, Mo.: University of Missouri Press, 1975); William A. Bullough, *Cities and Schools in the Guilded Age: The Evolution of an Urban Institution* (Port Washington, N.Y.: Kennikat Press, 1974); Ronald Cohen and Raymond Mohl, *The Paradox of Progressive Education: The Gary Plan and Urban Schooling* (Port Washington, N.Y.: Kennikat Press, 1979); David B. Tyack, *The One Best System: A History of American Urban Education* (Cambridge, Mass.: Harvard University Press, 1974); Meyer Weinberg, *A Chance to Learn: A History of Race and Education in the United States*

(Cambridge, Eng.: Cambridge University Press, 1977); David Hogan, *Class and Reform: Schools and Society in Chicago, 1880–1930* (Philadelphia: University of Pennsylvania Press, 1985); James W. Sanders, *The Education of an Urban Minority: Catholics in Chicago, 1833–1965* (New York: Oxford University Press, 1977). See also Michael W. Homel, *Down From Equality: Black Chicagoans and the Public Schools, 1924–1941* (Urbana: University of Illinois Press, 1984). On settlements see Allen F. Davis, *Spearheads for Reform: The Social Settlements and the Progressive Movement, 1890–1914* (New York: Oxford University Press, 1967); Louise C. Wade, *Graham Taylor: Pioneer for Social Justice* (Chicago: University of Chicago Press, 1964). On planning see Roy Lubove, *The Urban Community: Housing and Planning in the Progressive Era* (Englewood Cliffs, N.J.: Prentice-Hall, 1967); Mel Scott, *American City Planning Since 1890* (Berkeley and Los Angeles: University of California Press, 1969); Stanley K. Buder, *Pullman: An Experiment in Industrial Order and Community Planning, 1880–1930* (New York: Oxford University Press, 1967); David F. Burg, *Chicago's White City of 1893* (Lexington: University of Kentucky Press, 1979); Thomas S. Hines, *Burnham of Chicago: Architect and Planner* (New York: Oxford University Press, 1974); Judd Kahn, *Imperial San Francisco: Politics and Planning in an American City, 1897–1906* (Lincoln: University of Nebraska Press, 1980); William H. Wilson, *The City Beautiful Movement in Kansas City* (Columbia: University of Missouri Press, 1964); Richard E. Fogelsong, *Planning the Capitalist City: The Colonial Era to 1920* (Princeton, N.J.: Princeton University Press, 1986).

ENDNOTES

[1] Daniel Rodgers, "In Search of Progressivism," *Reviews in American History* 10(December 1982):120.

[2] *Ibid.*, 125.

[3] Robert Wiebe, *The Search for Order, 1877–1920* (New York: Hill & Wang, 1967).

[4] Christopher Wilson, "The Rhetoric of Consumption: Mass Market Magazines and the Demise of the Gentle Reader, 1880–1920," in *The Culture of Consumption* eds. Richard W. Fox and T. J. Jackson Lears (New York: Pantheon Books, 1983), 61.

[5] Ruth Rosen, *The Lost Sisterhood: Prostitution in America, 1900–1918* (Baltimore: Johns Hopkins University Press, 1982).

[6] Wiebe, *op. cit.*, 157.

[7] Joseph Huthmacher, "Urban Liberalism in the Age of Reform," *Journal of American History* 49(September 1962):231–41; John D. Buenker, *Urban Liberalism and Progressive Reform* (New York: Scribner's, 1973).

[8] Buenker, *op. cit.*, 206.

[9] Huthmacher, *op. cit.*, 238–41.

7

Cities in an Age of Metropolitanism: The Twenties and Thirties

NEW URBAN GROWTH

The 1920 federal census marked a milestone in American history: its figures revealed that for the first time a majority of the nation's people (51.4 percent) now lived in cities. Of course this revelation can be misleading: Massachusetts and Rhode Island had been predominantly urban long before 1920. Moreover in 1920 a city was defined as a place inhabited by at least twenty-five hundred people—hardly a rigorous criterion. Nevertheless the 1920 tallies were symbolically important. In 1890 the Census Bureau had signaled the end of America's youth by announcing that the frontier no longer existed. Now, thirty years later, the figures confirmed that the nation had evolved into an urban society. The city, not the farm, had become the locus of national experience.

The traditional, agrarian way of life, with its slow pace, moral sobriety, and self-help ethic, had been waning ever since urbanization accelerated early in the nineteenth century. To be sure, by the 1920s the demise was far from complete. Several social-reform movements and much political rhetoric looked nostalgically backward to the simple virtues of an imagined past. But everywhere signs pointed to an urban ascendance. A precipitous drop in commodity prices after 1920 spun small farmers into distress. Convinced that there was a better life elsewhere, an estimated six million Americans gave up the struggle to make a living from the land and poured into cities like Pittsburgh, Detroit, Chicago, Denver, and Los Angeles. Many more whites pushed into nearby cities in the South. After lagging behind the rest of the nation for nearly a century, the South now became the most rapidly urbanizing region in terms of proportionate population growth. Memphis, Atlanta, and Chattanooga experienced extraordinary expansion. The epitome of southern urbanization was Birmingham, Alabama. A burgeoning steel-making center in the late nineteenth century, Birmingham developed a diverse industrial, commercial, and service economy in the 1920s. This expansion attracted workers and their families from all over the South, who boosted the population of the metropolitan area from 310,000 to 431,000 during the decade (the population of the city proper was 260,000 by 1930). Smaller cities, many of them created by textile companies who had left New England to take advantage of cheap southern labor and readily available hydroelectric power, also helped boost the urban population of the South to thirteen million by 1930. The depression years heightened farmers' impoverishment. Continuing declines in crop prices, drought, foreclosure, and bank failures sent hundreds of thousands more rural men and women to the cities in search of work. Although popular journalism highlighted depression incidents of urban families returning to the land, and murals painted in the thirties depicted farm men and women as the prototypical Americans, the depopulation of the countryside continued.

Agrarian depression was only part of a broader development. All forms of primary economic activity—mining and other extractive industries as well as agriculture—were receiving a diminishing share of national wealth while tertiary activities—retail and service establishments—were mushrooming. These latter functions created an ever larger white-collar, urban middle class that became increasingly influential in local and national affairs. At the same time, some critics added a disdain for rural society to a general cynicism toward social conventions. Edgar Lee Masters' *Spoon River Anthology* (1915), Sherwood Anderson's *Winesburg, Ohio* (1919), Sinclair Lewis's *Main Street* (1920), and Thomas Wolfe's *Look Homeward Angel* (1929) assaulted the drabness of village and small-town life. The term "hick" became a widely used derogatory adjective, equating something clumsy or stupid with the farm. Much of the contempt for rural life represented a larger revolt against what writers called Puritan moralism—a revolt reflected in the popularization of the writings of Austrian psychoanalyst Sigmund Freud. But the debunking of the sturdy yeoman and small-town folkways also underscored a cultural shift that accompanied the city's rise to numerical superiority.

During the 1920s urbanization took place on a wider front than ever before. Maturing industrial economies boosted the populations of many areas, particularly steel, oil, and automobile centers such as Pittsburgh, Cleveland, Detroit, Akron, Youngstown, Birmingham, Houston, Tulsa, and Los Angeles. New commercial and service activities primed expansion in regional centers such as Atlanta, Cincinnati, Nashville, Indianapolis, Kansas City, Minneapolis, Portland, and Seattle. The most exceptional growth, however, occurred in warm climate resort cities. Between 1920 and 1930 the population of Miami ballooned from 29,571 to 110,637. As the

The Age of the Skyscraper   A workman sits on the end of a beam and bolts together the framework of the Empire State Building. Completed in 1930, this skyscraper operated with huge financial losses during the first six years of the Depression. *(Photograph by Lewis Hine. Works Project Administration, The National Archives.)*

prime beneficiary of the Florida real-estate explosion of the twenties, Miami attracted thousands of land speculators and home builders. A citrus-crop failure and two disastrous hurricanes punctured the boom in 1927, but the expansion of warm-climate cities continued: Tampa and San Diego doubled their populations during the twenties.

Urban populations in this period revealed a decline in foreign-born residents. Even before World War I the expansion of industrialization in Europe had begun to provide employment for uprooted peasants. The war completely stopped the flow of foreign migration, and after the war a feverish urge for national unity merged with anti-immigrant prejudices and fears to fuel sentiment for restricting immigration. Support for an end to free immigration had been building since the 1880s among urban reformers as well as unions and nativist conservatives. By 1919 humanitarians who had formerly opposed restriction were willing to admit that the melting pot had not worked and that many immigrants—particularly those from southern and eastern Europe—stubbornly resisted assimilation. Labor leaders, fearful that a new flood of unskilled aliens would depress wages, looked at the high postwar unemployment rates and increased their longstanding support for restriction. At first businessmen opposed the rising clamor out of self-interests: they hoped that a new surge of foreign workers would not only aid industrial expansion but also cut wage rates and curb unionization. But by 1924, when Congress was debating whether to close the doors more tightly, many industrialists were willing to support restriction because they discovered that mechanization and native migration from farm to city enabled them to prosper without foreign-born labor.

Congressional acts of 1921, 1924, and 1929 successively reduced the numbers of immigrants who could be admitted annually. A system of quotas, ultimately based on the number of descendants from each nationality living in the United States in 1890, severely limited immigrants from southern and eastern Europe, the very groups who had dominated urban cores since 1880.

The laws left the doors open only to Western Hemisphere countries. Mexicans now became the largest foreign group entering the country. Many came to work in the fields and vineyards of the Southwest, but others streamed into the region's booming cities. By the end of the 1920s, Chicanos made up more than half the population of El Paso, slightly less than half that of San Antonio, and one-fifth that of Los Angeles. Other Mexicans worked on the railroads or found employment in the automobile factories of Detroit and the steel mills, tanneries, and meat-packing plants of Gary and Chicago. By 1930, more than 15 percent of Mexican immigrants lived outside the Southwest. Chicano women looked for work in cities as domestics and in textile and food processing factories. Crowding into old barrios or forming new ones, Chicano migrants often were deprived of decent city services such as sanitation, schools, and police protection. But the barrio community provided an environment where immigrants could sustain customs and values of the homeland and develop institutions to protect them from the uncertainties of urban life. In the same period, Puerto Ricans began to arrive on the American mainland in significant numbers, primarily settling in neighborhoods in Brooklyn and Manhattan, identified by their Puerto Rican *bodegas* (grocery stores), restaurants, and boardinghouses.

The most visible contingents of native migrants from World War I onward were the millions of blacks who moved into northern and southern cities. Pushed off their tenant farms by failures in the cotton fields and lured by jobs in labor-scarce cities, hundreds of thousands of black families packed up and boarded the trains for Memphis, New Orleans, Chicago, Detroit, Cleveland, and New York. When the war cut off the influx of cheap foreign labor, some companies began to hire blacks, sending recruiters south to promise instant wealth to potential migrants in much the same way that railroads and industries had recruited laborers in Europe a generation or two earlier. By 1920 four-fifths of the country's blacks residing outside the South lived in cities. During World War I Chicago's black population increased by fifty thousand, almost doubling in two years—in 1920 only one of every seven blacks in Chicago had been born in Illinois. As migrations continued during the 1920s, New York's black population increased from 152,000 to 328,000, Chicago's from 109,000 to 234,000, Philadelphia's from 134,000 to 220,000, Detroit's from 41,000 to 120,000, and Cleveland's from 34,000 to 72,000. Blacks now constituted between 5 and 10 percent of the population of each of these places. Black migration continued in the 1930s as New Deal crop subsidies paid to landowners prevented black tenant farmers from making their customary living.

Like other migrants who preceded them, blacks squeezed into low-rent districts of the inner city. In many places blacks had earlier resided in unofficially delimited districts, embryonic ghettos recognized and accepted by both races. New York's Harlem, on the other hand, was a middle-class district transformed after 1900 into a slum by property owners, including black realtor Philip Payton, Jr., who tried to profit from demand by packing three or four black families into quarters originally designed for just one. In some places, notably where blacks made up only a minute fraction of the total population, they lived scattered among several neighborhoods. After the war, however, huge numbers of newcomers overflowed old districts and pressed against white neighborhoods. Racial prejudice and fear sizzled along the edges of expanding ghettos, from which whites fled or where they desperately tried to protect homes and neighborhoods acquired after long struggles to escape the inner city. In Cleveland and some smaller western cities black neighborhoods did not congeal into large, homogeneous ghettos as rapidly as they did in northeastern and southern cities. Nevertheless in many places nonwhite people were an increasingly significant urban presence.

Urban America's coming of age was proclaimed by the establishment of its own academic discipline. The study of city life was institutionalized at the University of Chicago's school of sociology, where Robert E. Park and Ernest W. Burgess trained a generation of scholars to draw relationships between city people and their environment in much the same way that biologists examined interactions between plants and animals and their surroundings. The Chicago school's approach to the city was known as human ecology. Park and his associates believed that human life had a cultural dimension that plant and animal life did not. This cultural dimension and the forms of communication it facilitated were what held human communities together. Migration to cities, according to the Chicago sociologists, broke the traditional forms of communication and community and created an atomized and disorganized society that isolated individuals amid rapid change.

How did people stabilize their social existence in these circumstances? The Chicago sociologists believed that they could understand the chaos of the city by studying its various "natural areas"—new types of communities, such as downtowns, slums, ethnic neighborhoods, suburbs, and artist's colonies, that formed as people adapted to the urban environment. Thus they set out to collect data—numbers, characteristics, maps, ratios, interviews, and the like. The data then formed part of the general theory that neighborhood communities had become the cores of individual and group life in the city and that these communities held the keys to the adjustment of people to urban society.

These ideas were central to such studies as Burgess's concentric-ring thesis, which depicted urban growth in terms of a series of concentric zones radiating outward from the urban core; Harvey W. Zorbaugh's *The Gold Coast and the Slum,* which outlined the life patterns of contrasting neighborhoods; Louis Wirth's *The Ghetto,* which probed the development of a single residential type; Frederick Thrasher's *The Gang;* and Roderick D. McKenzie's *The Metropolitan Community.* These scholars often failed to identify relationships within families and among neighbors that inner-city residents preferred to keep invisible to outsiders, and critics have charged that their emphasis on neighborhood looked nostalgically backward toward an imagined preurban village. Still, the Chicago school's commitment to urbanism as a legitimate field of inquiry, like the census milestone, unmistakably marked the city's importance in twentieth-century culture.

SUBURBANIZATION AND METROPOLITANISM

Ironically, at the same moment the United States was being labeled as an urban nation, important patterns of suburban development began to challenge the city's economic viability and political centrality. For one thing, industry began to decentralize. Electric power gave factories flexibility in location and made possible the assembly line, which gave factory management complete control over the pace of work, but assembly-line production required sprawling one- and two-story plants, not compact multistory ones like those in the city. Corporations constructed factory districts outside city limits, where land was cheaper and tax burdens less onerous. Industrial satellite suburbs like East Chicago, Hammond, and Argo outside of Chicago, Lackawanna outside of Buffalo, East St. Louis and Wellston near St. Louis, Norwood and Oakley beyond the Cincinnati city limits, and Chester and Norristown near Philadelphia became the location of factory employment. As the proportion of factory employment located within city limits began to decline, city tax bases suffered a corresponding loss.

In the same period as industrial decentralization, suburban areas were increasingly likely to reject municipal expansion through annexation and consolidation. Upper-class residential suburbs had been resisting central-city annexation since the late nineteenth century, but now corporate leaders exerted economic and political influence in local governments and in state legislatures to assure that the political independence of suburbs would be maintained. As one suburban editor explained, "Under local government we can absolutely control every objectionable thing that may try to enter our limits, but once annexed we are at the mercy of City Hall." As increasingly sharp racial, ethnic, and class divisions separated city and suburbs, new laws made incorporation easier and annexation more diffi-cult, and suburbs were able to gain access to improved services without annexation. Newer southern, midwestern, and southwestern cities such as Memphis, Atlanta, Kansas City, Indianapolis, Los Angeles, Houston, and Dallas were able to continue to successfully annex suburban areas, insuring that urban growth and economic vitality would continue unabated in these places. But older American cities came to be ringed by incorporated sub-urbs that emphasized their distinctiveness from rather than their ties to cities.

When industry moved out of the central city, many workers followed to be near their jobs. The wider availability of relatively inexpensive auto-mobiles (by 1908, twenty-four American companies produced simply con-structed automobiles at relatively low prices) allowed even more workers to reside beyond and between the reaches of urban mass transit. In 1908, Henry Ford unveiled his Model T, an inexpensive, durable motorcar pro-duced by assembly-line techniques, and in 1910 moved his own auto pro-duction factory outside of Detroit to Highland Park.

Suburban real-estate interests, the construction industry, and as they developed, the auto, rubber, and oil industries joined automobile owners in pressing for new roads and road surfaces for high-speed travel. Automo-bile wheels destroyed whatever was left of the older, lower-speed gravel surfaces. But smoother pavements and wider streets encouraged even more urban residents to invest in automobiles, generating more traffic and demands for additional roads. The building of expressways and parkways encouraged still further suburban migration.

In 1920 the growth rate of suburbs exceeded that of the cities for the first time. Between 1920 and 1930 suburbs around Los Angeles, Milwau-kee, Atlanta, Cleveland, Detroit, and Buffalo doubled and redoubled in population. Among the most rapidly growing suburbs were Elmwood Park, Berwyn, and Wilmette near Chicago; Beverly Hills and Inglewood near Los Angeles; Grosse Point and Ferndale near Detroit; and Cleveland Heights and Shaker Heights near Cleveland. Of seventy-one new towns incorpo-rated in Illinois, Missouri, and Michigan in the 1920s, two-thirds were Chicago, St. Louis, or Detroit suburbs. Many were residential suburbs for the upper and the middle classes, and many were industrial suburbs where factory workers constituted a fifth or more of the population.

As more and more people moved to the suburbs, retailing also fol-lowed a pattern of centrifugal development. Outlying secondary business centers at street-car transfer points were paralleled by those springing up at major highway intersections. Neighborhood banks, movie theaters, office buildings, branches of major department stores, and chain stores such as Woolworth's, Kresge's, A&P, and Walgreen's brought the amenities of downtown to the suburbs. The twenties witnessed the birth of the country's suburban shopping center. In 1922, Jesse C. Nichols, a Kansan well versed in land economics, built the Country Club Shopping Center as the commercial hub of his huge real-estate development in Kansas City. A few years later Sears Roebuck and Company began to build stores in outlying districts to reap sales from growing suburban populations. The major proliferation of shopping centers would occur as part of the suburban boom following World War II (see Chapter 8), but throughout the twenties and thirties, doctors, saloon keepers, restauranteurs, and independent merchants followed clients and customers out to expanding residential areas until business districts speckled every quadrant of a city's metropolitan area. By the time of the economic collapse in 1929 there were more than twenty-six million autos on the road, and the population of the suburbs was growing twice as fast as that of central cities. The more industry and retailing decentralized, the more roads were built; the more roads were built, the more automobiles became a social and economic necessity for suburban residents.

Streetcars, once the marvels of progress, declined as automobile suburbanization proceeded. After World War I, the cumulative effect of publicized abuses of streetcar franchises, strikes of streetcar employees, and accidents was that streetcars lost public support during precisely the period when companies were seriously strained by postwar inflation, overextended lines, and competition from automobiles. Millions of Americans continued to depend on mass transit to get to work through the 1930s, but by the end of the decade the number of mass-transit riders began to decline. As automobile use made central city streets more congested, streetcars could no longer provide a quicker ride to work, and the further away a commuter lived from downtown, the more benefits accrued from car travel. In the 1920s, cars counted for between 20 and 30 percent of the daily traffic into the central business district even in older cities such as Boston, New York, and Chicago, and as much as 50 to 66 percent in newer cities like Kansas City, Milwaukee, and Washington D.C. Streetcar company revenues began to fade, and even with rate increases, the companies could no longer earn enough to meet operating expenses.

Instead of mass transit, city and state government invested heavily in street improvement, traffic regulation, and new road construction. From early in the twentieth century, highway building had been subsidized by the government as contributing to public welfare in a way that mass transit, considered a private investment, had never been. By the 1920s, street and highway construction was the second largest item in municipal and state budgets. Between 1915 and 1930 the city of Chicago widened and opened 112 miles of streets at a cost of $114 million. New York City parkways built between 1923 and 1937 opened up for development seventeen thousand acres around the city. Urban road building failed to relieve congestion in the central business district or even keep pace with the spread of auto use but did encourage car travel, overloading streets and thoroughfares as soon as they were built and ultimately stimulating travel between outlying areas that avoided the central business district altogether.

Increasing long-distance travel made highways a state and national concern. Although cities were unable to secure much direct assistance from state capitols or from Washington in meeting local traffic needs during the twenties, urban interests were successful in influencing the evolution of national highway policy. As early as the first years of the twentieth century urban merchants and industrialists had organized the Good Roads Association because they believed that more and better highways would aid business. But among the most influential advocates of federal assistance were agrarian interests, such as the National Grange Association, which wanted to improve transportation between farm and market. The first attempt to initiate federal aid to highway construction reflected this rural base. In 1902 Congress considered, but did not pass, a bill that would have created a Bureau of Public Roads within the Department of Agriculture and would have provided $20 million in matching funds to states wishing to construct rural roads. The bill prohibited cities from receiving any appropriations.

It was not long, however, before metropolitan interests helped to swing federal highway policy to an urban axis. By 1915 increasing truck traffic gave urban businessmen stronger arguments for the construction of arteries to aid freight transportation between cities rather than to help farmers bring their crops to market. The Federal Roads Aid Act of 1916, the first legislation to create federal responsibility for highway improvement, revealed an ambivalence between support for arterial commerce between cities and aid for farm-to-market routes. The act authorized the secretary of agriculture to make matching grants to state highway departments (thereby forcing states to create their own highway departments) for the improvement of post roads. World War I intervened before most projects could begin. The war demonstrated the nation's need for trunk highways, especially after the railroads became overburdened and the Council for National Defense was forced to use trucks to relieve rail congestion. As a result Congress passed the Federal Highway Act of 1921, which provided federal aid to primary state roads that would contribute to a system of connecting interstate highways. More important, the act also created the Bureau of Public Roads, which by 1923 was planning a national highway system that would connect all cities of fifty thousand or more inhabitants. The new highway system reflected the emerging dominance of metropolitan interests in national affairs even before federal funds were designated for road construction within cities in the 1930s.

At the same time that manufacturing was relocating outside the city, the proportion of communications, finance, management, clerical and professional services situated downtown increased. The spreading out of factories on the periphery and the proliferation of skyscraper office buildings downtown represented a new stage in corporate organization, the separation of the production process from administrative functions. The massive scale of corporations expanded by vertical and horizontal integration made such a separation advantageous, and transportation between offices and factories via streetcars and highways and communication over the telephone made separation possible. By 1929 the editors of *The American City* could count 377 buildings at least twenty stories tall. Although New York claimed nearly half of them, Syracuse, Memphis, and Tulsa also boasted of their own. Just as booming brick factories and monumental railroad stations symbolized prosperity and growth in nineteenth-century cities, skyscrapers offered visual proof of progress in twentieth-century cities. Offices of newly expanded corporations, along with the banks, law offices, and advertising agencies that serviced them, now towered over downtown streets. Cleveland's fifty-two-story Terminal Tower, Chicago's thirty-six-story Tribune Tower, and New York's 102-story Empire State Building represented the reorientation of downtown space in the transition from industrial to corporate city.

Rising land values helped to specialize downtown space. Competition from suburban shopping districts and the reorganization of downtown threatened the major department stores, which found sales slipping by the 1920s. To recoup revenues, stores went to great lengths to entice customers to shop downtown. According to historian William Leach, "the department store became a zoo (Bloomingdale's and Wanamaker's in New York had enormous pet stores), a botanical garden (floral shops, miniature conservatories, roof gardens), a restaurant (some of the major stores had lavish restaurants bigger than any other in their cities), a barber shop, a butcher shop, a museum (gift and art shops, art exhibits), a world's fair, a library, a post office, a beauty parlor."[1] Downtown nightclubs, movie palaces, cabarets, and restaurants could afford premium space only by raising prices and cultivating a following among the wealthy and those aspiring to a similar life-style. Unable to meet high rents, many small retailers relocated in secondary business centers on the periphery. Older neighborhoods near high-rent sections continued to be characterized by a mix of commercial, industrial, and residential space. But as office towers replaced and displaced the factories, small retail businesses, apartments, and tenements that had previously jumbled together downtown, streamlined buildings and specialized land use defined what was valuable in the central city, and older, more varied neighborhoods came to be seen as slums.

Acceptance of the new specialization of space and especially of a suburban mentality dominated the thinking of political, social, and physical reformers who planned cities and formulated policy from the 1920s up until the 1960s. A commitment to decentralization implicit in its title characterized the Regional Planning Association of America (RPAA), convened in 1923, which included among its members architect and former settlement-

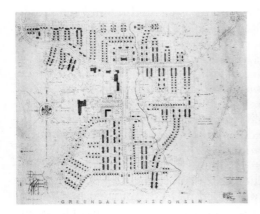 

A Green-Belt Town *Left,* a plan of Greendale, Wisconsin, prepared in 1936 by the Department of Suburban resettlement of the U.S. Resettlement Administration. *Right,* a photograph of Greendale in September, 1939. *(Both photographs courtesy of the Library of Congress.)*

house worker Clarence Stein and fellow architect Henry B. Wright plus intellectuals Lewis Mumford and Benton McKaye. Members of the RPAA had a broader view of planning than nuts and bolts concerns with housing, streets, water supply, and transportation. They argued that the physical totality of a city and its surrounding environs should provide the setting for the solution of modern problems. Wright and Stein asserted that uncontrolled expansion was causing unnecessary congestion and that decentralization would relieve the pressures of housing and traffic.

Following the English model of Ebenezer Howard's Garden Cities—new, planned communities with limited populations and surrounded by open land—the RPAA tried to prove the merits of decentralization by planning two projects near New York City. In 1924 it sponsored Sunnyside, a limited-dividend housing corporation in Queens planned by Wright and Stein and intended for low-income residents. Radburn, New Jersey, a genuine garden city, was begun in 1928 on a large tract seventeen miles from New York. Although Sunnyside and Radburn won much publicity for their advanced design, both were too expensive to build to offer a feasible model for low-income housing or a solution to the problems of urban overcrowding.

Impulses toward decentralization did not halt with Sunnyside and Radburn, however. In the 1930s, New Deal faith in the beneficial effects of modern suburbanization prompted Rexford Tugwell, head of the U.S. Resettlement Agency, to plan a network of garden suburbs that he visualized as Green-Belt cities. These were to be of limited size (about ten thousand people), located on the outskirts of metropolitan centers, surrounded by farms and open lands, built with federal funds, and leased to cooperatives of local residents. Tugwell hoped that his Green-Belt cities would relieve slum congestion, provide low-cost housing, and rebuild community cohesion. Tugwell planned twenty-five Green-Belt cities, but only three were actually built: Greenbelt, north of Washington, D.C., in Maryland; Greenhills, near Cincinnati; and Greendale, southwest of Milwaukee. Private developers' opposition to plans to house low-income people in Green-Belt cities, and to government-sponsored planned communities in general, squelched the program. For example, building-and-loan associations in Milwaukee sued to prevent Greendale from being built. In 1938 the Resettlement Administration was abolished, and after World War II the communities were sold to nonprofit corporations.

The RPAA's commitment to planning for a region rather than simply within city limits generated schemes for comprehensive planning, such as the New York Regional Plan, presented in 1931. Initiated by planning advocate Charles D. Norton, financed by the Russell Sage Foundation, and directed by planner Thomas Adams, the New York Regional Plan consisted of eight volumes of survey material and two volumes of proposals. It was the most extensive planning project yet attempted. Its recognition of the interrelationships among the different regions and different functions of a metropolis influenced similar projects envisioned in other cities. Surveys were taken for the metropolitan areas of Philadelphia, Chicago, Boston, San Francisco, and Cleveland. Civic leaders held conferences and appointed commissions to discuss regional problems of highways, land use, and water supplies, but political and economic rivalries and suburban insistence on political independence prevented substantive reforms such as consolidation of cities with their surrounding territories. Schemes to combine city and county governments by Cleveland, St. Louis, and Seattle were defeated, and efforts to integrate planning in Cook County, Illinois (the Chicago region), were tabled. New Deal agencies like the National Resources Planning Board and the Tennessee Valley Authority merged urban and rural planning into regional coordination. But the orientation of much regional planning was to accept growth as inevitable and to celebrate the automobile as the best possible means of transportation, underemphasizing possibilities for controlled growth and giving highways precedence over mass transit.

More narrowly defined planning strategies such as zoning and traffic control, popularized in the 1920s and 1930s, had a similar effect of rigidifying the divisions between urban and suburban space. Originally intended as a means of confinement, zoning became a tool of exclusion that still governs land-use patterns today. Copied from Germany and elsewhere abroad, zoning is a type of local police power that restricts certain types of buildings or land use to certain districts of the city. The earliest comprehensive zoning ordinance was passed by New York in 1916 to prevent skyscrapers and high-rise garment-industry lofts from encroaching on the fashionable Fifth Avenue retail district. By 1924 every major city, plus hundreds of smaller cities, had established zoning regulations. Although loopholes left room for easy circumvention, the laws generally controlled areas and heights of buildings, determined boundaries of commercial and residential zones, and fixed density limitations.

The U.S. Supreme Court upheld the zoning principle in *Village of Euclid, Ohio* v. *Ambler Realty Co.* (1926), a landmark case that had important consequences for future urban land-use policies. The court ruled valid a local law that zoned a parcel of land as residential and that prevented a property owner—in this case the Ambler Realty Company—from using residentially zoned land for industrial purposes. According to the court, zoning was a legitimate use of police power under which local government had the authority to "abate a nuisance." A nuisance could be defined as noise, traffic, fire hazard, or any other danger to the safety, health, morals, and general welfare of a residential area. In such an instance concern for the common good overrode an individual's or company's property rights.

This decision gave local governments much stronger prerogatives against formerly sacred rights of property owners, but zoning proved to be no panacea for urban ailments. Zoning laws aimed to establish stability in existing districts and orderly growth in newer regions, but they primarily protected the interests of real-estate developers and owners of commercial property by insuring that residential or commercial zones would not be invaded by unwanted features such as multiple-family dwellings and factories. Later, zoning would commonly be used to exclude "undesirable" people from the suburbs. In the 1920s zoning became the principal activity of the scores of planning commissions established in cities across the country. Planning staffs spent much of their time drawing maps that identified patterns of land use, traffic, health, lighting, utilities, and other aspects of the urban environment. Such projects proved helpful in systematizing policy planning, but they mainly ratified the status quo. Zoning maps could not renovate dilapidated housing stock, abolish want and crime, or improve the quality of life for all city dwellers.

Unplanned urban sprawl, new suburban expansion, and "automobility" unbound by tracks or schedules drew the country and the city closer together. Automobiles quickened travel speed, extended distances that could be traversed easily, and gave tourists access to rural areas as a recreational playground. On weekends, thousands of cars pierced the countryside, carrying picnicking and sight-seeing families, many of whom thought that farmers' fields were appropriate places for pitching tents and disposing of tin cans and that farmer-grown produce was theirs for the picking. Service stations, motor camps, and tourist restaurants sprouted along highways, and as farmers relied more heavily on automobiles for purchasing necessary goods, small cross-roads market centers lost their general trade and service functions to larger rural towns. With access to urban stores, goods, and services, farm families were less culturally isolated from urban

life. Suburbs remained economically tied to cities, because suburban residents depended on cities for employment, and adjacent towns were satel-
lites of large urban centers connected by ever expanding transportation
and commercial networks.

These regional networks formed metropolitan districts—regions
that included a city and its suburbs. In 1910 the Census Bureau gave the
concept official recognition by identifying twenty-five areas with central-
city populations of over 200,000 as metropolitan districts. By 1920 the total
of metropolitan and near-metropolitan districts had grown to fifty-eight,
and together they contained two-thirds of the nation's urban population.
By 1930 there were ninety-three cities with populations of over 100,000. In
1933 a member of the government-sponsored study on modern social
trends described the decentralization of urban space and centralization of
rural space as the national paradigm:

> The large center has been able to extend the radius of its influence. . . .
> Moreover, formerly independent towns and villages and also rural territory
> have become part of the enlarged city complex. . . . Nor is this new type of
> metropolitan community confined to great cities. It has become the commu-
> nal unit of local relations throughout the entire nation.

The rise of urban America had been eclipsed by the metropolitan age.

CONSUMING PASSIONS: GOODS AND LEISURE IN EVERYDAY LIFE

The end of World War I marked the emergence of the United States as a
mature industrial power. As corporate profits soared, investors looked for
new areas of expansion, investing abroad and creating new markets and
new products at home. Rising productivity and technological innovations
intensified the pace of the workday, shortened the hours of work, and
sharpened distinctions between working and nonworking time. In 1920 the
six-day, sixty-hour work week had been common. By 1929 most people
worked only five and a half days and forty-eight to fifty-four hours. Although corporate profits and investment returns rose much faster than
industrial wages, the prospering economy nevertheless gave many Americans time and money for amusements such as movies, sports, and radios.

As in previous eras cities stood in the center of economic change.
City dwellers, now constituting a majority of the country's population, more
than ever provided workers and consumers for expanding industry and
related services. The proliferation of urban commercial and service establishments reflected the rise of a mass-consumer economy on a national
level. American industrialists during the twenties utilized mass-production

techniques to market commodities that many white-collar and skilled work-ers' families could afford. Aided by advertising and new forms of consumer credit, producers promoted a dazzling array of goods. Installment buying ("a dollar down and a dollar forever") made acquisition of automobiles, radios, washing machines, vacuum cleaners, refrigerators, electric toasters, and kitchen cabinets possible. Advertising—an expanding professional service—helped to make acquisition desirable by celebrating consumerism in the popular media: newspapers, pulp magazines, radio, billboards, and motion pictures. Advertising strategies shifted from merely developing con-sumer loyalty to particular brand names to associating the possession of these products with states of well-being and the absence of them with anxi-ety and inadequacy. "You have to *create* a demand for a product," lectured one advertising man. "Make the public want what you have to sell. Make 'em pant for it."

Most advertising campaigns were aimed at urban consumers, particu-larly at the expanding middle class, because these were the people who had the money to buy new products—or at least to make a down payment. Between 1920 and 1929 farmers' share of the national income dropped from 16 percent to 9 percent, while skilled industrial and white-collar work-ers' incomes, most of which went to urban households, expanded. More-over the proportion of urban dwellings wired for electricity rose from 10 percent in 1920 to over 50 percent by 1930, whereas even at the later date few farmhouses had electricity. Thus most household appliances, van-guards of the new materialism, could be sold initially to urban and subur-ban families.

Many products were designed for use in the home. Advertisers claimed that refrigerators, washing machines, stoves, canned goods, and ready-made clothing would transform housework and "liberate" wives from "constant drudgery." Toastmaster proclaimed itself "The *Toaster* that FREED 465,000 homes." Recent studies, however, have shown that access to running water and stoves significantly lifted housewives' burdens but that most of the other new household conveniences and appliances failed to actually cut labor time spent in housework because rising standards of cleanliness kept housewives just as busy. Washing machines meant that households no longer sent their dirty clothes out to commercial laundries; vacuum cleaners changed rug cleaning from a once-a-year to a weekly or daily task. The decentralization of retailing made marketing more time consuming because goods previously available downtown now had to be purchased at stores scattered throughout the suburbs. Whether working as domestic producers or as domestic consumers, urban women with children at home found household responsibilities continuing to weigh heavily on them.

Another type of consumption basically supported by city dwellers was the expanding range of leisure activities. A mania for sports, movies,

More Leisure Time for City Dwellers   Crowds of bathers jam a Lake Michigan beach in Chicago, ca. 1925. *(U.S. Office of War Information, The National Archives.)*

music, and fads gripped every city in the nation. Passionate interest in sports had been building since the late nineteenth century, involving participants and spectators in contests that followed rules, offered keen competition, and engaged partisan loyalties of both male and female fans. In 1923, 300,000 fans attended the six-game World Series of baseball between the New York Yankees and the New York Giants. In 1926 the attendance of 130,000 at the first Jack Dempsey–Gene Tunney heavyweight championship prize fight in Philadelphia broke all records. But the return bout the next year shattered the newly set marks: 145,000 spectators jammed Soldier Field in Chicago, paying $2,650,000 to view the contest—even though many seats were so far from the ring that thousands were unable to see Tunney win. Each week millions of sports enthusiasts practiced baseball in sandlots and filled tennis courts, golf links, and beaches.

Popular drama, musical comedy, and vaudeville shows packed in family audiences during the 1920s. The rise of show business had paralleled the rise of sports, maturing with the growth of cities. Talented promoters turned vaudeville into big business, presenting the most popular live entertainment, including magic and animal acts, juggling stunts, comedy (especially ethnic humor), and song and dance. Playing continuously for hours, vaudeville's variety made it attractive to mass audiences. Music halls, cabarets, and nightclubs brought performers and audiences closer together, dancing to new kinds of ragtime and jazz band music in an informal setting that celebrated pleasure and a more explicit sexuality.

The Palatial Urban Movie House   First-nighters crowd the sidewalk in front of the opulent Warners' Theatre in New York, August 6, 1926, for the opening of *Don Juan,* starring John Barrymore. Note the lavish use of electricity—for lighting as well as for air conditioning. *(U.S. Office of War Information, The National Archives.)*

Motion pictures attracted enormous crowds in the 1920s. The movie industry used advertising to sell its dreams: as one advertisement appearing in the *Saturday Evening Post* in 1924 promised,

> Go to a motion picture . . . and let yourself go. . . . Before you know it, you are living the story—laughing, loving, hating, struggling, winning! All the romance, all the excitement you lack in your daily life are—in Pictures. They take you completely out of yourself into a wonderful new world. . . . Out of the cage of everyday existence! If only for an afternoon or an evening—escape.

During the banner years from 1927 to 1929, weekly movie attendance reached an estimated 110 million people—at a time when total population was just over 120 million and total weekly church attendance was under sixty million. Many moviegoers were country folk who streamed into the Bijou on Main Street in a thousand towns and villages. But many more were city dwellers who stood in line for one of the six thousand seats in Roxy's in New York or for the luxury of one of the ornate Balaban and Katz movie palaces in Chicago. Silent movies could attract a linguistically diverse urban audience, although by 1927 familiarity with English was widespread enough for the introduction of sound in *The Jazz Singer* to make movies even more appealing. Mass spectacles such as Cecil B. de Mille's *The Ten Commandments* (1923), sexually charged romances such as *The Four Horsemen of the Apocalypse* (1920) and *The Sheik* (1920) starring Rudolph Valentino, and slapstick comedies featuring Fatty Arbuckle, Harold Lloyd, Buster Keaton, and Charlie Chaplin, which often poked fun at authority were widely popular.

Radios brought the new world of entertainment and advertising into many homes in the 1920s. In 1922 three million homes had radios; by 1930 radios were a fixture in twelve million homes, approximately 40 percent of all American households, and radio production had become a billion-dollar industry. Stations sprouted in hundreds of cities. In Nashville a local insurance company pioneered new marketing techniques by operating its own radio station to sell its product through advertising and by creating a new entertainment institution, the "Grand Ole Opry," as the station's chief listener attraction. In 1926 a network of stations was formed by the National Broadcasting Corporation. To prevent chaotic expansion, the federal government in 1927 created the Federal Radio Commission, which distributed broadcasting licenses and frequencies among 412 cities. National radio programming included comedy shows such as "Amos 'n Andy' and "The Rise of the Goldbergs," routines performed by old vaudeville acts like Burns and Allen, advice shows like "Housekeeper's Chat," and variety shows like "Arthur Godfrey's Time." Radio broadcasting linked households in new ways, giving listeners a taste of sharing a common experience with a national audience. Radio advertising brought the message of consumption into every listening household.

A dizzying succession of games and other fancies passed through the cities. During 1922 and 1923 the Chinese game of mah-jongg was the rage. A new pastime, the crossword puzzle, emerged in 1924. Newspapers boosted sales by printing daily puzzles, and crossword puzzle books broke into the best-seller lists. At the end of the decade, fun seekers were adopting miniature golf as their newest diversion. By 1930 thirty thousand courses had filled empty lots in scores of towns and cities.

But all the new products, services, and entertainments paled when placed beside the automobile—the economic and social wonder of the age. Originally an expensive curiosity for the wealthy, autos were mass produced in the 1910s, and automobile registrations tripled between 1920 and 1930. Studies have estimated that just under 50 percent of nonfarm families owned cars in 1929. The automobile's effects on the economy were extraordinary. By the mid-twenties the automobile industry used 20 percent of the nation's steel output, 80 percent of its rubber, and 75 percent of its glass. It revamped the petroleum industry from one of illumination and lubrication to one of propulsion. It created a vast new service network of filling stations, repair shops, and parts and accessories dealers. Automobiles were a major subject of advertising and financing operations. General

Motors began to finance purchase of its own cars in 1919, and by 1922, consumers depended on installment buying to finance 73 percent of all car sales. At the same time as credit sales expanded the market for cars, the industry used advertising campaigns to differentiate between types of cars. Advertisements focused on styling and details of annual model changes in trying to develop a market for new cars, replacement cars, and second cars.

Historian Joseph Interrante has pointed out the important ways in which inequality continued to shape the consumption of automobiles even though the opportunity to consume became more widespread.[2] Car ownership reflected differences in wealth, region, and locality. Professionals and salaried employees owned cars more often than industrial workers did; California had a higher percentage of car owners than any other state; farmers and people in small communities had higher rates of ownership than did people in big cities; cities dependent on automobile manufacturing had a higher-than-average working-class ownership of automobilies. The increasing heterogeneity of car ownership was accompanied by a more pronounced differentiation between types of cars. During the mid-twenties a Ford Model T sold for under $300; a Chevrolet coupe sold for $700, and a used car could be had for $60 ($5 down and $5 a month). Automobiles were a highly visible expression of family means.

The attraction of new goods and commercial amusements in the 1920s pulled city people into what historians have labeled a culture of consumption, a culture of abundance. A new emphasis on spending, consuming, and playing replaced older values of frugality, hard work, and self-denial; external characteristics of "personality" substituted for internal strength of character. New techniques of display emerging in the 1920s heightened the intensity of what historian Neil Harris has labeled "the drama of consumer desire."[3] New use of glass, lighting, and mirrors transformed store interiors; improvements in color printing and engraving permitted full-page color advertisements; film's use of close-ups and lighting techniques focused attention on objects as part of screen imagery, and the profusion of brands and model changes presented consumption as a significant statement of choice.

The glitter and glamour of city life beckoned from the urban settings that radio and films projected. Cars, new goods and services, and nightlife infused cities with an expansionist spirit during the 1920s. But by middecade dark clouds were gathering. Speculation in securities was draining private capital from mortgage markets and pushing the costs of home ownership beyond the reach of many families. Housing construction ebbed in the inner cities and the outskirts. As prices for land and buildings soared, real-estate operators used inflated paper profits as security on loans obtained for stock-market speculation. Moreover advertising and consumer credit had created huge new demands for products, but demands themselves could not raise buying power. To be sure, the new prosperity had lifted the wages and living standards of urban workers, but a rising proportion of private incomes was spent on interest payments for installment purchases, instead of on goods and services. The economy of the urban nation was teetering on a weakening base—a base that crumbled in 1929.

CITIES AS A CULTURAL BATTLEGROUND

Commercial amusements drew on diverse cultural traditions for their popular appeal. White suburbanites trekked to Harlem nightspots to hear the hottest black jazz bands, and white dancers based their routines on toned-down black dances. Immigrant singers like Fannie Brice and Sophie Tucker and black dancer and comedian Burt Williams won loyal followings on the vaudeville circuit, although often their humorous appeal depended on perpetuating familiar and demeaning stereotypes of their own group experience. But urban commercial culture's potential for undermining older patterns of separation and mixing ethnic groups and races was a source of great concern to other urban residents. Issues like prohibition, labor organizing, and immigration restriction sharply divided urban populations, and race riots bared deeper tensions lying underneath surface accommodations. The city in the 1920s was often a battleground as various groups within the population struggled for dominance.

The triumph of national prohibition and rebirth of the Ku Klux Klan seemed to be last gasps of fading rural resistance to urban civilization. However, important segments of city populations contributed to the initial successes of these campaigns, while other urban groups brought about their ultimate failure. In 1917 Congress capped a long drive for prohibition by proposing the Eighteenth Amendment to the Constitution. The measure prohibited the manufacture, sale, and importation of intoxicating liquors. Within one year a sufficient number of states had ratified, and at the end of 1919 Congress passed the Volstead Act, which enforced the amendment. Although rural groups, particularly small-town Methodists and Baptists, had been in the vanguard of the dry crusade, a number of urban interests were also attached to the Great Cause. Middle-class Protestants in the cities (with the exception of Episcopalians and Lutherans), mostly residents of peripheral and suburban districts, supported prohibition as a reform instrument. They linked liquor with poverty, vice, and corruption. And they believed that enforced abstinence would improve worker efficiency, fortify family life, and blunt the power of political machines.

It is probable that national prohibition would not have passed without support from urban groups. On the other hand city dwellers were also instrumental in crippling the crusade. Prohibition simply could not prohibit. Large numbers of people refused to renounce the bottle. Although enforcement of the law worked well at first, smuggling and illegal distilling were increasing rapidly by the mid twenties. The Volstead Act forged new contacts between local police and federal agents in the attack against boot-legging. But it was impossible to dry up the cities. Not only were local efforts less than energetic but federal enforcement was sporadic, under-manned, and inept.

The results are well known. Speak-easies blossomed in cities across the country, and crime became a big business. By the early twentieth cen-tury those operations had adopted business techniques that utilized pay-rolls, modern communications, and coordinated management. But the pub-lic desire to evade prohibition gave organized crime new opportunities and dimensions in the twenties. As Mark Haller has remarked regarding Chi-cago, "Because bootlegging provided such resources in money and organi-zation, an unprecedented consolidation and centralization of organized crime occurred."[4] Like other twentieth-century businesses, crime had been rationalized. In New York, Chicago, Detroit, Cleveland, Kansas City, Buf-falo, New Orleans, San Francisco, and other cities big-time criminals ex-panded from illegal activities into labor racketeering and into control of small businesses, such as restaurants, barbershops, and dry cleaners.

The most notorious feature of organized crime in the 1920s was the use of violent extortion and wholesale murder to win customers and elimi-nate competition. Merchants who refused to accept gang-controlled busi-ness, such as slot machines or bootleg beer, or who refused to pay protec-tion money, were beaten and their property was destroyed. Between 1925 and 1928 over four hundred gang-related bombings of business establish-ments occurred in Chicago alone. Rivals who contested a gang leader's will were assassinated, and their bodies, feet encased in cement slippers, were dumped into nearby rivers and harbors. In Chicago a dispute over the bulk of illegal liquor traffic burst into a violent war when henchmen of crime boss Johnny Torrio murdered arch rival Dion O'Banion in O'Banion's florist shop in 1924. Torrio and his lieutenant, Al Capone, were consider-ate enough to send a basket of flowers to O'Banion's lavish funeral, but the gesture failed to console the florist's gang, now led by Hymie Weiss. The gang went on a bullet-filled rampage, driving Torrio into retirement, and Capone assumed full control of Torrio's legions. Combat raged for more than four years, climaxing on St. Valentine's Day, 1929, when Capone's agents, posing as policemen, trapped seven members of the O'Banion gang in a North Side garage and executed them with submachine guns. By this time Capone ruled the Chicago suburb of Cicero and had spread his influ-ence from bootlegging into a huge network of rackets that included ninety-one trade unions. He was earning over $100 million a year, and his flamboy-ant habits made him as famous as Charles Lindbergh and Babe Ruth. He was not yet thirty-two years old.

During the twenties Chicago, New York, Kansas City, and Detroit witnessed hundreds of gangland killings, almost all of which went unsolved. These were only the most grisly features of what had become a big business. Other factors besides prohibition contributed to the rise of big-time crime. Trucks and automobiles gave criminals and illegal commerce new mobility. Submachine guns and other weapons inherited from World War I made crime more threatening. And the times themselves had given birth to an indiscriminate worship of swagger. But also, crime itself—long a fact of life for inner-city residents—had come to serve important functions. Crime provided a ladder of social mobility, a means of "making it" for immigrants and other downtrodden groups forced to live on the margins of society. A 1930 report of 108 crime leaders in Chicago revealed that 32 were Italian, 31 Irish, 22 Jewish, and 13 black. Barred from any legitimate paths to success, some immigrants and blacks found profits in illicit activity. Crime, like politics, furnished opportunities to inner-city youths whose ambitions might otherwise have been blocked. By supplying liquor, gambling facilities, and prostitutes, organized crime served real wants of a consuming public. Thus Al Capone, who amassed a huge fortune by ignoring the law, saw himself as an ordinary businessman. "Prohibition is a business," he once remarked, "All I do is to supply a public demand. I do it in the best and least harmful way I can."

By 1933 Capone was in jail and prohibition was repealed. The return of legal liquor swept away most of the bootlegging but left behind more sinister underworld activities that had accompanied the growth of organized crime in the twenties—extortion, racketeering, narcotics (activities in which gangsters created demand far more than they served existing needs.) These areas gave the underworld its future.

Race relations became explosive when the unprecedented influx of black migrants during the Great Migration unsettled prior patterns of racial accommodation. Tensions over wartime housing shortages, inflation, fears of black voting strength, and the labor movement's unsuccessful initiatives in the face of postwar labor surpluses and new antiunion offensives inflamed racial hostilities building along the shifting boundaries separating black from white residential areas. A race riot in East St. Louis in 1917 was precipitated when blacks, having been beaten repeatedly by white gangs, shot into a police car. In the dusk they mistook it for another Ford automobile containing white joyriders who had shot up black homes earlier in the evening. In 1919 a race riot in Longview, Texas, occurred after blacks shot whites who entered a ghetto seeking a teacher who had reported a recent lynching to the major black newspaper, the Chicago *Defender*. The event that triggered a 1919 riot in Elaine, Arkansas, was when blacks returned the fire after two white law enforcement officials shot into a black church. In the summer of 1919, race riots broke out in a total of twenty-six cities. The most violent rioting occurred in Chicago. When the city was finally quieted, 38 people had been killed (23 blacks and 15 whites), 520 were injured (342 black and 172 white), and 1000 black families were left homeless by arsonists and vandals. Riots erupted in cities as diverse as Omaha, Knoxville, Charleston, and Washington, D.C. The 1921 riot in Tulsa, Oklahoma, originated when a crowd of armed black people assembled before the courthouse to prevent the lynching of a black arrested for allegedly attacking a white girl. The blacks shot at the white police and civilians who attempted to disperse them.

Unlike previous race riots in which blacks had been relatively passive victims of white mob action, the typical pattern in all these blowups was black retaliation against white acts of persecution and violence. Whites perceived this retaliation as an organized, premeditated conspiracy to "take over," which then unleashed the armed power of white mobs and police. In the face of overwhelming numerical superiority, black resistance ordinarily collapsed fairly early during the riots, especially in the South. Still, the riots left deep scars and divided communities.

Partly in response to race riots and threats, thousands of blacks in northern cities joined movements that called for black independence. The most influential of these black nationalist groups was the Universal Negro Improvement Association (UNIA), headed by Marcus Garvey, a fiery and flamboyant Jamaican immigrant who believed that blacks should separate themselves from a corrupt white society. Proclaiming, "I am the equal of any white man," Garvey cultivated racial pride through militant mass meetings and parades. His newspaper, the *Negro World,* refused to publish advertisements for hair straighteners and skin-lightening cosmetics, and his Black Star Shipping Line was intended to help blacks emigrate to Africa. The UNIA declined in the mid-1920s when the Black Star Line went bankrupt (unscrupulous dealers had sold the line dilapidated ships) and when antiradical fears prompted government prosecution (ten of the organization's leaders were arrested on charges of anarchism, and Garvey was deported for mail fraud). Nevertheless the organization had attracted a huge following in New York, Chicago, Detroit, and other places, and Garveyites would resurface in later years as the leaders of future movements for black rights.

White fears of black urban migration underlay the reemergence of the Ku Klux Klan in this period. D. W. Griffith's 1915 film *The Birth of a Nation,* based on a popular novel that had become a hit Broadway play, dramatized northern commercial corruption by glorifying the post–Civil War Ku Klux Klan and ridiculing newly enfranchised black voters. Griffith's technical innovations gave emotional power to the film's racist sentiment, and one result was the founding of a modern Klan by William J. Simmons, an Atlanta evangelist and insurance salesman who made his mission the purification of southern culture. The new invisible empire revived the hoods, intimidating tactics, and mystical rituals of its forerunner.

The Klan grew slowly until 1920, when Simmons hired two public relations experts, Edward Clarke and Elizabeth Tyler, to recruit members.

By sending agents into Masonic lodges and other organizations, Clarke and Tyler were able to build membership to a figure between two and four million by 1924. Using threatening assemblies, violence, and political pressure, the Klan made its presence felt in many communities in the early 1920s, and for a time the organization wielded frightening power in Arkansas, California, Indiana, Ohio, Oklahoma, Oregon, and Texas. Although, like its predecessor in the 1860s and 1870s, the new Klan vowed "to maintain forever white supremacy," its constitution also pledged Klansmen "to conserve, protect, and maintain the distinctive institutions, rights, privileges, principles, traditions and ideals of pure Americanism." Feeding on the fears and tensions spawned by post–World War I disillusion and reaction, the Klan added anti-immigrant, anti-Catholic, anti-Jewish, and antifeminist venom to its racist poison. From 1921 onward Klansmen paraded, harangued, and assaulted in the name of Protestant morality and Anglo-Saxon purity, meting out vigilante justice to bootleggers, wife beaters, and adulterers, forcing schools to adopt Bible readings and stop teaching the theory of evolution, and campaigning against Catholic and Jewish political candidates.

Although the Klan flourished in rural districts and small towns of the West and South—areas where people feared and distrusted the city—it also enjoyed considerable success in metropolitan areas. Kenneth T. Jackson has estimated that half the Klan's membership lived in cities of over fifty thousand people. Detroit, Atlanta, Indianapolis, Memphis, Philadelphia, Portland, and Denver had sizable contingents. Chicago, with an estimated fifty thousand Klansmen, contained the largest single operation in the country. In many cities the urban Klan thrived in the zone of emergence, the belt of modest neighborhoods that separated the inner core from the periphery. Here, working-class and lower-middle-class white Protestants, one step removed from the slums, grew increasingly apprehensive over nearby inner districts that were bulging with black and foreign migrants. As blacks, Catholics, and Jews began to spill into zone neighborhoods and to press upon housing markets, many white families, still on the lower rungs of the socioeconomic ladder, grasped for some means of soothing their anxieties and reinforcing their identification with "100-percent Americanism." The Ku Klux Klan, with its ceremony, secrecy, and emotionalism, served this need.

In the rural countryside the Klan's activities included parades, cross burnings, and lynchings. In the cities Klansmen often turned to politics rather than using violence and display to achieve their goals. Usually operating within one of the two major parties rather than independently, the KKK was partially successful in influencing local elections: it helped to elect a Republican mayor of Indianapolis and Democratic mayors in Denver and Atlanta. But after 1924, racked by scandals and dissidence, the "Invisible Empire" swiftly declined. The Klan waned locally because its political machinations failed to bring substantive results. Politics provided the only avenue where nativists could translate 100-percent Americanism into policy, but even the election victories produced only short-term effects. Moreover by the mid-twenties Catholics and Jews, along with liberal Protestants, could outvote it. As Professor Jackson has written, "The Ku Klux Klan provided a focus for the fears of alienated native Americans whose world was being disrupted. In the city the Invisible Empire found its greatest challenge, and in the city it met its ultimate defeat."[5] By 1930 the Klan had resubmerged into the current of intolerance that has flowed beneath the stream of American history, but racism and nativism in the twenties opened new sores that still have not healed today.

Anti-immigrant sentiments appeared to have been responsible for the 1921 conviction of Nicola Sacco and Bartolomeo Vanzetti, two immigrant anarchists accused of murdering a guard and paymaster during a robbery in South Braintree, Massachusetts. Sacco and Vanzetti's main offense seems to have been their radical political beliefs and Italian origins, since evidence failed to prove their involvement in the robbery. Judge Webster Thayer openly sided with the prosecution, privately calling the defendants "those anarchist bastards." Appeals by thousands of protesters organized in scores of cities failed to win a new trial, and the two Italians were executed in August 1927. In the same years some urban reformers joined the movement to restrict immigration, seeing this legislation as a means of controlling poverty and quickening the assimilation of foreign groups. Although ethnic communities strongly opposed immigration restriction, they did join in the debate over assimilation, with upwardly mobile and prosperous ethnic leaders urging Americanization and others holding out to defend religious orthodoxy and cultural traditionalism.

Besides joining rural-based movements for moral purity such as prohibition and the Ku Klux Klan, disgruntled, native-born city residents also provided a base of support for new waves of religious fundamentalism. A literal interpretation of the Bible and unquestioning faith provided not only a means to salvation but also a traditional and highly comforting defense against the skepticism and irreverence of what they saw as materialistic and hedonistic urban society. The most famous religious clash of the decade occurred in Dayton, Tennessee in July 1925. Here, at the trial of John Thomas Scopes, a high-school biology instructor arrested for teaching the theory of evolution, the issue was joined between fundamentalists and modernists, the unquestioning religion of the country and the scientific "higher criticism" of the city. The battle lines sharpened when the prosecution enlisted the counsel of William Jennings Bryan—self-proclaimed defender of the faith—and the defense obtained the assistance of big-city lawyers Clarence Darrow, Arthur Garfield Hays, and Dudley Field Malone. Although the jury found Scopes guilty of breaking a Tennessee law prohibiting instructors in state-supported schools from teaching that humans had descended from some lower order of animal, it was a Pyrrhic victory for the fundamentalists. Scores of newspaper reporters conveyed the circuslike event to a national audience and made the trial an object of ridicule, especially after Darrow cross-examined Bryan and bared all the ambiguities of literal interpretation of the Bible. Afterward humorist Will Rogers remarked, "I see you can't say that man descended from the ape. At least that's the law in Tennessee. But do they have a law to keep a man from making a jackass of himself?"

It appeared, then, that cosmopolitan urban culture could shrug off the challenge of rural old-time religion. Yet at the same time, pietistic fundamentalism, with its "holiness," "pentecostal," and storefront churches, was surging dramatically in cities across the country. In part this upswing accompanied the move of black Americans to northern and southern cities in the twenties. Blacks transplanted their churches from the rural countryside and looked to them for solace, adjustment, and identification. The majority of urban fundamentalists were white, however. Like the Ku Klux Klan, urban fundamentalist churches drew much of their membership from groups caught between the middle and lower classes. "Insecure, frustrated, feeling inferior and different," William G. McLoughlin, Jr., has written, "most of them were struggling not so much to get into a higher social bracket as to keep from sinking into a lower one."[6] Many were rural migrants attracted by the friendliness, lack of dogma, and closeness to God that the various storefront churches and gospel tabernacles promised.

Most leaders of these churches were professional evangelists, charismatic figures who operated outside of the regular Protestant denominations. Using the ballyhoo and pageantry of the new advertising age, they attracted huge followings and stirred up a revivalistic fervor. In Los Angeles Aimee Semple MacPherson, the widow of a missionary, established the Four Square Gospel Temple, where she produced extravaganzas of religious vaudeville. Sister Aimee's sumptuous services, flowing gowns, and moving sermons captivated thousands of newly arrived midwesterners and southerners. Her Sunday evening "shows for the Lord" were broadcast by her own radio station, KFSG, throughout southern Calfornia each week. Similar cults, founded by evangelists and graduates of Bible institutes, appeared in a host of other cities. They included Clinton H. Churchill's Evangelistic Tabernacle in Buffalo, Paul Rader's Chicago Gospel Tabernacle, Katherine Kuhlman's Denver Revival Tabernacle, E. J. Rolling's Detroit Metropolitan Tabernacle, T. H. Elsner's Philadelphia Gospel Tabernacle, Karl Wittman's Tabernacle in Toledo, and Luke Rader's River Lake Gospel Tabernacle in Minneapolis. Most of these churches had their own radio programs or stations and their own newspapers, Bible camps, and foreign missionaries.

Yet fundamentalist churches, along with prohibition and the Klan, were not unique responses by native Protestants trying to infuse their urban experiences with ideals of a romanticized past. Rather these institutions were part of a larger organizational impulse that pervaded all of urban society. City populations were too large and diverse to sustain a unified sense of community that many believed once existed in small towns and villages. In a fragmented society people turned to new forms of association that revolved around interest-group identities. Membership rolls of middle-class organizations such as Rotary, Kiwanis, Lions, Elks, and women's clubs swelled during the twenties. Football, baseball, and basketball games brought people together in new forms of community identification. Community chests, public campaigns for support of local welfare projects, increased in number from 12 in 1919 to 363 in 1930. Each of these activities and associations reflected a kind of social adjustment to the new urban society, where tight and tiny communities no longer existed and where people tried to bring order to the complexities of group and personal loyalties. The impulses of group organization had always been characteristic of the city, but the tensions and self-consciousness of the decade between World War I and the Depression heightened the search for identity.

URBAN POLITICS IN THE 1920s

The scope of public initiative in cities expanded broadly during the twenties. In addition to traffic signals and electric fire alarms, most cities began to purchase police cars and to equip them with radio receivers. Local governments bought snowplows, garbage trucks, and school buses. Pittsburgh, Chicago, Cincinnati, Cleveland, St. Louis, Denver, and Rochester took steps (seldom successful) to control smoke pollution. As air transportation became a reality, several cities began to construct facilities for the airlines. By mid-decade Philadelphia, Detroit, Boston, Kansas City, and Cleveland had municipal airfields. Cities literally roared with the sound of public construction as projects planned before World War I and postponed during it began to reach completion: government office buildings, parks, belt-ways, libraries, stadiums, and terminals.

Although the supply of quality housing for low-income residents remained generally inadequate, the notion that government needed to do more to relieve housing problems began to win limited acceptance. Rising rents and prices pushed new housing beyond the reach of most working-class families. Home ownership in the inner cities declined while slum congestion increased. To relieve the housing shortage that occurred during World War I, two federal agencies, the Emergency Fleet Corporation of the U.S. Shipping Board and the Housing Corporation of the U.S. Department of Labor, had built and operated housing units for war workers—the first direct federal program to provide low-cost housing. Congress abolished these programs after the war, and although reformers such as Clarence Stein and Henry Wright continued to advocate housing subsidies and government construction, the concept of public housing generated little support. Nevertheless officials in several cities encouraged private, nonprofit groups who sponsored housing construction for workingmen. A 1919 Wisconsin law permitted Milwaukee and other cities to help finance limited-dividend cooperative-housing companies (that is, companies that would limit profits in order to hold down prices). A few years later New York City received authorization to grant tax exemptions to limited-dividend housing projects—although the legislature stifled efforts by Stein and Governor Alfred E. Smith to amend the state constitution to enable creation of a state housing authority that could acquire land and construct public housing.

Behind the flurry of activity urban politics were readjusting to new conditions. To be sure, bosses and reformers still contested for the reins of power, but now both had to be more sensitive to each other's presence as well as to changing patterns within the electorate. For one thing the curtailment of European immigration, by World War I and later by legal restriction, shut off one important source of urban population growth. However, other sources remained. Newcomers by the hundreds of thousands still poured into many cities, but these were poor rural southerners, black and white, and dark-skinned Latin Americans from Mexico and the Caribbean. At the same time, the children of those who came during the peak immigration years of the early 1900s were reaching the voting age. In 1907, the year of the heaviest foreign influx, two thirds of all school-age children in the nation's thirty-one largest cities had foreign-born fathers. During the twenties these children became adults—voters, workers, parents. Their impact upon urban politics and society now bore considerable weight.

In the 1910s and early 1920s it was usually the Democratic party, already established as the party of new-stock voters, that recognized the potential of these trends and that made efforts, often unconsciously, to narrow the gap between boss and reformer. The first politician to bridge the gap substantially was New York's Alfred E. Smith—legislator, governor, and the nation's first Catholic presidential candidate. Smith's early career almost duplicated the backgrounds of the Tammany bosses who ruled the city during his youth. Born in a Lower East Side tenement, Smith left school at an early age to support his widowed mother. His toughness and ambition led him into Tammany Hall, where he rose rapidly within the organization and within the Democratic party. In 1903 he won a seat in the state assembly and attracted attention for his legislative acumen. As a lawmaker Smith managed to satisfy Tammany chieftains and at the same time ally with prominent progressive reformers such as Robert F. Wagner and Frances Perkins. His vice-chairmanship of a committee that investigated New York City's Triangle Shirtwaist Company fire in 1911 heightened his social awareness, and he continually supported welfare and labor-reform legislation. Smith ran successfully for governor of New York in 1918 and served from 1919 to 1921 and again from 1923 to 1928.

Smith's political success and broad appeal made him a logical presidential candidate. His attempt to win the Democratic nomination in 1924 failed, but in 1928 he could not be denied. His campaign against Republican Herbert Hoover, although provincial and impolitic, was vigorous and boisterous, stressing labor reform and an end to prohibition. Although both candidates tried to avoid religious issues, bigots managed to hurl some malicious barbs at Smith's Catholicism. But prosperity was the major issue, and in 1928 the country was still prosperous. Hoover and his party readily accepted credit for the good times, and Smith was badly beaten at the polls. Nevertheless the voting returns revealed some suggestive results. In almost every major city Smith drew a significantly higher proportion of the total vote than had any other Democratic presidential candidate for the past generation. For the first time since 1892 the Democrats carried several large cities in the presidential election. Hoover and the Republicans managed to retain large majorities in places like Indianapolis, Akron, Kansas City, and Portland where native white Protestants still predominated, but Smith carried immigrant cities as diverse as Providence, Jersey City, New Orleans, Milwaukee, and St. Paul.

Though he lost the election, the "Happy Warrior" had ratified a new political situation, one that had been evolving for over a generation. His Catholicism, his Irish-immigrant ancestry (somewhat exagerated by Smith himself), and his rise from the slums provided urban immigrants and their children with what students of politics call a "vicarious identification." He gave urban ethnic voters a symbol and pulled them into national politics. In 1924 just over half of those eligible to vote did so; in 1928 over two thirds voted. Much of the increased turnout occurred in cities. In heavily Catholic Boston, for example, 44 percent more people voted in 1928 than in 1924. Although successes of Democratic candidates for national office in off-year elections were not consistent enough in the cities to justify calling 1928 the year of the "Smith Revolution," his candidacy nevertheless signaled the emergence of urban America as a strong factor in presidential politics, a factor that reinforced the census returns.

The growing importance of the city on the national scene was also reflected in the expanding relationships between municipal functions and the federal government. Congress extended these responsibilities during and after World War I when it pumped funds into the construction of highways, airports, and even some housing. Increasingly, federal contracts and payrolls sustained a share of urban work forces—although the proportions were still small and many of the funds were filtered to the cities through the states. At the same time, several metropolitan areas had grown so large and complex that they rivaled the states of which they were parts for influence in the federal system. New York, Chicago, Philadelphia, Los Angeles, and Detroit—each with a population over one million by 1930— were rising above the screen of state government, which had formerly intervened between municipalities and Washington. These metropolises and the thirty-two others whose 1930 populations ranged between 250,000 and one million, were economically and politically powerful enough to constitute a third, urban partner to traditional federal-state relationships. When the economic crash of 1929 and its ensuing depression wiped away urban self-sufficiency, the lines of assistance and communications that had been stretched between cities and the federal government in the 1920s became the framework for the structure of government activities that was built in the 1930s.

ONSET OF THE GREAT DEPRESSION

After nearly a decade of optimistic economic expansion, something very uncharacteristic happened to the American nation in the autumn of 1929: a wildly plummeting stock market dissolved $30 billion worth of fortunes and pushed the country into a decade of sacrifice and deprivation. In retrospect the signs of imminent decline seem clear. Farmers had been suffering long before 1929. The construction industry had weakened after 1926. Automobile manufacturers and related industries had overextended production relative to the buying power of the general public. Unbridled speculation, encouraged by irresponsible banking practices, had created huge paper profits that perverted the economy's productivity. The stock-market crash bared these weaknesses, and during the last weeks of October an era of expansion gave way to an era of depression. In spite of considerable trauma American cities survived the ensuing decade. But economic collapse pulled them and the federal government into a new alliance, one in which Washington became the dominant partner. The American economic system now depended heavily on a national network of cities, and government could not ignore how vital that network had become. It was during the 1930s that urban problems became national problems.

Just as (or perhaps because) prosperity in the 1920s had been most visible in the cities, economic crisis struck city dwellers with particular severity. The effects came slowly, however. At first the depression seemed far away, a temporary setback that had bankrupted a few New York investors. Workingmen in Minneapolis and Houston joked about frantic stockbrokers jumping out of hotel windows, and advertisers in Atlanta and Los Angeles continued to celebrate the virtues of credit and consumerism. But the crash generated a brutal recession that gradually deepened in every city. Factories and stores cut back their payrolls. Families were forced to consume less. Private loans and IOUs circulated widely. In the public schools of Chicago, Cleveland, Milwaukee, and Grand Rapids teachers went without paychecks for months. In New York the International Apple Shippers Association sold crates of surplus apples to six thousand unemployed workers, who then peddled the fruit at five cents apiece. Relief rolls in the automobile capital of Detroit swelled while assembly lines slowed to a snail's pace. Everywhere savings accounts dwindled, insurance policies lapsed, and mortgage payments fell delinquent.

The major source of hardship was unemployment. The depression spun a vicious cycle: the more the business community contracted production in order to economize, the more people it threw out of work, and the more it diminished the nation's purchasing power. By 1932 between twelve and fifteen million Americans were jobless. The figures were astronomical in big cities: one million unemployed in New York, 600,000 in Chicago, 298,000 in Philadelphia, 178,000 in Pittsburgh, and 53,000 in Cincinnati. The weight of unemployment fell most heavily on the unskilled, the young, and the black. Employers laid off those who were needed least, and many factory owners downgraded skilled workers so they could fill unskilled jobs. Local surveys revealed that joblessness among people in their late teens and early twenties ran twice as high as among other age groups. Much of the unemployment resulted from the fact that young people entering the job market for the first time simply could find no work. Although blacks were able to retain jobs in some industries—meat packing, for example—the aphorism "last hired and first fired" rang true for them in the depression. A census of unemployment in 1931 found that in fourteen of sixteen northern and western cities the percentages of blacks out of work were much higher than those of whites. In Chicago, Pittsburgh, and Philadelphia rates of joblessness among employable blacks reached 50 percent and higher.

RESPONSES TO THE DEPRESSION

The profound displacements of the depression crisis saddled local governments with unprecedented responsibilities. President Herbert Hoover believed that the crisis should be attacked at the local as well as the national level. On November 15, 1929, he began a series of meetings with business leaders in which he urged more construction and plant expansion in order to maintain wage rates and employment. A week later he sent out a flood of telegrams calling upon governors and mayors to initiate public-works projects to provide jobs for the unemployed. In 1930 Hoover appointed the Emergency Committee for Employment, reorganized in 1931 as the Organization on Unemployment Relief, to encourage local communities to care for their jobless citizens. But at the same time, he emphasized the need for balanced budgets that he believed would stabilize all levels of the economy.

Municipal governments responded quickly to the economic challenge. Even before the stock-market crash, Cincinnati's city manager, C. O. Sherrill, partly influenced by the local Citizens' Party, a group of political independents, organized a committee to survey possibilities for public works, job training and placement, and other aspects of employment. After the onset of the depression other cities copied the Cincinnati model. According to Blake McKelvey, the city of Rochester appropriated $800,000 for work relief in 1930, and its city manager requested $1 million for 1931.[7] By the end of 1930 the seventy-five largest cities were spending $420 million annually on public-works projects. Yet even the most generous efforts failed to keep people out of bread lines and off the relief rolls. In 1929 Detroit spent $2.4 million on relief; in 1931 it spent $14.9 million. Over those same two years relief expenditures rose from $620,000 to $2.9 million in Milwaukee, and from $582,000 to $3.5 million in Philadelphia.

The problem for cities was basically a financial one, but underlying that were serious political and ideological issues. The depression caught municipalities between two millstones. On one side the need for services hiked costs of government operations, while on the other side unemployment and falling business reduced municipal revenues. One of the most universal problems was property-tax delinquency. In 1930 among the 145 cities with fifty thousand or more inhabitants, about 11 percent of the local taxes went unpaid. By 1933 the rate had reached 25.2 percent. To collect more revenue some cities, such as Dayton and Des Moines, agreed to accept late payments without penalizing the delinquents. But business leaders charged that such breaks only encouraged irresponsibility among taxpayers. Other cities drew and spent budgets based on anticipated full collection of tax revenues or borrowed against uncollected revenues, thereby falling deeper into debt. In an attempt to increase their incomes some municipalities levied a sales tax. Introduced in West Virginia in 1921, the sales tax won few advocates during the good times of the twenties. But between 1930 and 1935 twenty-one states and several cities, including New York and New Orleans, began taxing the sale of certain goods, mainly luxury items. By 1940 New York City's 3-percent sales tax was raising $60 million annually.

On top of revenue problems lay financial burdens inherited from the past. During the expansion years of the early 1900s, and especially during the 1920s, cities had floated large bond issues that came due in the 1930s. Unable to make payments on either principal or interest, many cities defaulted. Others were able to meet their obligations only by depleting their sinking funds—emergency monies to be used to relieve debt only in the last resort. As a result the prices for municipal bonds plunged. By 1933 bond issues of Detroit and of Greensboro, North Carolina, were worth forty cents on the dollar. In Los Angeles debt charges (that is, interest payments and retirement of principal) accounted for 78 percent of the 1934–35 budget. Local officials were quick to point out that rates of default by municipal governments were much lower than those by private corporations. Nevertheless the financial problems of cities affected a greater number of people. Some governments were forced to take drastic steps in reaction to the fiscal plights of local businesses. In 1932, during the depths of the depression, many people became distrustful of failing banks and hoarded so much currency that the amount in circulation declined precipitously. The shortage became so acute in the South that a few cities—Richmond, Knoxville, and Atlanta, for example—began to print their own scrip to pay public employees and relief recipients.

The cities' failures to meet their debt obligations raised cries for state control of local finances that echoed the charges of irresponsibility that reformers had leveled at boss-ridden city governments in the 1870s and 1880s. Now, a half-century later, reformers revived proposals that state officials intervene in local affairs and insure fiscal stability by reviewing budgets, limiting debts, and supervising tax levies. The real tug, however, was less between city and state than between those who advocated prudence and those who favored more debt and liberal public spending. Many civic leaders, such as Milwaukee's socialist mayor Daniel W. Hoan and the members of the International City Managers Association, believed that public funds should be conserved to protect the solvency of local governments. They adopted a pay-as-you-go policy toward relief projects, approving only those that would not drain the public till. Others, such as mayors Frank Murphy of Detroit and later Fiorello La Guardia of New York, preferred to expend whatever money was available and borrow more for relief, even if it mean paring budgets of other municipal services. Both policies—economizing and spending for relief—severely limited the activities of those departments deemed nonessential. Planning boards, underfinanced even during the 1920s, shrank to skeletons in the early years of the depression. In 1933, 57 percent of the nation's 739 city-planning boards received no appropriations, and 25 percent received less than $1000. Between 1929 and 1933 total expenditures by parks and recreation departments in 795 cities and towns decreased by 50 percent. Public-parks programs in Fall River, New Bedford, Providence, and San Antonio were completely eliminated; the parks were saved only by private donations.

In one respect the drive for economy produced beneficial results—by consolidating departments whose functions duplicated or overlapped one another. For example, to conserve funds Fresno, California, and New Haven, Connecticut, combined previously separate parks and recreation departments. More important, city and county departments were merged to create more centralized administration and a more regional recognition of metropolitan needs. The Chicago Park District, created by the Illinois State Legislature in 1933, consolidated the nineteen independent park districts of the Chicago area under one board. Cincinnati's welfare responsibilities were absorbed by Hamilton County, and in New Jersey and New Hampshire state agencies assumed welfare functions formerly handled by their various cities. In other places city and county health departments were combined. Local officials recognized that they could not drop services that had gradually expanded for a half-century or more, and that to preserve them meant questioning and rearranging administrative structures.

Whether or not public leaders favored belt tightening or more spending, the epidemic of hardship brought intense pressures for the relief of hunger and unemployment. Public and private agencies everywhere struggled through the early years of the depression, groping for ways to help. During the fall of 1931 the National Association of Community Chests and Councils, following President Hoover's suggestion, sponsored a drive that raised $85 million for relief in cities and towns throughout the nation. That sum, according to Blake McKelvey, was hopelessly inadequate. In Milwaukee all municipal salaries were reduced by 10 percent, which freed a million dollars for temporary job relief in 1932. The next year, however, the city voted a drastic tax reduction, thereby eliminating a large portion of public revenues and forcing money saved by salary cuts to be used to support essential services. Through coordinated efforts by public and private organizations Cincinnati and Minneapolis, among other cities, were able to forestall severe destitution during the winter of 1931–32. But the depression continued to deepen, and many families who had teetered on the margins of subsistence for two or three years succumbed and applied for relief. Faced with mounting hardship and shriveling tax revenues, even the most resourceful municipalities began to run out of funds. (Per-capita government expenditures in cities with over 100,000 people dropped from $78 in 1929 to $67 in 1933, while per-capita expenditures on relief rose from $0.90 to $2.94.)

Inevitably cities looked to Washington for help. In May 1932 at the invitation of Mayor Murphy, twenty-six mayors met in Detroit and appealed to the federal government for $5 billion to finance public-construction projects. This group of mayors became the nucleus of the United States Conference of Mayors (USCM), the first permanent organization (it was formally constituted in early 1933) formed to bring urban concerns before the president and Congress. By making Washington what Mark Gelfand has called an "arena for urban lobbying activities," the USCM opened a new era in American urban history.[8] Frustrated by rural-dominated state governments and overcome by economic and social pressures, urban officials came to believe that the best road to relief led to the federal government. In 1934, after a year of urban lobbying and resulting federal programs, Louis Brownlow, a New Deal adviser and former city manager, remarked that "it has been said that the Federal Government has discovered the cities; it is equally true that the cities have discovered the Federal Government."

In 1932, however, Washington approached urban problems gingerly. President Hoover rejected the mayors' request but did approve the Reconstruction Finance Corporation (RFC), an agency that was to loan money to banks, railroads, and other big businesses in hopes that by stabilizing these institutions it would enable recovery to filter down to the rest of society. Later the RFC was authorized to make loans to local government agencies for self-liquidating projects. Money trickled into the cities at a very slow pace, however, and the bankers who increasingly assumed control as cities defaulted on debt payments could offer little help except to institute further retrenchment. Moreover the RFC failed to bring relief to the unemployed, who needed it most. Hoover vehemently opposed direct assistance and squelched congressional proposals for public-works projects designed as unemployment relief. Instead he continued to push voluntaristic efforts.

Mayors, city managers, and other civic leaders were not uniformly in favor of greater assistance from the federal government. A number of these men were longtime Republicans, supporters of Hoover's policies who accepted the RFC as a meaningful reform. Yet, with their local economies and services continuing to collapse, by the fall of 1932 many civic leaders had begun to ponder what would happen if the Democratic presidential candidate, New York's governor Franklin D. Roosevelt, should win and carry out his promise for a new deal. When Roosevelt did win, cities were quick to revive their pleas and the new government was quick to respond. In his acceptance speech at the Democratic National Convention in the summer of 1932 Franklin Roosevelt had proclaimed, "I pledge you, I pledge myself to a new deal for the American people." In time *a* new deal became *the* New Deal—the legislative and administrative measures generated by Roosevelt and his advisers to bring about relief, recovery, and reform. Once in office the new president galvanized his programs quickly. Within one hundred days he had instituted measures affecting banking, agriculture, industry, and conservation. These and similar measures affected cities only indirectly, if at all. In fact several New Deal measures revealed a bias against cities. FDR was a lover of nature, and he responded favorably to programs aiming to revive small, rural communities. A back-to-the-land intent was clearly part of the Subsistence Homestead Division, a program inaugurated in 1933 to remove slum dwellers to some one hundred government-sponsored rural communities, and of the Tennessee Valley Authority, the government experiment in regional reconstruction.

Yet the New Deal policy makers did accept the fact that large-scale cities had become the principal centers of the national experience. To be sure, concern was directed not so much at urban life itself as toward the ways in which urban problems existed as part of the national economic crisis. Still many of the bills that were passed and the agencies that were created grew out of the urban experience, where thrift, self-help, and rugged individualism had always shared the stage with mutual benefit and public responsibility. The effect, if not the intent, of the New Deal was to meet traditional needs of city dwellers.

Relief and Welfare

Unemployment loomed as one of the most serious problems facing FDR when he assumed office. Its impact upon cities had been devastating. Hoover's programs had not reached the urban masses. By 1933 unemploy-

Working for Uncle Sam   These CWA workers are refurbishing the dome of the Colorado State Capitol in Denver in 1934. This was one of the thousands of projects devised to relieve unemployed laborers. *(U.S. Information Agency, The National Archives.)*

ment rates were 40 percent in Chicago, 30 percent in New York, and 26 percent in Cincinnati. As one newspaper remarked, "What this relief business needs is less RFC and more PDQ." Roosevelt responded first by proposing the Federal Emergency Relief Administration (FERA). Created by Congress in May 1933, the FERA distributed $500 million to the states for direct relief. Although the program was not explicitly designed to aid city dwellers, 42 percent of the 1933 appropriations were spent in five heavily urbanized northern states.

By the winter of 1933–34, almost eight million families (comprising twenty-eight million individuals) were receiving federal relief. The heads of nearly half of these households were enrolled in work-relief projects sponsored by the Civil Works Administration, an agency created in November 1933 to give jobs to the unemployed. Before it was dismantled and absorbed by the FERA in April 1934, it had pumped a billion dollars into the economy and had carried millions of people through the winter, providing them with incomes to purchase needed goods and services. The CWA, like the FERA, was meant to apply to the entire nation. But many of its 400,000 projects were located in, and directly benefited, cities. CWA workers built five hundred airports and improved that many more. Many of the fifty thousand teachers employed by Harry Hopkins offered adult-education classes in city schools. Millions of construction workers developed city parks, dug city swimming pools, and laid city sewer lines. Moreover wages

The Joys of the Streets   Although reformers viewed them with concern, children still found ways to turn city space into playgrounds. A New Deal photographer captured one such instance of children playing in a vacant lot in 1939 for the Federal Arts Project Series, One Third of a Nation. *(The Museum of the City of New York.)*

paid for CWA jobs were spent in business-starved city establishments—barbershops, shoe stores, drugstores, and clothiers. The Public Works Administration (PWA), a similar work relief agency, also proved beneficial, especially to cities. It built a new water-supply system in Denver, a municipal auditorium in Kansas City, and thousands of new schools and hospitals across the country.

In 1935 the Roosevelt administration responded more radically to continued cries for more jobs and security. Early that year the president asked Congress to turn over care of unemployables to the states and localities while retaining federal responsibility for providing work relief to needy employables. As a result Congress created the Works Progress Administration (WPA) to finance public projects, many of which were located in municipalities. Although it never employed as many as the CWA, the WPA included over two and a half million workers on its payrolls by 1936. Under the guidance of Harry Hopkins the WPA sought to fill needs that had been neglected or postponed by private enterprise and civic initiative. Between 1936 and 1941 almost one fifth of the nation's work force was employed by the WPA at one time or another. WPA workers built almost 600 airports and landing fields, 500,000 miles of roads and streets, 100,000 bridges and viaducts, 500,000 sewerage connections, and 110,000 libraries, schools, auditoriums, stadiums, and other public structures. Like the FERA and CWA, many of the WPA projects pumped new life into civic improvement. Indeed the U.S. Conference of Mayors, now headed by New York's Fiorello La Guardia, strongly influenced the size of WPA appropriations by pressing urban needs before the White House.

The Social Security Act, passed in August 1935, had a more permanent impact than did the relief agencies. The act created programs of old-age insurance, unemployment insurance, and federal assistance to the blind, the disabled, and dependent children. The consequences of these programs were not felt at the time, but the Social Security Act set a momentous precedent for the nation and its cities. Care of the aged and the distressed was now accepted as a national rather than a local concern, and the path had been broken for a long line of antipoverty programs that would follow. Collective responsibility for the relief and prevention of poverty, long a major issue of urban growth, had been nationalized.

Housing

Between 1929 and 1935 the volume of new housing construction in this country shriveled to almost nothing. In 1932 the editors of *Fortune* magazine wrote, "At least half of America's 30,000,000 families are not even decently housed." And the specter of eviction threatened millions of home owners. Between 1926 and 1933 the number of annual mortgage failures quadrupled, and by the latter date home mortgages were being foreclosed at the rate of one thousand per day. These plights made housing an early concern of the New Deal. The Roosevelt administration adopted a two-pronged approach: an insurance program to stabilize financial conditions for home owners and for mortgage lenders, and publicly sponsored construction and slum-clearance projects to improve housing conditions for the poor and boost employment in the building trades. Both programs set the pattern for subsequent urban growth. Mortgage insurance made possible a new and massive wave of suburbanization after World War II. Public housing and slum clearance brought the federal government into the urban core.

During the whirlwind of activity in its first one hundred days, the New Deal Congress created the Home Owners' Loan Corporation (HOLC) to bail out endangered home owners and stabilize mortgage markets. The HOLC was established almost exclusively to serve urban interests—the

Emergency Farm Mortgage Act passed almost a month earlier was designed to prevent rural foreclosures. The HOLC was empowered to refinance private loans with government money carrying interest of 5 percent; the borrower had fifteen years to repay. The loans were to enable home owners to escape foreclosure, to pay taxes, and to make needed repairs. The HOLC did not reduce a person's debt, but it did save millions from defaulting. In its three years of lending the HOLC granted $3 billion in loans to one-fifth of the nation's nonfarm households and held about one-sixth of all urban home-mortgage debt. In keeping with prevailing biases against inner-city ethnic and racial minorities, however, the HOLC established appraisal criteria that rejected financing in "redlined" neighborhoods that were dense, black, or aging.

Mortgage relief was only a stopgap measure; it did little to aid either the construction industry or housing markets. Thus at FDR's instigation, in June 1934 Congress passed the National Housing Act, which created the Federal Housing Authority (FHA), an agency to insure loans made by private lending institutions to families wishing to renovate or build homes. Over the next six years the agency underwrote $4.25 billion for the modernization of 3 million existing units and the construction of over 600,000 private homes and 600 rental units. The FHA drastically revised the nature of mortgage lending and by doing so initiated a new housing trend in metropolitan areas. Because the FHA would guarantee a borrower's mortgage (the borrower had to pay only a small fee for the guarantee), lending banks could reduce the interest rates to as low as 4 percent and could stretch out loans over twenty-five to thirty years. These new terms broke sharply with the loans of five to seven years and interest rates of 6 to 12 percent that had been common in the preceding half-century. Applicants for FHA insurance had to demonstrate their ability to afford a new home. Nevertheless long-term, federally insured mortgages made home building and home owning much easier than in the past. In effect, federal mortgage insurance created subsidies for low-density, detached, owner-occupied single-family housing, virtually excluding other types of dwelling units. Their mortgage terms deflected investment money away from the central city and encouraged neighborhood decay and blue-collar as well as middle-class flight to the suburbs because families could more easily and inexpensively finance a new home in a development springing up along a highway outside the city than repair or modernize an older building in an inner-city neighborhood.

But the HOLC and FHA had little effect upon the one-third of the nation whom President Roosevelt described as "ill-housed, ill-clad, ill-nourished." The plight of these groups raised to national dimensions the specter that had haunted urban reformers for a century: the slum. By amplifying local decay the depression alerted even the most economy-minded leaders to the costs of physical deterioration. Studies of Cleveland and Boston early in

1930 revealed that maintenance of city services in slum areas was much more expensive than in other districts. Such studies galvanized new efforts to abolish blight and provide low-income groups with adequate housing. These had been long-standing reform goals, but the new component was the increasing belief that projects should be financed with public funds. As one official admitted in 1934, "If housing costs the taxpayers something, in the long run it probably saves them more." For decades most Americans had cast only a cursory glance at the impressive public renewal projects in European cities such as Paris, Glasgow, Vienna, and Berlin. By the 1930s, however, many civic leaders were able to view fiscal and physical decay as part of the same problem, and they paid more attention to European precedents.

Early in the summer of 1933 the Emergency Housing Division was attached to the PWA. This agency financed local projects for slum clearance or for construction of low-cost modern housing. Although the work was done by private contractors, the projects were intended to provide job relief for people on PWA rolls. In four years the PWA Housing Division received about five hundred loan applications, fifty of which were financed. The first was in Atlanta, where workers leveled eleven slum blocks and replaced them with Techwood Homes, a group of low-rent apartments. Other slum-conversion projects included Lakeview Terrace in Cleveland, Jane Addams Houses in Chicago, and Williamsburg Houses in Brooklyn. PWA funds financed the construction of some twenty-two thousand dwelling units. Yet most projects failed to help those in need of better housing. Rents averaged twenty-six dollars per month, still too high for the many working-class families whose incomes were under a thousand dollars a year. Clearance programs only pushed these people into the slums. The first wide-scale federal participation in housing reform resulted in the demolition of some of the worst urban eyesores and the construction of better facilities for some lower-middle-class groups. But because it placed its major emphasis on work-relief and self-liquidating projects, it failed to address the most acute problems.

The obstacles to housing programs were political. As in the past public officials were reluctant to lead government, whether local or national, into the hallowed region of housing construction and maintenance. Even President Roosevelt preferred that Congress support private housing rather than public. Opposition to direct federal participation won the upper hand in 1935 when a U.S. district court, in the Louisville Lands Case, ruled that the federal government could not condemn private property for low-cost housing. Although subsequent court action eventually reversed the ruling, the original decision had the effect of steering federal programs away from direct supervision and toward indirect grants-in-aid or loans to municipalities, which could then use the funds at their own discretion.

This, in effect, was the strategy adopted by the U.S. Housing Authority (USHA), created as an agency of the Department of the Interior by the Wagner-Steagall Housing Act of 1937. Passed by Congress only after Sena-

Black Housing During the 1930s   These shanties in a black neighborhood in Atlanta typified the quarters that the U.S. Housing Authority attempted to replace. *(Courtesy of the Library of Congress.)*

tor Robert F. Wagner of New York, long a champion of public housing, had secured the reluctant support of President Roosevelt, the bill authorized $500 million for loans and grants to state and local authorities for slum clearance and housing developments. The law stipulated that tenants in USHA units be in the lowest income third of the population, and it particularly benefited blacks. Some 47,500 federally financed, low-cost dwelling units, nearly a third of those built in northern and southern cities, were occupied by black families. Critics charged that USHA-sponsored public housing was undermining the private market, but most of the accusations were false. Without the aid of public funds, private enterprise was unable and unwilling to clear slums and construct modern, low-cost housing. Units built under the USHA averaged $2,720 in cost, about 25 percent less than the cost of privately erected housing but still too high for the poorest families most in need of housing. Yet the USHA was more important for the precedent it established than for its accomplishments. It cleared more slums than had any other program in the previous half-century, but it only dented the problem, and it left millions of families still without decent housing.

Public concern with housing during the New Deal era split into two points of view, each with its own constituency. Differences between the two sides were subtle but also vital. On one side stood philanthropists, social workers, and economic liberals who wanted government to assume responsibility for removing slums and assuring a supply of decent housing. Slum clearance was this group's chief goal. The U.S. Housing Act defined a slum as "any area where dwellings predominate which, by reason of dilapidation, overcrowding, faulty arrangements and design, lack of ventilation, light, or sanitation facilities, or any combination of these factors, are detrimental to health, safety, or morals." Slum-clearance reformers adopted this definition as part of their goal of linking public housing with social improvement. Thus they believed that government must assist people to achieve better health, safety, and morals by sponsoring slum clearance and construction of low-cost housing.

On the other side of the reform thrust stood landowners and business people who were worried about falling property values and rising taxes. Their concern was with *blight,* the deterioration in an area that made it no longer profitable to maintain or improve. These people, then, were concerned with profits rather than with social conditions. Their motives were not pure greed; they simply believed that only a profitable area could be a vital one and that if an area was economically viable, its effects would filter down to benefit all groups. Thus they sought government aid, mostly in the form of loans and clearance projects, to protect their investments, but they opposed public housing because it interfered with private enterprise. Passage of the Housing Act crystalized these two points of view, and with their formation a debate began that became central to federal policies concerning urban renewal and redevelopment after World War II.

CHANGES AND CONTINUITIES IN URBAN LIFE AND POLITICS

The New Deal etched its mark on cities in many other ways as well. The National Recovery Administration (NRA) mustered local producers and consumers behind industrial codes of fair trade and price limits, and it boosted local labor organization by guaranteeing collective bargaining. The Wagner National Labor Relations Act, passed in 1935 after the Supreme Court had dissolved the NRA, rescued and reiterated the NRA labor provisions, clearing the way for successful unionization drives in the next decades in many occupations, including municipal employees. The NRA, the Wagner labor bill, and the Fair Labor Standards Acts of 1938 were not aimed at cities, but they did implement some of the goals of over half a century of urban reform: minimum wages, maximum hours, an end to child labor and the sweatshops, and licensing of business. Still, many black and women workers were excluded from Social Security coverage and minimum wage provisions because these did not extend benefits to waiters, cooks, hospital orderlies, janitors, farm workers, or domestics. Other NRA codes allowed pay differentials based on gender, so that women's minimum wages were frozen at a lower rate than those for men. An expanding low-wage unprotected labor market for blacks and women in cities was the result.

The depression years also left a heritage of urban protest. As early as 1930 in Chicago, Los Angeles, and Philadelphia the unemployed had marched on city halls, agitating for jobs and food and fighting evictions. In 1932 fifteen thousand black and white unemployed World War I veterans and their families made a historic journey to Washington, D.C., demanding immediate payment of veteran's bonuses due in 1945. Chicago schoolteachers protested dramatic budget cuts by pulling down the 1933 World's Fair flag and storming City Hall. The Congress of Industrial Organizations (CIO) used new tactics like the sit-down strike to mobilize broad-based community support for unionization, and unorganized groups as diverse as laundry workers in Chicago and dime-store clerks in Detroit also sat down to protest unfair working conditions. In northern cities, blacks protested the persistence of racial discrimination by boycotting stores as part of Don't Buy Where You Can't Work campaigns, launching Jobs for Negroes movements and starting tenants' unions to fight high rents. In 1939 in Chicago, Saul Alinsky began to directly apply the principles of labor organizing to neighborhood problems, setting up a model for community organizing with the Back of the Yards Neighborhood Council. Depression-era protest gave a generation of urban residents experience with organizing that would be a frequently utilized resource in the years to come.

New Deal programs had been committed to getting Americans spending again, and the decade of the 1930s shows the remarkable resilience and even expansion of consumer values despite economic collapse. For example, the New Deal passage of the Rural Electrification Act after 1935 brought electricity to isolated rural households and helped what were now labeled as "urban conveniences" to penetrate the countryside, shortening the distance between city and farm. Attendance at baseball and football games, which dropped between 1930 and 1935, revived later in the decade. Even during the depths of the depression, however, the World Series averaged forty thousand fans per game. Big city tabloids tripled their circulation during the thirties, mostly by publicizing public-interest stories such as the kidnapping of the son of Mr. and Mrs. Charles A. Lindbergh, the birth of the Dionne quintuplets, and the killing of bank robber John Dillinger, Public Enemy Number One.

Radio became even more important in the 1930s, especially after FDR began to depend on it to broadcast his "fireside chats," reaching out to many Americans with sets in their own living rooms. After 1933 the bulk of daytime radio programming was provided by soap operas such as "Stella Dallas," "Guiding Light," and "Search for Tomorrow," which translated social distress into individual domestic tales of woe, making housewives feel less alone and that their problems were not unique. Movies also continued

Family Life in the Depression, 1935   Note the care with which this family furnished their rooms behind a store in the Williamsburg section of Brooklyn, New York, and the pride and spirit of survival that the photographer captured on their faces. *(The New York City Housing Authority.)*

to be popular in the 1930s. Although a third of the nation's movie houses shut down in the early years of the depression, remaining movie theaters offered reduced prices, ladies' nights, sneak previews, and raffles to keep up attendance. Horror films like *Dracula* (1932), *Frankenstein* (1932), and *King Kong* (1933), films of adventures on the high seas such as *Mutiny on the Bounty* (1936), historical films detailing the tribulations of a bygone era such as *Gone With the Wind* (1939), and animated dreams of fantasy such as *Snow White and the Seven Dwarfs* (1937) attracted audiences of eighty-five million viewers per week.

Not even extreme deprivation and fiscal collapse could block the march of mass culture; indeed they often encouraged the search for escape. The Parker Brothers' fantastically successful board game Monopoly enabled would-be entrepreneurs to "make a killing" in real estate when economic conditions of the period all but prohibited such results in real life. And even the depression did not loosen Americans' dependence on their automobiles. Gas-station retail sales resumed their rise by 1935; sales and ownership figures fell between 1929 and 1932 but rose after 1933. As the Lynds observed in Middletown, although upper-class commentators saw cars as a luxury item that should be the first thing to go in hard times, working-class people viewed

Movie Dreams, 1939 The world Hollywood created in films was all the more compelling in the Depression. A photographer working for the Farm Security Administration captured this image of a young boy in Memphis, Tennessee, outside the entrance to a movie house on Beale Street. *(Library of Congress.)*

their cars as a symbol of achievement, which they equated with their own self-respect.[9] Industrial designers popularized streamlining in the 1930s, designing model changes and packaging for everything "from a lipstick to a locomotive," hoping that imagery of flight and technological promise would inspire consumption to refuel the economy.

Urban consumers continued to dictate popular tastes across the country. A major reason for the expansion of popular culture was that Americans had more time for it. The depressed conditions in industry plus the ceilings on hours set by the NRA shortened the work week more dramatically than had any previous combination of events and reforms. By the late thirties the forty-hour, five-day work week had become the rule, and Saturday closings were common in most cities. The focus on consumption heightened the pressure on men to provide, making unemployment especially humiliating, and drew married women and daughters into the expanded clerical and service workforce in order to raise their families' standards of living. Although consumption patterns sharpened the distinctions between people, the promise of a better life gave new meaning to Americanism and a new entitlement to workers demanding wage increases and unionization as the path to job security. The culture of consumption's focus on the results of labor rather than work itself, on leisure time instead of working time, paralleled the divisions between home and work, between suburb and city that were the hallmark of the metropolitan era.

The New Deal shifted urban political loyalties. By the mid-thirties, two-thirds of the populations of the eleven cities with over a million inhabitants were first- or second-generation immigrants, most of whom had few loyalties to rugged individualism and few scruples about state interference. These were the same people who had come to expect positive assistance in times of need from their leaders and who had exerted a strong influence on the development of an urban liberalism. Roosevelt responded to these new-stock city dwellers more than had any previous national leader. During Roosevelt's early career in New York politics boss "Big Tim" Sullivan had told him, "The people who had come over in steerage . . . knew in their hearts and lives the difference between being despised and being accepted and liked." As President, FDR remembered this advice. He exuded warm-heartedness, and his New Deal agencies offered direct relief with a minimum of questions. Thus support flowed to FDR because the effects of many of his national programs resembled what bosses and machines traditionally had done on the local level.

But New Deal support in the cities was more than another kind of boss constituency: it included a coalition between new-stock, working-class interests and elements of social and economic reform, a coalition that had begun to form in the late nineteenth century. The various regulatory agencies, relief programs, labor laws, and Social Security measures implemented many of the goals that had been part of reform crusades for half a century. Important New Deal personalities such as Rexford Tugwell, Harry Hopkins, Frances Perkins, Robert F. Wagner, and Harold Ickes had backgrounds in urban reform, and they helped shape federal programs into the framework of a national urban policy during the thirties.

Urban voters voiced their reactions to the New Deal in the presidential election of 1936, and Roosevelt won a resounding victory by carrying every state but Maine and Vermont. Support for FDR was particularly strong in the cities. The nation's ten largest cities contributed one third of Roosevelt's eleven-million-vote margin over Alfred M. Landon. Smaller places, many of them traditionally Republican, also piled up huge majorities for the Democratic president. Duluth, Gary, Scranton, Canton, Youngstown, and other cities that had supported Hoover in 1932 gave nearly three-fourths of their votes to FDR. In 1936 six million more voters went to the polls than in 1932, and it has been estimated that Roosevelt attracted five million of them. Immigrants and their children, who had responded to Al Smith's candidacy in 1928 and to other Democrats earlier in the 1920s, moved solidly behind FDR. A new segment of the electorate, urban black voters, joined the Democratic fold. Although the New Deal in many ways was insensitive to racial problems, it had at least dispensed relief with less discrimination than had any previous government effort. The effect on blacks was to break their ties with the party of Abraham Lincoln and to draw them into FDR's camp. The ghetto districts in Chicago, Cleveland, Detroit, and Philadelphia, which had given majorities to Hoover in 1932, now swung to the Democrats and became ever important fixtures of the party's national base.

If the federal government now began to assume the positive functions of machine politics—relief, jobs, and security—what now happened to the boss? Certainly bossism did not wither away. Some of the most powerful urban leaders survived and flourished during the New Deal: Crump of Memphis, Hague of Jersey City, Pendergast of Kansas City, and Kelly of Chicago. Although a number of bosses originally supported Al Smith for the Democratic nomination in 1932, almost all accepted Roosevelt by the time of the election. FDR maintained good relations with these men, and they often turned to the president for assistance.

Yet the New Deal did alter the nature of boss politics in several important ways. Most fundamentally, the New Deal diluted some of the boss's personalized services while embellishing his function as a broker between ordinary citizens and their government. Political machines could not handle the traumas of depression. The Christmas turkeys, burial money, summer outings, and free shoes for schoolchildren no longer sufficed. As the federal government assumed responsibilities for offering relief and insuring security, it scaled down the boss's power. To be sure, many New Deal benefits were filtered to the needy through local politicians, but the recipients knew the jobs and cash were coming from Washington. Equally important, by fostering a huge expansion of organized labor the New Deal indirectly gnawed away at several functions of bossism. Under the CIO and other unions more laborers than ever before had access to jobs, protection on the job, and unemployment compensation. Moreover union halls offered new social centers to workingmen, sometimes replacing saloons, and union leaders organized picnics, speeches, and other affairs that had previously been the prerogative of political machines. Because the labor vote became an increasingly important political force, the craft and industrial unions commanded the attention of city halls, state capitals, and Washington. Thus bosses now had to share their role as spokesmen for the working classes.

On the other hand, the New Deal gave some bosses unprecedented opportunities. By spreading its influence over local affairs, the federal government created new sources of patronage jobs, paid with federal money but controlled by local leaders. Particularly in cities where ward and precinct divisions had remained (that is, where district representation had not been replaced by city councils or city commissions elected at large), such as Pittsburgh and Chicago, the reinvigorated Democratic party offered employment possibilities to many people. In Pittsburgh, as Bruce Stave has shown, the New Deal helped the Democrats oust the Republicans from power and install David Lawrence as a powerful boss. In Boston, according to Charles Trout, Mayor James Michael Curley and his successors used New Deal programs such as the PWA and WPA to reward party faithful, especially Irish-stock voters.[10] Public officials grudgingly cooperated with the federal government, but very few of them caught the spirit of social reform and national unity that the New Deal represented. Thus although they supported President Roosevelt and benefited from his policies, Boston politicians were guided more by local conditions and ethnic rivalries than by a New Deal philosophy.

As bosses adjusted to the increased powers of the federal government, their intermediary functions became more important. They not only acted as information agents, telling constituents where and how to obtain services now offered by the federal government, but also built political bridges, increasingly supporting reform projects such as schools, cultural centers, and better housing. These issues often brought bosses into the camps of their traditional enemies, businessmen and social reformers. But only those bosses who recognized the need for new flexibility could survive after the New Deal. They could still control patronage, nominations for political office, and elections, but to do so meant acquiring a broader image.

At the mayoral level the depression and New Deal further blurred the distinction between machine politician and social reformer. Now, with prolonged hard times facing them, all mayors had to deal with pressing needs for money and jobs. Those who were most successful were the ones who could combine reform qualities of professional expertise with a boss's display of personal concern.

The epitome of this merger and the best-known mayor of the New Deal era was Fiorello La Guardia of New York, a former insurgent congressman who could outduel any machine politician in popular appeal. La Guardia was born in the Lower East Side of New York, but he spent his youth in Arizona, where his Italian immigrant father was a bandmaster for the U.S. Army, and his young manhood in southeastern Europe, where he worked for a U.S. consulate. In 1906 he became an interpreter on Ellis Island, the famous entry station for immigrants coming to the New York port. Here young La Guardia acquired firsthand experience with the plight of newcomers to the American city. He attended New York University Law School at night and then entered politics. Squeezing his way up through the Republican party, he won a seat in Congress in 1916, where he quickly gained notoriety as a people's advocate. He then made some frustrated attempts to unseat Tammany Hall from power in New York City and finally was elected mayor on a Fusion-Republican ticket in 1933, after Jimmy Walker, the scandal-tainted Democratic mayor, had been removed from office. La Guardia immediately became a national spokesman for the urban cause. Along with Mayor Murphy of Detroit, he took a leading role in the newly formed U.S. Conference of Mayors. In New York La Guardia's fiery, dynamic personality won him great affection, particularly from the city's many ethnic groups. As one observer wrote,

> La Guardia *is* melting-pot America—first-generation Italian-American, with a Jewish great-great grandparent. . . . The Mayor is adept in all branches of political fanfaronade: he can lead the Fire Department Band, he can dress up in a sand-hog's helmet to inspect new tunnels, he can step into the pitcher's box on opening day at the Yankee Stadium and cut loose with a high hard one in the general direction of home plate.

As mayor, La Guardia not only succeeded in obtaining large shares of PWA and other federal relief funds but also started a local program of public works and slum clearance, restored the city's credit, improved public facilities, obtained a new city charter, and initiated low-rent public housing. He was reelected twice, serving until 1945.

By the end of the 1930s the rising prominence of cities in national affairs had prompted new initiative on the local and metropolitan levels. Planning commissions revived surveys and projects postponed by the depression. Responding to new pressures from automobile traffic, New York, Los Angeles, Detroit, Pittsburgh, and Cleveland planned or constructed belt highways and freeways, often with the aid of federal funds. Studies by sociologists, economists, geographers, and political scientists examined a host of issues, ranging from urban land values to mental illness.

Still, however, the efforts of local planners, builders, and scholars paled beside the activity of the federal government. The New Deal had tightened the federal-city knot, and local officials were reluctant to loosen the bonds—especially since state governments maintained their traditional hostilities toward their cities. Skeptics like Harold Buttenheim, editor of *The American City,* warned that Uncle Sam was becoming "Boss Sam," but most urban leaders accepted federal programs and appropriations without fear of interference by Washington in local affairs.

It is significant that at this time the federal government sponsored the first national study of urban life. In 1937 the Committee on Urbanism within the National Resources Committee, a branch of the Department of the Interior, published a report entitled *Our Cities: Their Role in the National Economy.* This study, headed by Clarence Dykstra, former city manager of Cincinnati, was intended as a complement to the report of the Country Life Commission, which had examined rural society for President Theodore Roosevelt three decades earlier. In its foreword the National Resources Committee clearly recognized the central themes of the evolution of America as an urban nation:

> The city has seemed at times the despair of America but at others to be the Nation's hope, the battleground of democracy. Surely in the long run, the Nation's destiny will be profoundly affected by the cities which have two-

thirds of its population and its wealth. . . . The failures of our cities are not those of decadence and impending decline, but of exurberant vitality crowding its way forward under tremendous pressure—the flood rather than the drought.

The report urged the federal government to pay more attention to the needs of city dwellers. After a brief outline of the process of urbanization in the United States, it catalogued the nation's unsolved urban problems (no less than thirty-six of them) and presented a list of recommendations. The solutions proposed were nothing new. They included public housing for low-income groups, more planning, increased and more equitable welfare services, removal of slums, streamlined local governments, and more research. But the fact that these suggestions were now being offered by the federal government presaged a new era in the country's urban history.

BIBLIOGRAPHY

On general patterns of urban growth in this period see William H. Wilson, *Coming of Age: Urban America, 1915–1945* (New York: John Wiley & Sons, 1974); Blaine Brownell, *The Urban Ethos in the South, 1920–1930* (Baton Rouge: Louisiana State University Press, 1975). On the context of academic thinking about cities see Howard Gillette, Jr., "The Evolution of Neighborhood Planning: From the Progressive Era to the 1949 Housing Act," *Journal of Urban History* 9(August 1983):421–44.

On suburbanization and metropolitanization see Kenneth T. Jackson, *Crabgrass Frontier: The Suburbanization of the United States* (New York: Oxford University Press, 1985); Jon C. Teaford, *City and Suburb: The Political Fragmentation of Metropolitan America, 1850–1970* (Baltimore: Johns Hopkins University Press, 1979); Patrick J. Ashton, "The Political Economy of Suburban Development," in *Marxism and the Metropolis: New Perspectives in Urban Political Economy*, ed. William K. Tabb and Larry Sawers (New York: Oxford University Press, 1978), 64–89; Carol O'Connor, *A Sort of Utopia: Scarsdale, 1891–1981* (Albany: State University of New York Press, 1982); Zane Miller, *Suburb: Neighborhood and Community in Forest Park, Ohio, 1935–1976* (Knoxville: University of Tennessee Press, 1981).

On automobiles and their impact see Joseph A. Interrante, *A Moveable Feast: The Automobile and the Spatial Transformation of American Culture, 1890–1940* (forthcoming); John Rae's two studies, *The American Automobile: A Brief History* (Chicago: University of Chicago Press, 1965) and *The Road and the Car in American Life* (Cambridge, Mass.: M.I.T. Press, 1971); Warren Belasco, *Americans on the Road: From Autocamp to Motel, 1910–1945* (Cambridge, Mass.: M.I.T. Press, 1979); Mark S. Foster, *From Streetcars to Superhighways: American City Planners and Urban Transportation, 1900–1940* (Philadelphia: Temple University Press, 1981); Paul Barrett, *The Automobile and Urban Transit: The Formation of Public Policy in Chicago, 1900–1930* (Philadelphia: Temple University Press, 1983); Glenn Yago, *The Decline of Transit: Urban Transportation in German and U.S. Cities, 1900–1970* (New York: Cambridge University Press, 1984). See also Howard L. Preston, *Automobile Age Atlanta: The Making of a Modern Metropolis* (Athens: University of Georgia Press, 1979); Robert

Fogelson, *The Fragmented Metropolis: Los Angeles, 1850–1930* (Cambridge, Mass.: Harvard University Press, 1967).

On department stores in the new downtown see William Leach, "Transformations in a Culture of Consumption: Women and Department Stores, 1890–1925," *Journal of American History* 71(September 1984):319–42; Susan P. Benson, "Palace of Consumption and Machine for Selling: The American Department Store, 1880–1940," *Radical History Review* 21(March 1980):199–214; Benson, *Counter Cultures: Saleswomen, Managers, and Customers in American Department Stores, 1890–1940* (Urbana: University of Illinois, 1986); Neil Harris, "The Drama of Consumer Desire," in *Yankee Enterprise: The Rise of the American System of Manufactures*, eds. Otto Mayr and Robert C. Post (Washington, D.C.: Smithsonian Institution Press, 1981), 189–216, esp. 199–205. On the development of nightlife in downtown see Lewis A. Erenberg, *Steppin' Out: New York Nightlife and the Transformation of American Culture* (Westport, Conn.: Greenwood Press, 1981); Kathy Peiss, *Cheap Amusements: Working Women and Leisure in Turn-of-the-Century New York* (Philadelphia: Temple University Press, 1986).

On regionalism and decentralization see Roy Lubove, *Community Planning in the 1920s: The Contribution of the Regional Planning Association of America* (Pittsburgh: University of Pittsburgh Press, 1963); Lubove, *The Urban Community: Housing and Planning in the Progressive Era* (Englewood Cliffs, N.J.: Prentice-Hall, 1967); Daniel Schaffer, *Garden Cities for America: The Radburn Experience* (Philadelphia: Temple University Press, 1982); Joseph C. Arnold, *The New Deal in the Suburbs: A History of the Greenbelt Town Program, 1935–1954* (Columbus: Ohio State University Press, 1971). On planning and zoning see M. Christine Boyer, *Dreaming the Rational City: The Myth of American City Planning* (Cambridge, Mass.: MIT Press, 1983); and S. J. Makielski, *The Politics of Zoning: The New York Experience* (New York: Columbia University Press, 1966).

On the spread of new patterns of consumption and leisure see Robert S. Lynd and Helen Lynd, *Middletown: A Study of Modern American Culture* (New York: Harcourt, Brace and World, 1929); Lynd and Lynd, *Middletown in Transition: A Study in Cultural Conflict* (New York: Harcourt and Brace, 1937). See also the essays in Richard Fox and T. J. Jackson Lears, eds., *The Culture of Consumption: Critical Essays in American History* (New York: Pantheon Books, 1983); Warren Sussman, *Culture As History: The Transformation of American Society in the Twentieth Century* (New York: Pantheon Books, 1984); and Stuart Ewen and Elizabeth Ewen, *Channels of Desire: Mass Images and the Shaping of American Consciousness* (New York: McGraw-Hill Book Co., 1982). On advertising see Stuart Ewen, *Captains of Consciousness: Advertising and The Social Roots of Consumer Culture* (New York: McGraw-Hill Book Co., 1976); Roland Marchand, *Advertising the American Dream: Making Way for Modernity, 1920–1940* (Berkeley: University of California Press, 1985); Michael Schudson, *Advertising: The Uneasy Persuasion* (New York: Basic Books, 1984). On the transformation of the household see Susan Strasser, *Never Done: A History of American Housework* (New York: Pantheon Books, 1982); Ruth Schwartz Cowan, *More Work for Mother: The Ironies of Household Technology from the Open Hearth to the Microwave* (New York: Basic Books, 1983). On sports see Benjamin G. Rader, *American Sports: From the Age of Folk-Games to the Age of Spectators* (Englewood Cliffs, N.J.: Prentice-Hall, 1983). On movies and radio see Lary May, *Screening Out the Past: The Birth of Mass Culture and the Motion Picture Industry* (New York: Oxford University Press, 1980); Garth Jowett, *Film: the Democratic Art* (Boston: Little, Brown & Co., 1976); Eric Barnouw, *A History of Broadcasting in the United States*, Vol. 1, *To 1933* (New York: Oxford University Press, 1966). On industrial design in the 1930s see Jeffrey L. Meikle, *Twentieth Century Limited: Industrial Design in America, 1925–1939* (Philadelphia: Temple University Press, 1979).

On prohibition see K. Austin Kerr, *Organized for Prohibition: A New History of the Anti-Saloon League* (New Haven, Conn.: Yale University Press, 1985). For the development and effects of urban crime see Mark H. Haller, "Urban Crime and Criminal Justice: The Chicago Model," *Journal of American History* 57(December 1970):619–35; Haller, "Organized Crime in Urban Society: Chicago in the Twentieth Century," *Journal of Social History* 5(Winter 1971):21–34; and Humbert S. Nelli, *The Business of Crime; Italians and Syndicate Crime in the United States* (New York: Oxford University Press, 1976).

On nativism in this period see John Higham, *Strangers in the Land: Patterns of American Nativism, 1860–1925* (New Brunswick, N.J.: Rutgers University Press, 1955); Kenneth T. Jackson, *The Ku Klux Klan in the City, 1915–1930* (New York: Oxford University Press, 1967). Ethnic conflict is discussed in Ronald H. Bayor, *Neighbors in Conflict: The Irish, Germans, Jews, and Italians of New York City, 1929–1941* (Baltimore: Johns Hopkins University Press, 1979). Race riots are discussed in Richard Hofstadter and Michael Wallace, eds., *American Violence: A Documentary History* (New York: Alfred A. Knopf, 1971); William Tuttle, Jr., *Race Riot: Chicago in the Red Summer of 1919* (New York: Atheneum Publishers, 1970); David Allen Levine, *Internal Combustion: The Races in Detroit, 1915–1926* (Westport, Conn.: Greenwood Press, 1976); Elliott Rudwick, *Race Riot at East St. Louis, July 2, 1917* (Carbondale, Ill.: Southern Illinois University Press, 1964); Scott Ellsworth, *Death in a Promised Land: The Tulsa Race Riot of 1921* (Baton Rouge: Louisiana State University Press, 1982); Robert V. Haynes, *Night of Violence* (Baton Rouge: Louisiana State University Press, 1976); William Ivy Hair, *Carnival of Fury: Robert Charles and the New Orleans Riot of 1900* (Baton Rouge: Louisiana State University Press, 1986). On Harlem in the 1920s see Nathan Huggins, *Harlem Renaissance* (New York: Oxford University Press, 1971); Jervis Anderson, *This Was Harlem: A Cultural Portrait, 1900–1950* (New York: Farrar Straus and Giroux, 1982); David Levering Lewis, *When Harlem Was In Vogue* (New York: Alfred A. Knopf, 1981). See also Judith Stein, *The World of Marcus Garvey: Race and Class in Modern Society* (Baton Rouge: Louisiana State University Press, 1985). On religious responses to urbanization in this period see William G. McLoughlin, *Modern Revivalism: Charles Grandison Finney to Billy Graham* (New York: Ronald Press, 1959).

The depression in the cities is discussed in Blake McKelvey, *The Emergence of Metropolitan America, 1915–1965* (New Brunswick, N.J.: Rutgers University Press, 1968); and Richard O. Davies, *From Metropolis to Megalopolis: A History of Urban America Since 1930* (Cambridge, Mass.: Schenkman Publishing Co., 1980); Harvard Sitkoff, *A New Deal for Blacks* (New York: Oxford University Press, 1978). For memories of families in the depression see Russell Baker, *Growing Up* (New York: Congdon and Weed, 1982); Studs Terkel, *Hard Times: An Oral History of the Great Depression* (New York: Pantheon Books, 1970); and Jeane Westin, *Making Do: How Women Survived the 30s* (Chicago: Follette Publishing Co., 1976). For contemporaneous reports see Robert S. McElvaine, ed., *Down and Out in the Great Depression: Letters from The "Forgotten Man"* (Chapel Hill: University of North Carolina Press, 1983). For an analysis of urban survival strategies see Lois Rita Helmbold, *Making Choices, Making Do: Black and White Working Class Women's Lives and Work During The Great Depression* (forthcoming).

On politics in the depression years see Bruce Stave, *The New Deal and the Last Hurrah: Pittsburgh's Machine Politics* (Pittsburgh: University of Pittsburgh Press, 1970); Lyle W. Dorsett, *Franklin D. Roosevelt and the City Bosses* (Port Washington, N.Y.: Kennikat Press, 1977); Charles H. Trout, *Boston, The Great Depression and the New Deal* (New York: Oxford University Press, 1977); J. Joseph Huthmacher, *Robert F. Wagner and the Rise of Urban Liberalism* (New York: Atheneum Publishers, 1968);

Roger Biles, *Big City Boss in Depression and War: Edward J. Kelly of Chicago* (Dekalb: Northern Illinois University Press, 1984). See also Alan Brinkley, *Voices of Protest: Huey Long, Father Coughlin and the Great Depression* (New York: Alfred A. Knopf, 1982). For an engaging memoir of the period see James Michael Curley, *I'd Do It Again* (Englewood Cliffs, N.J.: Prentice-Hall, 1957).

Mark I. Gelfand's *A Nation of Cities: The Federal Government and Urban America, 1933–1965* (New York: Oxford University Press, 1975) provides indispensable perspectives on the development of federal urban policy during the New Deal. Other important works are the Urbanism Committee to the National Resources Committee, *Our Cities: Their Role in the National Economy* (Washington, D.C.: Government Printing Office, 1937); and Phillip J. Funigiello, *The Challenge to Urban Liberalism: Federal-City Relations During World War II* (Knoxville: University of Tennessee Press, 1978).

On labor and neighborhood organizing in the 1930s see James R. Green, *The World of the Worker: Labor in Twentieth Century America* (New York: Hill & Wang, 1980); Frances Fox Piven and Richard A. Cloward, *Poor People's Movements: Why They Succeed and How They Fail* (New York: Vintage, 1979); and Robert Fisher, *Let The People Decide: Neighborhood Organizing in America* (Boston: Twayne Publishers, 1984).

ENDNOTES

[1]William Leach, "Transformations in a Culture of Consumption: Women and Department Stores, 1890–1925," *Journal of American History* 71(September 1984):326.

[2]Joseph Interrante, "The Road to Autopia: The Automobile and the Spatial Transformation of American Culture," *Michigan Quarterly Review* 15–16(Fall 1980—Winter 1981):502–17; and "You Can't Go To Town in a Bathtub: Automobile Movement and the Reorganization of Rural American Space, 1900–1930," *Radical History Review* 21(Fall 1979):151–68.

[3]Neil Harris, "The Drama of Consumer Desire," in *Yankee Enterprise: The Rise of the American System of Manufacture* eds. Otto Mayr and Robert C. Post (Washington, D.C.: Smithsonian Institution Press, 1981), 189–216, esp. 199–205.

[4]Mark Haller, "Urban Crime and Criminal Justice: The Chicago Case," *Journal of American History* 57(December 1970):624.

[5]Kenneth T. Jackson, *The Ku Klux Klan in the City, 1915–1930* (New York: Oxford University Press, 1967), 249.

[6]William G. McLoughlin, Jr., *Modern Revivalism: From Charles Grandison Finney to Billy Graham* (New York: Ronald Press, 1959), 147.

[7]Blake McKelvey, *The Emergence of Metropolitan America, 1915–1965* (New Brunswick, N.J.: Rutgers University Press, 1968), p. 80.

[8]Mark I. Gelfand, *A Nation of Cities: The Federal Government and Urban America, 1933–1965* (New York: Oxford University Press, 1975).

[9]Robert S. Lynd and Helen Lynd, *Middletown in Transition: A Study in Cultural Conflicts* (New York: Harcourt, Brace and World, 1937).

[10]Bruce Stave, *The New Deal and the Last Hurrah: Pittsburgh's Machine Politics* (Pittsburgh: University of Pittsburgh Press, 1970); Charles Trout, *Boston: The Great Depression and the New Deal* (New York: Oxford University Press, 1977).

8

Contested Cities: The Politics of Growth in an Age of Suburbanization, 1945–1974

THE IMPACT OF WORLD WAR II ON CITIES

The New Deal had failed in its fundamental goal of putting people back to work. As late as 1938 over ten million men and women were still jobless. It was the massive government military spending for the Second World War that really ended the depression. The unprecedented level of federal activity during the 1930s paled in comparison to the awesome expanse of federal mobilization for defense from 1941 to 1945. When Japan's surrender on August 14, 1945, brought an official end to the war and crowds surged into the streets to celebrate the exhilarating moment of release, no one knew what the postwar economy would deliver—depression or prosperity. Wartime emergency circumstances had effected enormous changes in American life, and it remained to be seen how these would shape postwar recovery.

The most outstanding phenomenon of wartime America was full employment. In 1944, at the height of the war, only 1.2 percent of the labor force were jobless. The efficiency of the conversion from civilian to military production tripled the manufacture of durable goods. Government investment created totally new industries, such as that producing synthetic rubber. Cost-plus, fixed-fee contracts, generous tax write-offs, and exemption from antitrust prosecution encouraged companies to compete for government contracts totaling $175 billion from 1941 to 1944, most of which were awarded to the one hundred largest firms. Corporations doubled their net profits between 1939 and 1943, and employee wages and salaries rose more than 135 percent from 1940 to 1945. The pace of agricultural mechanization increased to make up for farm laborers lost to the front or war indus-

260

tries. The federal bureaucracy increased its size from 1.1 million workers to 3.4 million. The wartime emergency expanded the American economy to all-time record levels of growth.

Wartime opportunities uprooted millions of Americans and unsettled older patterns of community life. Just when men were going off to war, industry had to recruit enormous numbers of new workers to supply the rapidly expanding need for military equipment. Afro-Americans, southern whites, teenagers, Mexicans and Mexican-Americans, and married women filled these jobs. After the threat of a wartime march on Washington proposed by A. Philip Randolph, president of the black Brotherhood of Sleeping Car Porters, President Roosevelt had issued an executive order requiring that defense industry employment be open "without discrimination because of race, creed, color, or national origin," heralding a new era of employment possibilities.

To secure defense jobs, 1.6 million blacks migrated from the South to industrial cities of the North and West in the 1940s, more than the total migration of the previous thirty years. Almost three-fourths of these settled in the urban-industrial states of California, Illinois, Michigan, New York, Ohio, and Pennsylvania. More than half a million became active members of CIO unions such as the United Auto Workers, the United Steel Workers, and the United Rubber Workers, an experience that would be an invaluable resource in later civil rights struggles. Over 400,000 black women quit work as domestic servants to enjoy the better working conditions, higher pay, and union benefits of industrial employment. Hundreds of thousands of others abandoned menial jobs in restaurants, dime stores, laundries, and hospitals for war jobs.

Other groups were on the move as well. Reversing the depression policy of repatriation, the wartime government began in 1942 to admit Mexicans to the United States as braceros on short-term work contracts to meet the wartime need for farm and industrial labor. Although the newcomers continued to experience discrimination and segregation, they seized the economic opportunities that had become available. More than fifteen thousand Mexican railroad workers were relocated as far away as Chicago. In Los Angeles, seventeen thousand people of Mexican descent found shipyard jobs where before the war there had been none available. Similarly, displaced white coal miners and marginal farmers from the hills of West Virginia and Kentucky left Appalachia to work in the booming war industries of Detroit, Cleveland, Columbus, and Cincinnati.

Well over six million women entered the labor force during the war years, increasing the number of working women 57 percent in less than five years. Most of them worked in cities. Two million took clerical jobs; another 2.5 million worked in manufacturing. Seventy-five percent of the new women workers were married, and nearly two-thirds were not only married but also mothers. Women in industry were offered skilled jobs previously available only to men; they became riveters, welders, crane operators, tool makers, and blast-furnace cleaners. To take these jobs women had to up-root themselves, and over seven million women moved from their home counties to new locations during the war. Many women found jobs in the expanding aircraft industry, which increased its employment from four thousand women in December, 1941, to 310,000 by 1943. By 1944, three million children, one-third of those between the ages of fourteen and eighteen, were also employed.

New patterns of employment, wartime dislocation, and the mixing of peoples in defense industries generated explosive social tensions. Blacks and southern whites competed for defense jobs, scarce wartime housing, and seats on buses; they jostled against each other in overcrowded city schools, parks, and beaches. White workers staged walkouts to object to black employment and promotion. Black membership in civil rights organizations like the NAACP soared, suggesting that blacks were increasingly ready to protest discrimination. Mexican-American youth in Los Angeles flaunted wartime clothing rationing by wearing bootleg "zoot suits," suits with exaggerated padded shoulders and tapered pants identified with black urban jazz culture and rebellion. The 1943 zoot suit riots, initially confined to Los Angeles, emerged out of confrontations between white servicemen on shore leave, outraged by zoot-suiters' defiant posturing, and gangs of Mexican-American youth, asserting their dissatisfaction with wartime society. During the ensuing week of rioting the ritualistic stripping of zoot-suiters became the major means by which servicemen asserted their dominance over gangs of Mexican and black youth. Sporadic incidents broke out in other cities as well, particularly New York, Detroit, and Philadelphia. Nearly 250 racial conflicts broke out in forty-seven cities that summer. The worst of the 1943 race riots bloodied the streets of Detroit in June. At the end of thirty hours of violence, twenty-five blacks and nine whites lay dead, and more than seven hundred were injured. White mobs, undeterred by police, had roamed the city attacking blacks. Blacks had hurled rocks at police and hauled white passengers off of streetcars. In August 1943 a riot in Harlem began with a confrontation between a white policeman and a black soldier that left both men wounded. Rumors of the attack on the black serviceman spread through Harlem, and black residents responded with rage, looting, and vandalism. Wartime pressures brought underlying social divisions to the surface.

Federal intervention in the wartime economy encouraged local migration in the direction of suburbs, and national migration to the Sunbelt. Between 1939 and 1946 the federal government built an average of over $2.5 billion worth of industrial buildings every year. This was more than twice the average of private industry for the same years. Lacking adequate space in the cities, most of these plants were constructed in suburbs. When the war ended, these production facilities were turned over to private industry, often at nominal cost. In this manner, federal construction had the impact of regionalizing the national economy, particularly supporting the development of southern and western cities as the location of military installations and the aircraft industry, direct recipients of the defense budget. Between New Deal projects and military spending the federal government paid for capital facilities in southern cities that northern cities had bought for themselves in earlier decades and on which they were still paying off debts. The economies of Phoenix, Tucson, Alburquerque, San Diego, Los Angeles, San Francisco, Portland, and Seattle expanded substantially in the war years and after.

Wartime tensions were expressed in political shifts as well as racial outbursts. The New Deal coalition had already weakened in the war years as southern white farmers, white factory workers, and northern blacks discovered conflicting interests. Republican victories in 1942 raised the specter of an alliance between southern Democrats and Republicans. In 1942 and 1943 the conservative coalition began to dismantle New Deal relief and social-welfare agencies. Roosevelt's 1944 victory was his narrowest, and his return to the White House was almost completely dependent on the urban vote. Wartime population shifts explained the cities' political clout. New war workers—southern whites who had been lifelong Democrats and southern blacks who had never before voted—had migrated to urban industrial centers. Postwar layoffs, with 1.8 million people out of jobs within ten days of the victory over Japan and as many as 2.7 million seeking work in March 1946; labor strife, with more people out on strike in 1946 than there had been even in 1919; and inflation caused deep concern. Republicans won a majority of both houses of Congress in the elections of 1946. Challenges from the labor-left coalition that supported Henry Wallace and the Progressive Party in 1948 and from the right-wing Dixiecrats who bolted the Democratic Party after it adopted a civil rights platform shook what was left of the New Deal voting bloc, but big city voters, black voters, and most of the labor movement rallied to elect Harry S Truman president in 1948. Still, the conservative challenge to social legislation provided the context for policy initiatives with important ramifications for city life in the postwar years.

SPATIAL PATTERNS OF GROWTH

Veteran's Administration, low-interest GI loans combined with Federal Housing Administration (FHA) mortgage insurance to subsidize construction of thousands of new suburban real-estate developments in the years after the war. New housing starts climbed from 326,000 in 1945 to over one million in 1946, approaching two million by 1950. Suburban housing developers like Arthur Levitt and Sons built planned communities with mass-production techniques using interchangeable materials and designs, erecting rows of nearly identical houses on uniform treeless lots. By 1948, Levitt had perfected his production system, turning out thirty-five colonial-style houses per day, 150 houses per week, and completing a new house every fifteen minutes in his new community of Levittown outside of New York City.

Federal highway construction on an unprecedented scale played an important role in opening up rural land for suburban developments. In 1947 Congress authorized a 37,000 mile national highway network and designated funds for nearly three thousand miles of roads in or near 182 large cities. From the 1930s onward highway planners had conceived of urban road networks in terms of a hub (the downtown) and a wheel (radial arteries fanning out from the center and beltways circling the city on its outskirts). Federal road building supported the redefinition of downtown from a mixture of commercial, occupational, and residential uses to a commercial center with direct access to and from suburban residential areas. Cities also continued to spend funds on limited-access freeways. During the first half of the 1950s, New York City laid out the Cross-Bronx Expressway, Detroit began construction of the John Lodge and Edsel Ford superhighways, and Chicago built the Congress Street (later Eisenhower) expressway. By 1956 there were an estimated 376 miles of urban freeways in the nation's twenty-five largest cities, with at least 104 additional miles under construction.

The Interstate Highway Act of 1956 and creation of the Federal Highway Trust Fund strengthened these patterns. The highway act was proposed as a means of eliminating downtown traffic congestion, although primary arguments emphasized civil defense needs for high-speed travel between cities. Federal funds spent on highways swelled from $79 million in 1946 to $429 million in 1950 to $2.9 billion in 1960. Interstate access routes leveled some older downtown neighborhoods and cut right through the middle of others. The Federal Highway Trust, supported by gas-tax revenue, ensured that the freeways would be self-propagating, because more freeways encouraged more automobile travel, generating more gasoline revenue that could only be used to build more highways.

By 1950 the population of suburbs, aided by new highway construction, was growing ten times as fast as that of central cities. Between 1950 and 1970 Chicago and New York City lost population while their suburban rings grew 117 percent and 195 percent respectively. Detroit's population fell by 20 percent, and its suburban population expanded by 206 percent. The same patterns held in Boston, Washington, D.C., Cleveland, St. Louis, Minneapolis, Pittsburgh, and Baltimore. The only cities that continued to grow were southern and western cities that expanded with annexation, and even there, suburban growth overtook central-city increases. While Los Angeles's population grew by 43 percent from 1950 to

The Postwar Housing Explosion Signs in an undeveloped section outside San Diego advertise the types of housing and government support that invigorated suburbanization after World War II. *(Courtesy of the Library of Congress.)*

1970, its outer ring grew by 141 percent. Dallas's and Houston's populations grew by 94 percent and 104 percent; their outer rings grew by 107 percent and 330 percent.

Beltway construction in the 1950s and an increased reliance on trucking for intercity freight traffic provided renewed incentives to industrial relocation in suburban areas, and by the 1960s new factories lined peripheral highways, boosting the tax base of suburban communities at the cost of central cities. The decentralization of jobs began to leave central cities with a net loss in employment. Between 1954 and 1963, for instance, in the twenty-four metropolitan areas with populations greater than one million the central cities lost more than five hundred thousand jobs while their suburbs were gaining over 1.5 million. From 1954 through 1956 roughly 90 percent of the capital committed to the construction of new factories in the New York metropolitan area was invested in suburban areas beyond the boundaries of New York City. Between 1947 and 1954 the number of manufacturing plants in Chicago suburbs doubled, and in suburban Detroit there was a 220 percent rise in the number of factories. In 1957 Massachusetts completed Route 128, a freeway around the circumference of the metropolitan area about ten miles from downtown Boston, and by the end of that year manufacturers had already invested $94 million in ninety-nine plants employing seventeen thousand people located along the highway. By 1963 more than four hundred factories lined Route 128. Some communities developed industrial parks, special outlying tracts zoned exclusively for industry. Industrial Hayward and Milpitas, California, were as characteristic suburban developments as the more stereotypical residential

The Highway and the City   This complex of highways, photographed in 1946, provides access from Long Island to New York City and has made possible explosive suburban growth along its arteries. *(U.S. State Department, The National Archives.)*

enclaves of Lakewood, California, and Park Forest, Illinois. The declining urban tax bases that resulted from the suburban flight of industry were responsible for the downward economic cycle that would be apparent in the 1970s as the fiscal crisis.

Businesses naturally followed the residential expansion—although in some instances they located ahead of actual settlement in outlying districts—and formed secondary commercial centers near principal highway interchanges. As early as the 1920s this process foreshadowed the decline of downtowns. Now, in the mid-twentieth century the planting of these business districts began to take on a more formalized character. Shopping centers, complete with closed arcades of shops, large anchor department stores at the ends of arcades, and sprawling parking lots, became major retail marketplaces for the metropolis. As population radiated outward, it became increasingly convenient for a family to fill its material needs in shopping centers rather than in old central business districts. The various malls and plazas could boast of every service the consumer might desire: specialty shops, department stores, drugstores, groceries, movie theaters, restaurants, cocktail lounges, insurance offices, and, best of all, free parking. A New Mexico shopping center built in the early 1960s even intended to double as a bomb shelter in case of atomic attack, and it advertised that it could accommodate eight thousand people underground for up to two weeks. For a prepaid fee of $250, customers were guaranteed "organized schools, movies, games, and survival . . . to minimize panic and depression." As one researcher predicted in 1962, "It's not far-fetched to say that the shopping centers will become downtown areas." The centers themselves, their size (many now cover over one hundred acres), and their glitter became new objects of boosterism as each year chauvinists from a different community boasted that they had the biggest shopping mall in the state/region/country/world. Thus outward movement energized a new multiplier effect. Access to highways attracted residents, who in turn lured businesses, who then brought jobs and more enticement for residential development.

The division between cities and suburbs increasingly assumed a racial dimension—whites on the outside, people of color on the inside. The FHA refused to guarantee suburban loans to poor people, nonwhites, Jews, and other "inharmonious" racial and ethnic groups. Restrictive covenants and, after these were declared illegal in 1948, unspoken agreements among realtors and exclusionary zoning practices kept all but the most economically secure and assertive black families from buying homes in the new developments. A few suburban developments sprang up to house black

Rebuilding Downtown   While housing starts boomed in the suburbs during the 1950s, the roar of construction also vibrated through downtown areas. This view shows iron workers on the thirty-second floor of New York's Esso building in 1954. *(Records of the United States Information Agency, National Archives.)*

middle-class residents, but the great majority of suburban developments were exclusively white.

In the same years, central cities were becoming increasingly non-white. The mechanization of cotton harvesting in the 1940s and 1950s displaced more than four million people, ensuring that depopulation of the southern countryside would continue. Between 1949 and 1952 alone the demand for unskilled agricultural labor in the Mississippi Delta counties dropped by 72 percent. Approximately five million black people, primarily from the deep South, moved into the central cities between 1950 and 1970, in the same years that seven million white people moved out. In particular cities, racial population shifts were even more dramatic. In New York City the white population declined 7 percent between 1950 and 1960, and the black population rose 46 percent. In Chicago the white total dropped 13 percent, while the number of black residents rose 65 percent. Between 1940 and 1960, blacks increased from 8 to 23 percent of Chicago's population. In 1950 only one-sixth of the populations of Detroit, Cleveland, and St. Louis were black, but within ten years each of these cities was 29 percent black. Washington, D.C., was the first major American city with a black majority, and cities such as Detroit and Newark were changing from over-whelmingly white to predominantly black within a single generation. In other cities other nonwhite groups were a significant presence. As early as 1930, Chicanos had constituted more than half the population of El Paso, slightly less than half of San Antonio, and one-fifth the population of Los Angeles. The number of Puerto Ricans continued to increase in New York and Chicago, and significant numbers of Cubans settled in Miami, and Asians in San Francisco, Los Angeles, and New York.

Residents of older urban neighborhoods were increasingly likely to be either poor white ethnics, who could not afford to move out to the periphery, or new black migrants. A fierce struggle for available housing and an escalating anxiety in white communities adjacent to swelling black areas resulted from the sudden rise in minority populations. If the war and northern migration had heightened black expectations for equality and demands for better jobs and better housing, the residents of nearby ethnic enclaves saw their hard-won gains of home ownership and community stability threatened by those demands. Neighborhoods shifted composi-tion, but racial dividing lines persisted. In Cleveland, blacks dominated the East Side and white ethnics from southern and eastern Europe were the majority on the West Side. Chicago's South Side and West Side ghetto neighborhoods expanded, but the northern half of the city remained white territory, and most racial incidents in the city between 1945 and 1950 involved the competition for housing. White housing and black housing remained segregated, even though blacks were bursting out of the confines of traditional ghetto neighborhoods.

Older, central-city residential neighborhoods that had been vital communities before the war showed signs of transition and change. Large and bustling ethnic enclaves were reduced by the movement to the suburbs in the 1940s and 1950s. As columnist Mike Royko described the changes in the Chicago working-class neighborhood where he grew up: "When the younger couples started moving out . . . the neighborhood got older and never really recovered. . . . The vitality of the neighborhood was tremendous—until the move to the suburbs."[1] Cities after 1945 were plagued by

TABLE 8-1   Central-City, Black, and Metropolitan Populations for Selected American Cities, 1940 and 1970

	1940			1970		
CITY	CENTRAL CITY	BLACKS	METRO AREA	CENTRAL CITY	BLACKS	METRO AREA
Atlanta	302,288	104,533	558,842	496,973	255,051	1,390,164
Baltimore	859,100	165,843	1,139,529	905,759	420,210	2,070,670
Boston	770,816	23,679	2,209,608	641,071	104,707	2,753,700
Buffalo	506,775	17,694	958,487	462,768	94,329	1,349,211
Chicago	3,396,808	277,731	4,569,643	3,366,957	1,102,620	6,978,947
Cincinnati	455,610	55,593	787,044	452,524	125,000	1,384,851
Cleveland	878,336	84,504	1,267,270	750,903	287,841	2,064,194
Dallas	294,734	50,407	527,145	844,401	210,238	1,555,950
Denver	322,412	7,836	445,206	514,678	47,011	1,227,529
Detroit	1,623,452	149,119	2,377,329	1,511,482	660,428	4,199,931
Houston	384,514	86,302	528,961	1,232,802	316,551	1,985,031
Indianapolis	386,972	51,142	460,926	743,155	134,320	1,109,882
Kansas City (Mo.)	399,178	41,574	686,643	507,409	112,005	1,256,649
Los Angeles	1,504,277	63,774	2,916,403	2,816,061	503,606	7,032,075
Louisville	319,077	47,158	451,473	361,472	86,040	826,553
Memphis	292,942	121,498	358,250	623,530	242,513	770,120
Miami	172,172	36,857	267,739	334,859	76,156	1,267,792
Milwaukee	587,472	8,821	829,629	717,099	105,088	1,403,688
Minneapolis	492,370	4,646	967,367	434,400	19,005	1,813,647
Nashville	167,402	47,318	257,267	447,877	87,876	541,108
Newark	429,760	74,965	1,291,416	382,417	207,458	1,856,556
New Orleans	494,537	149,034	552,244	593,471	267,308	1,046,470
New York	7,454,995	458,444	8,706,917	7,894,862	1,668,115	11,571,899
Philadelphia	1,931,334	250,880	3,199,637	1,948,609	653,791	4,817,914
Pittsburgh	671,659	62,216	2,082,556	520,117	104,904	2,401,245
Portland (Ore.)	305,394	1,931	501,275	382,619	21,572	1,009,129
Providence	253,504	6,388	695,253	179,213	15,875	789,186
Rochester	324,975	3,262	438,230	296,233	49,647	882,667
St. Louis	816,048	108,765	1,464,111	622,236	254,191	2,363,017
Salt Lake City	149,934	694	211,623	175,885	2,135	557,635
San Francisco	634,536	4,846	1,461,804	715,674	96,078	3,109,519
Seattle	368,302	3,789	593,734	538,831	37,868	1,421,869
Washington, D.C.	663,091	187,266	967,985	756,510	537,712	2,861,123

Source: Bayrd Still, *Urban America: A History with Documents* (Boston: Little, Brown, 1974), derived from Table 4.1, pp. 356–59.

rising taxes, declining services, and expanding minority populations. In contrast the suburbs beckoned with space, the possibility of home ownership, low taxes, good schools, and racial and economic homogeneity.

RESHAPING DOWNTOWN: PROGROWTH COALITIONS AND URBAN RENEWAL

In the heyday of the suburban boom, central cities lost population, mass-transit systems lost riders, downtown department stores lost shoppers, and downtown hotels lost guests. As postwar observers looked at downtown, they saw the white exodus from old central city neighborhoods, the disappearance of manufacturing investment, and an increasing impoverished, nonwhite population. They lumped all these together as signs of central city decay. "Attacking blight" and stimulating downtown investment became priorities for city officials, business leaders, and members of Congress, who connected visible urban poverty, postwar housing shortages, and downtown decline under the rubric of slum clearance.

In 1945 Senators Robert F. Wagner of New York, Allen J. Ellender of Louisiana, and Robert A. Taft of Ohio cosponsored a housing bill that set a goal of 1.25 million new housing units a year to be built for all classes during the next ten years, with liberal government loans and subsidies for the construction of 810,000 public housing units for low-income groups to be built in the next four years. The Housing Act of 1937 had already created the United States Housing Authority and committed the federal government to public housing on a permanent basis, although conservative interests in Congress had limited USHA's appropriations and the National Association of Real Estate Boards (NAREB), joined by the U.S. Chamber of Commerce and the U.S. Building and Loan League, lobbbied strenuously against any public housing at all. Instead, realtors and builders supported broad government sudsidy for private redevelopment of what they labeled "blighted" (meaning unprofitable) tracts in the inner cities. NAREB labeled public housing as socialist interference with the private housing market, although the real-estate lobby accepted and even demanded government intervention to acquire and clear land and government subsidies for redeveloping land for private profit. NAREB argued that this kind of redevelopment would add to municipal tax bases, clear away acres of blighted buildings, and bring downtowns back to life.

Champions of public housing, such as social workers, housing officials, and labor leaders, sought public or subsidized housing for the broadest possible range of urban residents with only so much emphasis on slum clearance as was necessary to secure sites for this housing. Conservative opponents of the 1937 Housing Act had previously managed to tilt its emphasis from public housing to slum clearance. Now again the redevelop-

ment interests lobbied against the 1945 Housing Act. Still the public housing advocates had the votes in Congress to maintain their program. Professional planners from the American Institute of Planners entered the
debate, tending to favor redevelopment proposals, arguing that a sole emphasis on housing neglected the larger urban framework.

After four years of debate the bill that finally passed in 1949 as the
Taft-Ellender-Wagner Housing Act was an omnibus bill, containing several
types of measures: slum clearance, public housing, and expanded mortgage insurance through the FHA. Title I of the bill established the principle of urban redevelopment. In essence the provision committed federal
funds to the clearance of slums by local redevelopment agencies. The law
mandated that redevelopment programs be "predominantly residential."
But this meant either that areas earmarked for redevelopment had to be at
least 50 percent residential in character before they were cleared or that the
new construction in cleared, residential areas had to include 50 percent
residential units—*but not necessarily both.* Thus redevelopment projects
could level poor residential areas labeled as slums and replace them with
office buildings, shopping complexes, luxury apartments, and parking
lots—land uses that were supposed to raise property values, assist private
investment, increase tax revenues, and restore economic vitality.

Title II of the bill put public housing on a permanent basis, authoriz-
ing 810,000 units over the next six years. The AFL, CIO, U.S. Conference
of Mayors, various veterans groups, and the NAACP strongly supported
Title II and the omnibus bill as a whole. Public-housing advocates were
skeptical of the redevelopment provisions in Title I but believed that an
omnibus bill was the only way public housing could be achieved, and they
lobbied hard for the act. Because of the public-housing provision, NAREB
and the Savings and Loan League opposed the bill.

The 1949 Housing Act committed the nation to providing "a decent
home and suitable living environment" for every American family, set
public-housing production targets, and created a new and powerful mechanism for transforming land use in central cities. But almost immediately the
1949 Housing Act disappointed its liberal supporters. In 1951 New York
City planner, park commissioner, and highway builder Robert Moses demonstrated a pattern for local implementation of the act. He proposed to
build a colosseum and luxury housing at Broadway and 57th Street. By
including a few run-down tenements sheltering less than three hundred
people, Moses used urban redevelopment to gain control of more than two
square blocks of thriving commercial property. With $26 million in federal
assistance, Moses built an exhibition center, a parking structure, and luxury
housing on the site. Moses's action clearly demonstrated that the 1949
Housing Act could be used not to meet housing needs of the urban poor
but to advance redevelopment agendas for downtown.

In 1954 Congress, backed by the Eisenhower administration,

amended the 1949 provisions, and urban renewal replaced urban redevelopment. The amended housing act now recognized the need for rehabilitation of dilapidated structures rather than massive slum clearances, although provisions for clearance were retained. Thus in most cases redevelopment and renewal were combined into the latter term. The amendments included a new provision that allocated 10 percent of federal grants-in-aid to projects in nonresidential areas. That is, localities could now use a tenth of federal funds for projects that did not fit the loose "predominantly residential" criterion of the 1949 act. Further amendments in 1961 boosted the proportion of nonresidential funds to 30 percent, removing redevelopment further from the solution of housing problems.

Downtown revitalization in the 1950s became the rallying cry for a whole generation of postwar mayors, who built political organizations based on what political scientist John Mollenkopf has labeled "pro-growth coalitions." Big-city politicians, businessmen, building-trades labor unions, planners, and urban renewal executives joined forces in downtown renewal schemes. In Pittsburgh, R.K. Mellon, heir to a fortune that included Pittsburgh Consolidated Coal, the Mellon Bank, and Gulf Oil, brought together a group of young innovative executives to establish the Allegheny Conference on Community Development (ACCD) to develop plans for what would be the Golden Triangle, a new central business district for the city. Mellon and ACCD joined with David Lawrence, Democratic mayor and head of a considerable political machine, Republican corporate leaders, downtown merchants and real-estate interests, and the construction trades to orchestrate the Pittsburgh Renaissance, a downtown redevelopment program that eventually cleared railroad yards and commercial "blight" to create a historical park, six high-rise office structures, a luxury hotel, and an underground parking garage. In Philadelphia the business-dominated Greater Philadelphia Movement joined with reform mayors Joseph Clark, Jr., and Richardson Dilworth to build a shiny new high-rise office complex called Penn Center to replace an aging railroad terminal and railroad viaduct. New Orleans mayor DeLesseps S. Morrison joined the business community in replacing downtown inner-city neighborhoods with a civic-center complex and railroad terminal. In St. Louis a businessmen's alliance known as Civic Progress joined forces with Mayor Raymond Tucker, labor unions, religious groups, and other organizations to win approval for a $110.6 million bond issue that would clear downtown areas for expressways, street improvements, bridges, and hospitals. Most of these projects lured private investment money with generous property-tax abatements and reduced assessments, so that for at least the immediate future these projects would yield the city no tax revenue. A revitalization was to be generated by the jobs and other economic benefits these projects would create.

In some cities the financial and employment opportunities accompanying renewal activities were adequate to develop a new type of political machine whose supporters were loyal to progrowth politicians. In other cities, political changes that diminished the power of downtown neighborhoods and increased the input of business leaders were required before progrowth coalitions could emerge. In Boston the state legislature moved in 1949 to reform the city's charter, abolishing district elections of city councillors. The New Boston Committee, a business lobby, helped John Hynes defeat James Michael Curley as mayor in 1951. Once in office, Hynes initiated the West End Project, building luxury housing that displaced over twenty-six hundred families in a downtown neighborhood bordering on government offices and major hospitals.

In 1959 a group of Boston business leaders dubbed "the Vault" organized behind John Collins as a mayoral candidate. Among the Vault's members were Gerald Blakely, prime mover in a Route 128 development project, Ralph Lowell, retired chairman of Boston Safety Deposit and Trust Co. and director of numerous Boston corporations, Carl Gilbert, chairman of Gillette and director of Raytheon, Lloyd Brace, chairman of the First National Bank of Boston, and other bankers and executives of insurance and utility companies. With their backing, Collins hired Ed Logue, New Haven's innovative urban-renewal executive, to direct redevelopment in Boston and initiate a "New Boston" renewal program that ultimately subjected 10 percent of the city's land area to redevelopment. In cooperation with Mayor Collins and the Vault, Logue won federal funding for the construction of a government center, including a monumental new city hall and a group of towers to house federal and state agencies as well as private business concerns, and the redevelopment of the waterfront with high-rise luxury apartments. Critics charged that urban renewal in Boston was black and ethnic removal, and indeed the areas designated as slums included all the multiethnic West End, most of the racially mixed South End, and nearly all of Lower Roxbury, the center of the black community. The impact of urban renewal in Boston was to deeply intensify the competition for a diminishing low-rent housing supply between the city's poor white ethnics and newly displaced black residents.

In Richmond, downtown businessmen and professional leaders organized a "Greater Richmond" movement. A new city charter passed in 1948 provided for a city manager and a small city council to be elected at large on a citywide basis, effectively placing local government in the hands of the white elite for the next 30 years, even though Richmond had a black majority by the 1960s. The master plan for Richmond called for freeways to be built through the city and a larger, more exclusively commercial downtown. Richmond leaders used federal urban-renewal legislation to make it possible to remove black residents from locations desired by white businessmen and industrial interests.

In San Francisco, business leaders formed the San Francisco Planning and Urban Renewal Association (SPUR) to build support for urban renewal.

In 1959 an activist urban-renewal planner M. Justin Herman was appointed head of the city's redevelopment agency. With backing from SPUR, major city property owners, most trade unions, and after 1967, Mayor Joseph Alioto, who had been chairman of the redevelopment agency in the late 1950s and was supported by labor, real-estate, and corporate interests, Herman undertook to redevelop such large areas adjacent to the central business district as the city's produce market, its Japanese neighborhood, its major black neighborhood, and a variety of other low-rent sites.

The fate of postwar public housing was affected by shifting political currents. The upsurge of conservative political reaction bent on undoing the New Deal expanded to fight social-welfare programs, singling out public housing for attack as "creeping socialism." Congressional opponents of the program successfully cut annual appropriations, and between 1949 and 1955 barely 200,000 dwelling units out of the proposed 810,000 were actually completed. NAREB and the real-estate lobby conducted a massive campaign to hold local referenda against public housing, defeating twenty-five of the thirty-eight that were held. In one public-housing battle in Los Angeles, Mayor Fletcher Bowron and the city council had backed a public-housing plan to construct ten thousand dwelling units at a cost of $110 million. One of the largest of the eleven proposed projects was to be constructed in Chavez Ravine, a 315 acre parcel of land near the center of downtown Los Angeles and settled by Mexican-Americans and a smaller number of Chinese. Prominent Los Angeles architects Richard Neutra and Robert Alexander designed a combination of high-rise and two-story buildings for the parcel. As the residents of the Ravine were moved out, their homes and active community life demolished, a cluster of groups and individuals including the California real-estate lobby, the Home Builders Association, the chamber of commerce, and the *Los Angeles Times* began to attack the public-housing program. Mayor Bowron continued to defend the program and was supported by local AFL and CIO unions, the League of Women Voters, and various church, veterans,' and citizens' groups. But these organizations were out-bought and out-shouted in the press by the antihousing forces, who labeled public housing as socialist and collectivist. The California Senate Committee on Un-American Activities investigated the California Housing Authority, and by the end of 1951 the majority of the city council shifted from supporting public housing to canceling the city's contract with the California Housing Authority. After various legal battles, a citizen's referendum won by antihousing forces, and the defeat of the mayor by an antihousing candidate in 1953, plans for over half the public housing were scrapped, and the federal government resold the Chavez Ravine property to the city. The city finally found an acceptable public use for the land; in 1957 Los Angeles signed a contract with Walter O'Malley, owner of the Brooklyn Dodgers, promising the now-cleared Chavez Ravine and $2 million for site improvement for a new Dodgers stadium.

Where public housing was built, legal battles and neighborhood conflicts over its location meant that many years often passed between land clearance and the completion of new units. Facing diminished financing and rising costs, postwar housing planners had rejected the low-rise designs of the 1930s and built instead high-rise construction, grim rows of gray and brown towers in New York City, Boston, Chicago, and Philadelphia. There were never enough units built to house all the people who needed a place to live, and housing appropriations were never sufficient for adequate maintenance. In Boston the 1949 political change to an at-large council meant that whatever claim on resources public-housing residents had been able to demand from ward politicians was now lost. In that city public-housing placements became politically and racially charged as city leaders integrated public housing in response to militant civil rights demands for decent black housing *and* as a means of weakening ethnic working-class neighborhoods and thus eliminating the base of the defeated political machine. In Chicago, public housing seemed to be an instrument of segregation; black tenants occupied two-thirds of the city's public-housing units in 1955 and 85 percent by 1959.

Between 1950 and 1960 federal programs destroyed more homes than were built; those that were destroyed were primarily low-rent buildings; and most of the structures built were high-rent apartments. Although

The Impact of Urban Renewal and Redevelopment   *Left,* demolition of a slum. This photograph shows the systematic destruction of a so-called blighted area of Providence, Rhode Island in the early 1950s. A neighborhood consisting of over a thousand structures—mostly multiple-family dwellings—was completely leveled and replaced by a shopping center, a school, apartment houses, and town houses.

Right, the new neighborhood. These apartments were built on some of the cleared land depicted at left. The redevelopment project represented here included both low- and medium-priced rental units, but not all projects were as diversified. Often lower-class homes were removed and replaced by more costly housing designed to attract middle- and upper-income families back into the city. *(Both photographs, Providence Journal-Bulletin.)*

redevelopment laws specified that housing assisted by federal funds could not discriminate by race, creed, or color, the high rents in effect excluded most blacks from the new housing constructed on cleared land. Experts estimate that as a result of slum clearance and urban-renewal programs the United States *lost* a net of 200,000 housing units a year between 1950 and 1956 and 475,000 a year between 1957 and 1959. Thousands of local small businesses were destroyed, and their contributions to the city's tax base lost, while the redevelopment projects were built with deferred or diminished tax arrangements. Other renewal projects cleared land for the expansion of tax-free universities and hospital complexes into black or white ethnic working-class neighborhoods. Freeways and access routes also required generous portions of downtown areas, where planners argued that dilapidated buildings needed to be torn down anyway. Highway builders did not intentionally seek out poor neighborhoods to destroy, but they carefully avoided high-rent areas, where construction would disrupt private investment. Land in the path of a proposed highway rapidly declined in value, small neighborhood-oriented shops moved away, and low-income housing became more and more difficult to find. Promises of revitalization increasingly rang hollow as the redevelopment schemes failed to stem the tide of residential and economic movement out of the city.

CURRENTS OF PROTEST

Civil rights, labor, and neighborhood protest activism had continued through the 1940s. Civil rights agitators committed to nonviolent direct-action techniques to challenge segregation formed the Congress of Racial Equality in 1942 and organized picketing and sit-ins to test exclusionary public accommodations. Questioning the priorities of peacetime conversion with profits reaching an all-time high and wages and salaries declining, over 4.5 million men and women left their jobs to strike in 1946, more even than in 1919. Housewives organized meat boycotts to protest postwar inflated meat prices, and neighborhood tenants' groups lobbied for the retention of wartime rent controls. Union members had expanded the reach of their political participation by forming CIO Political Action Committees to support FDR in 1944, and many of these were active in Henry Wallace's third-party presidential campaign in 1948.

These social movements cross-fertilized one another. Some CIO unions took an active stand in support of civil rights and public housing. The strength of the labor and civil rights movements after the war opened up the chance for Chicanos to build alliances, and in 1948 and 1949, community organizers from Saul Alinsky's Industrial Areas Foundation supported the founding of a Community Service Organization (CSO) in the Los Angeles barrio. The organization worked on voter registration, ultimately registering twelve thousand new Hispanic voters in the Ninth Council District. Working in an ethnically mixed area, Ed Roybal put together a coalition of Armenians, Russians, blacks, and Jews, as well as Chicanos, to become the first Hispanic on the city council since 1881. CSO tactics were not highly demonstrative; letter-writing campaigns, lawsuits, and appearances at city hall were far more common than pickets and marches. But by 1960, CSO boasted of thirty-seven chapters, 217,000 newly registered voters, physical improvements in hundreds of barrio neighborhoods, and challenges to ethnic segregation in schools and public accommodations. But postwar protest organizations were under attack in the early 1950s, fractured and besieged by charges of Communist leanings. To anti-Communist crusaders, support for civil rights became an indicator of un-Americanism. Chicano labor leaders were particularly subject to political suppression through the threat of deportation. The reactionary political climate made protest suspect.

Still, a rising black challenge to segregation would not be silenced. Urbanization brought black people into direct exposure to the promises and frustrations of mass consumer society and the myth of opportunity. On tenant farms blacks felt the sting of poverty and discrimination, but the range of choices was narrow. White society, with all its comforts, was distant, almost unattainable. In the cities, however, blacks acquired more cash to spend on magazines, radios, television, and movies—all that celebrated the materialism of white middle-class urban (and suburban) culture. Here, the harder blacks tried to join consumer society, the more they discovered they were shut out. They not only were given inferior jobs, housing, schooling, and health care, but also were excluded from white-owned motels and restaurants, were forced into separate sections of bus stations and airports, and were subjected to usurious credit arrangements. Segregation and inferior services had always haunted blacks, but by the 1950s these conditions aroused new angers about discrimination. The city, which had kindled expectations and thwarted opportunities, had primed blacks to push for a more equitable share of the American promise.

Early in the campaign against discrimination the most momentous events occurred in southern cities, for it was here that social forces laid bare the conflicts between equal rights and local autonomy. For half a century civil-rights groups such as the NAACP and the Urban League had been working to eradicate the separate-but-equal doctrine that the U.S. Supreme Court had upheld in 1896 as justification for Jim Crow segregation laws passed by southern cities and states after Reconstruction. Using the courts, these organizations began to weaken the barriers. The breakthrough came in 1954 when the Supreme Court, in *Brown* v. *Board of Education,* stated that "in the field of public education the doctrine of 'separate but equal' has no place." The Court ordered an end to legislated school segregation "with all deliberate speed," but most southern communities balked. Would the federal government enforce the Court's order? The issue was tested before the nation in 1957. That year the school board in Little Rock, Arkansas, a moderate, emerging southern city, decided to allow a few black students to enroll in previously all-white Central High School. The decision to accede to the federal court order incensed Governor Orval Faubus, who sent troops from the Arkansas National Guard to bar blacks from the school. President Eisenhower, concerned about this threat to federal prestige, nationalized the guard and sent a thousand paratroopers into Little Rock to escort nine black teenagers to school. The troops patrolled the school's corridors for the rest of the year.

School-integration victories, however minor, encouraged other efforts toward gaining broader civil rights. Again cities provided the major theaters of action. In 1955 when Rosa Parks's personal protest against segregated seating on a bus led to her arrest in Montgomery, Alabama, the local black Women's Political Council distributed forty thousand flyers urging Montgomery's black community to boycott the bus company, which normally depended on a 70 percent black ridership. The year-long boycott, led by a young black minister, Dr. Martin Luther King, Jr., was supported by nearly 100 percent of Montgomery's black community. The boycott's success (the Supreme Court invalidated Alabama's segregation laws) proved to be less important than the means by which it was achieved—mass nonviolent action. Enough blacks now lived in cities for collective resistance to be effective. Soon Dr. King's "weapon of love" spread to other places. In Greensboro, North Carolina, in 1960 a group of students, black and white, sat at a Woolworth's lunch counter and refused to leave after being denied service. Their tactics began a wave of passive sit-ins, lie-ins, and wade-ins at segregated restaurants, stores, and swimming pools. By the end of 1961 lunch counters had been desegregated in two hundred cities, most of them in the upper South. Then, in 1963 Dr. King, now leader of the influential Southern Christian Leadership Conference, spearheaded a massive march against discrimination by employers and merchants in Birmingham, Alabama.

In the mid 1960s the civil-rights movement reached a climax as protesters began to draw attention to the de facto segregation (racial separation in fact and custom, though not in law) in the North as well as the de jure (legislated) segregation in the South. Under persistent prodding from President Johnson, Congress in 1964 passed the Civil Rights Act, which outlawed racial discrimination in public accommodations. In the Voting Rights Act of 1965, also pushed by President Johnson, Congress authorized federal agents to register voters who had been illegally denied suffrage.

Frustrations concerning the limits of legislative solutions provoked further reactions from blacks and whites, particularly in cities where numbers of blacks were large enough to exert significant pressure for more civil rights. As the quest for equality moved into the North, it stirred white fears about schools and housing. White residents in Chicago, Detroit, Boston,

The Challenge of Civil Rights   Martin Luther King, Jr. leads a march down Columbus Avenue in Boston, Massachusetts in 1965. Note the broad support for civil rights and integration that the banners and marchers proclaim. *(The Boston Public Library.)*

and Philadelphia organized to fight open housing and school busing. The increase in segregationist violence and antiblack activism cast doubt on the civil rights movement's commitment to nonviolent tactics, and new black political strategies called for black majorities to organize to make use of "black power" rather than to wait for what looked like utopian integrationist hopes for "blacks and whites together." A new restlessness spread through the civil rights movement, and internal debates dissolved prior consensus.

By 1968 the faith of two decades of struggle lay shattered. Martin Luther King was dead, the victim of an assassin's bullet, and the cores of a dozen cities were pocked with burned-out districts, the remnants of four of the most violent summers in the nation's modern history. The refrain of "We shall overcome" was now replaced by epithets like "Burn, baby, burn." Tensions exploded during the hot summers of 1965 through 1968. Ugly riots racked scores of cities and cast a gloom over urban America. No region of the country escaped racial outbursts. Fires, stonings, snipings, and lootings occurred in Los Angeles, San Francisco, Portland, Kansas City,

Omaha, Chicago, Milwaukee, Atlanta, Miami, Nashville, Cincinnati, Dayton, Cleveland, Rochester, New York City, Philadelphia, Washington, Boston, and many other cities. During a three-week period in the summer of 1967 a riot in Newark left twenty-six dead and twelve hundred injured, and a frenzy of violence in Detroit killed forty-three and injured two thousand.

Nearly all of the seventy-five or so riots of these years followed the same general pattern. They began as minor incidents involving the police and ghetto dwellers. Crowds collected, threw bricks and bottles at the police, and tensions mounted. Then windows were broken and social control dissolved. If police could not restore order at this point, the riot exploded into arson, looting, and sniper fire. Unlike most racial violence of the past, the riots of the sixties did not involve confrontations between blacks and whites over contested neighborhoods. Instead they were what Morris Janowitz has called "commodity riots"—outbursts within the ghetto against property and retail establishments, most of them owned by whites. Most deaths and injuries occurred in clashes between rioters and the police, not in fighting between black and white citizens.

Although violence also struck smaller cities, conditions were most explosive in big cities. The growth of huge ghettos, with their racial homogeneity and inferior services, created large populations of distressed blacks who could spontaneously mobilize once a riot broke out. Investigators estimated that roughly 10 percent or more of the ghetto populations of Detroit, Newark, and Watts (Los Angeles) participated to some extent in the riots in those cities. In each case this would mean that tens of thousands were involved, certainly too many for any local police force to handle. Moreover in big cities blacks had frequent occasion to view the disparities between their own situations and the middle-class white consumer culture that they constantly confronted. This is why so many became looters when ghettos erupted. As one Detroit rioter explained, "On Twelfth Street everybody was out, the whole family, Mama, Papa, the kids, it was like an outing. . . . The rebellion—it was all caused by the commercials. I mean you saw all those things you'd never be able to get. . . . Men's clothing, furniture, appliances, color TV. All that crummy TV glamour just hanging out there."

As cities smoldered, black militancy seemed to spread with the smoke. A new breed of young black leaders rallied behind the "black power" slogan, first popularized during a civil-rights march in Mississippi in 1966. Exploring the implications of this stance, black militants rejected integration, condoned armed self-defense, and proposed more aggressive strategies as a means of attaining political and economic power. In part this urge for independence reflected racial pride in the emergence of new black nations in Africa. More important, black nationalism in America stemmed from the urbanization experience itself, emerging from the confrontation with thwarted opportunities and the need for self-identity in a socially complex environment. By the 1930s remnants of Marcus Garvey's black nationalist crusade of the 1920s had merged with religious cults such as the Moorish Science Temple (a sect that, like many others, had developed to meet the needs of uprooted black migrants in the cities) to form the Black Muslims, a militant separatist organization. Under their founder, W. Fard Muhammad, and his successor, Elijah Muhammad, the Muslims achieved considerable influence among urban blacks, although actual Muslim membership remained small. By the early 1960s the Muslim creed of self-help had aroused a new militancy among disaffected blacks such as Malcolm X (who had rejected his "slave name" of Little). "You need somebody who is going to fight," Malcolm X once asserted. "You don't need any kneeling or crawling in."

Malcolm X was brutally assassinated in 1965, ironically just as he was beginning to explore tentative possibilities for cooperation with white allies, but his words foreshadowed the fragmentation of the civil-rights movement. Urban life had promised so much, yet yielded so little. In every city conditions seemed the same: police harassment, inadequate housing, inferior schools and municipal services, neglect by public officials, discriminatory courts, discriminatory consumer-credit practices, unemployment, and underemployment. Even blacks who had achieved some success were often excluded from many white neighborhoods. Thus the Kerner Commission, appointed by President Johnson to investigate the causes of the riots, speculated that "what the rioters appeared to be seeking was fuller participation in the social order and the material benefits enjoyed by the majority of American citizens. Rather than rejecting the American system, they were anxious to obtain a place for themselves in it."

As a number of black leaders, many of them graduates of the civil-rights movement in the cities, began to retreat from integration as a major objective, they turned back to the ghetto itself to try to find there a means to win a place in the American system. Race pride, which had grown during the equal rights crusades, now blossomed as African fashions, soul music, and soul food became symbols of identity and solidarity rather than ordinary features of ghetto life. Militants demanded a place for black history and black studies in high-school and college curricula, which ordinarily excluded the black experience altogether. A new cohort of black leaders sought to develop independent bases of political and economic power. This strategy aimed to utilize blacks' greatest resource in the city: their numbers. The Reverend Jesse Jackson of Chicago first rose to national prominence as a fiery spokesman for black capitalism, whose boycott campaign against the A&P food chain prodded the company to hire seven hundred black workers, market black products, deposit in black-owned banks, advertise in black media, and contract with black construction firms and service companies. Jackson's Operation Breadbasket was used against other companies and had spread to fifteen other cities by 1970. "We are going to see to it," he stated in a 1969 interview, "that the resources of the ghetto are not si-phoned off by outside groups. Right now, black exterminating companies don't even get the contracts to kill the ghetto's rats. But that's going to change. If a building goes up in the black community, we're going to build it. And we're going to stop anyone else from building it." (2) In 1973 Lonnie King, director of the Atlanta branch of the NAACP, offered the city a plan that abandoned school integration and busing in return for nine black appointments to the city's seventeen-member school board. (The plan so undermined the NAACP's long-standing goal to integrate schools that the national organization threatened to revoke the Atlanta chapter's char-ter.) In many cities black political candidates were seeking office they never would have considered a generation ago—only now they could command the votes that made their chances altogether possible. In 1970 fifty cities had black mayors, and by 1974 black men had been elected mayor of six major cities—Atlanta, Cleveland, Detroit, Gary, Los Angeles, and Newark (and two were appointed mayors—of Cincinnati and Washington, D.C.) (see Chapter 9). Many of these black politicians pledged services to all races, and some received considerable white support. But their positions reflected the widening of black influence on local politics.

The tactics of the civil rights movement set the terms for various kinds of community protest during the next decade. Increasingly in the late 1960s blacks and whites who lived in cities connected their deteriorating situation with the impact of redevelopment. Between 1964 and 1968 urban riot areas were also the sites of major renewal efforts. The Woodlawn Organization in Chicago fought a long battle against a renewal plan cospon-sored by the University of Chicago and the city that would annex a mile-long strip of the neighborhood for university expansion. After sit-ins and demonstrations, Woodlawn residents gained concessions from Mayor Rich-ard Daley, including a majority of seats on the project supervisory commit-tee and a guarantee that no neighborhood demolition would take place until new housing was built for displaced residents.

Community groups turned on local redevelopment agencies as the most visible agent of displacement and housing shortages. In San Francisco in 1967, black residents of the Western Addition area protested the destruc-tion of a thriving commercial and residential neighborhood by forming a broad-based community organization whose members picketed San Fran-cisco Redevelopment Authority offices, seized the stage at public hearings, and lay down in front of bulldozers. In Boston in 1968, community activists in renewal neighborhoods occupied city redevelopment offices and built a tent city over a parking lot to dramatize displacement of the poor families previously housed there. In Cambridge, neighborhood residents fought to save neighborhoods slated for destruction for highway construction. The highway plan was supported by local government officials, local universi-ties, and good government and civic associations, but a protracted struggle

Stopping the Highways   This mural, entitled "Beat the Belt" (acrylic on masonry), was painted in 1980 by artist Bernard La Casse on the side wall of a Cambridge, Massachusetts supermarket. The mural commemorates the broad-based movement to save inner city housing and neighborhoods by stopping the proposed inner belt bighway, and celebrates the continuing struggle to maintain affordable housing and economic diversity in local neighborhoods. *(Photograph by James D. Smith.)*

finally forced the governor of Massachusetts to declare a moratorium on all highway construction in the Boston metropolitan area in 1970. By the late 1960s, neighborhood activism successfully disrupted the progrowth consensus, raising the social cost of renewal and redevelopment to prohibitive levels.

FEDERAL RESPONSE TO URBAN CRISIS

During the 1950s the course of federal policy toward cities had generated new favors for private interests. The problems of the poor had been exacerbated by the impact of highway building and downtown development. Postwar national prosperity, particularly during the first Eisenhower administration, had deflected direct concern with the total problems of cities. Federal leaders had paid little attention to the huge in-migrations of poor people pressing against all the facilities of central cities.

In the 1960s this trend changed. President John F. Kennedy's reference to a New Frontier and his promise of federal support for schools, medical care, urban transportation, and planning particularly caught the interest of civic leaders. Kennedy sought to fulfill his commitments by pumping new funds into old programs for housing, renewal, pollution control, and mass transit. His President's Committee on Juvenile Delinquency initiated several projects that organized slum communities to work out solutions to their own problems, a tactic that later became central to the War on Poverty. These policies and the metropolitan emphases of cabinet members such as Arthur Goldberg and Abraham Ribicoff were directed at inner cities and inner suburbs, where Kennedy had elicited considerable voter support. However, Kennedy's attempt to create a cabinet department of urban affairs failed when southern congressmen balked his intention to nominate a distinguished black housing expert, Robert C. Weaver, as secretary. Creation of the Department of Housing and Urban Development was delayed until 1966. Once again, the only way advocates of comprehensive federal action in the realm of urban policy could win broad support was by emphasizing housing.

President Lyndon Johnson and his advisers mounted an even greater attack against urban problems, particularly against poverty, in their attempt to build the Great Society. In 1964 Johnson pressed Congress to pass the Economic Opportunity Act, which created the Office of Economic Opportunity. This agency directed a number of programs designed to end domestic poverty: Job Corps, a community skill-training program for young people; Head Start, an educational boost for preschool children with disadvantaged backgrounds; Volunteers in Service to America (VISTA), a domestic Peace Corps; Legal Aid; and the Community Action Program, which encouraged "maximum feasible involvement" of neighborhood residents in policy planning. Other legislation expanded the food-stamp program, funded old and new housing programs, and provided federal monies to modernize hospitals. In 1966 the Johnson administration launched the Model Cities program, a new variant of renewal that targeted federal funds to special districts where locally elected boards had hammered out a coordinated plan for the improvement of housing, health, education, employment, and welfare. Like War on Poverty measures, Model Cities emphasized neighborhood participation in community projects, an objective that often stirred conflict among community organizations and professional politicians, social workers and planning consultants who were used to making decisions for the community. Although federal officials tried to approve only those Model City projects that would not undermine locally elected officials, many funded projects had the opposite effect. Antipoverty programs informed the poor of their legal right to welfare and how to assert it. Welfare-rights groups sprang up that disrupted welfare offices and staged demonstrations to demand more adequate benefits in New York City, Baltimore, Los Angeles, Boston, Chicago, San Francisco, and Cleveland. These were organized by welfare recipients and poverty-program workers, some of whom had been former civil rights activists. Public-assistance lawyers tested the legality of renewal displacements. Black and Hispanic leaders challenged political machines through their presence on community-action councils, and one political scientist has estimated that almost one-fourth of all blacks elected to city executive posts, city councils, and state houses of representatives between 1964 and 1977 gained political experience working in community-action programs. Great Society urban spending may have been an attempt to consolidate urban support for the Democratic party and to quiet black discontent with poverty funding, but its actual impact neither ended poverty nor quelled urban protest.

In 1960 there were forty-four federal grant programs allocating $3.9 billion to the nation's largest cities. By the beginning of 1969 the number of these programs for urban America had risen to over five hundred, and annual appropriations had climbed to $14 billion. When Richard M. Nixon and the Republicans moved into the White House in 1969, they did not stem this flow of federal funding. Instead, federal aid to cities rose to $26.8 billion in 1974. But Nixon did attempt to restructure federal policy to eliminate the programs that emphasized neighborhood participation in policy-making and that undercut the authority of elected city officials. Thus in 1972 Nixon convinced Congress to terminate the Model Cities program. Although Democrats in Congress were able to increase funding for social security and food stamps, the president impounded funds from federal housing and rehabilitation programs in 1973.

In place of these programs Nixon proposed to establish a New Federalism, the return of policy-making decisions to state and local levels. The keystone of this policy was revenue sharing, the distribution of federal funds directly to local governments rather than through federal agencies. Despite strong opposition the State and Local Fiscal Assistance Act passed Congress in 1972, and during the succeeding winter checks totalling $5.3 billion were distributed to thirty-eight thousand state and local governments. Two-thirds of the money went directly to cities and towns to be used in nine possible areas: public safety, administration, transportation, health, environmental protection, capital expenditures, libraries, recreation, and social services for the poor and aged. Beyond these priorities the money could be spent without federal guidelines—except that discrimination by race, sex, ethnicity, or religion was prohibited. Nixon also proposed special revenue-sharing block grants to be distributed explicitly for use in education, law enforcement, manpower training, and urban community development.

As president, Nixon and his administration fomented racial polarization, taking a public stand against civil rights. In 1970 newspapers disclosed a memo written by Daniel Patrick Moynihan, Nixon's advisor on urban affairs and social welfare, that recommended that "the issue of race could benefit from a period of benign neglect." Attorney General John Mitchell tried to delay school desegregation in Mississippi and to prevent extension of the 1965 Voting Rights Act. Nixon's judicial appointments included G. Harold Carswell, a self-identified segregationist. In opposition to the 1971 Supreme Court decision *Swann v. Charlotte-Mecklenburg,* which upheld a school integration plan that relied on extensive cross-town busing, Nixon proposed a Congressional moratorium on busing and publicly denounced busing as a reckless and extreme remedy for segregation. A product himself of the Sun Belt, Nixon's political strategy was to cultivate conservative southern support for the Republican party.

Racial polarization in Boston expressed the spirit of the Nixon years. The Boston public schools had become increasingly segregated in the 1960s because when the city's black population increased considerably, the Irish-dominated School Committee used techniques of district gerrymandering, busing, and student transfers to keep white schools white. A long campaign by black parents for access to improved educational facilities for their children, which had involved running candidates for the school board, staging sit-ins at the School Committee, and organizing a voluntary busing program, finally culminated in a challenge in federal court accusing the Boston School Committee of illegal segregation. Boston's white ethnic groups blamed federal intervention and black migrants for a redevelopment economy of scarce blue-collar jobs and housing and rising taxes and rents. When Judge Arthur Garrity ordered the School Committee to begin a program of school desegregation and busing in the fall of 1974, white neighborhoods organized antibusing groups to protest school desegregation with motorcades, rallies, demonstrations, boycotts, and violent attacks on black students in white neighborhoods. A Pulitzer Prize–winning photograph captured a crowd of antibusing protesters attacking a black professional on his way to work in front of city hall, running at him with the sharp end of a flagstaff flying an American flag.

Part of Nixon's politics of polarization was his campaign to separate the working poor from the unemployed by his attacks on welfare recipients and what he referred to as the "welfare mess." During the 1960s the number of welfare recipients in this country mushroomed. Much of the new pressure on the welfare system resulted from the government's own urban policy. The community-action programs of the Kennedy administration and particularly the Johnson administration had encouraged poor people to organize in their own interest. Welfare-rights movements, plus continuing in-migrations of poverty-stricken rural and minority families forced a tremendous welfare expansion, especially in big cities. Moreover, as Frances Fox Piven and Richard A. Cloward have asserted in *Regulating the Poor,* fears of racial violence in the mid-sixties moved local officials to expand welfare rolls as a means of soothing tensions.[3] As a result, relief cases tripled in many cities between 1960 and 1970. By 1970 the New York City welfare rolls contained a million people, a population larger than those of fifteen states. In 1971 one out of every ten residents of the nation's twenty largest metropolitan areas depended on some form of public relief. The most common forms of welfare included Aid to Families with Dependent Children, unemployment compensation, food stamps, housing supplements or public housing, and free medical care. Although state and federal agencies supported some of these programs, local government carried most of the burden. In 1970 the welfare budget of New York City alone was $1.4 billion. Cities also received most of the criticism for sustaining welfare cheaters. Sometimes charges were warranted, but more often the needs of the genuinely poor overwhelmed cities, straining local revenues with millions of cases like that of a nineteen-year-old New York woman who wrote on her welfare application, "I have no one to help me. I was living with my grandmother, but she put me out on the street with my two children."

Frequently the burdens of poverty have fallen most heavily on women. The experience of a black welfare mother named Johnnie Tillmon is illustrative. She grew up in Arkansas, working there for fifteen years in a laundry before she moved with her six children to California. In 1963 she became too sick to work any more, and as she explained it, friends there helped her to go on welfare. Tillmon wrote in 1972, "Welfare's like a traffic accident. It can happen to anyone, but especially it happens to women." Welfare mothers became a vocal pressure group in many big cities. These women—black and white, married and unmarried—were caught between the self-help ethic on one side and requisites of family support on the other. They also received considerable abuse from welfare critics. Civil rights activities and community-action programs have brought these women together, so that they constitute the vanguard of welfare-rights and tenants' organizations. Welfare mothers participated actively in local hearings and lobbied forcefully for day-care centers, housing reform, job training, fairer relief allotments, and more humane treatment by public officials.

CRACKS IN THE PICTURE WINDOW: LIFE IN THE SUBURBS

The suburbs beckoned as an escape from city problems of downtown developers, desegregation, and demonstrations. The 1970 census revealed that more people lived in suburbs than in cities. Of two hundred million people, seventy-six million lived in suburban rings around cities, sixty-four million lived in cities themselves, and sixty million lived in nonmetropolitan areas. Almost three-fourths of the total housing stock in the United States has been built since 1940, two-thirds of it single-family detached homes, the majority of it in suburbs. Single-family housing, yards, shopping malls, and freeway boundaries characterized the bedroom communities that were the housing of choice for the millions of Americans who could afford to move out.

The 1950s were years of early marriages and young families, the very occupants for whom the suburbs seemed best suited. The presumption was that husbands would go off to the city to work, leaving wives at home to care for children. The daytime suburban world would be a community of women and children, joined by men at night and on the weekends. Suburban home design reflected these presumptions. Each house in Levittown was intended to be a self-contained world marked off by a white picket fence. Inside were a standardized living room with television set built into the wall and a kitchen with a Bendix washing machine built into the laundry alcove. The houses' large lots and grassy lawns emphasized privacy; plans for public space and social services were sacrificed to private acreage. Most communities required automobiles for access to stores and schools.

The suburban ideal was widely pictured in mass culture. Even "Duckburg," where comic-book character Donald Duck lived with his nephews, was clearly a Los Angeles suburb characterized by single-family homes and freeways. In *Life* magazine's special 1956 issue on American women the most space was devoted to a suburban woman, aged thirty-two and mother of four. A high-school graduate who had married as a teenager, *Life's* model mother was a hostess, volunteer, and "home manager" who sewed her own clothes, entertained fifteen hundred guests a year, and was supported by a husband whose annual income was $25,000. "In her daily rounds she attends clubs or charity meetings, drives the children to school, does the weekly grocery shopping, makes ceramics, and is planning to learn French," *Life* revealed as it followed the housewife from domestic chores to social events. "A conscientious mother, she spends lots of time with her children, helping with their homework . . . listening to their stories or problems." The suburban housewife was the model of domesticity in the 1950s. Born in the depression, most suburban homemakers appreciated the security and standard of living represented by a suburban life-style. A Gallup poll taken in 1962 reported that "few people are as happy as a housewife." But the poll also predicted future changes when most women interviewed revealed their hopes that their daughters would have more education and marry later than they did. Ninety percent of the women interviewed hoped that their daughters would not "lead the same kind of life they did."

Women's lives even in the suburbs were already changing in two important ways. First of all the demographics of early marriage and child rearing meant that suburban women more quickly than their mothers would come to a point in their lives when their responsibilities for children would lessen. More than half their adult lives would be spent neither having children nor caring for them. Second, married women, and in particular married women with children, were more likely each year to be at work. In the 1950s the demand for low-paid, qualified workers in such occupations as sales, service, and office work grew. Clerical jobs multiplied so quickly that by 1960 one of three women wage earners held one. At the same time, young women's likelihood of marrying and having children early limited the supply of single working women. Postwar inflation meant that families often needed a second income, even at the low wages that women commanded, to maintain homes and cars and to save for children's education. The rising proportion of working mothers would shift suburban life-styles; with less time for laundry, carpools, and gardening, working mothers would ultimately join women activated by civil rights and antiwar struggles in the new women's movement. The climate in the 1960s that fostered movements to attain equal rights for minorities and publicized their tactics alerted women to the nature of economic and social discrimination and prodded them to attempt to transcend their circumscribed roles, calling for new kinds of equality in the workplace and a new division of household labor at home.

Suburban communities were themselves more varied than mass culture images revealed, ranging from wealthy and exclusive suburbs in Marin County near San Francisco to heavily ethnic and working-class Cicero, Illinois, and Hamtramck, Michigan. By the 1970s the range of suburbs stretched from residential to industrial, wealthy to modest, white to black. Aging housing stock in inner suburban rings around such places as Chicago, New York, Washington, D.C., and St. Louis increasingly made these suburbs indistinguishable from the adjacent urban core. Although suburbs grew as places of single-family homes, much recent suburban construction was of apartment buildings for three reasons: (1) the communities needed the tax revenues that multiple-dwelling structures provide; (2) inhabitants of these communities no longer could afford homeownership; and (3) suburbs that once housed young families were aging. One result of this trend was that some suburban school systems began to flounder from lack of pupils and finances. Analysts estimate that by 1990, for example, the proportion of children under 14 in suburban Long Island will decline by 40 percent from 1970 levels, forcing many schools to close.

Even the most widely recognized characteristic of suburban life, commuting, has undergone changes. The companies that moved into urban outskirts brought thousands of jobs with them and jumbled commuting patterns. In the early 1960s alone the central cities of metropolitan areas with over 250,000 people lost 338,000 manufacturing jobs while their suburbs added 443,000 such jobs. White-collar employment in suburbia expanded even more rapidly. Pollsters in 1980 found that over 70 percent of suburban residents worked in their own or another suburb. In the New York area one-third of suburban workers were employed in a suburb other than their own, and only one-fifth commuted to the city.

Shifts in the political loyalties of suburbanites paralleled their rising share of the population. In the 1950s suburban voters led the march toward Eisenhower Republicanism. In 1956, for example, the Republican vote in suburbs around Philadelphia, New York, Chicago, St. Louis, and San Francisco was large enough to supersede Democratic majorities inside those cities and thereby to make significant contributions to President Eisenhower's reelection. In the 1960s, however, sizable proportions of suburbia dwellers voted for Democratic candidates. In 1964, for example, Lyndon Johnson captured nearly two-thirds of the suburban vote, although Republican majorities in nonpresidential elections were maintained in the suburbs. By the 1970s it became much more difficult to identify suburban voters with one party or another. Political analysts uncovered wide incidences of ticket splitting (a voter casting ballots for candidates of both major parties rather than for all candidates from one party) in national, state, and local elections. As all Americans, and suburbanites in particular, became better educated and more affluent, party identification became less secure and more voters declared themselves to be independents.

These fluctuations in party affiliation indicated that middle-class white suburbanites really had several loyalties. On the one hand they were pursuing an old American dream: security in private surroundings, a flirtation with nature, small-community political autonomy, and escape from the disorganization and complexities of crowded cities. These have been the ideals of the ambitious, aggressive family, and during this century they attached to the ideology of the Republican party. On the other hand many of the families now populating middle-class suburbs were second- and third-generation immigrants only once removed from the inner city. The expansion of the aircraft industry in southern California brought unionized workers to Los Angeles suburbs. By the late 1970s three-quarters of all AFL-CIO members were purchasing their homes on long mortgages. Many brought with them remnants of urban liberalism, that bundle of welfare and labor goals traditionally attached to the Democratic party. Yet the new suburbanites have sought to protect their stake in the middle-class dream by strongly supporting measures to keep out "undesirables": blacks, Chicanos, and other minority groups. (In 1970 only 5 percent of the nation's black population lived in suburbs.) Thus to protect their interests suburbanites became issue oriented, not party oriented. And they reached to protect these interests at the expense of others. Finally suburbs, particularly those closest to the city, have begun to experience the problems of urban life that suburbanites originally sought to escape—soaring taxes, crowding, creeping decay, pollution, and crime. The growth of these problems has forced many suburban officials to abandon a self-help stance and to seek aid from metropolitan, state, and federal agencies. The lines dividing suburbs from city had begun to blur.

BIBLIOGRAPHY

For an overview of this period see Kenneth Fox, *Metropolitan America: Urban Life and Urban Policy in the United States, 1940–1980* (Jackson: University of Mississippi Press,

1986) and Jon C. Teaford, *The Twentieth Century American City: Problem, Promise and Reality* (Baltimore: Johns Hopkins University Press, 1986).

On the impact of World War II on cities see Roger Lotchin, ed., *The Martial Metropolis: American Cities in War and Peace* (New York: Praeger, 1984); Mauricio Mazon, *The Zoot-Suit Riots: The Psychology of Symbolic Annihilation* (Austin: University of Texas Press, 1984); Dominic J. Capeci, Jr., *The Harlem Race Riot of 1943* (Philadelphia: Temple University Press, 1977); Alfred Lee and Norman Humphrey, *Race Riot* (New York: Dryden Press, 1943); Harvard Sitkoff, "Racial Militancy and Interracial Violence in the Second World War," *Journal of American History* 58 (December 1971):661–81. On Appalachian whites in Chicago see Todd Gittlin and Nanci Hollander, *Up Town: Poor Whites in Chicago* (New York: Harper and Row Publishers, 1970).

On the emergence of the Sunbelt after World War II see Carl Abbott, *The New Urban America: Growth and Politics in Sunbelt Cities* (Chapel Hill: University of North Carolina Press, 1981); Alfred J. Watkins and David C. Perry, eds., *The Rise of Sunbelt Cities* (Beverly Hills, Calif.: Sage, 1977); Richard Bernard and Bradley Rice, eds., *Sunbelt Cities: Politics and Growth Since WWII* (Austin: University of Texas Press, 1983); Bradford Luckingham, *The Urban Southwest: A Profile History of Albuquerque, El Paso, Phoenix, Tucson* (El Paso: Texas Western Press, 1982); Franklin J. James, *Minorities in the Sunbelt* (New Brunswick, N.J.: Rutgers University Press, 1984). On individual southern and western cities see Don Doyle, *Nashville Since the 1920s* (Knoxville: University of Tennessee Press, 1985); David McComb, *Houston: A History*, rev. ed. (Austin: University of Texas Press, 1981); Francisco Rosales and Barry J. Kaplan, eds., *Houston: A Twentieth Century Urban Frontier* (Port Washington, N.Y.: Associated Faculty Press, 1983); David R. Johnson, John A. Booth, and Richard J. Harris, eds., *The Politics of San Antonio: Community, Progress, and Power* (Lincoln: University of Nebraska Press, 1983); Carl Abbott, *Portland: Planning, Politics and Growth in a Twentieth Century City* (Lincoln: University of Nebraska Press, 1983); Christopher Silver, *Twentieth Century Richmond: Planning, Politics and Race* (Knoxville: University of Tennessee Press, 1984). See also David Goldfield, *Cottonfields and Skyscrapers: Southern City and Region, 1607–1980* (Baton Rouge: Louisiana State University Press, 1982).

On highway building see Mark Rose, *Interstate: Express Highway Politics, 1941–1956* (Lawrence: University of Kansas Press, 1979). See also K.H. Schaeffer and Elliot Sclar, *Access for All: Transportation and Urban Growth* (Baltimore: Penguin, 1975). For a discussion of the transformation of the roadside see Karal Ann Marling, *The Colossus of Roads: Myth and Symbol Along the American Highway* (Minneapolis: University of Minnesota Press, 1984); Chester Leibs, *Main Street to Miracle Mile: American Roadside Architecture* (New York: New York Graphic Society, 1985); Thomas Schlereth, *U.S. 40: A Roadscape of the American Experience* (Bloomington: University of Indiana Press, 1985). See also Stan Luxemberg, *Roadside Empires: How the Chains Franchised America* (New York: John Wiley & Sons, 1985).

On progrowth coalitions and urban renewal programs in various cities see John Mollenkopf, *The Contested City* (Princeton, N.J.: Princeton University Press, 1983); David Tucker, *Memphis Since Crump: Bossism, Blacks, and Civic Reform, 1948–68* (Knoxville: University of Tennessee Press, 1980); Frederick Wirt, *Power and the City* (Berkeley: University of California Press, 1975); Robert Dahl, *Who Governs: Democracy and Power in an American City* (New Haven, Conn.: Yale University Press, 1961); Roy Lubove, *Twentieth Century Pittsburgh: Government, Business and Environmental Change* (New York: John Wiley & Sons, 1969); Robert Caro, *The Power Broker: Robert Moses and the Fall of New York* (New York: Vintage, 1974); Edward Haas, *DeLesseps S. Morrison and the Image of Reform: New Orleans Politics, 1946–61* (Baton

Rouge: Louisiana State University Press, 1974). On urban renewal see Scott Greer, *Urban Renewal and American Cities* (Indianapolis: Bobbs-Merrill, 1965); James Q. Wilson, ed., *Urban Renewal: The Record and the Controversy* (Cambridge, Mass.: M.I.T. Press, 1966); Jewel Bellush and Murray Hausknecht, eds., *Urban Renewal: People, Politics, and Planning* (Garden City, N.Y.: Anchor Books, 1967). For a portrait of urban renewal's impact on one older ethnic neighborhood see *Mission Hill and the Miracle of Boston,* a documentary film distributed by Cine Research, 32 Fisher Ave., Boston, MA, 02120.

On the history of public housing see Anthony Jackson, *A Place Called Home: A History of Low-Cost Housing in Manhattan* (Cambridge, Mass.: M.I.T. Press, 1976); Richard O. Davies, *Housing Reform During the Truman Administration* (Columbia: University of Missouri Press, 1966); Lawrence M. Friedman, *Government and Slum Housing: A Century of Frustration* (Chicago: Rand McNally & Co., 1968); Devereux Bowly, Jr., *The Poorhouse: Subsidized Housing in Chicago, 1895–1976* (Carbondale: Southern Illinois University Press, 1978); Arnold Hirsch, *Making the Second Ghetto: Race and Housing in Chicago, 1940–1960* (New York: Cambridge University Press, 1983); Dominic J. Capeci, Jr., *Race Relations in Wartime Detroit: The Sojourner Truth Housing Controversy, 1937–42* (Philadelphia: Temple University Press, 1984). See also Neil Lebowitz, " 'Above Party, Class or Creed': Rent Control in the Central States, 1940–1947," *Journal of Urban History* 7(August, 1981): 439–70; Chester Hartman, ed., *America's Housing Crisis* (New York: Methuen, 1983). On Los Angeles see Thomas S. Hine, "Housing, Baseball, and Creeping Socialism: The Battle of Chavez Ravine, Los Angeles, 1949–1959," *Journal of Urban History* 8(February 1982):123–43. On Boston see *Down the Projects,* a documentary on the history of public housing in the city, distributed by Cine Research, 32 Fisher Ave., Boston, MA 02120.

On the origins of the civil rights movement see Rhoda Lois Blumberg, *Civil Rights* (Boston: Twayne Publishers, 1984); Aldon Morris, *The Origins of the Civil Rights Movement: Black Communities Organized for Change* (New York: Free Press, 1984); Doug McAdam, *Political Process and the Development of Black Insurgence, 1930–1970* (Chicago: University of Chicago Press, 1982); William Chafe, *Civilities and Civil Rights: Greensboro, North Carolina and the Black Struggle for Freedom* (New York: Oxford University Press, 1980); see also Frances Fox Piven and Richard A. Cloward, *Poor People's Movements: Why They Succeed and How They Fail* (New York: Vintage, 1979). On the 1960s riots see James W. Sullivan, *Race Riot: New York, 1964* (New York: Thomas Y. Crowell, 1964); David O. Sears and John B. McConahay, *The Politics of Violence: The New Urban Blacks and the Watts Riot* (Boston: Houghton-Mifflin Co., 1973); Hubert G. Locke, *The Detroit Riot of 1967* (Detroit: Wayne State University Press, 1969); Robert Fogelson, *Violence as Protest: A Study of Riots and Ghettos* (Garden City, N.Y.: Anchor Press, 1971); Hugh Davis Graham and Ted Roberts Gurr, eds., *Violence in America* (Washington D.C.: U.S. Government Printing Office, 1969). See also David Colburn, *Racial Change and Community Crisis: St. Augustine, Florida, 1877–1980* (New York: Columbia University Press, 1985). On the emergence of protest based in neighborhood organization see Harry Boyte, *The Backyard Revolution: Understanding the New Citizen's Movement* (Philadelphia: Temple University Press, 1980); Robert Fisher, *Let the People Decide: Neighborhood Organizing in America* (Boston: Twayne Publishers, 1984); Ira Katznelson, *City Trenches: Urban Politics and the Patterning of Class in the United States* (New York: Pantheon Books, 1981); Lloyd H. Rogler, *Migrant in the City: The Life of a Puerto Rican Action Group* (Maplewood, N.J.: Waterfront Press, 1986); Robert A. Slayton, *Back of the Yards: The Making of a Local Democracy* (Chicago: University of Chicago Press, 1986). On antihighway movements see Gordon Fellman in association with Barbara Brandt, *The Deceived Majority: Politics and Protest in Middle America* (New Brunswick, N.J.:

Transaction Books, 1973); Alan Lupo, Frank Colcord, and Edmund Fowler, *Rites of Way: The Politics of Transportation in Boston and the U.S. City* (Boston: Little, Brown, & Co., 1971); Richard O. Baumbach, Jr., and William E. Borah, *The Second Battle of New Orleans: A History of the Vieux Carre Riverfront Expressway Controversy* (Tuscaloosa: University of Alabama Press, 1981). On the emergence of tenants' organizing see Ronald Lawson and Mark Naison, eds., *The Tenant Movement in New York City, 1904– 1984* (New Brunswick, N.J.: Rutgers University Press, 1986). See also Henry Bedford, *Trouble Downtown: The Local Context of Twentieth Century America* (New York: Harcourt Brace Jovanovich, 1978).

On welfare see Frances Fox Piven and Richard A. Cloward, *Regulating the Poor: Functions of Public Welfare* (New York: Pantheon Books, 1971); and Michael B. Katz, *In the Shadow of the Poorhouse: A Social History of Welfare in America* (New York: Basic Books, 1986). See also Ann Withorn, *The Circle Game: Services for the Poor in Massachusetts, 1966–1978* (Amherst: University of Massachusetts Press, 1983); and Withorn, *Serving the People: Social Services and Social Change* (New York: Columbia University Press, 1984). On federal policy see James T. Patterson, *America's Response to Poverty, 1900–1980* (Cambridge, Mass.: Harvard University Press, 1981); Bernard Frieden and Marshall Kaplan, *The Politics of Neglect: Urban Aid from Model Cities to Revenue Sharing* (Cambridge, Mass.: M.I.T. Press, 1975).

On recent trends in suburbanization see Herbert J. Gans, *The Levittowners: Ways of Life and Politics in a New Suburban Community* (New York: Pantheon Books, 1967); Bennet M. Berger, *Working Class Suburbs: A Study of Auto Workers in Suburbia* (Berkeley: University of California Press, 1968); Scott Donaldson, *The Suburban Myth* (New York: Columbia University Press, 1969); Peter O. Muller, *Contemporary Suburban America* (Englewood Cliffs, N.J.: Prentice-Hall, 1981); Mathew Edel, Elliot Sclar, and Daniel Luria, *Shakey Palaces: Home Ownership and Social Mobility in Boston's Suburbanization* (New York: Columbia University Press, 1984); Jon C. Teaford, *City and Suburb: The Political Fragmentation of Metropolitan America, 1850–1970* (Baltimore: Johns Hopkins University Press, 1979); Robert Lake, *The New Suburbanites: Race and Housing* (New Brunswick, N.J.: Rutgers University Press, 1981); Thomas A. Clark, *Blacks in Suburbia: A National Perspective* (New Brunswick, N.J.: Rutgers University Press, 1979); Harold Rose, *Black Suburbanization* (Cambridge, Mass.: Ballinger Publishing Co., 1976); Michael Danielson, *The Politics of Exclusion* (New York: Columbia University Press, 1976). See also Dolores Hayden, *Redesigning the American Dream: The Future of Housing, Work, and Family Life* (New York: W.W. Norton & Co., 1984).

ENDNOTES

[1] Mike Royko, interview, in *The Good War: An Oral History of World War II* by Studs Terkel (New York: Pantheon Books, 1984), 137.

[2] "An Interview with Jesse Jackson," *Playboy.* 16(November 1969), 108.

[3] Francis Fox Piven and Richard A. Cloward, *Regulating the Poor: Functions of Public Welfare* (New York: Pantheon Books, 1971).

9

Prospects for Urban America: 1974–1986

TURNING POINTS

Between 1973 and 1974 an Arab embargo tripled the price of oil. The resulting energy crisis caused people to question the assumptions of suburban superiority for the first time in the twentieth century. Americans who had grown up with cheap and abundant energy were dependent on big, gas-guzzling cars to travel to work, and their single-family suburban homes were poorly insulated as well as crammed with electrical appliances. Government officials feared that the price of home air conditioning and heating would soar beyond the reach of even middle-class Americans. Gas shortages momentarily revived the attractiveness of mass transit, and the price of suburban real estate beyond the reach of public transportation began a temporary decline. Some people became wary of their commitment to automobiles and began to reconsider the advantages of downtown living.

The new downtown corporate economy, based on finance, banking, and insurance, plus expanding medical complexes and educational institutions provided employment opportunities for a highly educated and highly skilled work force, whose choice to live downtown near their jobs produced a market for high-rent luxury downtown housing. Young urban professionals participated in projects to remodel apartment houses and townhouses, often in the name of historic preservation and with government aid in the form of grants for renovations in registered historic districts. Renovation also was helped by federal loan programs like the Community Reinvestment Act of 1978, which pressured banks to invest some of their deposits in neighborhood businesses and housing. Increasingly downtown property owners tried to capitalize on renewed middle-class interest in inner-city neighborhoods by

Downtown Revival in Boston, Massachusetts City and state dignitaries in Massachusetts cut into a cake in the shape of the newly-restored Quincy Market to celebrate the reopening of the historic Faneuil Hall Market in 1976 as an upscale marketplace of restaurants, food stalls, shops and boutiques to attract tourists and suburbanites downtown. *(The Boston Redevelopment Authority.)*

converting old apartments into condominiums and offering the benefits—especially the tax breaks—of ownership without the worries of maintenance. Gentrification, the process by which wealthier groups occupy and restore run-down neighborhoods, propped up sagging tax bases by lifting property values but exacerbated housing problems for the poor by depleting the already short supply of low-rent housing and thus pushing low-income and minority groups out of their traditional neighborhoods.

The Census Bureau heralded these changes by reporting that 1974 migration patterns seemed to reverse the long-term trend of suburban growth at the cost of the central city. Growing numbers of single people living alone, childless and gay couples, and smaller families were also reshaping housing and consumption patterns. In 1973 and 1974 retail sales in downtown stores increased while suburban shopping centers began to falter. City movie houses, theaters, restaurants, and hotels were increasingly well patronized. The *Blue Book of Major Home Builders*, a survey of all builders who produce more than one thousand units a year, reported that

Gentrification in Older Downtown Neighborhoods   The houses along Montgomery Street in Baltimore, shown here in different stages of restoration, have attracted professionals to the old Federal Hill neighborhood, just one block from Baltimore's Inner Harbor, and the newly-built Maryland Science Center, National Aquarium, and the restaurant and shop-filled Harborplace. *(Photograph by Judith E. Smith.)*

by 1974 big builders were increasingly less likely to build detached single-family suburban housing and that in 1973 twice as many major home builders were rehabilitating older houses as in 1972.

The 1974 boost in the price of imported oil reverberated through the entire economy. High-cost fuel drove up both inflation and unemployment and considerably slowed overall economic growth. New office towers stood empty in New York and Chicago. New housing starts dropped from 2.4 million in 1972 to 2.1 million in 1973 to 1.5 million in 1974. As the national economy tightened, some employers sought to flee high taxes, energy costs, and labor costs by moving to newer, warmer, less labor-militant areas. Employees and their families migrated for similar reasons: cheaper living costs, less congestion, better job opportunities. An accelerating shift of businesses, jobs, and population from the northeastern "Frostbelt" to the southeastern, southwestern, and western "Sunbelt" had a profound impact on cities of all regions. Since World War II, the Sunbelt had captured a larger share of new growth industries such as defense, resort and retirement, petrochemicals, and aerospace, and a large proportion of new startups in both new and traditional industries. A band of fast-growing communities extended across the country's southern tier, among them the metropolitan areas of Tampa-Miami, Jacksonville, Dallas–Fort Worth, Phoenix, and the southern coast of California. Houston became the fastest growing city in the nation, with a population increase from two million to three million from 1970 to 1980 and boasted of more construction than any other American city. Meanwhile, northern metropolitan areas such as New York, Pittsburgh, Detroit, and Cleveland grew minimally or lost population.

Yet serious problems lurked in Sunbelt cities, problems of growth that resembled those of earlier eras. Although western cities deftly used annexation to prevent strangulation from suburbanization, their rapid growth left them disorganized, overly dependent on automobile transportation, and vexed by housing problems. The disorganization spilled over into social relations, and crime rates soared. Stories of muggings and murders made New York a feared city, yet in the late 1970s the homicide rates of Atlanta and Houston (almost 40 per 100,000 people per year) doubled that of New York. Phoenix, once a haven for people suffering from allergies and respiratory ailments, developed atmospheric pollution and pollen caused by the cars, flowers, trees, and shrubs brought to the city by its huge influx of northern immigrants.

Moreover, Sunbelt cities were plagued by poverty, though it in some ways differed from that in the North. Northern urban poverty was characterized chiefly by unemployed people who wanted to work but were unable to find jobs, and discouraged workers, those who were jobless because they did not believe they could find a job that would pay a satisfactory wage. In the Sunbelt, rates of unemployed and discouraged workers were much lower. Instead Sunbelt poverty consisted of involuntary part-time workers, people who wanted to work full time but could only find part-time jobs, and, more commonly, fully employed workers who were so underpaid that their earnings left them below adequate income levels. In the 1970s, El Paso, which attracted electronics firms and the garment industry from other parts of the country with its promise of available, low-paid Hispanic laborers, had the lowest per capita urban income in the Southwest. Sunbelt poverty was the direct result of the region's "good business climate," which attracted northern companies seeking large docile pools of low-wage workers. Thus Sunbelt cities suffered from poverty as much as Frostbelt cities did. Successful unionization drives to organize southern textile, garment, and hospital and service workers, despite bitter resistance from local companies drawing on enormous corporate resources, may in the end diminish the Sunbelt's "good business climate."

A changing federal-city relationship was presaged by passage in 1974 of the the Housing and Community Development Block Grant Act. This act, one of the first signed into law by President Gerald Ford, merged most federal grant programs into one program with single block grants totaling $8.4 billion over three years. These grants gave local officials more discretion over how to spend federal funds. Pledging that the act would avoid "red tape and excessive federal regulation," Ford announced that cities would have "greater certainty" about the level of funding they could expect and that officials could concentrate on comprehensive programs of community betterment rather than on seeking special or "categorical" grants for individual projects. Mayors and city managers, who were given ultimate authority over how to spend the grants, had only to apply annually, specifying their plans for community development and for meeting community needs, a program for eliminating or preventing housing deterioration, and a plan to serve housing needs of lower-income persons. Funds could be used for almost any purpose—public works, salaries, law enforcement, and special projects as well as for housing and job training. A formula based on population density, age of housing supply, and extent of poverty would determine how funds would be distributed to assure that needy cities would receive proportionately more than cities that were better off.

The goal of reinforcing local autonomy through revenue sharing and community-development block grants pumped new life into local planning efforts, but Supreme Court reapportionment gave the suburbs, fast becoming the new centers of population, political strength to secure funds at the expense of the cities. By 1970 only about twenty of the nation's 247 metropolitan areas were managed by fewer than ten local governmental bodies. Suburbanization and the proliferation of urban services had spawned thousands of new independent administrative authorities (municipalities, townships, school districts, and utilities districts). The Chicago area alone had over eleven hundred separate governments; Philadelphia, almost nine hundred; New York, almost six hundred. Not all these bodies qualified for revenue sharing, but their numbers raised fears among big-city officials that revenues would not be distributed according to need. Cities housing poverty-stricken racial minorities would not receive proportionately more than suburbs inhabited by affluent whites.

In practice, smaller cities, particularly the suburbs, benefited the most from revenue sharing: federal grants prevented local tax rates from rising, kept municipal salaries competitive, and funded new projects such as roads and sewage plants. In big cities, local officials had to spend most of their grants to avoid severe budget cuts and to sustain Great Society programs threatened by curtailment or impoundment of federal funds and by soaring inflation. Opponents of community development block grants complained that such grants encouraged corruption and blurred accountability. Under federal supervision, they argued, a city wishing to use federal funds to build a park had to create a public record of hearings, citizen participation, and a specific grant application. If no park was ever built, there were grounds for suspicion and even litigation. Block grants, however, contained few inherent checks on how they were spent and thus created greater opportunity for patronage and graft. The Community Development Act helped to create a new kind of city boss, one who personally held control over federal funds that the mayor could use almost at will. Both the Ford and Carter administrations used the disposition of block grants to gain political support. Local governments and cities became even more dependent on federal funding. The percentage of local governmental revenues from the federal government grew from 5.1 percent in 1970 to 12.9 percent in 1975; for municipalities, from 7.1 percent to 19.3 percent. In 1967, federal aid accounted for only 1 percent of St. Louis's budget and 2.1 percent of Buffalo's. By 1978 federal funds accounted for 54.7 percent and 69.2 percent, respectively. Federal aid also made up one-fourth to half of the operating revenues of countless other cities, including Baltimore, Philadelphia, Phoenix, Cleveland, and Detroit.

After his defeat of Gerald Ford for the presidency in 1976, Jimmy Carter tried to address urban problems, but the effects of Carter's federal policy were contradictory and confusing. Many efforts worked against each other. For example, the Carter administration strongly supported housing improvements, but the Federal Reserve Board, in its attempts to cool inflation, pushed interest rates to record high levels, forcing banks to restrict the financing of such improvements. And in 1980, at the same time that federal agencies were pumping money into declining cities, a report by Carter's Commission for a National Agenda for the Eighties suggested that some cities were not worthy of support because their decline was inevitable. Moreover, proliferating programs confounded any coordination of federal urban policy. In 1979, for example, the Department of Health, Education and Welfare, because of its huge aid programs, spent far more money on housing than did the Department of Housing and Urban Development.

In contrast, the impact of President Ronald Reagan's policies toward cities has been absolutely consistent. Cities' greater dependence on federal funds resulted in greater vulnerability to Reagan's budget cuts. Touting the virtues of private enterprise, Reagan began his first term as President by announcing pullbacks from public aid to cities and instead offering incentives to private investment, the benefits of which would supposedly trickle down to people in need of jobs, housing, and services. But urban "enterprise zones" and other programs promoted by the Reagan administration soon faded. Moreover, the resuscitation of private incentives, even with the accompanying economic upswing and plunge in interest rates, failed to alter the cities' problems of inequality. As an analysis of Reagan's early months in office concluded, "It is clear that the changes introduced make the distribution of income less equal and require some sacrifices by low-income families while granting large tax cuts to high-income families." As the impact of these "sacrifices" puts low-income families in the position of needing more services, cities will be unable to provide them because of loss of federal revenue and inability to raise local revenues.

FISCAL CRISIS

During the 1970s, urban administrations facing declining revenues tried to avoid tax increases and to balance city finances by cutting back department budgets. But to meet service obligations, such as road maintenance and sewer repair and to honor employees' union contracts, these departments often had to overspend their allotments. They escaped deficits by borrowing from the city's cash flow, hoping to repay such loans from anticipated revenues due the following year. The next year, however, they found it necessary to borrow again and to postpone balancing accounts another year. In this way, cities accumulated large internal debts. Initial revenue sharing funds helped pay back these cash advances, but the borrowing practices continued. As expenses mounted and sentiment against tax increases heated up, it became increasingly difficult for cities to repay and eliminate these loans. A sudden emergency could collapse the system and create a fiscal crisis. In 1979, for example, cleanup from a massive snowfall cost Chicago some $72 million. Once this bill was paid, however, the city had no cash left to meet other obligations, including its payroll. Only an emergency loan and a sharp tax hike forestalled a major catastrophe. And the federal administrations of Ford and Reagan were increasingly less willing to bail cities out.

The most publicized case of fiscal crisis occurred in New York City in 1974 and 1975. During the economic expansion of the 1960s the city borrowed large amounts of money from its banks; when the economic downturn in the early 1970s came, New York's budget was badly overextended. Nixon's new policy of fiscal federalism sharply curtailed aid to the city and reduced aid from the state as well, leading city officials to budget manipulation. Postponing payment on previous debts enabled newer obligations to be assumed. When the city's large banks withdrew from the New York bond market between October 1974 and March 1975, they pulled the rug out from under the city. In the end the banks did not scale down their loans to the city, but they raised the interest rates. By 1977, 20 percent of New York City's budget went to interest payments—the largest and fastest-growing single item.

Popular accounts of New York City's fiscal distress blamed greedy bankers, corrupt politicians, selfish municipal unions, and malingering welfare recipients for the city's troubles. Conventional explanations asserted that excessive municipal wages and exorbitant welfare payments caused the increased tax squeeze and that the solution was to "bite the bullet" and reduce those expenditures. At the time Treasury Secretary William Simon claimed that "New York spends in excess of three times more per capita than any city with a population over 1,000,000." News of the city's fiscal chaos unleashed a torrent of antiurban and often racist dismissal of the city's problems. The *New York Daily News* headline of October 30, 1975, paraphrased President Gerald Ford's public response to New York's dilemma: "FORD TO CITY: DROP DEAD."

A closer look at New York's finances revealed that the fiscal crisis was not caused by an excessive budget. Many of the services that in New York were provided by the city government were elsewhere provided by state, county, school-board, and special-district jurisdictions. When economists compared standard city functions alone, New York's per capita expenditures were less than those of many large, older cities such as Boston, Baltimore, and San Francisco and only slightly higher than those of Los Angeles. Philadelphia, Newark, and Baltimore each had more employees per capita. In real terms New York's welfare levels were lower than those of Chicago, Detroit, Philadelphia, and Milwaukee. The 12.6 percent of New York's population who received welfare benefits was lower than that of Baltimore (16.8 percent), St. Louis (16.4 percent), Philadelphia (16.4 percent), Boston (17.0 percent), and Washington, D.C. (14.9 percent).

The heart of New York City's fiscal crisis was the loss of 542,000 jobs as offices, plants, and stores moved to the suburbs and Sunbelt between 1969 and 1976. The city lost 40,000 more manufacturing jobs in the five years prior to 1976 than in the preceding twenty years. Job loss was inevitably followed by tax-revenue loss. Economists estimate that if the half million jobs that disappeared between 1969 and 1975 were still providing income for New Yorkers, the city would have received $1.5 billion in tax revenues and there would have been no fiscal crisis. New York was truly a victim of the economic shift to the suburbs and the Sunbelt.

Patterns of downtown development exacerbated New York's tax problem. If private towers occupied the land where the tax-exempt World Trade Center stood, the city would have received about $50 million in taxes. Instead, New York City taxpayers were (1) paying interest to the banks for the money lent to build the structure, (2) paying its operating deficit, (3) paying higher taxes to the state, which are turned over to the World Trade Center for high-cost office facilities, and (4) making up the tax reductions granted to other office buildings with vacancies due to offices moving to the World Trade Center.

Other cities faced similar job losses. Between 1965 and 1972 when New York City lost 16 percent of its jobs, Philadelphia lost 17 percent and New Orleans nearly 20 percent. Debt ceilings, taxpayer rebellion, and competition with other jurisdictions have placed limits on the cities' ability to raise funds. The general inability to make revenue sources stretch to fit expenditures mandated by the state and services demanded by the people has reached crisis proportions in many localities.

The long-term solution to New York City's fiscal crisis involved political decisions that were in line with previous patterns of corporate transformation of the central cities: business incentives for corporate investment and "planned shrinkage," dismantling services to low-income communities with the impact of pushing them out of the city. Announced in 1978 as the city's "New Urban Partnership" with business and heralded in a forty-six-page spread in *Business Week,* New York's package of business incentives included reduction of the corporate tax and commercial rent rates, lowering and capping of real property taxes, tax credits for the purchase of machinery, tax-exempt industrial bonds, and a generous program of tax abatements to stimulate construction. "Planned shrinkage" included cutting more than 160,000 off the city's welfare rolls, a cut of 60,000 in the city's work force, tuition fees at the formerly free City University, the closing of municipal hospitals, and skyrocketing subway fares. For many New Yorkers, especially minorities and the poor, the quality of life declined.

Dennis Kucinich, the white ethnic populist mayor of Cleveland, made different political choices in the face of Cleveland's problematic municipal economy. In his short term as mayor from 1977 to 1979, he killed a deal with Republic Steel to build a $20 million dock to handle one thousand–foot ore boats, charging that the plan would create few jobs and that what would amount to a $153.5 million public subsidy over the life of the agreement was too high a public cost for the city to bear. Over the objections of the city council, Kucinich stopped a tax-abatement program on the grounds that it only produced windfall profits to downtown developers and did not bring widespread benefits of growth to the city. Kucinich's refusal to follow the recommendation of local bankers and sell the city's public utility, Muny Light, to Cleveland Electric Illuminating Company, the city's private utility, led the banks to call in the city's loans and the city to default, the first by a major city since the depression. Although the media labeled Kucinich the cause of Cleveland's decline and his successor the architect of "Comeback City," economic analysis suggested that reports of Cleveland's demise under Kucinich were greatly exaggerated and that despite the efforts of new mayors, Cleveland's economic decline continues. Incidents of fiscal crisis illuminated the political conflicts under the surface of urban economic directions and suggest the hard choices facing cities looking into the future.

NEIGHBORHOOD INITIATIVES

The wide range of community protest in the 1950s and 1960s moved into city hall in the 1970s. Women's expanding political activism resulted in pioneer women mayors such as Kathryn J. Whitmire in Houston, Donna Owens in Toledo, and Diane Feinstein in San Francisco. Newly registered minority voters and district representation campaigns brought black, Hispanic, white ethnic, and gay voices into local government. By the mid-1970s, six major cities—Washington, D.C., Newark, New Orleans, Baltimore, Atlanta, and Gary—were over 50 percent black. A new generation of black mayors took over the reins of local government: Richard Hatcher in Gary, Indiana, Carl Stokes in Cleveland, Kenneth Gibson in Newark, Coleman Young in Detroit, Maynard Jackson and Andrew Young in Atlanta, Tom Bradley in Los Angeles, Marion Berry in Washington, D.C., Ernest Morial in New Orleans, Harold Washington in Chicago, Wilson Goode in Philadelphia, Richard Arrington in Birmingham, and Henry Marsh and Roy West in Richmond. Although in the South political "reforms" for reapportionment, at-large elections, annexation, and consolidation have been proposed to dilute black electoral strength, black voters have continued to hold onto their political influence.

As blacks have won the highest office in urban politics, they have sometimes inherited more of a problem than a prize. Black mayors have taken over cities when local revenues were drying up, when municipal expenses were skyrocketing, when the nation was in a recession, and when Reagan's budget cuts slashed federal aid to the cities. Nevertheless, blacks have fared significantly better in these cities because black mayors have been more likely to engage in vigorous affirmative-action efforts that have given blacks access to municipal jobs. City purchases from businesses owned by members of minority groups have increased, and community programs have helped to diminish crime. In other cities, like Chicago, black mayors have had to contend with entrenched machine interests that have blocked them from implementing their own policies. However, the focus of new black political activity extends beyond electoral campaigns to more broadly raising the political and social consciousness of black, poor, and working-class people in the cities and developing policy alternatives to enhance the quality of urban life for all people.

The presence of significant new immigration in the 1970s presents a continuing challenge to existing patterns of political representation and social coexistence. The new migration in this period has come primarily from Latin America and Asia, with smaller percentages from Europe and Canada. In particular cities new migrants have constituted a considerable political and social force. In Miami in 1980, Hispanic residents made up 55 percent of the population within city limits, and 35 percent of its metropolitan totals. In 1985 the city's first Cuban-born mayor was elected, defeating the Puerto Rican incumbent. In 1983, in New York City 36 percent of the five boroughs' population was born in other countries. This seems particularly significant when compared to the 42 percent foreign-born in New York in 1910 at the height of European immigration. Los Angeles, with a population by the early 1980s that was 10 percent Asian and 32 percent Hispanic, boasts the second largest Mexican urban population in the world.

In 1979–80, a quarter of the schoolchildren in Los Angeles County were less fluent in English than in one of a hundred other languages. As with earlier waves of migration, the new migrants will bring new vitality, new social, economic, and cultural institutions, new needs for services, and new claims for political inclusion to cities in the years to come.

Law suits charging that at-large representation has discriminated against minorities and grass-roots neighborhood campaigns for greater representation have revived district representation in cities like Albuquerque, Richmond, San Antonio, San Francisco, and Boston. Albuquerque citizens voted down nonpartisan, at-large representation, replacing it with a district council in 1974. In San Antonio a community organization, Communities Organized for Public Service (COPS), organized westside Chicano residents and challenged downtown development, urging that growth projects be redirected to urban neighborhoods. A 1972 annexation that stretched San Antonio's city boundaries to encompass 300 square miles was successfully challenged by the U.S. Justice Department in 1976 on the grounds that adding Anglo voters to the city by annexation would dilute minority power. The final court decision offered the city a choice between reversing its annexation or returning to a district electoral system. In 1977, elections based on local districts gave San Antonio's ethnic neighborhoods direct access to political office for the first time since 1914. In 1977 five Mexican-Americans and one black were elected to the city council, and in 1981 the city elected its first Mexican-American mayor, Henry Cisneros. In Richmond a similar court challenge redefined city council districts such that voters were able to elect a majority of black members to the city council in 1977.

In San Francisco, grass-roots activism to stop urban renewal helped to elect George Moscone as mayor on a neighborhood-oriented platform. In 1976 Moscone appointed a planning commission committed to neighborhood growth and to exploring the neighborhood consequences of downtown development, and residents voted for a city initiative calling for district elections for the board of supervisors. In 1977, newcomers brought into the board of supervisors by district elections included Ella Hill Hutch from the largely black Western Addition, gay activist Harvey Milk who represented a growing liberal and gay constituency in the Haight-Ashbury/Castro/Noe District, and Dan White, a former city policeman and San Francisco firefighter, representing the white, Catholic, ethnic lower-middle-class and working-class neighborhoods of Portola, Excelsior, Visitacion Valley, and Crocker-Amazon. A political analysis of the results of the district elections suggested that "the sources of power which had previously drawn strength from a city wide base—downtown business, organized labor, the two major papers—found their influence sharply reduced, while neighborhood groups grew in power and the role of campaign financing was downgraded."

District representation's new, progressive coalition building on issues such as limiting high-rise development and protecting low-rent housing stock with rent control were cut off in midstream by the tragic deaths of Mayor Moscone and Supervisor Milk at the hand of Dan White. White, apparently troubled by personal economic pressures and his own ineffectiveness as a supervisor and disturbed by the increasing presence of minorities and a gay subculture in the city, suddenly resigned his own supervisor's position. Under pressure from neighborhood supporters, he just as suddenly changed his mind and asked Moscone for his seat back. Moscone's liberal supporters including Milk pressured Moscone to accept White's resignation and replace him with a more liberal appointee who supported Moscone's policies. After several weeks of vacillation, Moscone did decide to replace White, who learned of the decision from a television reporter. The next day, feeling betrayed and humiliated, Dan White strapped on his old police service revolver, sneaked into city hall to avoid encountering a security metal detector, asked to see Moscone, and shot four bullets into him. With the mayor lying dead on the floor, White walked across the building to Harvey Milk's office, and within minutes he too was dead. The next mayor, Diane Feinstein, used her powers of appointment to install a more development-oriented planning commission and to fill supervisor vacancies with more moderate appointments. During her terms of office the short-lived district elections reform was repealed, the expansion of downtown accelerated, and the city's housing crisis grew more severe. Still, considerable activity among the neighborhood-oriented forces that Moscone and Milk represented is still pressuring for housing reform measures and more balanced growth in the city.

In Boston a return to district representation signaled a resurgence of neighborhood orientation, culminating in the 1983 mayoral election of South Boston populist Ray Flynn on a platform of shifting money and planning energies away from glamorous downtown and harbor-front development toward rebuilding Boston's neglected working-class neighborhoods. Prodevelopment candidates were eliminated in the primary, and Flynn ran against long-time black community activist Mel King. King had initially proposed a linkage plan connecting neighborhood economic development to downtown growth and the Boston Jobs for Boston People program establishing quotas on public jobs for minorities, city residents, and women, proposals that Flynn later endorsed. The two candidates' "populist appeals were so evenly matched" that *Time* magazine could not distinguish them, but in the end, Boston did vote along racial lines. Flynn beat King by a two-to-one margin, carrying 80 percent of the majority white vote and only a small fraction of the vote cast by people of color. King's 20 percent of the white vote was substantially higher than the proportion received by Harold Washington in Chicago or Andrew Young in Atlanta, and his 70 percent of the city's Latin vote (close to 10 percent of the city's population), 25 percent of the city's main Italian ward, significant totals in the Asian districts and in gay neighborhoods, as well as the overwhelming majority of the black vote gave real content to his campaign's claim to be a rainbow coalition. If present Boston population trends continue, by 1990 people of color will be the majority of the city and King's rainbow coalition the hope of transcending racial polarization in the future.

THE FUTURE OF CITIES

It remains to be seen whether ambitious programs of neighborhood housing, of rent control, and of controlled development can form effective political coalitions to change the direction of the massive financial, corporate, educational, and medical expansions that have reshaped our central cities. It remains to be seen whether northeastern urban patterns will be repeated in the Sunbelt as that area's cities mature and whether coordinated national action can keep capital investment and employers from abandoning current locations to search out low-wage labor markets outside the United States. It remains to be seen whether changes in social support systems, employment policies, and wage structures can keep cities from becoming a two-class society populated by the very rich and the very poor and can stem the feminization of poverty that condemns many urban youth to a childhood of deprivation. No one can predict if cities will survive their present predicaments, and if so, in what form. A recent satirical *Washington Post* editorial prophesied that the expansion of office buildings, hotels, restaurants, theaters, and boutique-style marketplaces would evolve into its most profitable form, a giant chocolate chip cookie chain stretching from Boston to Washington.

Still, eulogies for urban America seem premature. By the mid-1980s, better planning, declining interest rates, neighborhood involvement and activism, and creative leadership had fueled inner-city revival in cities as diverse as Baltimore, San Antonio, and Seattle. Although at a high cost, historic preservation and gentrification have sparked middle-class commitment to urban life. As a result, efforts have been made to give downtowns and waterfronts the kinds of attractions that made them dynamic, exciting places in the nineteenth century. Street fairs, free concerts, art in public places, walking tours, running races, ethnic festivals, and many more similar events have attracted people of different classes and races to city spaces and celebrations. Cities today remain what they have always been—the centers of economic, social, and cultural opportunity. As Mr. Dooley reasoned,

> Ye might say as Hogan does, that we're ladin' an artyficyal life, but, be Hivins, ye might as well tell me I ought to be paradin' up and down a hillside with a suit iv skins, shootin' the antylope an' the moose, be gory, an' livin' in a cave as to make me believe I ought to get along without sthreet cars an' ilictric lights an' illyvators an' sody wather an' ice. "We ought to live where all

Urban Celebrations   The annual Kite Festival in Boston's Franklin Park attracted upwards of 40,000 people in May, 1986, the nineteenth year in which the festival was held. *(Richard Heath/the Franklin Park Coalition.)*

the good things iv life comes from," says Hogan. "No," says I. "Th' place to live is where all the good things iv life goes to."

BIBLIOGRAPHY

On the fiscal crisis see William K. Tabb, "The New York City Fiscal Crisis," in *Marxism and the Metropolis: New Perspectives in Urban Political Economy* (New York: Oxford University Press, 1978); Charles R. Morris, *The Cost of Good Intentions: New York City and the Liberal Experiment, 1960–1975* (New York: W.W. Norton & Co., 1980); and Ken Auletta, *The Streets Were Paved with Gold* (New York: Random House, 1979). See also John Mollenkopf, *The Contested City* (Princeton, N.J.: Princeton University Press, 1983). On Cleveland see Todd Swanstrom, *The Crisis of Growth Politics: Cleveland, Kucinich, and the Challenge of Urban Populism* (Philadelphia: Temple University Press, 1985).

On new black mayors see Paul Kleppner, *Chicago Divided: The Making of a Black Mayor* (DeKalb: Northern Illinois University Press, 1985); Melvin G. Holli and Paul M. Green, eds., *The Making of the Mayor, Chicago, 1983* (Grand Rapids, Mich.: William B. Erdmans, 1984); Peter K. Eisinger, *The Politics of Displacement: Racial and Ethnic Tensions in Three American Cities* (New York: Academic Press, 1980); William

E. Nelson, Jr., and Philip J. Meranto, *Electing Black Mayors: Political Action in the Black Community* (Columbus: Ohio State University Press, 1977); Peter Eisinger, "Black Mayors and the Politics of Racial Economic Advancement," in *Readings in Urban Politics*, 2nd ed., eds. H. Hahn and C. Levine (New York: Longman, 1984). See also Norman L. Fainstein and Susan S. Fainstein, *Urban Political Movements: The Search for Power by Minority Groups in American Cities* (Englewood Cliffs, N.J.: Prentice-Hall, 1973); James Jennings and Monte Rivera, *Puerto Rican Politics in Urban America* (Westport: Greenwood Press, 1984).

On racial and ethnic politics in Boston in the 1970s and 1980s see Mel King, *Chain of Change* (Boston: South End Press, 1981); James Jennings and Melvin I. King, *From Access to Power: Black Politics in Boston* (Cambridge, Mass.: Schenkman, 1986); J. Anthony Lukas, *Common Ground: A Turbulent Decade in the Lives of Three American Families* (New York: Alfred A. Knopf, 1985); Alan Lupo, *Liberty's Chosen Home: The Politics of Violence in Boston* (Boston: Little, Brown, & Co., 1977). On the mayoral campaign in Boston in 1980 see the special double issue of *Radical America* 17–18 (November 1983–February 1984). The Mel King Campaign and Coalition Politics, especially articles by James Green, "The Making of Mel King's Rainbow Coalition: Political Changes in Boston, 1963–1983," 9–34; and James Jennings, "America's New Urban Politics: Black Electoralism, Black Activism," 35–40.

On neighborhood initiatives in San Francisco see Chester Hartman, *The Transformations of San Francisco* (Totowa, N.J.: Rowman and Allenheld, 1984); John D'Emilio, *Sexual Politics, Sexual Communities: The Making of a Homosexual Subculture in the United States, 1945–1970* (Chicago: University of Chicago Press, 1983); Frances Fitzgerald's articles on gay politics in San Francisco, "A Reporter at Large—the Castro—1," *The New Yorker*, July 21, 1986, pp. 34–70, and "A Reporter at Large—the Castro—2," *The New Yorker*, July 28, 1986. An Academy Award winning documentary on Harvey Milk and the Milk-Moscone murders is *The Life and Times of Harvey Milk*, made by Robert Epstein and Richard Schmeichen, distributed through Black Sands Educational Productions.

Index